126268

THE ECONOMICS
OF
MEDICAL
MALPRACTICE

*A Conference Sponsored by
the Center for Health Policy Research of the
American Enterprise Institute for Public Policy Research*

THE ECONOMICS OF MEDICAL MALPRACTICE

Edited by Simon Rottenberg

American Enterprise Institute for Public Policy Research
Washington, D.C.

ISBN 0-8447-2111-5 (Paper)
ISBN 0-8447-2112-3 (Cloth)

Library of Congress Catalog Card No. 78-6364

Printed in the United States of America

MAJOR CONTRIBUTORS

Galen Burghardt, Jr.
Division of Research and Statistics
Board of Governors
Federal Reserve System

Guido Calabresi
John Thomas Smith Professor of Law
School of Law, Yale University

Ross D. Eckert
Associate Professor of Economics
University of Southern California

Richard A. Epstein
Professor of Law
School of Law
University of Chicago

H. E. Frech, III
Associate Professor of Economics
University of California, Santa Barbara

Jerry R. Green
Associate Professor of Economics
Harvard University

Bruce C. N. Greenwald
Lecturer in Economics
Wesleyan University

Clark C. Havighurst
Professor of Law
School of Law
Duke University

Michael D. Intriligator
Professor of Economics
University of California, Los Angeles

Barbara H. Kehrer
Senior Economist II
Mathematica Policy Research, Inc.

Mark C. Kendall
The Times, Mooresville, Ind.
Publisher, Mooresville (Ind.)
formerly at the National Planning Association

Judith K. Mann
Assistant Professor of Economics
University of California, San Diego

Marnie W. Mueller
Assistant Professor of Economics
Wesleyan University

Patricia Munch
Economist Associate
The Rand Corporation

Albert L. Nichols
Instructor in Public Policy
John Fitzgerald Kennedy School of Government
Harvard University

Melvin W. Reder
Isadore Brown and Gladys J. Brown
Professor of Urban and Labor Economics
Graduate School of Business
University of Chicago

Simon Rottenberg
Professor of Economics
University of Massachusetts

Steven Shavell
Assistant Professor of Economics
Department of Economics
Harvard University

Dennis Smallwood
Associate Professor of Economics
University of California, San Diego

Richard Zeckhauser
Professor of Political Economy
John Fitzgerald Kennedy School of Government
Harvard University

CONTENTS

PREFACE

These papers were first delivered at the American Enterprise Institute's conference on medical malpractice held in Washington, D.C., in December 1976. The underlying issues addressed at that conference are still with us today, and the articles contained in this collection continue to be of prime importance for those who wish to think and work on the control and quality of medical care in contemporary America. Nonetheless it is possible, and appropriate, to note the subtle, but clear, change in tone and nuance between 1976 and today. When the conference was held, the medical malpractice problem was the source of much immediate anxiety to all parties concerned—physicians, hospitals, patients, insurance companies, and federal and state governments. These papers somewhat reflect the tension of that moment. While concern about the problems of medical malpractice and the possible alternatives to it still remain, much of the anxiety present at the conference has been dissipated.

There are two very broad explanations for the cooling down that has taken place with medical malpractice. The first concerns the internal operation of the legal system. It is common knowledge that substantive changes within the common law liability system during the past decade or so have worked to increase the exposure of physicians and other health care providers to medical malpractice liability. It is, however, sometimes forgotten that these legal changes operate in a system in which the power of decision in individual cases is split between judge and jury. The effect of these innovations has been to allow cases to reach the jury which under previous legal regimes would have been decided for the defendant by the judge, often on a summary basis. There is little about these innovations which demands juries to find for the plaintiff, once the judge gives them the ultimate power of control. What seems to have happened, quite independently of any fresh formal changes in the legal rules, is that more of the close cases—particularly those involving the exercise of medical judgment—are in fact being decided for defendants. The exact shifts in jury sentiment are hard to pin down, and the phenomenon may yet turn out to be temporary. But now it seems clear (in the short run at least) that a plaintiff's chances before a jury are less promising than they were in 1975 or 1976, and that perception has influenced the entire process. It gives signals about which malpractice actions are worth bringing and which are not, and it influences the dollar settlements in difficult cases. The short-term effects across the system have been considerable, even in the absence of any major legislative reform.

The second reason for the cooling down comes from quite a different source. One of the major sources of distress in 1976 (and even more so in 1975) was the sharp and unanticipated increase in medical malpractice insurance premium rates, coupled with the withdrawal of many insurance firms from the market, and the bankruptcy, or near bankruptcy, of some that remained. The new insurance rates required major short-term adjustments, and they fed fears that further increases of similar dimensions were in the offing. Now that problem has crested. Premiums generally have been relatively stable, certainly as compared with inflation, and in some instances have declined. Private physicians and medical institutions have had a chance to "catch up" on costs and to make necessary internal adjustments in their methods of doing business, again without any formal independent changes in the law.

The true picture is doubtless more complicated than this brief sketch suggests. And it is quite possible that the current equilibrium will turn out to be fragile and short lived. But no matter which way the future turns out, the essays in this collection should help in understanding the many-faceted issues about medical malpractice whose fundamental importance to our medical care systems remains undiminished.

ROBERT B. HELMS
February 1978

INTRODUCTION

Simon Rottenberg

The delivery of medical care is a risky business. Even a prudent medical practitioner cannot be completely certain that his diagnosis or the therapy he prescribes is correct; if he is wrong, the patient is not cured and the illness or disease is not arrested. Furthermore, even if he is right the patient may suffer from side effects.

Therapies have side effects that are adverse to some patients. The probabilities of the occurrence of side effects of different magnitudes may be known or unknown. If they are known, the expected value of the gain to a patient of the prescription of a particular therapeutic regime may be sufficient to warrant running the risk of a side effect. But the therapy may induce adverse effects without curing the patient; at worst, it may cause his death.

And, finally, providers of medical care are of diverse quality; the standards of practice of some are high and those of others, low.

Outcomes in medical practice fall somewhere on a continuum from failure, in the sense of an absence of cure coupled with an adverse side effect of some severity, through failure without side effects or success with side effects, to success without side effects.

When injury is done a patient by a medical practitioner, there are a number of possible ensuing arrangements. One rule might be, for example, that the patient run the risks associated with medical treatment and that the practitioner not be held responsible for maloccurrence. In that case, the patient might either purchase commercial insurance to reimburse him the costs of repairing the injury and compensate him for the damage he suffers, or the patient might self-insure against such damage.

Another rule might require the practitioner to repair injury and compensate for damages on the simple showing that medical injury has occurred. A strict liability rule or a "no fault" arrangement has this effect.

Another rule might require the practitioner to bear the cost of repair and compensation only if it is shown that the injury was produced by imprudent behavior on his part.

Or, finally, patients and practitioners might be permitted to choose from this array. any arrangement for fixing liability and allocating costs that suited their convenience. In such cases, the price of medical service would presumably reflect the allocation of risk: the price would be lower if the patient bore the risk, and it would be higher if the risk were borne by the practitioner. Such an arrangement is called contractarian.

The rule that currently prevails in the United States is one that requires that practitioners bear the cost of medical injury only if they have acted imprudently.

When patients or their survivors seek to be compensated for injuries which they claim were produced by diagnostic or therapeutic practice by physicians, they make what is called a malpractice claim.[1] Malpractice occurs when the physician commits an error which causes harm to the patient. The error may be one of commission or omission; the physician may have done something he should not have done, or he may have omitted to do something he should have done.

Claims for damages brought against physicians may lie in various branches of the law. Some allege, for example, breach of contract or assault. Usually, however, malpractice suits involve the application of tort law.

The law of torts assumes that there is an implied contract between the practitioner and the patient in which the duty of the practitioner is defined by law. It is the practitioner's duty "to possess that degree of knowledge and skill necessary to treat a particular condition; . . . to exercise that degree of care, judgment, and skill which other physicians . . . exercise . . . under like or similar circumstances; . . . to exercise that degree of care . . . which other physicians of good standing of the same school or system of practice usually exercise; . . . (to exercise) that degree of care . . . which other physicians . . . exercise in the same or similar localities; . . . having due regard to the advanced state of the medical profession at the time in question." [2]

The law of torts is sometimes called negligence law, and suits brought in this branch of the law allege negligent conduct. Negligence is careless conduct that causes unintentional harm. The conduct is measured by the standard of care one would expect from a reasonably prudent person. The plaintiff in a negligence suit must show that the defendant was under a duty to be careful toward him, the defendant violated that duty by careless action or inaction, the plaintiff was injured

---

[1] Malpractice claims may be made not only upon physicians but also upon hospitals, sanatoriums, nurses, paramedical personnel, and other health care providers. This paper will discuss only malpractice of physicians; many of the principles are transferable to other objects of claim.

[2] C. Joseph Stetler and Alan R. Moritz, ed., *Doctor and Patient and the Law*, 4th ed. (St. Louis: C.V. Mosby Company, 1962), p. 308ff.

or damaged, and there was a clear connection between the defendant's conduct and the damage to the plaintiff.

The courts write a kind of implicit manual of prudent and non-negligent behavior by medical practitioners in deciding the cases that come to them. A few cases will illustrate what the courts have come to define as malpractice.[3]

> The plaintiff came to the defendant physician with a swelling on his knee. . . . The physician examined the patient manually, placed him on a diet, and injected a solution into his blood stream. Severe injuries followed. It was shown at the trial that the usual practice among physicians in the community under these circumstances was not only to take the history of the patient but also to make an x-ray study, a blood test, and a biopsy. These were not considered alternate tests. All of them were required. The defendant was held guilty of negligence for failing to make these diagnostic tests.

> The plaintiff alleged that the defendant physicians had prescribed the drug stilbestrol for her. . . . After using the drug for approximately three years, the plaintiff developed cancer of the breast, necessitating removal of the breast. She alleged that stilbestrol—being a synthetic estrogen containing properties which may produce cancer of the female breast—should not be administered to women who have a family history of cancer, as she did. . . . [The appeals court allowed] the complaint to stand, since it stated a good cause of action.

> The plaintiff, suffering from bursitis in her right shoulder, received x-ray treatments from the defendant radiologists. During the treatments she experienced nausea. Subsequent to the seventh treatment, her shoulder began to itch, the skin turned red, blisters formed and then ruptured, and the skin peeled, leaving raw flesh of the shoulder exposed. Scabs formed and lasted for several years. Her condition was diagnosed as chronic radiodermatitis caused by the x-ray therapy. A judgment against the physician was affirmed.

> The plaintiff was a 49-year-old housewife, the mother of four children. She entered the defendant hospital for a vaginoplasty. A large dose of spinal anesthetic was administered, after which an attempt was made to change her position on the operating table. There was a mechanical failure in the table and it was necessary to shake it. The patient experienced respiratory difficulties and suffered a cardiac arrest. The

[3] The cases are all drawn from Statler and Moritz, *Doctor and Patient,* p. 312ff.

patient's life was saved by a thoracotomy, but spontaneous respiration did not return for an hour. The patient suffered anoxia and, although she partially recovered, brain damage was permanent. A suit against the surgeon, two anesthesiologists, and the hospital was settled.

The plaintiff was operated on by the defendant and another physician for an extrauterine pregnancy. Immediately following the operation, she developed severe pain in her abdominal region at about the same place where defendant had made the incision. In a second operation, two years later, the defendant removed from the plaintiff's large bowel a cloth sack approximately 10 inches wide and 16 inches long. On appeal [the court instructed that the plaintiff had grounds for her claim.]

The patient consented to the performance of an operation on the septum of her nose. During the operation the surgeon also removed her tonsils. The court affirmed judgment against the surgeon for unauthorized surgery.

The patient sustained a fracture of his leg. The defendant physician reduced the fracture and set the leg in a cast in the customary fashion. On the following two days he saw the patient, who was suffering excruciating pain in the leg and had no feeling in the toes. After the second examination of the patient, the physician left town without making any arrangements for the care of the patient. Nine days later, when the physician returned to town, he refused to render any further medical care to the patient, although he was requested to do so. He refused a similar request after another seven days. The leg ultimately had to be amputated. A judgment was rendered against the physician for his abandonment of the patient, for his refusal to treat him, and for his failure to make any provisions or give any directions for his care and treatment.

The law distinguishes among injury, negligent conduct, malpractice, and malpractice claims. Not all injuries are produced by negligence and not all negligence produces injury. Malpractice occurs when there is injury due to negligent conduct, but not all malpractice generates malpractice claims.[4]

Injuries can also be distinguished by their progenetic properties. There are injuries that *can* be forestalled by the exercise of caution, like those caused by the surgeon's omitting to remove a sack from the bowels when he sutures his incision. There are injuries that *cannot* be

---

[4] It is reported that about 8 percent of hospitalized patients sustain identifiable injuries and that about 10 percent of all injuries lead to malpractice claims.

forestalled by the exercise of caution, as when a therapeutic procedure produces a set of possible outcomes to each of which is attached some probability that it will occur that includes adverse side effects, and when probabilities are known, and the distribution of outcomes among individual patients is random.[5] There are, finally, "injuries" that *cannot* be forestalled in the sense that diagnostic and therapeutic decisions are made with less than perfect information (whatever the quantity of resources employed in the production and assimilation of information), so that, even in the absence of adverse side effects, treatment can be expected ex ante to produce a probability set of outcomes on a continuum from complete failure (the pain is not diminished at all) to complete success (the pain is completely gone and never recurs); "injuries" can be defined to comprehend failure in this sense.

Much litigation over medical malpractice claims is devoted, in sometimes long, complex, and arduous court proceedings, to distinguishing cases of failure and injury that are caused by the physician's imprudent behavior from those produced by other causes. It is a distinction that is not easily drawn.

The expected value of malpractice claims made upon a physician can be perceived as a component of the price he pays for the right of access to the income-earning opportunities of practicing medicine. The expected value of malpractice claims is the sum of professional liability insurance premiums (or, for the self-insured, the product of the probability of successful suits and the estimated magnitudes of awards)[6] and the value of loss of reputation produced by successful, and possibly even by unsuccessful, malpractice suits. Damage to a physician's reputation finds pragmatic expression in diminished income. There appears to be no commercial market for insurance against loss of reputation.

This component of the price of access to income-earning opportunities in medicine is positive and nonuniform. It can be expected to affect the allocation of resources to and in medical practice at a number of points, including the following:

(1) the establishment and abandonment of practice, and thus the

---

[5] It is assumed, in this case, that the values of therapeutic gains and the costs of adverse side effects are of such magnitudes that the prescription of the relevant drug/procedure is indicated. There would be fewer injuries if there were fewer prescriptions, but this could not appropriately be called cautionary behavior; there would be fewer cures as well.

[6] Until recently, almost all practicing physicians in the United States have been insured by commercial insurers and almost none has been self-insured; self-insurance now appears to be a growing phenomenon in some states.

size of the industry, for which the number of practitioners is a proxy; [7]

(2) the allocation of practitioners among specialties;

(3) the spatial distribution of medical practice—urban versus rural, by city size, and by practice in home visits, outpatient clinics, and hospitals;

(4) size of firm—solo versus group practice;

(5) the allocation of those trained in medicine between medical research and medical practice;

(6) the allocation of practitioners among cases differentiated by diagnostic and prescriptive difficulty and by the degree of risk-aversion of patients;

(7) the ratio of physicians to paramedical personnel in delivering medical care; and

(8) the choice of diagnostic procedures and the choice of therapies appropriate to diagnostic estimates.

These allocational effects will occur because the risk of malpractice claims can be expected to vary among the subsets indicated in (1) through (8) above. The effects might be small for some members of that set and large for other members. Whether effects are large or small will depend upon whether the value of the risk of a claim is a large or small part of the price of entry into activity in which choice occurs. It might be reasonably surmised that allocative effects will be small upon rates of entry into medical practice but that they will be large upon the choice of diagnostic and therapeutic procedures by practitioners.

To the extent that there *are* effects, however, the relative risks of claims in medical practice and in other occupations, and the relative risks of malpractice claims in alternative activities open to choice within the medical profession, produce a relative price set. That set becomes an incentive system partially governing choice. If it is suboptimally arranged, the allocation of medical skills will be suboptimal. The arrangement of the price set is partially determined by the conventions of the law as the courts apply them.

---

[7] "One out of every 21 health-care providers (doctors, dentists and hospitals at risk) was the object of a malpractice claim in 1970." U.S. Department of Health, Education, and Welfare, *Report of the Secretary's Commission on Medical Malpractice* (Washington, D.C., 1973), p. 8. Physicians against whom a number of successful malpractice suits have been pressed, especially where damage awards are relatively large, will be unable to find a commercial insurer that will carry them, and rather than self-insure, will abandon practice.

Several factors determine the values of the risks of malpractice claims which attach to different activities. These are the probabilities of occurrence of injurious incidents, the estimated value of successful damage awards, the propensity of patients to claim, the cost of legal services, and the prevailing legal conventions with respect to the assignment of the nominal incidence of the cost of repairing (compensating for) damage and with respect to the cost of contesting at law.

The cost of contesting at law will be affected by considerations like the following: the courts' willingness to apply the doctrine of *res ipsa loquitur*, which shifts the burden of proof of (non-) negligence from plaintiff to defendant, that is, from patient to practitioner; the application of the discovery rule, which defines the time-point from which the statute of limitations begins to run; the treatment of oral guarantees (by the practitioner) of good results, which, if permitted, open the way to actions for breach of contract, thus permitting claims to be brought that may be foreclosed by a statute of limitations, if negligence actions are brought; the interpretation of the rule of informed consent, which can be construed as establishing the physician's duty to disclose, or as requiring him only to respond to his patients' inquiries; and rules governing the admissibility of evidence in court proceedings.

Different courts have interpreted these rules differently. Any interpretation will affect the distribution of the cost of litigation between plaintiffs and defendants. A set of interpretations that is favorable to the plaintiff will lower the cost of claiming and enlarge the number of claims.

Lawyers representing plaintiffs in medical malpractice claim cases are frequently paid for their services by "contingency fees," and the medical care provider community seems to believe that this arrangement generates claims that would not otherwise be made. In a contingency fee arrangement, plaintiffs pay their lawyers nothing if the case is lost, and some predetermined fraction of the award (usually about one-third, but sometimes as much as one-half) if the case is won. Another arrangement for the payment of the plaintiff's legal fees is "fee for service": the lawyer is paid his hourly fee for the number of hours spent on the case, win or lose.

Under the fee-for-service arrangement, claimants who assign a low probability to winning the claim or who believe that the amount of the award, if won, will not be large are reluctant to pursue a claim since they run the risk of losing the legal fees. Under the contingency-fee plan, lawyers who assign a low probability to winning a particular case or who believe the size of the award will not be large are reluctant to accept the case since they run the risk of losing time that might be more lucratively spent on other cases. In both fee arrangements, therefore, trivial and unlikely cases are screened out.

The question of which of these legal-fee arrangements will generate more claims, other things being equal, is complicated by possible differences between claimants' and lawyers' aversion to risk and capacity to make correct forecasts of the probability of winning and of the size of awards. The question is further complicated by the fact that the probability of winning is a partial function of the length of time spent by the lawyer exploring precedents, searching out evidentiary material, and preparing legal briefs.

It should be noted that lawyers employed to defend against medical malpractice claims are almost always employed on salaried or fee-for-service terms.

The price set previously referred to can be seen, alternatively, as a set of costs of doing business of diverse kinds or as a set of taxes on diverse activities in which the tax is proportional to output. Either way, the analytical implications for the allocation of resources to medical care and to caution in medical practice are unaffected.

An application of the analytical principles of the incidence of taxation seems to produce fruitful insights. We have referred to the risk of a malpractice claim as a tax on a medical activity.[8] In a purely formal sense, it is not the risk of claim that is the tax but rather the risk of injury per se. Doctors and patients transact healing services; the one sells, the other buys. The risk of injury is a tax on the transaction. The magnitude of the tax is determined by the expected value of the injury, which is the product of the probability that it will occur and the value of the damage done, if it does occur.

The tax may be nominally paid by the practitioners. This is the case both under strict liability, where doctors must repair damage upon simple proof that injury has occurred, and under tort law, where proof of negligence must be established.[9] On the other hand, the tax may be nominally paid by patients. This is the case in a legal context where malpractice claims may not be brought.

We know, however, that nominal rules defining the payers of a tax do not define the true incidence of the tax. Usually the burden of a

---

[8] Specifically, the reference was to risk of claim as a component of the price of entry into an activity; it will be recalled that "activities" include entry into and exit from the profession, choice of specialty, of locus of practice, of factor combination, of procedures, and so on.

[9] It is in this case that the pure tax-risk of injury comes to be operationally expressed as a risk of malpractice claim. Operational expression in this form requires, however, *both* risk of injury and the existence of the convention permitting malpractice claims to be pursued.

tax is borne by both buyers and sellers. The consequences of the risk of injury are shared by doctors and patients, whatever the formal, legal assignment of nominal liability. The shares of the consequences falling upon each will be determined by the degree of responsiveness of buyers and sellers of medical care services to changes in the prices of those services, or what economists call the schedule elasticities.

The risk of injury associated with a medical activity will diminish the quantity of that activity that is done. The magnitude by which the quantity diminishes will be determined by the magnitude of the risk of injury and by schedule elasticities. If risks of injury and schedule elasticities vary among activities, as they probably do, the existence of risk of injury in medical practice will shrink different medical practice activities in different amounts. Whatever these outcomes, they are generated by the existence of the risk of injury and are unaffected by the nominal rules assigning liability for the repair of damage from injury.

Implicit in the treatment of the incidence and allocative effects of a risk-of-injury tax is an assumption that both buyers and sellers of healing services are optimally informed of the existence of risk and of the distribution of risks among activities. If patients did not know there were risks of injury, risk would have a zero value in the calculus of their choice; if they did not know how risk was distributed among activities, they would make random choices with respect to this variable. If they did not know (and could not learn; that is, would never know) of the existence of the risk of injury attached to an activity, the objective existence of the risk would not cause the quantity of the activity to shrink. If they knew there was risk but did not know how risk was distributed among activities, shrinkage would occur, but it would be randomly distributed among activities. If patients *are* informed and shrinkage is appropriately distributed among activities, it is because caution has been exercised. We shall proceed on the assumption that there is optimal information in the market.

Physicians produce a joint product of probabilistic healing of illnesses and probabilistic injuries. Similarly, therapeutic strategies are investments that yield joint returns of probabilistic healing and probabilistic injuries. The ratios of injuries to healing vary among physicians and among therapeutic strategies.

Patients are confronted in the market by arrays of strategies and physicians offering diverse combinations of therapeutic power and injuries. If patients are more informed, they may choose among strategies directly. If they are less informed, they may choose among strategies vicariously by choosing among physicians. Vicarious choice of strategies will occur in the latter case, if patients know which physicians are leaders and which are followers in the prescription of innovative agents and procedures—that is, if they know even approximately the time distribution of physicians in the adoption of new therapeutic methods.

Patients will choose the strategy that will optimize for them some combination of therapeutic power (measured by the mean and variance of the probability of successful therapy associated with a strategy) and of forestalled injury. The optimal combination will be determined by the prices of different strategies of different powers, the price of forestalled injury (the price of cautionary resources), and the patient's preference set.

Suppose now that buyers of medical services are in pristine ignorance; they can rank-order neither therapeutic strategies nor physicians with respect to the combinations of healing power and injuries they represent. Patients will make random choices among physicians and will deliver to physicians carte blanche power of attorney to select among strategies. Ignorant patients prefer powerful healing physicians whose caution generates, *ceteris paribus*, few injuries, but they cannot distinguish those physicians from others who are less knowledgeable and more careless.

If liability is not assigned to them, physicians have, in this case, no incentive to be knowledgeable about medical practice or to exercise care. Good or bad, each will have the share of patients chance assigns to him. If, however, patients are entirely ignorant and the relevant rule of law requires physicians to repair injury, the physicians will employ cautionary resources. As a first approximation, they will push their precautions to the point where the cost of the last unit of cautionary resources is equal to the expected value of the damage that would be done if the last injury had not been forestalled by caution. But this is not strictly true, because the cost of caution—for instance, the cost of an incremental diagnostic test which can be expected to increase by a magnitude approaching zero the probability that the diagnosis is correct—is not borne by the physician. Doctors who are reimbursed by patient charges for the cost of avoiding injury and who capture the gain of avoided injury (by saving the cost of repair of damage) will push caution too far; they will produce fewer injuries, so to speak, than patients would like.

This will also occur in a world in which patients are somewhat, but not completely, ignorant. Suppose patients are not trained in medicine; they cannot diagnose and they cannot prescribe therapy. They assign power of attorney to physicians to select medical strategies.

Suppose, however, that medical licensure statutes inform patients that, shortly after leaving medical school, physicians knew enough of the art of medical practice to pass muster with an examining board;

suppose that patients are informed of the medical specialties in which physicians qualify and that, by examining framed degrees on the walls of medical offices, they know the schools where physicians were trained and can approximately rank-order those schools on an index of quality; they know the physicians to whom the rich and powerful are attracted when they are ill; they are told by family and friends which doctors have given good, and which bad, service in the past; they are informed by newspapers when malpractice judgments are entered. In such a world, a somewhat intelligent ordinal ranking of physicians is possible. Patient choice of physicians is no longer random. A physician's reputation counts for something. He will want to produce fewer injuries to advance his reputation and to attract custom.

Suppose in that world patients bear the cost of caution and the legal convention requires physicians to bear the cost of repairing damage when they do injury to patients. By avoiding injury, physicians capture two gains: cost of repair avoided and cost of lost reputation (and custom) avoided. In this case, too, they can be expected to push caution beyond the point desired by utility-maximizing patients.

They can be expected to practice what has come to be called defensive medicine. Defensive medicine is the "conducting of a test or performance of a diagnostic or therapeutic procedure which is not medically justified but is carried out primarily (if not solely) to prevent or defend against the threat of medical-legal liability" or the nonperformance of "a procedure or (non-) conduct of a test because of the physician's fear of a later malpractice suit, even though the patient is likely to benefit from the test or procedure in question." Fifty to 70 percent of physicians polled reported that "they engage in various forms of so-called defensive medicine." [10]

More formally, physicians apparently engage in operations that generate higher incremental costs than gains and do not undertake operations that would generate higher incremental gains than costs. They do things that informed, utility-maximizing patients would not choose to have done; they do not do things that informed, utility-maximizing patients would choose to have done. They require x-rays and laboratory tests, office visits, consultations, and hospitalizations to excess. [11]

Thus, it turns out that the assignment of liability (that is to say, the assignment of the cost of repairing damage) can be expected to

[10] U.S. Department of Health, Education, and Welfare, *Report of the Secretary's Commission on Medical Malpractice,* p. 14.

[11] Ibid., Appendix, p. 39ff. See also Donald McDonald, ed., *Medical Malpractice* (Santa Barbara, Calif.: Center for the Study of Democratic Instiutions, 1971), p. 3.

leave resource allocation (including the allocation of resources to the avoidance of injury) unaffected in an informed world, but not in an uninformed world, and possibly not even in an optimally uninformed world.

Malpractice claims, to be successful under tort law principles, must establish negligence by the physician; the physician must be found to have been "at fault." No-fault insurance arrangements have been offered as an alternative system for the repair of injurious damage. Under such an arrangement, it would suffice to establish that injury had occurred as a result of medical activity for compensation to be paid to the victim. The premise of such a system would be that "compensation for medical injury should be tied to the degree that a given result from a medical procedure or treatment deviates from a set of expected results for like medical procedures." [12]

Figure 1

EXPECTED OUTCOMES OF AN ILLNESS WITH AND WITHOUT TREATMENT

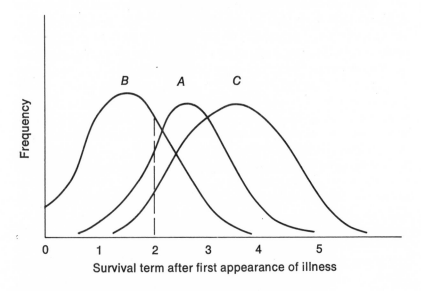

Broken line indicates the survival term of a hypothetical patient.
A is the set of expected outcomes without treatment.
B is the set of expected outcomes with inept treatment.
C is the set of expected outcomes with efficient treatment.

---

[12] McDonald, *Medical Malpractice,* p. 13.

The problem here lies in the definition of a compensable incident. Medical procedures produce a distribution of outcomes. The "expected results" are not a single event but a frequency distribution of events on a continuum from very bad to very good. A patient falling anywhere in the distribution has an expected result. In such a context the notion that given results deviate from expected results is not sensible. Suppose "results" are operationally defined to mean the period of survival after the first appearance of the symptoms of an illness. Without medical treatment, there would be a distribution of survival terms; with inept (injurious) treatment, the distribution is pushed to the left; with efficient treatment, the distribution is pushed to the right.

But suppose the distributions overlap. In the case illustrated in Figure 1, it is known only that, for a given patient, the results were survival for two time periods after the first appearance of the illness. How will a compensating agency know whether the patient suffered medical injury?

One of the defenses for no-fault insurance in medicine is that it would encourage innovative behavior by physicians. Tort law imposes the cost of repair of injury upon a physician if he has not exercised "that degree of care, judgment, and skill which other physicians exercise under like or similar circumstances." This is said to discourage innovative practice; practitioners are induced by the rule to apply establishmentarian procedures. There is another rule which diminishes innovation, namely the principle of informed consent. A physician may not treat a patient unless he has the patient's "informed consent"; if he treats the patient without the patient's consent he commits assault and a malpractice claim may ensue. The larger the quantity of information which must be given the patient to satisfy the informed consent rule, the larger the number of refusals to consent. The larger the number of refusals to consent, the smaller the quantity of medical experimentation that is done. The smaller the quantity of experimentation, the slower the advance of medical knowledge—and the less well served the future.

A rule requiring informed consent, therefore, implies a stronger preference for the present over the future (the economist's "time discount rate") than would occur in the absence of such a rule. The more information must be conveyed to the patient in order to secure his consent, the higher the implicit discount rate.

Malpractice claims are not uniformly distributed in space. The premium cost for a constant level of coverage for professional liability insurance for surgeons was over twice the national average in California and New York City in 1972, and it was less than one-third the national average in Wyoming, Vermont, South Carolina, Rhode Island, and New

Hampshire.[13] One possible explanation for spatial nonuniformity is that, adjusted for quality, legal services are cheaper in some places than in others and there are incentives, in those places, to settle disputes through litigation. On the other hand, the spatial distribution of claims may simply reflect the nonuniform spatial distribution of practitioners in medical specialties against whom claims are concentrated. Almost one-fifth of all malpractice claims in 1970, for example, were made against orthopedic surgeons, who make up far less than one-fifth of all practitioners. It is not credible that orthopedic surgeons are, on average, grossly more negligent than practitioners in other specialties.

A sensible hypothesis to explain why malpractice claims are concentrated upon a few specialties is that the cost of litigation forecloses petitions in cases except those in which the damage from negligent practice is serious and, therefore, awards can be expected to be large. The mean magnitudes of the consequences of error in medical practice vary among specialties.

In recent years, in the United States, the number of medical malpractice claims has increased greatly, as has the average size of awards and settlements made on those claims. The increase in the number of claims is said to reflect the increase in damage to patients as riskier cases are accepted for treatment and an increase in the propensity to bring suit against medical care providers. As a result of the rising incidence of claims, companies selling professional liability insurance have substantially increased the premium rates they charge.

It is sometimes thought that increased malpractice insurance premium rates increase the total cost to society of medical care. This is, however, not true. The cost to society of medical care is the sum of the value of the foregone uses of real resources employed in health care delivery and the value of the damage to patients arising from the ministrations of health care practitioners. That sum is unaffected by the magnitude of malpractice insurance premium charges. If more and larger payouts are made in malpractice trial awards and settlements than previously, this means only that a larger fraction of the cost of repairing medical injury is being borne by physicians than previously and a smaller fraction of that cost is being borne by patients. The distribution of that cost is affected, but the magnitude of the cost is unchanged.

A changed distribution of the cost of repairing damage might, however, have behavioral effects. If it induces, as has been suggested,

---

[13] U.S. Department of Health, Education, and Welfare, *Report of the Secretary's Commission on Medical Malpractice*, Appendix, p. 540. See also Sidney Shindell, " 'Epidemiology' of Professional Liability Losses," *Journal of the American Medical Association* (November 30, 1964), p. 824.

the practice of defensive medicine which employs resources in unnecessary and superfluous activities, it will, indeed, tend to enlarge the cost of medical care, both because resources are used in the delivery of medical care that have a marginal value larger than the value of the diagnostic and therapeutic gains they produce and because the increments of medical care delivered have the probabilistic capacity to injure patients. If, similarly, it produces an inappropriate allocation of medical practitioners in space, among specialties, and among patients, it will also enlarge medical care costs.

Premium rates for medical professional liability insurance are said to be high because the insurance contracts are written on an "occurrence" basis. That is to say, an insurance company selling coverage to a provider for some given year undertakes to pay damage claims against the provider that grow out of incidents occurring in that year, even if the claim awards are made years later. Medical occurrences commonly have "long tails"; long intervals tend to intervene between incidents giving rise to claims and the award of claims.

Would the elimination of the tail diminish insurance premium rates? Insurance policies could be written on a "claims made" basis. In that event, insuring companies would pay awards and settlements occurring in the year in which the payout is made, irrespective of the time when the originating incident occurred. Such an arrangement would redistribute premium payments over time, but it would not alter the aggregate of premiums paid over a "lifetime." Premiums would be less in early years of practice but they would be larger in later years. And, while insurance contracts written on an occurrence basis need no longer be purchased after retirement from practice, claims-made insurance would go on being purchased after retirement and, indeed, might be purchased by the practitioner's estate after his death, to protect survivors' interests in the estate from malpractice claims.

Some commercial insurance firms selling professional liability insurance policies to medical practitioners have withdrawn from the market. It is sometimes said that their withdrawal is a result of the large awards made by the courts and of the uncertainty confronted by the insurance companies with respect to the payouts they will be required to make when they write policies on an occurrence basis. Neither of these circumstances should be expected to prompt withdrawal from the professional liability market; both circumstances can be compensated for by raising premium rates. If withdrawal does occur, therefore, it is more likely to be the result of regulation by the public authorities preventing premium rates from rising high enough to cover payouts and administrative costs.

15

Recent increases in the number of physicians who self-insure are possibly a reflection of the joint occurrence of rising premium rates and inappropriate experience rating for malpractice insurance. Some experience rating is now done. The risk that a malpractice suit will be brought and will be successful is higher for some medical specialties than for others and it is higher in some regions and cities than in others. Insurance companies take account of those differences in risk by charging higher premium rates for malpractice insurance in some specialties than others and in some regions and cities than others. Nevertheless, there remain, within a given experience class thus defined, some practitioners for whom the risk of successful claims is low and others for whom the risk is high. All members of the class are charged the same premium rate. That rate will seem high to practitioners against whom successful claims are unlikely. They will tend to drop out of the commercial liability insurance market and to self-insure; they might also redefine their practice to eliminate the more risky components. The insurance companies might, of course, define the experience classes more narrowly by drawing finer distinctions than they now do. But drawing distinctions is administratively costly and it does not pay to push refined class differentiation too far. In addition, if differentiating is pushed to the limit, each practitioner has his own risk defined for him and is charged a premium related to that risk. Effectively, each becomes self-insured, and the socially useful property of insurance—aggregating or pooling risk—is lost.

In medical practice, we do not always know the magnitudes of the probabilities of cure and of the occurrence and severities of side effects. Where we do know, the magnitudes are different for different illnesses and, for given illnesses, they are different for different therapeutic strategies. The benefits of successful therapy have different values for different diseases (an end to paralysis is worth more than an end to the common cold for a given patient) and the benefits of given curative treatments have different values for different patients. Different therapeutic strategies also have different costs when costs are measured in terms of the real resources employed in their execution. Patients, meanwhile, are distributed on continua defined by the strength of income constraints and by their aversion to or preference for risk.

In the best of all possible worlds, informed patients, covering their own medical costs, would choose therapeutic regimes by satisfying equimarginal conditions, taking account of the cost of therapy, the value of cure, the expected value of side effects, and their own risk preferences. Where costs are borne by a third party—insurance or an agency of the state, for example—the cost of therapy becomes less relevant to patient choice, but it is still possible to define optimal solutions to therapeutic choice problems.

Where the patient is uninformed or lacks the capacity to reason or where he is merely a passive participant, someone else—say, his physician—must be his surrogate and assume his decision function; the physician ought, in principle, to estimate the patient's values, run those values through the calculus of the decision process, and attempt to produce the outcome that the patient would have come to if he had been informed, reasoning, and active.

The risks associated with the administration of medical care exist even when medical care is prudently administered. Sometimes it is imprudently administered. The quantity of imprudent behavior by health care providers can be optimal or it can be suboptimally too much or too little.

It might be thought that any positive quantity of imprudent behavior is suboptimally too much. This is, however, not necessarily true. Prudent behavior implies the exercise of caution. The production of caution uses up resources. It follows that we cannot be correctly responsive to the question, How prudent should we optimally be in delivering medical care? without taking account of the cost of prudence. It is not impossible—indeed, it is probable—that the survival of some residual quantity of imprudence is socially indicated.

The papers delivered at this conference are concerned with a central question: How can society design and administer rules and pricing and incentive arrangements and processes that will cause patients to receive the kind of medical care they desire; will cause the appropriate quantity of caution to be exercised in its delivery; and will achieve those objects at the cheapest possible social cost?

17

LESSONS FROM THE ECONOMICS OF SAFETY

Richard Zeckhauser and Albert L. Nichols

Introduction

Policies for dealing with medical malpractice must address three classes of objectives. They should seek to:

(1) provide patients and their advisors with information that will help them to make informed choices of physicians and procedures,

(2) provide incentives for physicians to exercise levels of care that are appropriate given resource costs and patients' preferences, and

(3) provide equitable and efficient compensation to those who are injured through malpractice.

If the problem were merely to select a set of policies that would promote this set of objectives, malpractice would be less troubling than it is, at least conceptually. Major analytic difficulties, however, arise because of the complex intertwining of malpractice problems with other aspects of the medical care system. Third-party financing of most medical care, for example, through both private and public insurance programs, makes the threat posed by defensive medicine far greater than it would be otherwise. Broad-based national health insurance could well exacerbate this aspect of the problem. Conversely, if Professional Standard Review Organizations (PSROs) live up to the expectations of their most enthusiastic supporters, they might not only alleviate problems of excessive utilization associated with defensive medical practice (both by protecting the physician and by scrutinizing his use of medical resources), but also reduce the incidence of compensable events by improving the quality of care.

In sum, the malpractice problem is inexorably linked to all aspects of the medical care system which gave rise to it, as becomes clear when we consider such problems as the selection of practitioners and the

This research was supported in part by grants from the Robert Wood Johnson Foundation and the Commonwealth Fund through the Center for the Analysis of Health Practices, Harvard School of Public Health.

training they receive, the financing of care in alternative facilities, and quality control mechanisms. What is referred to as the malpractice crisis, then, might be viewed as a symptom of malfunction in the medical care system as a whole. This observation suggests two negative conclusions. First, symptomatic treatment of the malpractice problem, though possibly effective in its own arena, may well prove detrimental in its overall consequences for the medical care system. Second, many changes that will be undertaken in the medical care system for purposes quite unrelated to malpractice issues may end up affecting malpractice significantly. At the core, then, we would argue that the problem of malpractice is only an element of the more general difficulties we are experiencing with our medical care system.[1] These observations suggest a somewhat general policy of reform. We should seek to implement policies that will improve the overall functioning of the medical care system, hoping that the malpractice problem will diminish, and recognizing that if it does not, despite well-chosen policies, there must have been more than compensating gains elsewhere.

We were invited to present this paper not as experts on malpractice, which we are not, but rather as individuals who have looked at problems in other fields where health, low probabilities, and compensation are also critical elements. From an analytic standpoint, all of these fields involve the economics of safety. We attempt here to extrapolate principles from the economics of safety to the malpractice problem. We steer clear of specific recommendations, lest we be subject to the accusation of analytic malpractice.

Aspects of a Malpractice System

Interpreting Malpractice Costs. The medical malpractice problem gained prominence because of its costs, which were not only high but rising rapidly.[2] It is more than a simple problem of cost containment, however.

---

[1] There may be spillovers outside the medical care system as well. It is sometimes suggested that the excessive level of malpractice expense is but a symptom of our litigious society. To focus the problem more narrowly, our society presently has a large number of lawyers who earn their livelihood by enabling some people to sue others. Just as those states that initiated no-fault auto insurance have had an upsurge in other forms of litigation, so too policies to reduce the incidence of malpractice suits may increase litigation in other areas.

[2] From 1966 to 1972, national price indexes for malpractice coverage rose 398.3 percent for "physicians (class 2)" and 426.3 percent for "surgeons (class 4)" (U.S. Department of Health, Education, and Welfare, *Report of the Secretary's Commission on Medical Malpractice,* Washington, D.C., January 16, 1973, p. 13). The costs of malpractice coverage have continued to rise sharply since 1972. From 1972 to 1976, premiums for physicians insured under the Washington

The absolute levels of costs, indeed, should not be a matter of concern, except to the extent that they represent a misallocation of resources. If, for example, we were to develop a program to provide appropriate prenatal care for all pregnant women, it would probably cost a great deal. Yet those expenditures might be highly worthwhile. It could conceivably be the case that the rising level of malpractice payments indicates that justified claims that previously would have gone uncompensated are now being paid. In such a case, the rising costs could reflect an improved allocation of resources.[3] Our approach to the malpractice issue should focus on the extent to which resources are being misallocated. Misallocation can come about for any of the three reasons that we identified at the outset: inefficient incentives, inappropriate compensation, or poor information. Consideration of these possibilities is at the heart of our discussion of the lessons to be learned from the economics of safety.

Low-Probability Events. Instances of malpractice and, to a still greater extent, actual malpractice claims are low-probability events. Small probabilities are a pervasive difficulty in the economics of safety. Where low probabilities are involved, information is likely to be poor, inferences are difficult to draw, and individuals have difficulty making rational decisions. For many types of occupational illnesses, for example, it is often impossible to attribute any particular case of illness to a specific period of employment, and thus to assign liability.[4] Similar difficulties may present themselves in malpractice claims. Suppose the victim of an automobile accident is operated on and later fails to recover full use of

State Medical Association plan rose 144 percent for physicians in the lowest premium group and 240 percent for those in the highest (Health Policy Analysis Program, *The Malpractice Issue in Washington,* Department of Health Services, University of Washington, Seattle, November 1975, p. 6). In New York, the average cost of malpractice coverage per hospital bed rose 313 percent from 1974 to 1975 (Special Advisory Panel on Medical Malpractice, *Report of the Special Advisory Panel on Medical Malpractice, State of New York,* January 1976, p. 17).

[3] Any rapid transition to a new equilibrium, even if that equilibrium is superior, will inevitably involve dislocation costs. This lesson has been demonstrated most graphically in the environmental area. The introduction of appropriately calibrated environmental regulation will obviously raise the costs for some parties and lead to some deadweight loss; individuals thrown out of work, for example, must search for new positions. Compensating savings come from an improved environment.

[4] Many occupational health hazards simply raise the probabilities of contracting various diseases already found in the general population, such as lung cancer. Even in those cases where the worker contracts an identifiable occupational disease, such as pneumoconiosis ("black lung," a respiratory disease of coal miners), it may well be impossible to determine which of the worker's past employers should be held accountable.

his arm because a nerve has been severed. It may well be impossible to determine with any degree of certainty whether the nerve was severed in the accident or during the operation.

Reliance on statistics to identify poor physicians is likely to provide little insight. Even the poor physician is unlikely to have a large number of claims. Indeed, if the vast majority of physicians are both capable and careful, as we believe to be the case, most claims (even those that are legitimate) will be made against good physicians.[5] Suppose, for example, that 98 percent of all physicians are "good." Even if a "bad" physician has ten times the probability of making a negligent error in treatment, claims against good physicians will outweigh those against bad ones by a ratio of $(.98 \times 1)/(.02 \times 10)$, or 4.9 to 1. The problem of using claim frequency to identify poor physicians is further complicated by the fact that most potentially actionable physician errors do not result in suits, thus reducing low probabilities still further and slowing the accumulation of statistical evidence.[6]

The low-probability nature of malpractice-related events taxes the decision-making abilities of both individuals and institutions. As discussed above, small probabilities are difficult to measure accurately, even when large statistical samples are available. Even when probabilities can be measured, most individuals have difficulty incorporating them into their decisions in a rational way.[7] Most people cannot readily distinguish between 1 chance in 1,000 and 1 in 10,000, even though those probabilities differ by an order of magnitude. Thus a physician attempting to discuss alternative courses of action with a patient will have difficulty estimating the probabilities of various adverse outcomes, and the patient will have difficulty interpreting even the most accurate estimates. Given this limited information and individuals' difficulties in assessing it, the conditions required to ensure the efficiency of free contracting will not be met.

---

[5] See J. Ferreira, "Accidents and the Accident Repeater," in *Driver Behavior and Accident Involvement: Implications for Tort Liability,* U.S. Department of Transportation, Washington, D.C., October 1970, for a study of the difficulties involved in using accident records to identify high-risk drivers. The problem is more difficult with malpractice since the probability of suit is so small.

[6] Even if evidence piled up quickly, it is not entirely clear how our legal system would respond. Our present negligence arrangements do not permit statistical evidence from other instances to be brought to bear in a particular case.

[7] A. Tversky and D. Kahneman, "Judgment Under Uncertainty: Heuristics and Biases," *Science,* vol. 185 (1974), pp. 1124-31, present experimental evidence on the inability of most individuals to draw the correct inferences from probabilistic information. Kunreuther's analysis of survey data on decisions to purchase flood and earthquake insurance shows that below some threshold level of concern, most individuals fail to make even rudimentary attempts to assess probabilities; H. Kunreuther, "Limited Knowledge and Insurance Protection," *Public Policy,* vol. 24 (1976), pp. 227-62.

One solution under such circumstances is to rely on the tort system: establish some quality level for care, either by contract or implicitly by case law, and hold the physician liable if care fails to meet that level. Unfortunately the tort system itself is not very adept at dealing with low-probability events, particularly with sorting out causative factors when only statistical inferences can be drawn. Indeed, financial judgments scaled down to reflect uncertainty about causality, while they surely occur sometimes in practice, in theory are not permissible.[8]

Incentive Effects of Third-Party Financing. The fact that malpractice claims are low-probability, high-risk events leads virtually all physicians in the United States to carry malpractice insurance.[9] Unfortunately, once such insurance is introduced, the burden of loss is shifted to a third party, and the pecuniary incentives to deliver careful and appropriate care diminish substantially. The diminution of these incentives would not be so large if premiums were based on the records of individual physicians, or if policies involved large deductibles and significant coinsurance rates. In practice, however, most malpractice insurance policies, particularly those sponsored by state or local medical societies, base the premium solely on the physician's specialty, and not on his past record of malpractice suits.[10] Furthermore, most policies contain only trivial deductibles and have no provisions for coinsurance. (Similarly, in workmen's compensation insurance, a firm's premiums are not primarily dependent on its own accident record, but on its size, and the type of industry.[11])

---

[8] Rubsamen reports on such a case in California, where the jury awarded a "compromise" verdict because of uncertainty about the physician's negligence; D. S. Rubsamen, "Medical Malpractice," *Scientific American,* vol. 235 (August 1976), p. 21.

[9] The Secretary's Commission on Medical Malpractice observed: "Medical malpractice insurance is a necessity for today's health-care providers. . . . Few physicians would dare to practice without adequate insurance coverage." Department of Health, Education, and Welfare, *Report,* p. 38.

[10] Munch notes this opposition and points out that during the early 1970s in Los Angeles two insurance companies were able to offer preferred-risk physicians lower rates than they could get through the county medical association's group plan. P. Munch, "Causes of the Medical Malpractice Insurance 'Crisis': Risks and Regulations," in this volume, pp. 125-53.

More recently, several university-affiliated hospitals in Massachusetts have formed their own captive insurance company in order to take advantage of the fact that their malpractice losses are far lower than the statewide averages on which premiums are based.

[11] As a result, workmen's compensation does not provide appropriate safety incentives for most firms; A. Nichols and R. Zeckhauser, "Government Comes to the Workplace: An Assessment of OSHA," *The Public Interest,* no. 49 (1977), pp. 39-69.

Third-party financing plays a critical role in malpractice on the patient's side as well. Patients pay only a small fraction of the costs when they receive medical care.[12] Through public and private insurance and government and charitable support, the whole medical system is laced with subsidies that drive the marginal cost of care to the patient well below its true cost. Any analysis of medical malpractice should start with a recognition that incentives for overexpenditure are implicit in such a system, since the costs of marginal care are borne neither by the patient nor by his physician, and hence neither has much incentive to limit costs. Defensive medicine is cheap from the perspective of both the patient and the physician, if not from that of society as a whole.[13]

Third-party financing may also distort the mix of services used by the physician when practicing defensive medicine. An additional battery of tests is often fully covered; indeed, the physician may reap some additional revenue when he orders them. But a more careful review of the patient's chart, an extra hour spent keeping up with the relevant medical literature, or the exercise of greater care in the conduct of an operation will not be covered.[14] The physician's fee will be unchanged. These observations suggest that defensive medicine may well be overly intensive in the provision of covered services, but those will not generally include a greater devotion of the physician's time and attention to his cases. (Extra visits, say for followup, are probably exceptions.)

Cross-Elasticities of Risks. We have suggested that malpractice penalties designed to improve the quality of care are likely to lead to inefficient allocations of resources. In some instances the distortion of incentives may be so great that not only are resources wasted, but levels of health are actually lowered. Experience with the economics of safety makes it evident that when evaluating the potential effects of a change designed to improve safety in one area, it is important to consider its effects in

---

[12] In 1970, 59 percent of personal health expenditures and almost 87 percent of hospital bills were paid by third parties; M. Feldstein, "The Welfare Loss of Excess Health Insurance," *Journal of Political Economy*, vol. 81 (1973), pp. 251-80.

[13] Feldstein estimates that in 1969 the welfare loss from excess health insurance was probably in excess of $4 billion per year. Feldstein was not concerned with the malpractice protection aspects of overexpenditure. Including them would drive the welfare losses higher. Ibid., p. 277. The general absence of third-party financing of legal services, we would argue, makes the problem of legal malpractice, which has received increasing media attention, substantially different and ultimately less threatening.

[14] The issue of defensive medicine is widely discussed, but few data are available. The Secretary's Commission on Medical Malpractice called defensive medicine "one of the most pervasive impacts of the medical malpractice problem," but was unable to cite any measures of the magnitude of the problem. Department of Health, Education, and Welfare, *Report,* p. 14.

other areas as well. In the language of economics, this requires paying attention to the cross-elasticities of risks.

When incentives are provided to make one activity safer, the costs of that activity usually rise, leading to a shift of resources to other activities, some of which may be more dangerous.[15] For example, it is sometimes argued that very strict safety requirements for nuclear-based electric generating plants may actually lower overall safety. Although such requirements may make every reactor safer, they also raise the costs of nuclear-based power generation, thus causing some utilities to shift to coal-fired plants, which may well pose greater risks to human life and health in the form of air pollution and mining hazards.[16]

The physician's choice of patients and procedures may raise similar problems. Malpractice suits are won by demonstrating negligence (out-of-court settlements are obtained by showing that it may be possible to prove negligence), but negligence that does not result in injury is never brought to trial. If initial medical conditions could be monitored accurately, the physician's record could be evaluated on the basis of how well he had done with the situation at hand. In practice, however, the outcome is a critical variable. Thus, if the potential penalties are significant, physicians have an incentive to avoid treating patients who present a high risk of suffering an injury as the result of treatment. These tend to be high-risk individuals, those most in need of medical care. In a perfectly competitive market, this problem would not arise, for physicians would simply charge such patients higher fees to reflect their higher expected malpractice costs. Medical custom and ethics, and the payment schedules of third parties, however, preclude such differential charges.[17]

No-fault malpractice plans could well exacerbate the incentives problem. Under no-fault schemes, outcome alone would determine the physician's compensation costs, and thus the incentives to avoid treating high-risk patients would rise significantly. Instituting no-fault schemes might also bias the physician's choice of procedures since most such

---

[15] We should concentrate on the sum of safety costs plus resource costs, not either component alone. Peltzman's analysis of seat belts suggests that they may actually have increased highway fatalities since drivers now go at higher speeds. To see whether this has proved net beneficial, we should value these drivers' time to see whether gains in time saved outweigh increased fatalities. S. Peltzman, "The Effects of Automobile Safety Regulation," *Journal of Political Economy*, vol. 83 (1975), pp. 677-725.

[16] See, for example, R. Wilson, "Will the Past be Prologue?: The Past Health Effects of Fossil Fuel and Nuclear Electricity Generation," *Public Utilities Fortnightly*, vol. 99 (1977), p. 43.

[17] Clark Havighurst, " 'Medical Adversity Insurance'—Has Its Time Come?" *Duke Law Journal*, no. 106 (1976), suggests that high-risk patients may be referred to specialists, who are in fact able to charge higher fees.

plans would not cover all procedures and all patients. Suppose, for example, that one procedure were covered by the no-fault plan while an alternative procedure remained under current tort law. In such a situation, the physician would have an incentive to employ the procedure which fell under the plan with the lower expected cost.[18]

Efficient Compensation. In addition to providing appropriate incentives for health care providers and patients, policies for dealing with malpractice must address the issue of compensation for the victims of unfortunate medical outcomes. Tort law, the present remedy, takes as its general objective "making whole" the victim of negligence. Not only will this provide equitable compensation for those who have suffered unjustly, it is argued, it will also provide incentives for physicians to act with appropriate care.

The incentives argument suggests that if you charge the physician $100,000 when he imposes a loss of that magnitude, he will spend $100 of his own resources to reduce the probability of that untoward event by .001. This incentive would be just appropriate to lead him to take actions that would minimize the sum of losses plus the costs of actions taken to avoid such losses. (Risk aversion on the part of the physician would lead him to spend too much on loss avoidance; his insurance against malpractice claims will lead him to spend too little.) The charged losses should include pain, suffering, and anxiety, for they are costs that individuals would pay to avoid. In essence, the objective should be to structure incentives so that the physician acts for the patient as the patient, if equivalently informed, would act for himself.[19]

Our institutional mechanisms link the incentive and compensation aspects of damage claims. What the physician (or, more often, his insurance company) pays, the injured patient receives (minus legal fees).

---

[18] The financial incentive could run either way, although in most cases expected compensation costs would probably be higher under the no-fault scheme. Havighurst, one of the originators of the no-fault scheme called Medical Adversity Insurance, observes: "The obvious solution to this problem would be to add the undesirable outcome, perhaps even nonrecovery from the condition itself, to the list of compensable events, but this would not always be feasible." Ibid., p. 1267.

[19] The quantity we are after here is what economists refer to as willingness to pay. With events that are compensable under malpractice, it will be difficult to tally such a figure since individuals will have little experience with the types of losses contemplated, and because, with compensation, wealth positions will change dramatically. The appropriate question to compute willingness to pay would be of the following sort: You are undergoing an operation with a .002 risk of paralysis. How much would you pay to reduce this risk to .001? The question posed in this way eliminates problems associated with wealth effects; also by being placed in probabilistic context it gets some degree of realism. For a discussion of alternative approaches to assessing willingness to pay for lifesaving activities, see R. Zeckhauser, "Procedures for Valuing Lives," *Public Policy,* vol. 23 (1975), pp. 419-64.

Economists tend to ignore this linkage, thus implicitly reinforcing it, viewing compensation as a simple transfer payment without implications for efficiency. And indeed the efficiency effects would be minimal if the amounts involved were small, for shifting small amounts of money does not lead to significant risk-spreading losses. Nor would these efficiency effects be noteworthy if the losses being made whole were strictly financial, for individuals would voluntarily choose to insure themselves against such losses and thus the compensation paid would reflect the types of trades individuals would undertake voluntarily, assuming they had access to actuarially fair markets.

Unfortunately, the losses for which malpractice awards compensate are not primarily of a financial nature; rather, they are losses of health or physical function. Moreover, the magnitudes of the payments are often large.[20] In effect the current malpractice system forces the patient to buy, through higher medical fees, a lottery ticket that pays off if he is injured and can demonstrate that his injury resulted from the physician's negligence. To gauge the efficiency of this approach we must ask if individuals would choose to take this gamble.

Upon reflection, it becomes obvious that individuals would not accept the gamble offered. First, given the opportunity to secure what is in effect insurance, most would choose to insure themselves against an unfortunate outcome for the same dollar amount regardless of how the condition might come about. For example, leaving incentives aside, if it is rational to pay higher medical fees in order to be entitled to $50,000 compensation through a malpractice suit if the physician's negligence leads to a paralyzed arm, then one should also insure for $50,000 against that paralysis should it result from any cause, such as an automobile accident or a mugging. Yet with the malpractice system, the ultimate condition is only one determinant of compensation; negligence must also be demonstrated. Observations of this sort have in part been responsible for proposals that malpractice be replaced with a no-fault system for iatrogenic injuries.[21] Such proposals, however, do

---

[20] Rubsamen reports that from January 1974 through mid-1976, fourteen malpractice awards of more than $1 million were made in California; Rubsamen, "Medical Malpractice," p. 19.

[21] One such proposed plan is "Medical Adversity Insurance," put forth by Clark Havighurst and Laurence R. Tancredi in " 'Medical Adversity Insurance'—A No-Fault Approach to Medical Malpractice and Quality Assurance," *Milbank Memorial Fund Quarterly*, vol. 51 (1973), pp. 125-68 and elaborated more recently by Havighurst in "Has Its Time Come." The no-fault approach raises equity problems, some of which are discussed below. Specifically, we might wish to compensate more heavily individuals who we feel have been unjustly injured. Payments of this sort may enable society to feel that it has better atoned for its sins. Moreover, any no-fault approach will whittle away at the legitimacy of the entire tort law system.

not carry the argument to its logical conclusion. Compensation, again leaving aside incentive effects, should depend only on the physical state of the victim, not on whether the physician was in any way responsible for its occurrence.

In many circumstances where the loss is health, it is not appropriate to try to make the injured party whole. In some cases the question is moot, since no amount of money would be sufficient to bring the individual up to his original welfare level. No monetary payment, for example, would induce most individuals to accept blindness. Conceptually, at least, we can deal with this aspect of the problem. It is unlikely that the choice will be quite that stark, with blindness a certainty under one option. More realistically, we might inquire what savings in medical care costs would induce an individual to accept a .001 risk of blindness. Say that amount is $1000. Then providing the individual with $1000 before the risk is incurred, and letting him allocate it as he wishes on an actuarially fair basis, would, by definition, just make him whole. One possible allocation would be $1000 whether or not he is blinded. Alternatively, he might provide himself with $100,000 if blinded, for an actuarial cost of $100 = $100,000 × .001, and $901 if he is not, for an additional actuarial cost of $900. Or he could allocate the total amount to the blind state, in which case he would receive $1,000,000 if blinded, nothing otherwise.[22]

The point of this example is that the individual, confronted with a probability distribution on states of the world, is likely to have strong preferences about the contingent allocation of compensation. Rarely will he allocate all funds to the least favorable outcome. The point is seen most readily in the extreme case of a bachelor who might take a .01 chance of death in return for $1,000. He would hardly allocate this money in the form of $100,000 should he die, yet that is what is in effect done with malpractice. The simple point is that a tort system allocates monies highly inefficiently, concentrating large sums upon unfortunate physical conditions.

A more general point should be made. The tort system as originally defined was intended to provide incentives for an appropriate level of care as well as efficient compensation. Even if the first objective were being met (and we have argued that insurance for malpractice claims and third-party coverage of medical care tend to defeat it), the second

---

[22] If actuarially fair insurance is available, the individual seeking to maximize expected utility will allocate his funds so as to equalize the marginal utility of income across states (R. Zechhauser, "Coverage for Catastrophic Illness," *Public Policy*, vol. 21 [1973], pp. 149-72). See also P. Cook and D. Graham, "The Demand for Insurance and Protection: The Case of Irreplaceable Commodities," *Quarterly Journal of Economics*, vol. 91 (1977), pp. 143-56.

would not be. The incentive and compensation aspects of malpractice should be disentangled. Logically there is no reason why the amount of damages paid by the physician or his insurance company should be proportional to the level of compensation received by the injured victim.

Equity versus Efficiency. Malpractice engenders numerous issues of fairness or equity. The major contribution of the economics of safety to the equity discussion is to point out the competition between equity and efficiency, a long-standing concern of economists. We argued above that efficient compensation requires that a patient suffering disability as the result of his physician's negligence should receive no more than he would if the disability resulted from an act of God or any other cause. Many will disagree with this conclusion on equity grounds, feeling that an individual injured by another's negligence somehow deserves more compensation.

The economist might formulate the equity issue by examining individuals' ex ante positions, before they have been exposed to any risk of injury. Suppose a patient engages a surgeon whose skill and care are well established. There is some risk that the patient's left arm will be lost. What sort of compensation scheme would the patient choose if he had to pay its fair actuarial cost? If, for example, he proposed receiving $100,000 if the arm were lost (let us say that is the amount that would make him "whole"), and if the probability of that event were .001, he would have to pay $100. A right-handed white-collar worker might observe that while the loss of his left arm would make him extremely unhappy, it would not impair his ability to earn an income. By the arguments made earlier, in such a situation it might be quite rational for him to opt to receive no compensation at all for the loss of his arm, thus saving the cost of insurance. But then the surgeon operates, the 1 in 1,000 event occurs, the surgeon errs, and the arm is lost. At that point the patient would be unlikely to accept the idea that no compensation should be paid, and his complaint would have wide appeal; for although efficiency and indeed equity, as evaluated ex ante, would be served by his receiving no compensation, perceived equity would not be. To approach the issue by asking how the individual would have allocated funds across possible outcomes is not immediately appealing.

The usual conceptions of equity require attention to fault as well. Every state that has gone through the no-fault automobile insurance debate has confronted the argument that it hardly seems fair for a person whose car is slammed from the rear to have to pay his own deductible.[23] We suspect that considerations of this sort would make it virtually impossible to implement any no-fault malpractice scheme that closely tied a physician's premiums to his individual record of claims. Even under the current fault-based system, medical societies strongly resist attempts to experience-rate individual physicians. Under a no-fault scheme, this resistance would be all the stronger. Pressures probably would mount to fund compensation publicly, perhaps through some type of tax on health care expenditures, in which case all financial incentive effects on physicians would be lost.[24]

If physicians are to be subject to meaningful financial incentives, under either the current system or a no-fault plan, premiums must reflect the claims record of individual providers, or policies must include deductibles and coinsurance provisions. Any such attempts to tie the physician's costs more closely to his own record, however, will appear inequitable in many instances, particularly if claims are rare and dependent on capricious factors, such as the patient's personality. Even if a plan could somehow be devised that penalized only "bad" physicians, if the incentive effects were small the welfare loss from reduced risk spreading or equity might outweigh the efficiency gains.[25]

Equity, or at least concerns that are often labeled as such, will impinge strongly on any effort to reform malpractice. Any significant change will create some losers. Both our political system and our notions

---

[23] Indeed, in the authors' own state of Massachusetts, which pioneered no-fault automobile insurance, property damage coverage is now once again administered on a fault basis.

[24] In his dissent to the report of the Secretary's Commission on Medical Malpractice (Department of Health, Education, and Welfare, *Report*, pp. 127-29), Dr. Charles Hoffman, then president of the American Medical Association, advocates a form of no-fault compensation patterned after workmen's compensation and financed by employers. Havighurst, "Has Its Time Come," rightly emphasizes the necessity of tailoring physicians' premiums to their individual records if incentives are to be maintained under a no-fault scheme.

[25] A somewhat prosaic example drawn from another area may clarify the point. People who are overweight have a higher risk of suffering a variety of medical problems than people who are not. Yet health insurance premiums do not vary with weight, and hence fat people do not bear the full costs of their excess poundage; they impose a financial externality on other participants in their insurance plans, in the same way that "bad" physicians do for malpractice coverage. Suppose we wished to provide efficient incentives for people to maintain their proper weight by imposing a surcharge on health insurance premiums for overweight individuals. How one would evaluate such a plan would depend on a number of factors, but we suspect that most would find it much less attractive if it were discovered that most overweight individuals suffered from glandular problems, or simply from a very strong psychological propensity to overeat, that is significantly greater than the desire to maintain healthful weight levels. In that case the efficiency gains would be minimal, since behavior would change little, while the risk-spreading losses (assuming one did not yet know one's genetic endowment or fatness propensity) would be great.

of equity leave us disinclined to create losers. (Indeed, the malpractice crisis has arisen not because physicians were being driven to levels of welfare that would normally generate much sympathy, but rather because they were suffering significant losses.) This attitude tends to enshrine the status quo. Whatever system is in effect confers benefits on some individuals. As time passes, whatever the legitimacy or efficiency of the original distribution, these benefits are transformed into "rights." They will be difficult to take away, as some inevitably must be when society moves from one type of malpractice system to another. The groups whose rights are threatened are likely to complain bitterly, and if their screams are not quite sufficient to halt change, they will at least slow progress significantly.

The Drawbacks to Direct Regulation

A general theme emerges from our discussion. The malpractice area, characterized as it is by ill-defined low probabilities and vaguely understood causal relationships, will be one where patients, physicians, and adjudicators must be expected to make poor decisions. Moreover, given the maze of distorted incentives in the area, even good self-interested decisions by the actors involved are likely to be inconsistent with the maximization of social welfare.

Frequently under such circumstances the government steps in to regulate, particularly when human health is involved. Such governmental efforts range from preventing the sale of foods containing additives that can be shown to be carcinogenic, to prescribing certain physical conditions in workplaces, to banning unsafe consumer products from the market. In the malpractice area, the most significant interventions are likely to be some sort of quality assurance mechanisms, such as Professional Standard Review Organizations. Experience outside the medical realm suggests that direct regulation of safety is unlikely to prove successful. The recent flap over the Food and Drug Administration's ban on saccharin and the failure of the Occupational Safety and Health Administration to generate any noticeable reduction in occupational accidents, despite imposing substantial costs on the economy,[26] are cases in point.

The problems with attempts to regulate safety directly are apparent. Only a limited number of relevant variables can be monitored by the regulatory agency. With medical care, for example, it would be difficult to observe the level of care or sophistication of judgment exercised by

---

[26] See Nichols and Zeckhauser, "Government Comes to the Workplace," for an account of OSHA's performance.

the physician. Yet these may be the variables that have the greatest influence on outcomes.

Since only some factors can be monitored, there will be overinvestment in those areas if the regulatory mechanism has any teeth in it. Thus, because OSHA monitors capital equipment, expenditures on railings and rollover bars may be excessive relative to those on safety training. In the medical area, where quality-control mechanisms such as PSROs could determine whether a doctor had administered tests A and B, but not whether he was a bit tired from the night before, we can expect that tests A and B will be administered even in the most marginal of circumstances, but that physicians will not make every effort to be fresh and alert. Such regulation also tends to introduce undesirable rigidities. Doctors are supposed to perform in a manner that meets present standards and procedures, not those that would be determined to be best in an evolving and innovative world. This problem is most serious where there may be bureaucratic resistance to the evolution of new standards and where knowledge or technology is advancing rapidly—both of which appear to be characteristic of medical care. Direct regulation is thus not a very promising approach to promoting safety in this area.

Malpractice as a Symptom. The malpractice problem, we have argued, should be looked at as part of the larger problems that exist in our medical care system. The system suffers throughout from inappropriate incentives, unresolved conflicts between perceived equity and efficiency, and the general difficulty for many classes of participants in making firm determinations of the consequences of various actions, past and prospective. The medical care system—a modern leviathan, we are told—is on the brink of major changes and innovations. The malpractice problem will bob in its wake. For example, whatever its other virtues or faults, broad-based national health insurance without significant deductibles and coinsurance rates, or other incentives for cost control, would undoubtedly exacerbate the malpractice problem. (We distinguish here between the actual problem and the problem as it is perceived or measured, say by the level of insurance premiums. The first can get worse while the second gets better.)

Certain aspects of problems become salient in the political arena. With malpractice it was escalating the costs and premiums. A reform designed to deal primarily with these problems, we have suggested, may very well hurt the overall performance of the medical care system, in part through increases in such closely related inefficiencies as the excessive defensive medicine generated by fears of malpractice. Prescribing solely for malpractice symptoms is all the more futile because the medical care system itself is changing. A measure that may reduce claims in the context of the medical system of 1977 may actually prove counterproductive when the 1985 system is upon us.

Our purpose in this essay was diagnosis rather than prescription. Experts in the medical care area suggest that matters are not going well. Though we may be short of the collapse of the total system, there are certainly failures in many areas. The malpractice area is like the kidneys: it is a clearinghouse for unwanted wastes. Simply ministering to the kidneys of a patient suffering multiple failures will do little for the performance of the kidneys in the long run, or for the patient as a whole.

Proposed remedies in the malpractice area include placing ceilings on recovery, requiring patients to insure themselves, substituting no-fault compensation, developing contractual systems for the waiver of rights, and establishing new institutions for the arbitration of claims. None of these proposals should be adopted hastily in a crisis atmosphere. They should only be considered if they can be shown to have a high probability of superior performance. Our experience in making predictions in other fields is sobering. Consider the much simpler, though related, problem of no-fault auto insurance. In virtually no state is no-fault insurance working out as its supporters expected it would. It is just exceedingly difficult to make predictions when you tamper with one aspect of a system that involves complex incentives and limited information—one more reason why we should not try to treat malpractice as a problem in its own right.

The type of medical care system we have will strongly influence both the appropriate structure for compensating patients when they suffer adverse outcomes at the hands of a physician, and the penalties that should be levied on the physician. Moreover, the malpractice problem can only be ameliorated by improving the medical care system itself. Success with that larger task would yield benefits far in excess of any gains available by tinkering with malpractice. The malpractice crisis, though itself a significant concern, is most disturbing as a symptom.

THEORETICAL ISSUES IN MEDICAL MALPRACTICE

Steven Shavell

Introduction

This paper is concerned with medical malpractice as a problem in normative economics. Accordingly, it focuses on the connection between malpractice and two principal determinants of individual welfare, these being compensation for medical accidents and the quality and cost of medical services. It is assumed that individual utility depends on the probabilities of various alternative states of health and on the level of income which would be enjoyed in each possible state of health. These variables are known once the two determinants are specified. The accidents of special interest are iatrogenic, those which may be imputed to medical treatment itself rather than to a prior medical condition. By medical accident is meant any adverse medical event, whether or not it is in some sense "accidental" in nature. So far as the second determinant is concerned, emphasis is placed on the role of nonmarket institutions in assuring the quality of services. Assuring quality, in turn, is viewed as a dual problem: the typical physician [1] must be given the correct incentives to take care in the provision of medical services; and relatively unskilled physicians must be compelled or induced to get further training or to limit the scope of their activities. While there are other factors which clearly affect the quality and cost of medical services—consumer demand, the supply of new physicians, and the level of medical knowledge and technology—these are not emphasized.

The first two sections of the paper review theoretical issues pertinent to compensation and to assuring the quality of medical services. Then alternative approaches to liability for medical accidents are briefly

I wish to thank Kenneth Arrow, Ralph Berry, Guido Calabresi, Richard Danzig, Peter Diamond, Ted Frech, Victor Fuchs, Jerry Green, Robert Keeton, A. Mitchell Polinsky, Henry Steiner, and Richard Zeckhauser for comments and the National Science Foundation and the American Enterprise Institute for research support.
[1] The word *physician* is used for convenience; it is recognized that other providers (nurses, hospitals) of medical services are involved in the problems of malpractice.

compared; these are patient liability, strict liability, no-fault plans, and the negligence system (including proposals which would modify but not radically reform the system). The final section states the major conclusion of the paper—that special reliance on the courts for compensation of medical accidents is inappropriate—and also comments on the problem of assuring the quality of medical services.

The performance of the price system under perfect conditions is taken as a point of departure and standard for comparison. This is because under perfect conditions the price system results in an optimal outcome in Pareto's sense—it is impossible to simultaneously improve everyone's well-being. Moreover, given a suitable reallocation of ownership of resources, any Pareto optimal outcome can be achieved with the price system; complaints about economic outcomes are therefore reduced to complaints about the distribution of initial resources, notably income.[2] The conditions for an optimal outcome that are, perhaps, most important for the case of medical malpractice pertain to information about risks and the quality of medical services.[3] If information about both were perfect, there would be little difficulty with either compensation or assuring quality. Individuals would be aware of the true risks of medical accidents and would provide themselves with adequate insurance protection (given their income).[4] Individuals would recognize the true characteristics of medical care and would pay for services only in accordance with quality. Of course, much of the discussion here has to do with the consequences of individuals' lack of information about risks and the quality of medical services.

Compensation for Medical Accidents

In order to isolate issues related to compensation,[5] the probability of medical accidents and thus physician behavior is taken as fixed in this part of the paper.

---

[2] See for example Kenneth J. Arrow and Frank Hahn, *General Competitive Analysis* (San Francisco: Holden Day, 1971).

[3] See Kenneth J. Arrow, "Uncertainty and the Welfare Economics of Medical Care," *American Economic Review,* vol. 53 (December 1963), pp. 941-73. Throughout the paper the words *optimal, ideal,* and *appropriate* mean Pareto optimal.

[4] There are other obstacles to optimal insurance coverage which would also be eliminated in a hypothetical world of perfect information. These are discussed below.

[5] R. Keeton, "Compensation for Medical Accidents," *University of Pennsylvania Law Review,* vol. 121 (1973), pp. 590-617, contains an interesting discussion of the general subject of this section.

A Guide to Optimal Compensation. Whether publicly or privately provided, compensation for a medical accident ought to reflect the insurance coverage against the accident that a rational, well-informed individual with a socially acceptable level of income would have bought.[6] That is, the determination of optimal compensation ought to reflect a hypothetical decision about the purchase of insurance.[7] This point of view certainly does not imply that actual compensation should necessarily be left up to individuals and their insurance companies. As suggested in the introduction and stressed below, individuals may not make well-informed decisions about insurance (or may not have socially appropriate incomes).

In the next several subsections, aspects of the insurance purchase decision when made under perfect market conditions are considered. Then characteristics of the decision when made under more realistic circumstances are discussed.

Optimal Insurance Coverage versus Compensation for Economic Losses versus Compensation to Make a Person Whole. When buying insurance, an individual considers the cost of coverage, the likelihood of an accident, and—what is of particular importance here—the utility he would derive from income if he did not have an accident as compared to the utility he would derive from income if he did have an accident.[8]

Two examples make it clear that the level of coverage which an individual would select does not necessarily correspond to either of two perhaps appealing notions of optimal compensation: (1) the amount of purely economic damages, that is, forgone earnings plus costs of remedial treatment, and (2) the amount required to make a person whole, to restore him to his initial level of well-being, supposing that this were possible. Consider first an individual's decision to buy protection against

---

[6] Compensation is taken to include the amount received from *all* sources, that is, from private insurance, social insurance, out-of-court settlements, and court awards. By rights, the definition of ideal compensation for a medical accident involving a particular individual should reflect the arrangements for insurance that all interested parties (for example, employer, dependents) would wish to make; but this consideration is ignored for simplicity's sake.

[7] The justification for this is that (as stated above) under ideal conditions reliance on consumer preferences and on the price system results in a Pareto optimal outcome.

[8] The discussion in this subsection is most closely related to K. Arrow, "Optimal Insurance and Generalized Deductibles," *Scandinavian Actuarial Journal* (1974), pp. 1-42 and especially, Richard Zeckhauser, "Coverage for Catastrophic Illness," *Public Policy*, vol. 21 (Spring 1973), pp. 149-72; see also P. Cook and D. Graham, "The Demand for Insurance and Protection: The Case of Irreplaceable Commodities," in *Quarterly Journal of Economics*, vol. 61, no. 1 (February 1977), pp. 143-56. Appendix 1 contains a precise version and a proof of the statements of the subsection.

a permanently disabling medical accident. Assume that the (discounted) costs of treatment, chronic care, and therapy would be $200,000 and that of forgone earnings, another $200,000; assume further that an additional $100,000 would fully compensate pain and suffering. Finally, suppose that the individual has no dependents. In fact, this individual might buy, say, only $275,000 coverage, for money might have very little use to him when disabled yet be very valuable in his current state. In this case, therefore, optimal insurance coverage would not equal the economic damages, much less make the individual whole.

Now consider an individual who is about to buy coverage against the event that his appendix will have to be surgically removed. Assume that the sum of lost wages and medical expenses would be $2,000 and that $1,000 more for pain and suffering would be adequate to make him as well-off as before the contemplated event. If insurance is sold on an actuarially fair basis, this individual might buy only $2,000 coverage because, while he knows that surgery would be unpleasant and could be fully redressed by receipt of an additional $1,000, it may be that the utility he would derive from having the extra $1,000 after surgery is not sufficient to make his paying a higher premium worthwhile. (Equivalently, his need for money after surgery and after the $2,000 compensation for economic losses might be no different from what it had been beforehand.) In this instance, optimal insurance coverage would equal economic damages but fall short of making the individual whole.

In general, optimal insurance coverage would fail to make an individual whole when the marginal utility of income (net of payment of the insurance premium) if he does not have an accident exceeds the marginal utility of income (at the level which would make him whole) if he does have an accident. One guesses investigation would reveal that for most individuals and most accidents, optimal insurance coverage would not be sufficient to make a person whole and would in fact provide little or no benefits beyond the purely economic; furthermore, for accidents which do not involve permanent disability, optimal insurance coverage would probably equal economic losses (see Appendix 1). Of course, in theory almost any amount of insurance coverage could turn out to be optimal.

Cause as a Determinant of Optimal Compensation. Under perfect market conditions optimal insurance coverage would not ordinarily depend on the cause of a medical accident. Consider first the case of accidents due to factors (iatrogenicity, physician negligence) beyond the control of the patient. In this case, if the cost of each dollar of coverage per unit of probability of an accident does not depend on the cause of the accident, a rational individual would purchase the same amount of coverage for each cause. For example, suppose that a particular accident can occur in one of two ways, A and B, the latter being twice as likely as the former. Then if the premium for coverage applying in the event of B is twice that for coverage in the event of A, the amount of protection purchased for each would be identical.[9]

The example of an injured patient who wishes greater compensation because he wants to punish a negligent physician may not contradict this assertion. The patient's desire for *retribution* may not reflect an intrinsic need for additional *compensation*. His need for retribution might be satisfied by the physician's paying a fine to the state. It is only because the current negligence system is used that the compensation awarded to a patient and the monetary penalty paid by a physician (or his insurer) are the same.

However, the assumption that costs per unit of probability are independent of the cause is not always true. Suppose that a particular medical accident can be caused either by a factor which is random over the population or by an equally probable factor (an epidemic) which affects simultaneously a large group of individuals. Then the risk bearer, whether an insurance company or government, might have to charge a higher premium for insurance against the second factor. Nevertheless, in most cases considered below the premise about costs may be taken for granted.

Now consider the case of accidents in which the patient might have played a contributory role. In this case too it can be shown that optimal insurance coverage would not depend on cause, so long as the insurer could costlessly determine the actions of the patient (as would be true under perfect market conditions). This is explained in part below.

Obstacles to Compensation. Administrative costs are an obstacle to compensation which would be faced even under perfect market conditions.[10] Two types of administrative costs are noted here (see Appen-

---

[9] This is easily verified. Let the concave von Neumann-Morgenstern utility functions U and V give, respectively, the utility of wealth if there was no accident and if there was an accident. Let l be the monetary loss suffered in an accident, p_A and p_B be the probabilities of the accident's being caused by the (exclusive) events A and B, π the cost per dollar of coverage per unit of probability of the accident, and c_A and c_B the levels of coverage in the event of A and B. Then if y is initial wealth, c_A and c_B would be chosen to maximize expected utility $(1-p_A-p_B) U (y-\pi(p_A c_A + p_B c_B)) + p_A V(y-\pi(p_A c_A + p_B c_B)-l+c_A) + p_B V(y-\pi(p_A c_A + p_B c_B)-l+c_B)$ and the first order conditions imply that $c_A = c_B$ independent of π, p_A, and p_B.

[10] On administrative costs, see D. S. Lees and R. G. Rice, "Comment," *American Economic Review*, vol. 55 (1965), pp. 140-54; V. F. Bowland, "Comment,"

dix 2). The first are fixed costs: the costs of adding an individual's name to the list of insureds and the costs of collecting premiums. It is easy to show that given fixed costs, if it is optimal to purchase any coverage at all, it will be optimal to purchase full coverage (for once one has decided to purchase positive coverage and the fixed costs therefore have to be paid, additional coverage is purchased on actuarially fair terms—in which case full coverage is appropriate). But it will be optimal to purchase coverage only if potential losses are sufficiently high or if they are sufficiently uncertain. The second type of administrative cost is that of processing claims and of making payments. Given this type of cost, the optimal insurance policy is either full coverage against all losses or a kind of deductible (the use of deductibles reduces the number of claims), according to which approximately full coverage is paid if any coverage at all is paid.

There does not seem to be any general reason to believe that the public or the private sector has a special cost advantage. Cases need to be evaluated on an individual basis, taking into account at least three factors: (1) Economies of scale obviously exist in the provision of insurance. One suspects that these may often be fully enjoyed by numerous competing firms. Otherwise, efficiency would require that only a few firms service the entire market, and regulation might be needed to force them to pass on cost reductions.[11] (2) "Acquisition costs," the costs of selling insurance, face both public and private insurers, though the proportion of these which may be attributed to informative selling effort may well be higher for public insurers. (3) On the other hand, there is the often-heard argument that the private sector has a greater desire and a better opportunity (especially with respect to its personnel policy) to achieve efficiency.

Several well-known obstacles to compensation which arise under less than perfect market conditions need to be mentioned. It will become obvious that these obstacles are due in one way or another to lack of information. The first obstacle, called the *moral hazard*, is the tendency of insurance to reduce the incentive of the insured to avoid losses.[12]

American Economic Review, vol. 55 (1965), pp. 1172-73; Peter Diamond, "Insurance Theoretic Aspects of Workers' Compensation," mimeo. (Cambridge, Mass.: MIT, 1975); Arrow, "Uncertainty and Welfare"; and Appendix 2 of this paper.

[11] Depending on one's views of the effectiveness of the regulators and of their ability to ascertain true costs, the regulated insurer may or may not sell coverage at rates achievable by a public insurer.

[12] See Arrow, "Uncertainty and Welfare"; Mark Pauly, "The Economics of Moral Hazard: Comment," *American Economic Review*, vol. 58 (1968), pp. 531-37; Michael Spence and Richard Zeckhauser, "Insurance, Information, and Individual Action," *American Economic Review*, vol. 61 (1971), pp. 380-87; and Steven Shavell, "On Moral Hazard and Insurance," mimeo. (Cambridge, Mass.: Harvard University, 1977).

Two types of moral hazard are of potential interest. One is exemplified by the case of a person with insurance who takes less care to avoid a loss than an uninsured counterpart. This happens because the insurer is unable to observe costlessly how careful the insured person is; otherwise the insurer would certainly make the premium or the insurance payment depend on the level of care, thereby giving the insured an incentive to be careful. Insurers have partially offset this kind of moral hazard by spending to acquire information about the level of care or by using deductible and coinsurance schemes. Both practices give the insured an incentive to be careful.

In theory, this type of moral hazard alters the previous conclusion that cause is irrelevant to compensation for a medical accident. Suppose that an accident (paralysis) may occur in either of two ways (disease, surgical error). Suppose further that if it occurs in the first way, it is possible that the injured individual may have played a contributory role (failed to seek medical attention when symptoms first appeared). Then, because of the moral hazard, deductibles or coinsurance may be desirable. (Alternatively, the insurer may choose to offset the moral hazard by acquiring information about the level of care and then conditioning the premium or insurance payment on the observation of care; in this case if the information was imperfect, partial coverage would still be desirable.) Optimal compensation, therefore, may be less if the accident occurs in the first way than if it occurs in the second way. However, in this paper we will assume that individuals have little influence over the probability of occurrence of a medical accident. This reflects the admittedly casual judgment that in the cases of greatest empirical interest, the question of a contributory role of the individual is not important.

The other type of moral hazard is exemplified by the case of a person with health insurance who (together with his physician) spends more on treatment of a given medical condition than an uninsured individual with a similar condition. This happens because the insurer is unable to observe perfectly the true medical condition; otherwise the insurer would link the premium or the payment to the actual condition. Insurers have attempted to offset this kind of moral hazard in ways similar to those mentioned above.

A second obstacle to compensation is that it may be difficult or impossible for the insurer to distinguish between individuals as to risk. In this circumstance both relatively low- and relatively high-risk individuals have to pay equally for equal amounts of coverage. If risks are pooled, then, the usual consequence is that low-risk individuals pay too much and buy too little insurance (as compared to the optimum under perfect market conditions), while high-risk individuals pay too little and buy too much.[13]

A third obstacle to compensation is that an individual's perception of the risk he faces may be inaccurate.[14] If he overestimates the risk, his purchase of coverage will be too great, while if he underestimates the risk, his coverage will be too small. (A closely related difficulty is that, because an individual may find it distressing to contemplate the possibility of a medical accident, he may buy on an "irrational" basis.)

This problem may be remedied in several ways by the public sector; the motive and scope for action by private insurers seems limited. On the one hand, individuals can be educated to the true nature of the risk, but this may be very expensive and only partially attainable. Whatever the value of such education, the private sector is unlikely to invest in it sufficiently. An individual insurance firm would find it difficult to appropriate the benefits of its investment, for a better informed customer could just as well buy from the firm's competitors. Although a collective effort on the part of private insurers to inform the public of risks (at least of higher risks) might be worthwhile, such an effort could be hampered by the problem of "free riders."

Rather than attempting to educate individuals to the truth, the public sector can provide compensation on a compulsory basis or subsidize the purchase of insurance. (The case considered here is that individuals purchase too little insurance. If they bought too much, the consequences would be less serious; in any event, in this case a tax would be appropriate.) Compulsory protection alone may fail to individualize adequately compensation; and, ideally, compensation ought to be individualized, especially with respect to differences in forgone earnings associated with differencess in income earning capacity. However, there are two reasons why compulsory protection may fail to or, as a practical matter, ought not to individualize compensation. First, it may be difficult to determine a good approximation to optimal coverage on an individual basis. Second, it may be difficult to arrange to individualize payments (implicit premiums) to finance the compulsory compensation system; and if payments are not individualized, benefits should not be individualized. Court awards in malpractice cases are financed by physicians and, therefore, ultimately by patients. But the extent to which physicians usually charge patients higher fees

---

13 See, for example, Arrow, "Uncertainty and Welfare," and Michael Rothschild and Joseph Stiglitz, "Equilibrium in Competitive Insurance Markets," *Quarterly Journal of Economics*, vol. 90 (November 1976), pp. 629-50.

14 See Michael Spence, "Consumer Misperceptions, Product Failure, and Producer Liability," mimeo. (Stanford, Calif.: Stanford University, 1974).

when the latter would have wished for greater insurance coverage is unclear.

Subsidization alone would probably help to individualize compensation but still fail to induce individuals—particularly those who were overly optimistic about risk or financially constrained—to purchase correct coverage. Therefore, a compromise between compulsory and subsidized insurance seems attractive.

Court Awards and Insurance Purchases as Indicators of Optimal Compensation. To determine optimal compensation, it is unlikely that one should look to actual court awards. These awards, made after the fact, are apparently often based on the doctrine of making a person whole, a doctrine which, as we have seen, is not justifiable by economic theory. The awards may occasionally be based on payment of economic losses alone, another faulty criterion. Moreover, particularly in cases of malpractice, there is the suspicion that awards may sometimes be inflated to punish the physician or to ensure that the plaintiff is left with his rightful share after deduction of lawyers' fees. Also, juries are sometimes swayed by emotions in deciding upon an award.

Neither is it clear that the record of actual insurance purchases would furnish the right information. As mentioned above, if individuals misperceive the risks of adverse medical events or if they find the act of insuring against these risks psychologically burdensome, they will not purchase the correct amount of coverage. In addition, if premiums exceed by a large amount actuarial costs (through lack of competition or inordinately high acquisition costs), individuals will not purchase the correct amount of coverage.

Summary. (1) Compensation (the sum of accident benefits from all sources) for a medical accident ought to reflect the amount of insurance coverage an individual (with a socially appropriate income) would have bought against the accident if he were acting rationally and were cognizant of the relevant risks.

(2) Optimal insurance coverage may exclude attributions to pain and suffering and may fail to restore economic losses (costs of treatment plus forgone earnings).

(3) Furthermore, optimal insurance coverage ordinarily depends only on the circumstances of an injured individual. Causal factors such as iatrogenicity or physician negligence are irrelevant to optimal coverage.

(4) There are four major obstacles to compensation: administrative costs, moral hazard (reduced incentive for insureds to avoid loss), pooling of unequal risks, and misperception of risks.

(5) Misperception of risks can be remedied in several ways (education, compulsory or subsidized insurance) by the public sector. The motive and scope for action by private insurers in this regard seems limited.

(6) Neither court awards nor the actual record of individual insurance purchases may be good indicators of optimal compensation.

Assuring the Quality of Medical Services

Failure of Market Forces to Assure Quality. Demand and supply factors, technology, and certain nonmarket institutions of the medical sector jointly determine the quality and price of medical services. It has been argued that these nonmarket institutions are required because the operation of the price system alone would not be expected to result in a completely satisfactory outcome:[15] It is true that under ideal conditions, market forces would lead to provision of medical services of the correct quality and cost (as well as to an appropriate matching of patients to physicians), for patients would demand those services which best met their needs, taking quality and cost into account. However, in fact patients are presumed to be unable to judge adequately the quality of medical services. Society has therefore resorted to nonmarket institutions to guarantee quality, namely, to educational standards, licensure requirements, and a variety of professional and legal incentives. (Such nonmarket institutions also restrict supply of physicians and therefore tend to raise wages.) Furthermore, the medical profession has developed a set of ethical norms which help to maintain public trust in the quality of medical services.

Nonmarket Influences on Competence and Care. Emphasis in this subsection is on the effects of nonmarket institutions on the competence of and the care taken by physicians; there is no discussion of the effect of nonmarket institutions on other relevant variables (such as medical technology or the number of new physicians). *Competence* refers here to the skill and knowledge of a physician, reflecting both his training and his native ability, while *care* refers to the effort and time taken in the provision of medical services by a physician of given competence.

Consider first the effects of educational standards and tests for licensure. These do not usually raise levels of care, as the term has been defined, but they do influence competence. They encourage

---

[15] The point of view summarized in this paragraph is elaborated in Arrow's important paper, "Uncertainty and Welfare."

physicians to acquire new skills and they eliminate those who fail to meet prescribed standards. However, use of standards does not affect the competence of different physicians in the same way, for only those who consider failure a real prospect are (other things equal) most highly motivated to acquire new skills, and only those who are least able actually fail. This is not to deny the existence of other reasons for performing well nor is it to rule out the potential for graded licensing.

Nonmarket incentives—threats of financial or professional sanctions based on the performance or outcome of medical activity, along with positive incentives—influence both competence and care. Incentives clearly increase care; this is the subject of the next subsection. They also tend to improve competence in several ways: (1) physicians may acquire new skills, (2) they may decide to avoid certain medical activities altogether, and (3) they may be prevented from engaging in certain activities as a result of sanctions. Items (1) and (2) depend on the extent to which physicians actually assess their competence and act on that evaluation. Item (3) does not require such cooperation from the physician but has the drawback that it often applies only after harm has been done. Also, inasmuch as evidence of incompetence may appear rarely, sanctions may have to be imposed on the basis of incomplete information. It may be difficult to distinguish the unlucky from the incompetent. Presumably, evidence may appear rarely either because situations which truly test skills are infrequent or because it is difficult to obtain credible information.

The difference between the effects on competence and care of educational standards and tests for licensure on the one hand and of incentives on the other has relevance for the design of policy. For example, if physicians are on the whole sufficiently competent and most cases of malpractice are due to lack of care, stricter incentives might be necessary. But if under existing incentives adequate care is usually taken and most cases of malpractice are due to the incompetence of a small subgroup of physicians, then stricter licensure rather than stricter incentives might be advisable. Determination of whatever is the best policy is likely to be sensitive to the relative importance of the problems of adequacy of care and incompetence.

Incentives and Care. The discussion of nonmarket incentives and care logically belongs in the previous subsection, but because of its length, it is presented separately. It is assumed here that physicians are of equal competence.

Penalties (or rewards) under an incentive system may be made conditional on the *outcome* of a medical activity or on the degree of care taken during the activity, that is, on *process*. For example, a system under which surgeons had to pay damages whenever a patient died on the operating table (regardless of care taken), would be a purely outcome-oriented incentive system. A system under which surgeons' activities were under constant observation and fines imposed whenever care was insufficient (regardless of outcome) would be a purely process-oriented incentive system. A negligence system, under which inquiries were made into a surgeon's activity only after a patient had died on the operating table, and fines were imposed when care was found to have been insufficient, would be an incentive system that was both outcome and process oriented.

Outcome versus process-oriented incentive systems.[16] One justification for outcome-oriented incentive systems (when there is no question of contributory negligence) runs as follows. Suppose that whenever there is an accident, a penalty equal to the social loss incurred is imposed on the physician. Since the physician will then weigh the costs of taking care against the social loss which he would pay in the event of an accident, he will make a socially optimal decision. (If costs of taking care are relatively high compared to the social loss, the physician will take relatively little care, and so forth.) Furthermore, all that the designer of the incentive system needs to know is the magnitude of the social loss. There is no necessity for him to know the costs the physician bears in taking care, the technical relationship between care and the probability of an accident, or the actual level of care taken in a particular incident.

This justification for an outcome-oriented incentive system overlooks the effect of risk aversion on the part of the physician. Assume for now that the physician cannot buy insurance against a penalty he may have to pay. If he is averse to risk, he will either take more care than is desirable or he will insist on extra compensation for bearing risk, charging more for his services. By contrast, an ideal incentive system would induce the physician to take the optimal level of care without imposing risk.[17]

A perfect process-oriented incentive system can accomplish this. Suppose that the penalty is imposed only if the actual level of care is

---

16 The following is based in part on Steven Shavell, "Accidents, Liability, and Insurance," mimeo. (Cambridge, Mass.: Harvard University, 1977).

17 This would clearly be a superior situation, for either the potential injurer would be made better off by no longer having to bear risk, or else he would no longer need to be compensated for bearing the risk. Note that under the conditions most congenial to the market (in this case, perfect information about the quality of medical services), the physician is induced (by the prospect of a lower price) to take the right amount of care without having to bear risk.

below the optimal level. Then physicians would take the optimal level of care, would not fear the imposition of a penalty, and therefore would bear no risk. In other words, a perfectly accurate and costlessly operated process-oriented incentive system is better than an outcome-oriented system; information about the level of care is valuable.[18]

Now consider the possibility that physicians can purchase insurance against penalties imposed under an outcome-oriented incentive system. If the insurer observes the level of care, the insurance policy would depend on care, in effect making the incentive system process oriented. If the insurer does not observe the level of care, then the insurance coverage purchased will be only partial. This is because the insurer will face a problem of moral hazard of the first type outlined above.[19] With incomplete coverage, then, physicians would still be subject to some risk and a process-oriented incentive system would still be desirable.

Under a perfect process-oriented system, it is clear that there would be no motive to buy insurance against liability. Of course, in the usual case, when the process-oriented system makes use of inaccurate information, this statement no longer holds.

There are, however, important qualifications to be made about the case for a process-oriented incentive system. First, information may be costly to gather and evaluate, as is particularly true of information about the care exercised by a physician. Consequently, it may be advantageous to use a process-oriented system only part of the time—for instance, when there is, before acquisition of information about a case, some basis for thinking that the care taken was insufficient. Presumably, this is what is accomplished under a negligence system, since investigation of care is made only if there is a suit.

Second, information may be inaccurate. If information about care is not precise, a physician who in fact takes the optimal level of care is subject to the risk of penalty since his observed level may appear too low.[20]

Third, the standard of care (below which a penalty is imposed) may not be correctly chosen or consistently applied under a process-oriented incentive system. Choice of the correct standard requires knowledge not only of the loss imposed by physicians, but also of the costs physicians face in taking care and of the technical relationship between care taken and the quality of medical services. Therefore, the

---

[18] This fact is equivalent to the statement that the (first) problem of moral hazard is eliminated when the insurance payment can be made conditional on the level of care.
[19] For simplicity's sake, it is assumed that the insurer does not invest in information about care. If the insurer does, the argument is more complicated.
[20] See Shavell, "Moral Hazard."

47

opportunities for error and for inconsistent application of standards by the agents of the incentive system are probably substantial.

These last two qualifications provide different reasons why risks would be imposed on physicians, diluting the advantage of the process-oriented system and making it resemble an outcome-oriented system. If risks are imposed on physicians under a process-oriented system, the previous observation that they would not purchase insurance obviously fails to apply. The insurance coverage purchased, however, would be incomplete for the same reason that it would be under an outcome-oriented system. This does not necessarily imply that insurance against court awards would be incomplete, for there are costs other than the award itself which may not be insured.

Bias in patient selection. A problem which would arise, especially under an outcome-oriented incentive system, is a tendency toward bias in patient selection. Suppose that a physician has more detailed knowledge of the medical risks facing a patient than does the agency administering the incentives. Then the penalties imposed by the agency for adverse medical outcomes cannot be made to depend on all the circumstances which the physician recognizes as influencing risk. Consequently, a physician would (other things equal) choose to treat low-risk patients rather than high-risk ones. For example, surgeons might select patients at least partly on the basis of the risk of adverse outcomes. This criterion for patient selection is not generally desirable; for instance, high-risk patients might on average have a greater need for treatment than low-risk patients. In addition, physicians might needlessly expend medical resources in determining risks even though the level of risk would not always change the choice of treatment.

Patient-selection bias appears most likely under outcome-oriented incentive systems. Under process-oriented incentive systems, information concerning the true condition (risk) of the patient might be adduced by the agency administering the incentives; penalties could be made to depend on the condition of the patient. Knowing this, a physician would have less reason to select on the basis of risk. But the information acquired might be incomplete or inaccurate; patient-selection bias is therefore likely to remain under a process-oriented incentive system.

It must be admitted, however, that physicians could charge more to high-risk than to low-risk patients. This would not only lessen the selection bias but also could do positive good by increasing (from what may be a suboptimal level) the general recognition of patient risk.[21] Yet it would often be difficult to arrange differential charges for medical

---

[21] I owe this point to Peter Diamond.

treatment. First, the fact that patients usually prepay medical expenses through insurance plans would hinder the individualization of charges. And, second, the fact that patients would frequently be unable to verify easily their supposed risk category would make it hard for a physician to charge high-risk patients more.

Defensive medicine. Defensive medicine is the use of medical resources beyond the point that is justified by an evaluation of true social costs and benefits. As mentioned above, three factors can lead under a process-oriented incentive system to the imposition of risk on providers—and thus to unduly conservative action, defensive medicine. The three factors are the use of inaccurate information, the inconsistent application of standards, and difficulties in determining correct standards. The current negligence system is subject to these factors.

It also appears that the risks of penalty to physicians under the current negligence system go beyond the settlements which may be made with patients. The risks include the opportunity cost of time lost in handling claims and damage from loss of reputation. Physicians typically bear these risks. Because of the problems of moral hazard, the potential insurability of the financial risks is limited. The non-financial risks cannot be insured.

Two additional factors deserve mention. First, certain types of medical care (such as diagnostic tests or the administration of drugs) are readily observable. Realizing this, physicians may overemploy such types of care. Second, many individuals' medical expenses are covered by health insurance plans, suggesting an overuse of medical resources to begin with—the second moral hazard discussed above. In other words, the current negligence system may exacerbate an existing pattern of overuse of certain medical resources.[22]

Summary. (1) Nonmarket institutions (educational standards, licensure requirements, incentive systems) are needed to assure the quality of medical services because patients are presumably ill equipped to judge quality on their own.

(2) The quality of medical services depends on the competence of physicians and on the effort or care they exercise. The choice of policy depends on the relative importance of the problems of incompetence and adequacy of care.

---

[22] It is unclear whether one such resource is physician time per patient. For example, if under a health insurance plan a physician earns more over a given period the more patients he sees (the quality of services being constant), he might spend less time per patient than would be optimal.

(3) Educational standards and tests for licensure affect and distinguish competence but have little influence on the care taken by a physician of given competence.

(4) Incentive systems (threats of financial or professional sanctions) affect both competence and care. Competence is affected ex ante and ex post; care is affected primarily ex ante. Ex ante effects depend on physicians' recognition of their own characteristics and of the incentives. Ex post effects do not depend on this, but there are other problems with such effects.

(5) Penalties under an incentive system may be dependent on the outcome of medical activity or on the procedure or process itself. The advantage of a process-oriented incentive system over an outcome-oriented system is that the former reduces the risk borne by physicians since penalties are imposed only when there is negligence. (But the possibilities for physicians to insure themselves against the penalties of an incentive system must be taken into account.) However, the cost of employing a process-oriented incentive system suggests that it might be advantageous to use it only part of the time. In addition, inaccurate information, inconsistent application of standards, and difficulties in determining appropriate standards seriously limit the attractiveness of a process-oriented system by imposing risk on physicians.

(6) There are two additional potential problems with incentive systems. The first, patient-selection bias, arises because physicians may often be able to differentiate patients on the basis of risk of an adverse medical event and may shun high-risk patients. Patient-selection bias would be more significant under an outcome-oriented system. The second problem, defensive medicine, may be caused by the general factors which promote risk for physicians under incentive systems, but there are other special predisposing factors including (1) the physician's inability to insure against certain losses (such as damage to reputation), (2) the tendency for courts to focus attention on the use of certain medical resources (such as diagnostic tests) which may be easily observed, thus leading physicians to overemploy such resources, and (3) a pattern of overuse of certain types of medical resources initially (because of patient health insurance).

Approaches to Liability for Medical Accidents

Several approaches to liability for medical accidents are briefly considered here both as a means of compensation and as a means for assuring the quality of medical services. Of course, only if individuals would otherwise be underinsured does it make sense to judge a system of liability on how well it serves as a means of compensation.

Patient Liability, Strict Liability, and No-Fault Plans. By definition, patient liability has no role as a means of compensation. However, in regard to assuring the quality of medical services, it should be recognized that patient liability does not preclude the use of incentives, including financial penalties, to affect physician behavior.

As a means of compensation, strict liability has a serious drawback. The drawback is that compensation is given only if the accident in question is determined to be iatrogenic, that is, caused by medical treatment but not necessarily by negligent medical treatment.[23] This determination, which would often be costly and time consuming, has little value from the point of view of achieving optimal compensation, for it has been argued that the latter does not depend on the cause of an accident. As a means of assuring the quality of medical services, strict liability has the general disadvantages of any outcome-oriented incentive system, namely patient-selection bias, the imposition of risk on physicians, and defensive medicine.

A no-fault plan is probably best viewed as a system of strict liability. Under such a plan, physicians would contribute to a fund from which individuals would be compensated for a predetermined class of iatrogenic injuries. Thus, as with strict liability, compensation is not given for all accidents and there might be substantial operating costs owing to the possibility of having to decide a large number of cases in which it would be difficult to determine iatrogenicity. Proposed no-fault plans differ somewhat from strict liability with regard to assuring the quality of medical services. Under one no-fault plan, that of Senators Inouye and Kennedy, a mechanism would be established for collecting information about medical accidents. This information would supposedly be used to influence physician behavior, but few details are given.[24] Under another no-fault plan called Medical Adversity Insurance, the use of coinsurance and especially experience-rating would be emphasized.[25]

---

[23] Should the death of the patient during surgery be attributed to medical treatment itself or to a prior medical condition? See, more generally, Robert Keeton, "Compensation for Medical Accidents," *University of Pennsylvania Law Review*, vol. 121 (1973), pp. 590-617 and Richard Epstein, "Medical Malpractice: The Case for Contract," *American Bar Foundation Research Journal* (1976), pp. 87-149.

[24] S. 215, 94th Congress (1975) and H.R. 4881, 94th Congress.

[25] See Clark Havighurst, " 'Medical Adversity Insurance'—Has Its Time Come?" *Duke Law Journal* (1975), pp. 1233-80. The usefulness of experience-rating appears to be limited. Experience-rating has two effects. (1) It supplies an incentive to take care. In this respect the advantage it has over coinsurance is not

The Negligence System. As a means of compensation, the negligence system suffers from much the same drawback as strict liability. Under the negligence system compensation is not given to all injured individuals, but only to those who establish (or make a credible threat to establish) physician negligence; and the substantial costs of attempting to establish negligence are of dubious benefit in achieving optimal compensation.

As a means of assuring the quality of medical services, the current negligence system has two major disadvantages. First, it appears to be subject to the general factors mentioned above associated with process-oriented incentive systems which impose risks on physicians and which therefore contribute to the problems (including patient-selection bias and defensive medicine) associated with outcome-oriented incentive systems. Popular wisdom regards the risks faced by physicians as important, and the strength of demand for malpractice insurance confirms the belief. Second, medically irrelevant characteristics of the physician and the socioeconomic status and personality type of the patient are apparently important indicators of the likelihood of a malpractice claim.

Modifications of the negligence system. Many suggestions for mitigating the malpractice problem would modify the current negligence system. Most of these suggestions aim to reduce the risks and insurance costs borne by physicians.[26] Before we discuss several of the suggestions it may be appropriate to make a few remarks about rates, claims, and settlements. Rates are based on both experienced costs and projected costs. Projected costs are of particular importance since claims on present occurrences may easily be made as many as five or more years into the future. Experienced costs are determined by the volume of claims and by the expense per claim, comprising legal costs and settlements. Legal costs and the size distribution of settlements influence the motive to make claims and therefore the volume of claims.

(1) Ceiling on malpractice awards: This would reduce malpractice insurance rates in three ways: by lowering the size of settlements, by reducing the motive to make claims and therefore the number of claims, and by making prediction of costs easier and consequently by permitting insurers to reduce allowances for risk which they would otherwise build

---

clear. (2) Experience-rating also discriminates against physicians with bad records. Because these physicians may be unlucky rather than incompetent and there is no reason to penalize the unlucky, the optimal structure of experience-rating would strongly depend on the distribution of competence among physicians. The dangers of miscalculation would therefore be significant.

[26] Suggestions concerning screening, arbitration, and narrowing of defendant liability are not discussed here; see for example Epstein, "Medical Malpractice."

into rates. A ceiling on malpractice awards is, however, undesirable from the point of view of providing compensation since it would deny coverage to those in greatest need. A better approach would be to place a floor on awards and to base the size of awards in a predetermined way on the circumstances of injured individuals.

(2) Prohibition of contingent fees for lawyers:[27] The effect of prohibiting the use of contingent fees on the number of claims is unclear. Such a prohibition would shift the direct financial risk of losing a case to individuals. If lawyers are better able than individual patients to bear this risk, the typical patient would be less inclined to make a claim if his legal fees were not contingent, and hence the number of claims would fall. Present use of contingent fees suggests that lawyers are in fact the better risk bearers, but there are other (not necessarily competing) explanations. The prohibition would also diminish the incentive of lawyers to expend effort to win cases, further reducing the inclination of individuals to make claims. Because lawyers would not need to win their cases to collect fees, however, they would be more willing to accept tenuous claims, implying an increase in the number of claims.[28] The net effect on the *number* of claims is therefore ambiguous. Other things equal, the average *size* of claims would decline, since lawyers would have less reason to press large claims over small ones. However, as the total *value* of claims is determined by the total number and average size of claims, it does not seem possible to conclude that the total value of claims would fall.

The desirability of prohibiting contingent fees is likewise unclear. Consider first the issue, compensation. After prohibition, compensation net of lawyers' fees would be lower for those getting small amounts and higher for those getting large amounts than with contingent fees. While on average this change might be considered beneficial (those bearing greater losses being helped at the expense of those with lesser), the indeterminacy of the change in the total value of claims makes it impossible to conclude whether prohibition would make better or worse a problem of underinsurance against medical accidents.

Consider now the issue of assuring the quality of medical services. In this regard, the question is whether prohibiting contingent fees would lead to more rational use of the negligence system.[29] Ideally, the negli-

---

[27] Under a contingent fee plan, a lawyer is paid only if his client actually collects damages. See Reder's paper in this volume.

[28] It is fair to ask why tenuous claims might not be accepted today on a non-contingent fee basis. The answer is probably that the refusal of a lawyer to accept a case today on a contingent fee basis is a strong signal to the potential client that his claim is not a good one.

[29] I plan to investigate the question in subsequent work.

gence system ought to be employed only if the social costs of making an additional claim are less than or equal to the social benefits. While the social costs include the costs of running the courts and the legal expenses of both plaintiff *and* defendant, in the United States the private cost to the plaintiff usually includes only that of his own counsel. The social benefits of making another claim reside in the claim's effect in assuring quality. The relationship between the social benefits and the private benefits (the expected award or out-of-court settlement) is not clear. If it turns out, as I would suppose, that there are in fact too many claims, and if prohibition would reduce the number of claims, prohibition would have to be considered as beneficial in assuring the quality of services.

(3) Subsidization of small claims: Subsidization of small claims would no doubt increase the total number of claims. The objective of subsidization appears to be the provision of compensation through the medium of courts to a class of individuals who might otherwise be under-insured. This is an expensive way for society to buy insurance. As to assuring the quality of medical services, subsidization appears to be undesirable, in view of the considerations discussed in the previous paragraph.

(4) Use of "claims made" versus "occurrence" insurance:[30] The St. Paul Fire and Marine Insurance Company has introduced a "claims made" medical malpractice insurance policy. Suppose that in year one a physician treats a patient who decides in year two to sue for malpractice because he discovers evidence of malpractice only in year two. Under an "occurrence" policy, the usual kind of medical malpractice insurance policy, the physician would have purchased at the beginning of year one coverage against all claims—whenever they might be made—on incidents occurring during year one. Thus, his insurance would apply to the suit in question even though it was brought in year two. Under a claims-made policy, however, the physician's coverage purchased at the beginning of year one would have protected him only against claims made that year. But he would also have had the option of purchasing at the beginning of year two coverage protecting him against claims made during that year for occurrences in year one. The rate he would pay in year two would depend on the insurer's projection of costs at the beginning of that year. Thus, with claims made, the insurer would

---

[30] Although this is a modification of the terms of insurance rather than a modification of the negligence system, it seems appropriate to mention it here. See St. Paul Fire and Marine Insurance Company, "Preserving a Medical Malpractice Insurance Marketplace: Problems and Remedies," January 1975.

not have to bear the risk of unexpected changes in average claim costs for periods greater than one year; this risk would be borne by physicians. On the other hand, physicians would still be insured against the risk they fear most, that of having to pay a large award. If insurers are particularly averse to fluctuations in malpractice underwriting profits, then claims-made policies appear to offer a better means of risk sharing than occurrence policies.[31]

Concluding Remarks

The discussion of this paper has suggested that it would be undesirable to place special reliance on the courts for compensation of victims of medical accidents. This conclusion is based on the argument that compensation should ideally depend only on the circumstances of victims and the nature of their injuries, not on physician negligence or iatrogenicity. But whether compensation is given to victims by the courts does depend on the latter factors. Moreover, it was claimed that when compensation is given by the courts, the principles used in determining the size of awards are not generally appropriate. Additionally, inquiries into medical accidents by the courts are typically much more costly than would be the mere provision of insurance benefits to victims.

With regard to the goal of assuring the quality of medical services, this paper distinguished problems related to competence of physicians from problems related to adequacy of care taken by physicians. It was pointed out that educational standards and tests for licensure affect primarily the competence of physicians, while the risk of legal and professional sanctions following medical accidents provides incentives which affect not only competence but also adequacy of care. These incentives were discussed from a general theoretical perspective, and alternative approaches to liability for medical accidents were compared. However, the relative lack of information about the problem of assuring the quality of medical services made it difficult to conclude that one approach was better than another.

---

[31] The St. Paul company points out that an advantage of such policies would relieve young physicians of having to pay large premiums when they were starting their careers. Epstein in "Medical Malpractice" suggests that retiring physicians would be hurt by such policies since they would have to pay premiums after the end of their careers. This overlooks the fact that such premiums could be financed out of savings from premiums under occurrence policies which would have been paid before retirement. On the other hand, the consequences of unexpectedly early retirement would be more serious, imposing extra risk on physicians.

It should be mentioned that there are apparent accounting advantages to claims-made policies; insurers' required reserves are less under claims-made than under occurrence policies.

Appendix A: Optimal Insurance Coverage, Economic Losses, and Making a Person Whole

The discussion of the relationship among optimal insurance coverage, economic losses, and making a person whole (fully compensating pain and suffering as well as economic losses) makes reference to a simple example of an insurance decision; the example is similar to the one in an article by P. Cook and D. Graham.[32] Let p be the (fixed) probability of an accident, l the associated economic (monetary) loss, $U(y)$ the von Neumann-Morgenstern utility of wealth y if there is no accident, and $V(y)$ utility of wealth if there is an accident. Assume that in either state the individual is risk averse (U,V are concave), that the accident itself is not desirable (so $U(y) > V(y)$), and that insurance coverage is sold on an actuarially fair basis. Then the individual would select a level of coverage c to maximize his expected utility

$$(1-p)U(y-pc) + pV(y-pc-l+c). \qquad (1)$$

(The premium for coverage c is pc.) The first order condition (which in this case determines the optimal coverage c^*) of course equates marginal utilities of wealth in the two states,

$$U'(y-pc^*) = V'(y-pc^*-l+c^*). \qquad (2)$$

Let $\bar{c}$ be the amount of coverage such that the person would be made whole (assuming $\bar{c}$ exists), that is

$$U(y-p\bar{c}) = V(y-p\bar{c}-l+\bar{c}). \qquad (3)$$

Note that $\bar{c} > l$ since $U(y) > V(y)$ for any y. (The amount $\bar{c} - l$ compensates pain and suffering.) Then it follows (from (2) and the concavity of U and V) that

$$c^* < \bar{c} \text{ if and only if } U'(y-p\bar{c}) > V'(y-p\bar{c}-l+\bar{c}). \qquad (4)$$

Moreover, if $U'(y) > V'(y)$ for all y (marginal utility of wealth is lower after an accident at identical levels of wealth), (2) shows that $c^* < l$, optimal coverage is below economic losses and certainly the individual is not made whole. If $U'(y) = V'(y)$ for all y, $c^* = l$, coverage equals economic losses and again the individual is not made whole. If $U'(y) < V'(y)$ for all y, $c^* > l$, coverage exceeds economic loss—there is compensation for pain and suffering—and the person may or may not be made whole (it is possible that he would actually be better off after the accident and compensation). This is illustrated in Figure 1 and Figure 2. Obviously, cases in which U' and V' are not so simply related are also possible.

---

[32] P. Cook and D. Graham, "The Demand for Insurance and Protection: The Case of Irreplaceable Commodities," *Quarterly Journal of Economics*, vol. 61, no. 1 (February 1977) p. 143-56.

Figure 1

INDIVIDUAL (MORE THAN) MADE WHOLE

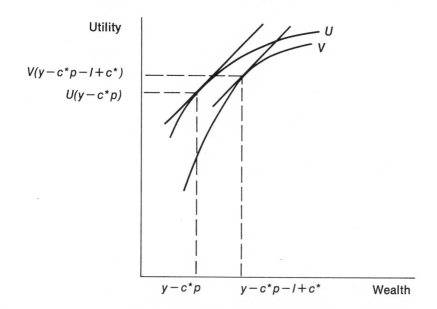

If an accident does not result in a permanent disability—would not result in any alteration of life style (given the same level of income)—the natural assumption would seem to be $U'(y) = V'(y)$; coverage should therefore equal economic losses and nothing should be given for pain and suffering. Only if the accident does result in lasting changes would one expect $U'(y)$ and $V'(y)$ to differ. I suspect that if the disability is not severe, so that income can still be enjoyed, it *might* be that $V'(y) > U'(y)$, coverage would exceed economic damages but would not make the individual whole in the cases which seem plausible to me. If the disability is severe (for example, the well-known case of Karen Quinlan, who is in an essentially vegetative state), $V'(y) < U'(y)$ would seem typical and coverage would fall short of even economic losses.

Appendix B: Administrative Costs of Insurance and Optimal Insurance Policies

Two types of administrative costs are considered: (1) *fixed costs* of opening a policy and of collecting premiums and (2) *claims-processing costs*. The problem is to describe optimal insurance policies given these

Figure 2
INDIVIDUAL NOT MADE WHOLE

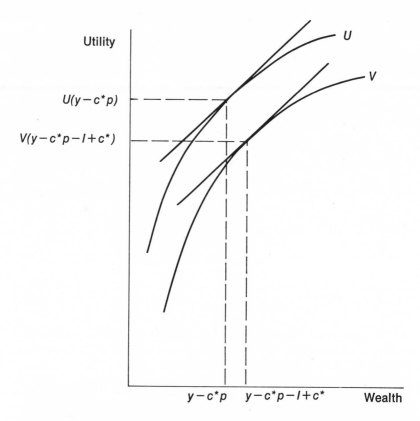

administrative costs. The relationship between this problem and a similar one discussed by K. J. Arrow [33] is discussed below. Denote by

$x_i > 0$	$i=1,\ldots,n$	possible losses
$p_i > 0$	$i=1,\ldots,n$	probability of loss of x_i
$p_o > 0$		probability of no loss
$q_i \geqq 0$	$i=1,\ldots,n$	payment by insurer if loss is x_i
π		insurance premium
$a \geqq 0$		fixed costs of opening a policy
$b \geqq 0$		claims-processing costs
y		initial wealth
$U(\cdot)$		utility of wealth

---

[33] Arrow, "Uncertainty and Welfare."

It is assumed that individuals act so as to maximize the expected utility of final wealth, that they always value increases in wealth $(U' > 0)$, and that they are risk averse $(U'' < 0)$. It is also assumed that $U(\cdot)$ is defined only over nonnegative levels of wealth (and therefore that $x_i \leq y$, $i=1,\ldots,n$).

An insurance policy is then specified by (π,q), with $q = (q_1,\ldots,q_n)$. It is assumed that the premium equals the insurer's expected costs, comprising both expected direct payments to the insured and expected administrative costs. Therefore, if $I = \{i \mid q_i>0\}$, the index set of losses for which positive insurance has been arranged, then

$$\pi = a + \sum_{i\epsilon I} p_i \,(q_i + b) \qquad \text{if } I \neq \phi \qquad (1)$$
$$= 0 \qquad \text{if } I = \phi \,.$$

$I = \phi$ means no losses are positively insured—no policy is purchased. Note that the claims-processing cost b is assumed to be independent of the size of a claim.[34] The expected utility associated with a policy (π,q) is

[34] The importance of this assumption is that claims-processing costs do not go to zero with the size of the claim.

$$p_0U(y-\pi) + \sum_{i=1}^{n} p_iU(y-\pi-x_i+q_i). \qquad (2)$$

The policy which will be purchased—the *optimal insurance policy*—maximizes (2) over (π,q) subject to (1) and $q_i \geq 0$, $i=1,\ldots,n$.

PROPOSITION 1: If the only administrative costs are the fixed costs of opening a policy $(a>0, b=0)$ and it is optimal to purchase positive coverage against some loss, the optimal insurance policy will in fact give full coverage against all losses.

The reason for this is clear. Once the decision has been made to buy a policy, fixed costs have to be paid. Then coverage can be bought on the margin on actuarially fair terms, in which case full coverage is optimal.

Proof: Since $I \neq \phi$ and $b=0$, (1) is just

$$\pi = a + \sum_{i=1}^{n} p_iq_i \qquad (3)$$

and the appropriate Lagrangean to consider is [35]

$$(4)$$
$$L(\pi,q) = p_0U(y-\pi) + \sum_{i=1}^{n} p_iU(y-\pi-x_i+q_i) - \lambda(a + \sum_{i=1}^{n} p_iq_i - \pi).$$

[35] In this case and those considered below, the constraint qualification (guaranteeing that the solution must be a critical point of the Lagrangean) obviously holds. In this case we have not explicitly incorporated the constraints that the q_i are nonnegative since it turns out that without doing so the q_i obey the constraints at the optimum.

At the optimum

$$0 = \frac{\partial L}{\partial q_j} = p_j U'(y-\pi-x_j+q_j) - \lambda p_j \tag{5}$$

or

$$U'(y-\pi-x_j+q_j) = \lambda. \tag{6}$$

Also

$$0 = \frac{\partial L}{\partial \pi} = -p_0 U'(y-\pi) - \sum_{i=1}^{n} p_i U'(y-\pi-x_i+q_i) + \lambda \tag{7}$$

so (using (6) and $p_0 = 1 - \sum_{i=1}^{n} p_i$),

$$U'(y-\pi) = \lambda. \tag{8}$$

Since $U'' < 0$, $y-\pi = y-\pi-x_j+q_j$ therefore $q_j = x_j$, which completes the proof.

The advantage in terms of expected utility of insuring is therefore

$$U(y-a-\sum_{i=1}^{n} p_i x_i) - [p_0 U(y) + \sum_{i=1}^{n} p_i U(y-x_i)]. \tag{9}$$

If a declines, (9) increases and is positive for all a sufficiently small. If x_i increases (to a maximum of y, by assumption), (9) increases but need not become positive. If p_0 is sufficiently close to 1, (9) is negative. However, as p_0 approaches zero, (9) is positive unless a is sufficiently large or $n=1$. Summing up, it will be optimal to purchase (full) coverage if administrative costs are sufficiently low. High losses make insuring more advantageous. If the probability of loss is sufficiently close to zero, no coverage will be bought, but if the probability of loss is close to (or equals) one, it may still be optimal to purchase (full) coverage.

PROPOSITION 2. Suppose that there are claims-processing costs and, possibly, fixed costs of opening a policy ($a \geq 0$, $b > 0$). Then if it is optimal to purchase positive coverage against some loss, the optimal insurance policy will either provide (i) full coverage against all losses or (ii) no coverage against some losses, in which case the policy will be a kind of deductible.

Note: Both (i) and (ii) are possible whether or not $a=0$. In (ii) the deductible policy referred to is such that if $q_i > 0$, then $q_i = x_i - d$ where $d > 0$. However, it is suggested that in an important case d is "close" to zero, that is, *the optimal policy is approximated by a policy which gives full coverage against loss whenever the optimal policy gave positive coverage*.

The explanation for this proposition is similar to that for the first. If it is optimal to positively insure against all of the x_i, then expected claims-processing costs (and any fixed costs) may be regarded as fixed costs. In this case the explanation for Proposition 1 applies and the optimal policy fully insures all losses. On the other hand, suppose that it is optimal to positively insure only some losses. Then optimality requires that for these losses, post-insurance-payment marginal utilities of wealth must be constant, that is $x_i - q_i = d$ for $i \epsilon I$. Why the deductible d is in fact positive is explained below; it is not because, on the margin, coverage is purchased at actuarially unfair rates for, on the margin, coverage is purchased at fair rates.

Two factors are shown below to militate against positively insuring a loss: low magnitude of loss and high probability of loss.[36] It is not worth insuring small losses, for as loss size goes to zero, the implicit "loading" (due to claims-processing costs) grows arbitrarily large. It is not worth insuring extremely likely losses, for if one is relatively confident of suffering a loss, he may as well shoulder the risk himself and avoid the claims-processing costs. However, as a practical matter, the first factor is probably the more important.

Proof: Suppose first that it is optimal to insure positively against each loss, so $I = \{1, \ldots, n\}$. Then (1) becomes

$$\pi = a + b \sum_{i=1}^{n} p_i + \sum_{i=1}^{n} p_i q_i \tag{10}$$

which is of the same form as (3). Hence, by the proof to Proposition 1, $q_i = x_i$, $i = 1, \ldots, n$.

On the other hand, suppose that it is optimal to insure positively only some losses, so $\phi \neq I \neq \{1, \ldots, n\}$. Then the appropriate Lagrangean may be written as [37]

$$L(\pi, q) = p_0 U(y - \pi) + \sum_{i \notin I} p_i U(y - \pi - x_i) + \sum_{i \epsilon I} p_i U(y - \pi - x_i + q_i)$$

$$- \lambda(a + \sum_{i \epsilon I} p_i(q_i + b) - \pi). \tag{11}$$

At the optimum, for $j \epsilon I$

$$0 = \frac{\partial L}{\partial q_j} = p_j U'(y - \pi - x_j + q_j) - \lambda p_j \tag{12}$$

or

$$U'(y - \pi - x_j + q_j) = \lambda. \tag{13}$$

Hence (as $U'' < 0$), $x_j - q_j$ is equal to a constant, say d, for $j \epsilon I$. We wish to show $d > 0$. At the optimum

---

[36] The second factor is noted in Diamond, "Insurance Theoretic Aspects."

[37] The constraints q_i nonnegative, $i \epsilon I$, have not been introduced for the reason cited in footnote 39.

$$0 = \frac{\partial L}{\partial \pi} = -p_0 U'(y-\pi) - \sum_{i \notin I} p_i U'(y-\pi-x_i) \tag{14}$$
$$- \sum_{i \in I} p_i U'(y-\pi-x_i+q_i) + \lambda.$$

Substituting (13) and solving for λ,

$$\lambda = (1 - \sum_{i \in I} p_i)^{-1} [p_0 U'(y-\pi) + \sum_{i \notin I} p_i U'(y-\pi-x_i)] \tag{15}$$

$$> (1 - \sum_{i \in I} p_i)^{-1} [p_0 U'(y-\pi) + \sum_{i \notin I} p_i U'(y-\pi)] = U'(y-\pi).$$

Thus $d > 0$, which completes the proof.

The first line of (15) says that at the optimum the marginal utility of wealth after insured losses ($i \in I$) is a (conditional probability) weighted average of the marginal utilities of wealth after uninsured losses or no loss. This indicates why the deductible d is positive if it is optimal not to insure at all against certain x_i (a zero deductible would make the marginal utility of wealth after insured losses equal to that if there were no loss, and thus less than the average of marginal utilities after uninsured losses or no loss).

However, in one important case the optimal policy might be closely approximated by fully insuring any loss which is positively insured, that is, by setting $q_i = x_i$ for $i \in I$ (even through $I \neq \{1, \ldots, n\}$). This case is that in which the probability of no loss is large compared to the probability of uninsured losses, for then, by (15), λ is approximately $U'(y-\pi)$. In any event, by (15) λ is always less than $\max_{i \notin I} U'(y-\pi-x_i)$, implying that the deductible d is less than the largest uninsured loss. (This would unfortunately increase the incentive to overstate losses.)

Now briefly consider the two factors mentioned above which may induce an individual to leave a loss x_j uninsured. First, if an x_j is sufficiently low, the optimal coverage $q_j = 0$: Suppose that $q_j > 0$ is optimal. Then the premium may be written as $\pi = z + p_j(b+q_j)$. Then expected utility may be written

$$p_0 U(y-\pi) + p_j U(y-\pi-x_j+q_j) + \sum_{i \neq j} U(y-\pi-x_i+q_i) \tag{16}$$

$$= p_0 [U(y-z) - p_j(b+q_j) U'(y-z) + e(y-z, -p_j(b+q_j))]$$
$$+ p_j [U(y-z) - (p_j(b+q_j) - x_j + q_j) U'(y-z)$$
$$+ e(y-z, -(p_j(b+q_j) - x_j + q_j))] + \sum_{i \neq j} U(y-\pi-x_i+q_i),$$

where $e(s,t) = U(s+t) - (U(s) + tU'(s))$. Now write expected utility for the policy modified only in that $q_j = 0$ (and the premium is accordingly reduced to z):

$$p_0 U(y-z) + p_j U(y-z-x_j) + \sum_{i \neq j} p_i U(y-z-x_i+q_i) \tag{17}$$

$$> p_0U(y-z) + p_jU(y-z-x_j) + \sum_{i\neq j} p_iU(y-\pi-x_i+q_i)$$

$$= p_0U(y-z) + p_j[U(y-z) - x_jU'(y-z) + e(y-z, -x_j)]$$

$$+ \sum_{i\neq j} p_iU(y-\pi-x_i+q_i).$$

To establish the claim, it is shown that if x_j is sufficiently low, the expression written after the equality sign in (17) exceeds the expression written after the equality sign in (16). Subtracting the latter from the former,

$$p_j\,[e(y-z, -x_j) + (p_j(b+q_j) + q_j)\,U'(y-z) \qquad (18)$$

$$- e(y-z, -p_j(b+q_j) - x_j + q_j)]$$

$$+ p_0\,[p_j(b+q_j)\,U'(y-z) - e(y-z, -p_j(b+q_j))].$$

As $U'' < 0$, $e(s,t) < 0$ if $t \neq 0$. By Proposition 2, $-x_j+q_j = -d < 0$. Hence the only negative term in (18) is $p_je(y-z, -x_j)$ whereas the positive terms are certainly bounded from below by $p_j^2bU'(y)$. Since $e(y-z, -x_j) \rightarrow 0$ as $x_j \rightarrow 0$, (18) is positive for x_j sufficiently low.

Second, if a loss probability p_j is sufficiently high, the optimal coverage $q_j = 0$: Suppose that $q_j > 0$ is optimal. Then, as in the previous paragraph, write $\pi = z+p_j(b+q_j)$ and expected utility of the optimal policy as

$$p_0U(y-z-p_j(b+q_j)) + p_jU(y-z-p_j(b+q_j) - x_j+q_j) \quad (19)$$

$$+ \sum_{i\neq j} p_iU(y-\pi-x_i+q_i)$$

$$< p_0U(y-z-p_j(b+q_j)) + p_jU(y-z-p_j(b+q_j) - x_j+q_j)$$

$$+ \sum_{i\neq j} p_iU(y-z-x_i+q_i).$$

The expected utility for a modified policy with $q_j = 0$ and premium of only z is

$$p_0U(y-z) + p_jU(y-z-x_j) + \sum_{i\neq j} p_iU(y-z-x_i+q_i). \quad (20)$$

It needs to be shown that if p_j is sufficiently high, (20) exceeds the expression following the inequality sign in (19). Subtracting the latter from the former,

$$p_0\,[U(y-z) - U(y-z-p_j(b+q_j))] + p_j\,[U(y-z-x_j) \quad (21)$$

$$- U(y-z-p_j(b+q_j) - x_j+q_j)].$$

When $p_j = 1$ (in which case $p_o = 0$), (21) equals $U(y-z-x_j) - U(y-z-b-x_j) > 0$, so that a continuity argument implies that (21) is positive for p_j sufficiently close to 1.[38]

---

[38] The variable z is implicitly determined by the probabilities and is not necessarily

The discussion of the problem of the administrative costs of insurance as presented here should be compared with Arrow's well-known result about deductibles. This result is that the optimal insurance policy must be the usual kind of deductible if the premium paid is based only on the expected payments which are made to the insured under the terms of the policy. If the administrative costs are just the fixed costs of taking out a policy, then Arrow's assumption holds (if $\bar{q}$ is expected payments, then $\pi(\bar{q}) = a + \bar{q}$), but Proposition 1 does not contradict his result, since he did not rule out a deductible of zero—full coverage. On the other hand, if there are claims-processing costs, the premium is not a function merely of expected payments to the insured. It also depends on the probability that positive payment will be made. Therefore, Proposition 2 does not contradict Arrow's result either.

---

continuous in p_j and p_o. However, as $z = \pi - p_j(q_j + b)$ where π is assumed to be the optimal premium, z is certainly bounded from above by $(1-p_j) \max_{\substack{h \\ i \neq j}} x_i$ (by Proposition 2, at the optimum $q_i \leq x_i$ or $\pi \leq \sum_{i=1}^{h} p_i x_i$) and from below by zero. Thus $z \to 0$ as $p_j \to 1$, so that it is clear that (21) is positive for p_j close to 1.

MEDICAL MALPRACTICE AND MEDICAL COSTS

Bruce C. N. Greenwald and Marnie W. Mueller

Do doctors and hospitals pass on the increased cost of their malpractice insurance? Do doctors move away from states where they think they are likely to be sued for malpractice? Are millions of dollars of scarce medical resources being used by doctors and hospitals for defensive medicine? Finally, have the suspicions generated by increased malpractice claims destroyed the therapeutically beneficial trust between doctors and their patients? Recent requests for legislative relief from the rising costs of malpractice suits and of insurance premiums have been justified by belief that the answer to each of these questions is affirmative. The purpose of this paper is to bring the weight of empirical evidence from cross-sectional data by state from 1970 to bear on these questions and to determine the likely magnitude of these effects.

The first section of the paper examines the effect of malpractice suits against doctors on doctors' services, while the second section examines the effect of malpractice suits against doctors and hospitals on hospital services. These sections are organized in parallel fashion. Each begins by constructing measures of the complexity of medical procedures appropriate to the area in question. These measures form the basis for analyzing the extent of the practice of defensive medicine and provide evidence of the influence of insurance coverage and income on medical procedures and through them on costs. Similar models of the market for doctors' services and of the market for hospital services are developed next. These models are then used to determine the final incidence of increases in malpractice insurance premiums through their direct impact on doctors' fees and hospital prices, on the demand for doctors' services and for hospital services, and on the location decisions of doctors. The third section concludes the paper with estimates of the additions to medical costs caused by the phenomenon of malpractice suits.

Malpractice Suits and Doctors' Services

Doctors who believe themselves threatened by the prospect of a malpractice suit will take defensive actions. Most obviously, they will buy

65

insurance against the expenses of settling claims. In addition, they will modify their usual way of practicing medicine, either because they are unable to purchase insurance against the full cost of a claim (including such things as loss of their own time from practice, damage to their professional reputation, psychic damage to their family) or because they can lower the probability of loss to themselves by a given amount more cheaply with insurance and a modification of their practice routines than with insurance alone.

While an obvious measure of the cost of insurance exists (an index of malpractice premiums), this is not true for those changes in standard medical practices which constitute "defensive medicine." However, since the extra resources used in defensive medicine constitute an important part of the real cost of the malpractice phenomenon, the first step in any analysis of malpractice costs and doctors' services must be to find a measure of differences in medical procedures across states and to analyze what determines these differences. This indicator then assumes the role of an independent variable in a model of the market for doctors' services.

While a measure of differences in standards of medical practice is needed for an analysis of defensive medicine, its usefulness is not limited to this area. Given the steady rise in medical outlays over time, it would be interesting to know the contribution to increased costs of the adoption of different procedures and to know also what was responsible for the changes in technique. Although it is not possible to provide a definitive answer to that question in this study, the effect of procedural complexity (as we measure it) on costs and the effect of insurance coverage and the level of income on the measure itself provide some indication of the forces involved.

Our measure of procedural complexity is a weighted average of the frequency of certain secondary procedures per ordinary office visit. The specific procedures chosen for constructing the index were laboratory tests, X-rays, and consultations, inasmuch as these procedures are often cited as being characteristic of defensive medicine.[1] For a measure such as this to represent differences in medical practices across states, (1) there must be significant variations in how doctors in different states handle similar situations, (2) those standards of practice must be determined to an important extent by the collective interaction (formal or informal) of all doctors in that state, and (3) the variation in the use of each of the procedures must be in the same direction (that is,

---

[1] See, for example, U.S. Department of Health, Education, and Welfare, Secretary's Commission on Medical Malpractice, *Appendix,* Washington, D.C., 1973, p. 39.

states where doctors use more X-rays should also be states where they use more laboratory tests).

The data used to construct this measure are from a sample of Medicare billings in different states in 1968. Because of the special nature of Medicare patients, variations in treatment resulting from differences in a state's demographic structure or from differences in prices should be minimized. On the other hand, if there is less malpractice exposure in treating patients over sixty-five because they sue less frequently or because they are given lower awards (or both), the defensive medicine practiced on this group may be an attenuated version of that practiced on the patient population as a whole.

Aside from price and demographic influences, the choices doctors make with respect to medical procedures in any state should be determined by the doctors' anxiety about malpractice suits, the general level of income in the state, the influence of standards of academic practice, and the character of insurance coverage.

The procedure used to derive weights for lab tests ($MCLAB$), X-rays ($MCXRAY$), and consultations ($MCCON$) to form the procedure index (CXD) is described in the appendix. The level of doctors' malpractice premiums ($PREMD$) is used to measure fear of suit;[2] premiums indicate both frequency and severity of claims, while the most obvious alternative measure, claims per doctor, indicates only frequency. Per capita income ($YCAP$) is used to measure income, and medical students per capita ($MEDSTU$)[3] is used as a proxy for the influence of a medical school. The effect of insurance coverage was measured in two ways: breadth of coverage by the percentage of the population covered by some form of private medical insurance ($COVH$) and depth of coverage by the percentage of private medical expenditures paid by private insurance for those people covered ($COMTO$). As additional procedures are insured, doctors will be more likely to use them, and their doing so in covered cases ultimately affects standards applied to all patients. Thus, the fact that the Medicare patients are almost fully covered does not preclude the possibility of measuring the effect of insurance coverage from Medicare data.

The following regression—and all other regressions reported in this study—were run in log-linear form, which means that the coefficients for the right-hand-side variables represent elasticities or the percentage

---

[2] This assumes that the perceptions of doctors and insurance companies, which are based on the same underlying data, are almost identical.

[3] Clearly this sort of thing is difficult to measure accurately. However, the number of medical students should be related to both the size and number of medical schools. It should, therefore, be a reasonably good proxy for the influence they exert.

change in these variables (in the frequency of secondary procedures in the case of this particular regression) resulting from a percentage change in the determining variable. T-ratios, which measure how likely it is that the coefficients differ from zero for reasons other than chance alone, are reported in parentheses below the regression coefficients. Because the magnitude of the population represented in each state varies so greatly, the observations were weighted so that the larger states would have greater weight. The ordinary least squares (OLS) technique was used to estimate this particular equation on the assumption that, while procedural complexity influences the determination of the price and quantity of doctors' services, procedural complexity is not itself influenced by interactions in that market. The equation was estimated as follows:

$$CXD = -5.93 + 0.362\,PREMD + 1.121\,YCAP + 0.038\,MEDSTU \quad (1)$$
$$ (8.00)\ (3.77) (2.03) (1.05)$$

$$+\ 0.101\,COVH + 1.567\,COMTO \quad \bar{R}^2 = 0.968$$
$$(0.19) (2.74)$$

Anxiety about suit, per capita income, and the depth of insurance coverage appear to be important determinants of different standards of medical practice in different states. The effect of academic standards appears to be slight, and the effect of breadth of insurance coverage virtually non-existent. The large impact of depth of coverage, on the other hand, may account for the discrepancy between the rather slight influence of insurance coverage found in studies of households and the rapid increase in medical expenditures as insurance coverage has increased over time.

We now turn to an analysis of the market for physicians' services. Normally in such discussions the forces which interact to determine price and quantity are categorized into those emanating from the producers of the product (supply) and those emanating from the consumers of the product (demand). Our model retains this dichotomy with appropriate modifications for the special institutional characteristics of markets for medical services (characteristics which differentiate these from a purely competitive market). Accordingly, the consumption side of the market is represented by a demand equation with allowance for the fact that, while patients may initiate contact with doctors, their final purchase of medical services is partially determined by the doctor acting as the patient's agent. The production side of the market could be represented by an equation determining the quantity per doctor (case load per doctor) and an equation determining the number of doctors in a state. While retaining the location equation, we have chosen to analyze the quantity-per-doctor relationship in the form of a price-setting equation on the assumption that doctors possess enough market power to be characterized more accurately as pricemakers than as pricetakers and also because one of the central concerns of our study is to determine how malpractice suits influence fees. The impact of the malpractice phenomenon on office-based care can thus be analyzed by looking at its effect on the price of doctors' services, the number of doctors in a state, and the demand for doctors' services.

Because the major effect of the threat of a malpractice suit (aside from its influence on defensive medicine) occurs as doctors pass on insurance premium costs, the price equation is central. While the theory of doctors' price-setting behavior has produced a considerable literature, the single major theoretical controversy that is pertinent to our interests is the question "What is being maximized when doctors set prices?" Here the issue is whether doctors are concerned only with their personal income and leisure (as in the case of the economist's traditional "selfish" utility maximizer) or in addition they are concerned with such things as providing service to the community or charging low prices.

For the purposes of this paper the significant fact is that the responses of a selfish utility maximizer to the malpractice threat differ from those of a more altruistically motivated person. The differences appear unambiguously in the nature of the income effect of a change in fixed costs. For the person interested only in income and leisure an increase in fixed costs reduces income and thereby reduces the value of leisure time relative to income. This decrease in the value of leisure time in turn reduces the marginal cost of providing services since leisure forgone constitutes the greater part of a doctor's marginal costs. Finally, the decline in marginal costs should reduce the price and increase the quantity of medical services supplied. Paradoxically, therefore, a selfish utility maximizer should lower his price in response to an increase in malpractice premiums or to an increase in the wages of assistants (to the extent that they are both fixed costs). This income effect also magnifies the impact of an increase in caseload on prices. An increase in patient loads pushes up prices directly; in addition, as workloads rise, income rises, the value of leisure relative to income increases, and the marginal cost of providing services rises. The income effect thus contracts the supply of doctors' services and further increases prices.

In contrast, the response of a nonconventional (altruistic) utility maximizer may be to increase prices as fixed costs rise. Consider the case of a doctor who derives satisfaction from being available to patients and from charging low prices. If this satisfaction were a normal good, an income-lowering increase in fixed costs would reduce the doctor's "consumption" of low prices and the rewards of public service. Indeed, the tendency to raise prices could outweigh the income effect on the value of leisure, if prices on balance increased. If the influence of this type of unusual income effect on prices is strong, then, as patient loads rise, it is conceivable that prices will decline: the tendency for prices to rise as doctors try to obtain more leisure time would be outweighed by an increased desire to consume low prices as income increases. This will be all the more likely to occur if patient loads tend to be controlled by nonprice appointment rationing. Thus, it turns out that we have an unambiguous test for the hypothesis that doctors are motivated only by concern for their own income and leisure: if fees increase when fixed costs increase and decrease when patient case loads increase, then physicians cannot be motivated solely by a concern for their own income and leisure.

The price equation was estimated from cross-sectional data for fifty states and the District of Columbia from the year 1970. The price series $(PBLS)$ used for the dependent variable was constructed from Bureau of Labor Statistics data. The BLS prices a standard market basket of doctor's services, heavily weighted in favor of office visits, in many metropolitan areas and rural regions. While a standard service bundle so heavily weighted in favor of one type of service normally would not be a comprehensive indicator of all services, the existence and wide application of the California relative value scale which prescribes fixed relative prices for various doctors' services, means that the BLS index probably is a fairly useful proxy. This index was then deflated by an overall cost-of-living index from the same BLS source to obtain a relative price.

The variables determining the doctor's price reflect costs and conditions of practice. The index of malpractice premiums $(PREMD)$ and an index of clerical wages $(WCLER)$, also deflated by a cost-of-living index, represent costs. The measure of procedural complexity (CXD) was included so as to determine the extent to which differences in procedures are reflected in the price of standard services. Average caseload (Q/MD) was included as a measure of the costs of a doctor's time and of the spread of fixed costs per patient. A greater availability of doctors per capita (MD/CAP) should reduce fees if any competition exists. Although the government pays for an important part of doctors' services, it is impossible to predict a priori how the percentage of physician expenditure paid for by the government $(\% \ PUBMD)$ will influence fees. While higher prices could result from breaking the financial link between patient and doctor, the government may use its superior bargaining power to obtain lower fees than the patient could obtain.

70

Because of the simultaneous determination of the variables of doctors' fees, caseloads, and the number of doctors in any state, the price equation was estimated by two-stage least squares (2 *SLS*). This statistical technique removes the effect of prices on caseloads and the number of doctors from the price equation so that the coefficients on caseload and number of doctors represent only the effect of caseload and number of doctors on price, not a mixture of the two effects; the hat over a variable indicates that it has been purged of the simultaneity bias.[4]

The price equation was estimated as follows:

$$PBLS = 1.645 + 0.091\,PREMD + 0.631\,WCLER + 0.064\,CXD \qquad (2)$$
$$(1.61)\quad(3.47)\qquad\qquad(2.90)\qquad\qquad(2.02)$$

$$-\,0.619\,Q\hat{/}MD - 0.132\,\%\,PUBMD - 0.192\,MD\hat{/}CAP$$
$$(4.66)\qquad\qquad(2.48)\qquad\qquad(2.40)$$

$$\bar{R}^2 = .999$$

The evidence indicates strongly that doctors are not selfish utility maximizers: the coefficients of all the cost variables are positive indicating cost "pass-along," and the coefficient of the caseload variable is negative.[5] In addition, the magnitude of the coefficient of the caseload variable is less than one, which suggests that some price rationing is taking place. If all costs were fixed except the doctors' time and if doctors aim at a target income, a 1 percent increase in caseload should lead to a 1 percent reduction in price. The significance and positive sign of the procedural complexity variable indicate that there are quality differences across states in the BLS standard unit of a doctor's services. The negative sign on doctors per capita indicates a slight degree of competition, while the negative sign on the percentage of expenditure on physicians by the government indicates that the government as a third party exerts a downward pressure even on quoted fees. The coefficients on malpractice premiums and clerical wages suggest that physicians are more than just passing on their fixed costs (these coefficients are greater than their respective percentages of the average physician's practice costs). In the case of wages this may occur because doctors use wages as a partial basis for gauging the income level to which they aspire. In the case of malpractice premiums (which in 1970 amounted to 2 to 4 percent of costs), the deterioration in doctor-patient relationships accompanying an increased incidence of suits may

---

[4] For a detailed explanation of such an instrumental variables procedure, see John Johnston, *Econometric Methods,* 2nd ed. (New York: McGraw-Hill, 1972).
[5] A positive coefficient would measure the slope of a positively sloped supply curve. A negative slope is difficult to explain in such a "normal" context.

lessen the social restraints helping to keep down doctors' fees. Thus, the cost passed on to the public may well exceed the total cost of premiums—with attendant serious consequences for medical costs.

The location decisions of physicians and hence the number of doctors per capita in each state (MD/CAP) should depend primarily on the pecuniary and nonpecuniary advantages available. Since net income of physicians reported to the Internal Revenue Service or to survey researchers does not reflect the leisure costs associated with different workloads, and since many elements of income are classified for tax purposes as business expenses, it is appropriate to measure all the characteristics that influence the financial conditions of practice in any area. For this purpose, average price ($PBLS$), clerical wages ($WCLER$), malpractice costs ($PREMD$) or claims per doctor ($CLMS$), and existing average patient loads (Q/MD) are independent variables in the location equation.

Measuring the nonpecuniary advantages of a particular state is an imprecise matter at best, but such factors are undoubtedly important. As a proxy for better schools, more social and cultural amenities, and a more congenial patient population, the percentage of high school graduates in each state ($HSGDS$) is included as an independent variable. The presence of training programs should provide benefits for local doctors in the form of off-call coverage, the reflected prestige of medical training institutions, and opportunities to maintain valuable human capital. In addition, doctors may simply choose to remain in the areas where they receive their training. Thus, the number of interns and residents per capita ($INRES$) is also included as an independent variable. Finally, fear of the uninsurable costs of malpractice suits may be a disincentive to locate in a given area. These costs are probably captured better by the number of claims per doctors ($CLMS$) than by the level of malpractice insurance premiums.

The location equation was estimated in the same manner as the price equation, with the following results:

$$MD/CAP = -7.042 - 0.014\,CLMS + 0.704\,HSGDS \qquad (3)$$
$$(4.27)\quad(0.29)(5.32)$$

$$+\,0.147\,INRES + 1.152\,P\hat{B}LS - 0.226\,WCLER$$
$$(5.42)(3.08)\phantom{P\hat{B}LS}(0.29)$$

$$+\,0.168\,Q\hat{/}MD \quad \bar{R}^2 = 0.655$$
$$(0.64)$$

The variables all have the appropriate signs and are significant in the cases of price, training programs, and educational levels. Caseload

(Q/MD) is not significant: high caseloads may be a mixed blessing, easing the establishment of a profitable practice but also intensifying the pressures of work. Also, the level of clerical wages is insignificant, possibly as a result of the limited variations in real clerical wages that characterize our sample.

Finally, concern about malpractice suits appears to have no influence on location decisions. Indeed, in a similar regression using *PREMD* instead of *CLMS,* the coefficient on *PREMD* was actually positive, though it was not significant. There are, however, two caveats to this conclusion. Although malpractice premiums in our sample differ by as much as a factor of four, they average no more than 5 percent of total gross receipts. Thus, our results may be of little relevance to current situations where massive increases in premiums must have sent malpractice premiums costs as a percentage of gross receipts to a level which should make these costs far more important in location decisions. Finally, malpractice suits vary considerably by specialty, and our aggregate measure of doctors per capita misses any differential migration by specialty.

Because there exists no measure of the physical quantity of doctors' services which is not hopelessly muddied by quality differences, we have chosen to use as the dependent variable in the demand equation total per capita expenditures on doctors' services in each state (*MDEXP*), deflated by the cost-of-living index. Since demand is being estimated as an expenditure function, the price coefficient should be less than one if the quantity of services demanded falls as prices rise, and greater than zero if demand is inelastic. One group of independent variables consists of the price and income factors which are the usual determinants of demand, such as *PBLS* and *YCAP.* In addition, variables are included to account for the influence of insurance coverage and the nonmonetary costs of consuming doctors' services (for example, travel costs or convenience). The insurance variable is the percentage of the population covered by doctor and hospital insurance in each state (*COVDH*). The main consequence of insurance coverage for expenditure on physicians should arise from differences in the hospital-related consumption of doctors' services between insured and uninsured households inasmuch as the discretionary office visits which account for roughly two-thirds of all spending on doctors' services are generally not covered by insurance. The depth of coverage should influence procedural standards which affect all patients equally and which should be captured by the separate inclusion of the index of procedural complexity. The number of general practitioners and pediatricians per capita (*PRIM*) is included as an independent variable to account for differences in the convenience costs of doctors' visits (initial visits being made predominantly to primary-care physicians).

The second group of demand determinants is made up of those which arise from the role of doctors and other agents in determining the consumer's choice. The index of procedural complexity (CXD) reflects the amount of treatment associated with an illness. The availability of hospital beds ($BEDS$) or doctors ($PRIM$) may reduce non-price rationing or may cause doctors to generate demand. While publicly financed expenditures ($\%\ PUBMD$) may generate new demand, if these services also displace more costly private ones, total expenditure may fall.

The expenditure function was estimated to be as follows:

$$MDEXP = 2.878 + 0.216\ CXD + 0.272\ P\hat{B}LS + 0.808\ YCAP \quad (4)$$
$$(0.80) \quad (2.38) \qquad\quad (0.38) \qquad\qquad (3.40)$$

$$+ 0.183\ P\hat{R}IM + 0.034\ COVDH - 0.270\ \%\ PUBMD$$
$$(0.73) \qquad\qquad (0.41) \qquad\qquad (2.88)$$

$$+ 0.227\ BEDS \qquad \bar{R}^2 = 0.968$$
$$(1.58)$$

The estimate of income elasticity of demand is 0.81, which is somewhat higher than those found in studies using data on individual households. Since household income is the independent variable in these studies, those income elasticities could not incorporate the "demonstration" effect—that is, could not come from observing health care consumed by neighbors as their income rises and adopting new standards in accordance with the observations. Because in the long run both the direct effect and the demonstration effect should determine the level of demand, our higher figure which is based on geographically aggregated cross-section data is more appropriate for projecting trends than figures based on individual data. The complexity index appears to raise doctors' expenditures by roughly 0.2 percent for each 1 percent increase. Consequently an increase in per capita income of 1 percent, which increases the complexity index by about 1.1 percent (see equation 1), should increase doctors' expenditures by .22 percent. If we add to this the direct 0.81 percent effect of income on demand, the total income elasticity would be 1.03—which, being greater than unity, helps explain why expenditures on doctors' services have increased over time at least as rapidly as per capita income.

A doubling in the complexity index leads to an increase of 22 percent in real physician expenditures per capita. Thus, while the coefficient on $COVDH$, or the direct impact of insurance on doctors' costs, is not significant, insurance influences medical costs indirectly through its effect on procedural complexity. Finally, since the coefficient of malpractice premiums in the complexity equation is 0.36, a 100 percent increase in doctors' premiums should add 8 percent to the costs of doctors' services through the practice of defensive medicine.

The hospital beds per capita and public expenditures coefficients are both significant. In the following section we estimate that a 1 percent increase in the number of hospital beds generates an increase in the demand for hospital services of about 0.6 percent (equation 8). If one-third of all doctors' expenditures are hospital related, a 1 percent increase in beds per capita would yield an increase in the demand for doctors' services of 0.2 percent—which is very close to our estimate. A doubling of the percentage of physicians' expenditures paid for by the government actually leads to a 27 percent decrease in total physician expenditures.

Neither the price variable nor the insurance variable is significant. The insurance variable may well be insignificant because its actual coefficient is almost undetectably small. Household data indicate that a 1 percent increase in families covered by insurance leads to about a 0.16 percent increase in hospital usage. Since hospital visits account for one-third of doctors' receipts, this would lead to an increase in demand for doctors' services of at most about 0.05 percent. Furthermore, if hospital-related care substitutes for noninsured office visits, the increase in hospital-related expenditures should be partially offset by a decline in expenditures for office-based care. Thus, 0.03 is not an unreasonably low figure for the insurance elasticity; given the limited range of variation in the extent of population covered across states, such a figure is unlikely to be measured precisely enough to be statistically significant. The insignificant price elasticity is also not surprising, given the uncertain and contradictory conclusions of previous demand studies. The estimated elasticity is -0.728 (being 1.0 less the coefficient in the expenditure equation) and its associated T-statistic is 1.05 (a significant effect would imply an expenditure equation coefficient different from one). Thus while the point estimate of the elasticity has the correct sign, the estimate is imprecise.

Malpractice and Hospital Costs

The malpractice suit phenomenon also affects hospital costs, most obviously because hospitals themselves are liable to such costs. While at one time they were protected from suit by charitable immunity, by 1970 this doctrine had been restricted in thirty-nine states. The doctrine of *respondent superior,* meanwhile, had been successfully applied to hospitals in thirty-three states.[6] Indeed in this same year a survey of claims closed revealed that 39 percent of all malpractice claims were made against hospitals. Clearly, as is the case with doctors, hospitals have an incentive to protect themselves from the financial consequences of claims.

The question of the way malpractice suits influence medical costs has an additional dimension, however, when the sector in question is the hospital industry, because of the special relationship between doctors and hospitals. While the exact weight of the medical staff vis-à-vis the hospital administration in hospital decision making remains a subject of controversy, the very fact that in the treatment of many illnesses doctors and hospitals require the use of each other's services to produce any output at all assures us that doctors have a significant influence over the allocation of resources in a hospital.

To be more specific, as Pauly and Redisch [7] have argued, doctors will have effective control over the use of many hospital resources and will use that control to maximize their own incomes. Overuse of hospital resources is, of course, costless to the doctors themselves. Thus, unless there are use constraints imposed by the hospital administration, the doctors will order such things as elaborate nursing care or the services of sophisticated hospital equipment up to the point where the revenue increase from the doctors' enhanced productivity equals the revenue loss from the price-induced decrease in patients. When the hospital part of the patient's expenses is covered partially or wholly by insurance, doctors will order a correspondingly more intensive use of hospital resources.

Since hospitals are the site of 75 percent of the incidents which result in claims against doctors,[8] doctors will obviously be highly motivated to devote hospital resources to defensive medicine (especially when there is extensive hospitalization insurance). Moreover, the hospital administration will have less reason to inhibit any physician's overuse of hospital resources because of the chance that the hospital itself would be named as a codefendant in suit. To measure the extent of the resulting defensive medical practices and their impact on hospital costs, we again construct a complexity index and develop a simultaneous model of hospital costs, demand, and facilities, using that index and

---

[6] U.S. Department of Health, Education, and Welfare, Secretary's Commission on Medical Malpractice, *Appendix,* p. 135.

[7] Michael Pauly and Michael Redisch, "The Not-for-Profit Hospital as a Physicians' Cooperative," *American Economic Review,* vol. 63 (March 1973), pp. 87-99.

[8] U.S. Department of Health, Education, and Welfare, Secretary's Commission on Medical Malpractice, *Appendix,* p. 10.

malpractice premiums as independent variables to determine the total effect of the current rise in claims.

The measure of procedural complexity developed in the section on doctors' services (CXD) was based on secondary procedures and data which are related largely to the practice of office-based medicine. Although areas characterized by sophisticated and costly office-based standards are likely also to be characterized by similar inpatient procedures, the practice of hospital-based medicine is sufficiently different in both nature and governing influences for the construction of a separate hospital complexity index to be desirable. Moreover, one of the most widely discussed—albeit least well understood—medical phenomena of recent years is the explosive change in the technology of hospital-based medicine. Thus, it is of more than passing interest to examine this phenomenon in two stages by looking just at the determinants of geographical differences in hospital techniques and then at the influence of these differences on costs for any light they may shed on the causes and impact of the dramatic changes in hospital technology.

Our measure of procedural complexity specific to hospitals is a weighted average of the percentage of hospitals, in any state, with intensive care units (ICU), cardiac intensive care units (ICCU), and electroencephalogram testing equipment (EEG). These particular facilities were chosen for several reasons, not the least of which was that information was available on their frequency of occurrence. These particular facilities were found in 47 percent (ICU), 42 percent (ICCU), and 36 percent (EEG) of hospitals across the nation so that their occurrence is neither so common as to be capable of explaining very little variance (as would be the case with recovery rooms) nor so rare as to be idiosyncratic (as would be the case with open heart surgery units). Moreover, these facilities should measure the use both of diagnostic and of treatment procedures. The growth of intensive care has indeed been one of the major innovations in inpatient procedures in recent years, providing new modes of care for familiar illnesses like heart attacks and making feasible operations which were formerly too complicated and risky to be undertaken. EEG measures new kinds of diagnostic procedures which would be missed by the CXD index.

The influences determining hospital procedural complexity (CXH) should be similar to those determining the measure of procedural complexity. Interns and residents per capita ($INRES$) indicates the presence of "cheap labor" to monitor patients using hospital facilities and of a demonstration effect of hospital training programs on practice standards. Since an important determinant of the complexity of facilities and treatment should be the economic base upon which hospitals can reliably expect to draw, the percentage of the population covered for hospital and doctors' services (COVDH) should be an important indicator of the effect of insurance. However, because insurance coverage once a patient is hospitalized is quite comprehensive in relation to the coverage for procedures in a doctor's office, a depth-of-coverage measure should have little or no impact here—in contrast to its impact in the case of the doctor's complexity index. Income (YCAP) will of course be important for paying for the services of facilities when insurance coverage of the population or of expenditure is less than 100 percent. Also, income is another important indicator of the extent of the economic base on which hospitals may draw. Finally, doctors may urge a hospital to acquire facilities which they believe will help to protect them from suit (PREMD).

As with all other equations, the hospital facilities equation was run in log-linear form with weighting of observations to reflect the different populations of each state. As with the other complexity equation, ordinary least squares was used for the estimation.

$$CXH = -2.162 + 0.773 \, YCAP + 0.304 \, COVDH \qquad (5)$$
$$ (3.60) \quad (2.06) \qquad\quad (2.30)$$

$$+ \, 0.071 \, INRES + 0.117 \, PREMD \qquad \bar{R}^2 = 0.844$$
$$ (1.46) \qquad\qquad (2.17)$$

Again, income, insurance, and malpractice threat appear to be important influences on medical procedures, although the values of these coefficients are lower than the values of the corresponding coefficients in the CXD complexity equation. However, since the index is defined up to a scalar multiple, only relative magnitudes matter, absolute differences having no empirical significance.

As is the case with doctors' services, the forces affecting the equilibrium price and quantity of hospital services are categorized into those emanating from producers and those emanating from consumers, with allowance made for the institutional characteristics peculiar to this market. Since patients rarely choose to hospitalize themselves, the demand equation contains variables representing a physician's part in the hospitalization decision. The supply side of the market is represented by a stock-of-beds equation and a pricing equation.

The pricing equation is again central for our analysis of the influence of the malpractice phenomenon on costs. While there are several hospital "prices" available for use as the dependent variable (most common among them revenue per patient day, cost per patient day, and room charges), we have chosen instead an index of hospital prices (PHOS) based on both room charges and charges for auxiliary services (operating rooms, pharmacy services, and the like) which constitute almost 40 percent of average hospital bills. This should be preferable to other measures inasmuch as revenue and cost per patient day both vary with the occupancy rate of the hospital as well as with its pricing policy, and inasmuch as room charges are at best a partial measure of prices.

The independent variables are those which describe input costs, quality levels, and competitive and institutional forces to which the hospital may be subject in setting prices. Health worker wages ($WHWK$) and doctors' prices ($PBLS$) represent the price of labor to the hospitals. An index of hospital malpractice premiums ($PREMH$) represents another element of costs. These and the dependent variables were deflated by a total cost-of-living index which should account for differences in materials prices (to the degree that those prices are related to the cost of living and to the degree that the price setters do not suffer from "money" illusion). The measures CXD and CXH are included to represent differences in the quality level of care provided in the hospitals. The occupancy rate ($OCRT$) fulfills two possible roles. On the one hand a higher occupancy rate where there are heavy investments in fixed costs will—with average-cost pricing—lead to lower prices. On the other hand, a higher occupancy rate may reflect greater demand and lead to higher prices. Beds per capita ($BEDS$) should measure competitive pressure, but given the decisive role of doctors in the choices of patients among hospitals, competition may take the form of improved services for the physicians and thus may actually lead to higher costs and prices. Finally, the percentage of hospital expenditures paid for by the government ($\%PUBH$) may indicate the strength of the pressure against increased costs because of the special nature of this particular third-party purchaser.

The price equation contains the simultaneously determined variables of occupancy rate and beds per capita and thus was estimated by the two-stage least squares technique ($2\,SLS$) in order to remove the effect of price on occupancy rate and beds from the regression coefficients. The results are as follows:

$$PHOS = 6.748 + 0.829\,WHWK + 0.544\,PBLS \qquad (6)$$
$$(2.93) \quad (4.43) \qquad\qquad (2.94)$$

$$+\, 0.034\,CXD + 0.245\,CXH + -0.258\,O\hat{C}RT$$
$$(0.768) \qquad\quad (3.53) \qquad\qquad (1.07)$$

$$+\, 0.089\,PREMH - 0.160\,\%\,PUBH + 0.246\,B\hat{E}DS$$
$$(3.20) \qquad\qquad (1.52) \qquad\qquad (2.14)$$

$$\bar{R}^2 = 0.998$$

Hospital prices are clearly affected by the anxiety doctors and hospitals feel about their liability for malpractice. The coefficient on the measure of simpler kinds of medical procedures (CXD) is low and not significant, probably because of its close relationship to the measure of hospital-based procedural complexity (the simple correlation between the two is 0.860). When CXD is omitted from the equation, the coefficient on CXH rises by the magnitude of the coefficient on CXD. The increase in hospital prices from both kinds of changes in medical practice as a result of a 100 percent increase in doctors' malpractice premiums would be 4.1 percent (0.362, the change in CXD due to a change in $PREMD$, times 0.034, the change in $PHOS$ due to a change in CXD, plus 0.117, the change in CXH due to a change in $PREMD$, times 0.245, the change in $PHOS$ due to a change in CXH). The change in hospital prices from a change in hospital malpractice premiums is 0.089. Since, in 1970, malpractice insurance costs for hospitals amounted to only .0005 percent of hospital costs, $PREMH$ is clearly measuring something in addition to a cost pass-along. Our regression contains a measure of simple routine tests (CXD) and sophisticated hospital facilities (CXH), but lacks a measure, which $PREMH$ may be picking up, of the kind of defensive medicine which would involve devoting resources to ensuring that no accidents happened to patients during the course of their hospital stay. For example, providing straps on X-ray tables and a second technician to double-check the use of the straps would considerably lower the probability that a disoriented patient would roll off an X-ray table. Our complexity indices appear to do only a partial job of measuring the total impact of defensive medicine.

Of the other independent variables, labor costs appear to be particularly important to hospital prices. Also, while neither is significant, the sign on occupancy rate supports the assumption of average-cost pricing, and the sign on $\%PUBH$ (as is the case with doctors' prices), implies that hospital prices are lower in states where publicly financed expenditures are relatively important. In contrast, however, to the negative effect of doctors per capita on doctors' prices, more hospital beds per capita actually increase hospital prices—which suggests that competition amongst hospitals takes place in service rather than in price.

Because the stock of hospital beds in a state, unlike the stock of doctors, is unlikely to be affected by the malpractice question, the equation explaining the stock of beds will be discussed only briefly. The number of short-term general hospital beds per capita ($BEDS$) in a state should reflect the age-sex-race demographic structure in the state

(*HUTIL*), the number of bed-days used as a result of factors other than health status (or the demographically adjusted bed-days, *DBDD*), the population density (*POPDENS*)—because in higher-density states hospitals are more highly concentrated, which leads to economies of scale in the number of extra beds necessary to handle random fluctuations in demand—and income per capita (*YCAP*). This equation was estimated with two-stage least squares:

$$BEDS = 0.244 + 0.184\ YCAP - 0.041\ POPDENS \qquad (7)$$
$$(1.54)\quad(1.67)\qquad\quad(4.00)$$
$$+\ 0.909\ D\hat{B}DD + 0.851\ HUTIL \qquad \bar{R}^2 = 0.973$$
$$(9.10)\qquad\qquad(3.98)$$

The dependent variable in the demand equation is a quantity measure, bed-days per capita adjusted for the demographic characteristics of the state's population (*DBDD*). Independent variables include price (*PHOS*), income (*YCAP*), and price of substitute (out-patient price or *OPP*). Education level (*HSGDS*) will negatively affect the demand for hospital days if education is associated with better information or ability to retain one's initial stock of health. If we control the effect of price on quantity by including price as a right-hand side variable, then beds per capita will be associated with an increase in bed-days if doctors are generating demand. The demand for bed-days will also be greater when quality (*CXD, CXH*) is higher, if quality and quantity in hospital services are complements. Since hospital services are rarely an end in themselves, it is more probable that quality and quantity are substitutes; if so, their effect on bed-days is likely to cancel out (that is, higher quality may raise admissions but lower average stays). Bed-days should be greater, of course, when a larger proportion of the population is covered for hospital and doctor expenses (*COVDH*).

Finally, the demand equation also allows us to investigate the question of the impact of malpractice on hospital use. Because our study is on the additions to medical costs as a result of the malpractice phenomenon, our focus has been on "positive" defensive medicine—that is, on undertaking procedures to avoid liability. Of concern also in any discussion of the effect of malpractice on the quality of patient care must be the practice of "negative" defensive medicine—that is, of not undertaking procedures which would otherwise be medically indicated, in order to avoid liability. If doctors are keeping patients in the hospital longer than otherwise warranted as a form of positive defensive medicine, bed-days should be positively associated with doctors' malpractice premiums (*PREMD*). On the other hand, because 75 percent of the injuries which result in claims against doctors occur in hospitals, doctors may, when possible, avoid hospitalizing patients in states where malpractice premiums are high and may also avoid procedures that are associated with hospitalization.

The demand equation was estimated in the same manner as the price equation and the beds equation:

$$DBDD = 0.847 + 0.301\ YCAP + 0.607\ B\hat{E}DS - 0.241\ PHOS \qquad (8)$$
$$(0.84) \quad (2.01) \qquad\qquad (5.83) \qquad\qquad (1.09)$$

$$- 0.122\ HSGDS + 0.077\ OPP + 0.157\ COVDH$$
$$(1.19) \qquad\qquad (1.73) \qquad\quad (2.28)$$

$$- 0.033\ PREMD + 0.004\ CXD - 0.003\ CXH$$
$$(1.39) \qquad\qquad (0.11) \qquad\quad (0.07)$$

$$\bar{R}^2 = 0.974$$

Income, insurance coverage, and beds per capita have plausible magnitudes and are significant. Price, price of substitutes, and educational level have the predicted signs and, while not significant, have magnitudes which differ from zero by more than their standard error. The procedural complexity measures clearly have no effect on bed-days per capita; either they truly have no effect or their effects on admissions and mean stay offset each other. The coefficient on doctors' premiums indicates that the overuse of hospital services is not a likely defensive reaction among anxious doctors; indeed there is, if anything, weak evidence that doctors are not hospitalizing patients as much as they probably should be, given usual medical practices, in suit-prone states.

Conclusions

We can now answer the question posed at the beginning of the paper. Do doctors and hospitals pass along the costs of the insurance premiums they have to pay? The evidence indeed indicates that, if anything, they more than pass on these increased costs. Doctors' fees rise by 9.1 percent for every 100 percent increase in doctors' premiums when these premiums represent only about 4 percent of total costs, and hospital prices rise by 8.9 percent for every 100 percent increase in hospital premiums when these premiums represent less than 1 percent of total costs (although it should be remembered that this probably measures some forms of defensive medicine not captured in our equations).

Do doctors avoid living in states where they fear they will be sued? We found no evidence to support this speculation from our analysis of 1970 data. In any case, the effect that migration from a state would have on fees in that state is problematic, since the presence of fewer doctors in a state tends to raise prices, but *higher caseloads per doctor tend to lower prices* (see equation 2).

Are medical resources being used by doctors and hospitals for defensive medicine? The evidence for this is also strong: a 100 percent increase in doctors' premiums leads to a 2.3 percent increase in doctors' fees and an 8 percent increase in doctors' services, and to a 4.1 percent increase in hospital prices—but no increase in hospital use.

Has the malpractice crisis led to a breakdown in doctor-patient trust? Our results are consistent with the notion that doctors are not merely concerned with their own incomes and leisure and that consequently they possess unexploited monopoly power. Our finding that the doctors' insurance premiums are more than 100 percent passed on provides some evidence of a deterioration in the doctor-patient relationship resulting from the malpractice phenomenon.

Finally, just what is the magnitude of the cost of the malpractice crisis? A rise of 400 percent in both hospital and doctors' premiums—such as that which occurred between 1970 and 1975—should lead ultimately (our cross-section data should measure long-run impacts) to an increase of $1.1 billion in doctors' costs and of $1.2 billion in hospital expenditures, as a result of higher prices and increased costs from the practice of defensive medicine. These increases in medical expenditures cannot be considered a dead loss—after all, patients are better off if there is a system for compensation for injury, and defensive medicine is probably successful in preventing injuries as well as in preventing lawsuits. Nevertheless, the sum of $2.3 billion is considerable and justifies the search for actions to deal with this crisis, even if it does not justify some of the remedies so far proposed.

Appendix A: Construction of the Procedural Complexity Indexes

If the conditions on pages 66–67 are fulfilled there will be a number of observable indicators (Y) each related to the underlying level of procedural complexity in each state. Their relationship to the level of procedural complexity (Z) which is unobservable can be written as:

$$Y_k = \alpha_k + \beta_k Z + \epsilon_k \qquad \text{where } k \text{ indexes the procedures and } i \text{ indexes the states.} \qquad [A.1]$$

If we ignore the constant term, a linear combination of the Y_k variables takes the form:

$$CX_i = \Sigma \mu_k Y_{k_i} = \Sigma \mu_k \beta_k Z_i + \Sigma \mu_k \epsilon_{k_i} \qquad [A.2]$$

83

If X_j variables represent forces determining the level of complexity:

$$Z_i = \gamma_0 + \gamma_1 X_{1_i} + \gamma_2 X_{2_i} + \ldots + \gamma_n X_{n_i} + U_i \qquad \text{[A.3]}$$

Considered as a system of simultaneous equations, [A.1] and [A.3] give us the unobserved component model, in line with the work of Zellner, Goldberger, Griliches and Chamberlain. Although we are interested in estimating the γ_i coefficients determining complexity, we are not concerned with the effect of complexity on the individual indicators (that is, the β_k). Instead we wish to find the linear combination of indicators most closely related to the unobserved level of complexity for use in our models of the markets for doctors' services and hospital services. If nothing is known about the intercorrelations of the ϵ_k errors and if they are distributed independently of the u errors, then the best sets of weights (μ_k) are those which maximize the correlation between CX_i (the resulting complexity index) and the "best" linear combination of the X_j variables. Those weights are designated $\mu_k{}^*$ and the index they produce $CX_i{}^*$. If the errors are normally distributed with the correlation properties described above, then the coefficients that result from the regression of $CX_i{}^*$ on the X_j variables are the maximum likelihood estimates of the γ_j coefficients that would be produced by the usual analysis of the unobserved components system [A.1] and [A.3].

The technique which produces the best μ_k weights and the γ_j coefficients estimates in this way is a cannonical correlation of the complexity indicators (Y_k) with the determinants of the level of complexity (X_j). A cannonical correlation to find these weights was performed after we took logs of both the left-hand and right-hand side variables and after we weighted the observations for heteroscedasticity.

Appendix B: Data Sources

VARIABLES

MCCON, MCXRAY, MCLAB: U.S. Senate Committee on Finance, *Medicare and Medicaid: Problems, Issues and Alternatives,* Washington, DC., 1970, Appendix H, Table 2. CXD = 0.471 MCCON + 0.03 MCXRAY + 0.573 MCCON

PREMD: U.S. Department of Health, Education, and Welfare, Secretary's Commission on Medical Malpractice, *Appendix,* DHEW pub. no. (05)73–88 (Washington, D.C., 1973), pp. 539–40.

YCAP: U.S. Department of Commerce, *Statistical Abstract 1971,* Washington, D.C., 1972, p. 313.

MEDSTU: U.S. Department of Health, Education, and Welfare, *Health Resources 1970,* Table 88; B. Cooper, N. Worthington, P. Piro, *Personal Health Care Expenditures by State,* vols. 1, 2, DHEW pub. no. (552) 73–11906 (Washington, D.C., 1975), vol. 2, p. viii.

CMTO, COVH, COVDH: Health Insurance Institute, *Source Book of Health Insurance Data 1970*, New York, 1970, pp. 26–27; U.S. Department of Commerce, *Statistical Abstract 1971*, p. 31; Cooper et al., *Personal Health Care Expenditures by State*, vol. 2, p. 34.

PBLS: U.S. Department of Labor, *Three Budgets for an Urban Family of Four Persons 1969–70,* Supplement to BLS Bulletin 1570–5 (Washington, D.C., 1972), pp. 16–27.

WCLER: U.S. Department of Labor, *Handbook of Labor Statistics 1974*, Bulletin 1825 (Washington, D.C., 1974), p. 258.

Q/MD: Cooper et al., *Personal Health Care Expenditures by State*, vol. 2, pp. 37–62; U.S. Department of Labor, *Three Budgets*, pp. 16–27; American Medical Association, *The Distribution of Physicians, and Hospitals, and Hospital Beds in the U.S., 1969*, vol. 1: *Regional, State, County*, Chicago, 1970, Table 9.

% PUBMD, % PUBH: Cooper et al., *Personal Health Care Expenditures by State*, vol. 2, pp. 37–62.

MC/CAP: American Medical Association, *The Distribution of Physicians*, Table 9; U.S. Department of Commerce, *Statistical Abstract 1971*, p. 31.

PRIM: American Medical Association, *The Distribution of Physicians*, Tables 9 and 11; U.S. Department of Commerce, *Statistical Abstract 1971*, p. 31.

BEDS: Cooper et al., *Personal Health Care Expenditures by State*, vol. 2, p. viii; U.S. Department of Commerce, *Statistical Abstract 1971*, p. 31.

MDEXP: Cooper et al., *Personal Health Care Expenditures by State*, vol. 2, pp. 37–62; U.S. Department of Labor, *Three Budgets*, pp. 16–27; U.S. Department of Commerce, *Statistical Abstract 1971*, p. 31.

CLMS: U.S. Department of Health, Education, and Welfare, Secretary's Commission, *Appendix*, p. 8.

HSGDS: U.S. Department of Commerce, *Statistical Abstract 1973*, Washington, D.C., 1974, p. 119.

INRES: U.S. Department of Health, Education, and Welfare, *Health Resources 1970*, Table 85; American Hospital Association, *Hospital Statistics 1971*, Chicago, 1972.

ICCU, ICU, EEG: American Hospital Association, *Hospital Statistics*, pp. 38–40.

$$CXH = 0.252 \text{ ICU} + 0.574 \text{ ICCU} + 0.321 \text{ EEG}$$

PHOS: American Hospital Association, *Survey of Hospital Charges as of January 1972*, Chicago, 1972, Tables A2, B2, A19, B19, A21, B21.

OCRT: American Hospital Association, *Hospital Statistics 1971*, Table 3.

PREMH: U.S. Department of Health, Education, and Welfare, Secretary's Commission, *Appendix*, p. 543.

POPDENS: U.S. Department of Commerce, *Statistical Abstract 1970*, Washington, D.C., 1971, p. 12.

HUTIL: U.S. Department of Commerce, *U.S. Census of Population 1970*, Washington, D.C., 1971, pp. 297–303.

DBDDS: American Hospital Association, *Hospital Statistics 1971*, Table 3; source for HUTIL.

OPP: American Hospital Association, *Hospital Statistics 1971*, Table 8.

AN ECONOMETRIC MODEL OF MEDICAL MALPRACTICE

Michael D. Intriligator and Barbara H. Kehrer

Introduction: the Growing Medical Malpractice Problem

Recent dramatic increases in premiums for medical malpractice insurance coverage, withdrawals of insurance carriers from the medical malpractice market, and physicians' protest strikes have brought the growing medical malpractice problem into the public arena. Moreover, although evidence is scattered, there appear to have been large increases in the number and monetary value of malpractice claims and in the awards or settlements received by patients injured as a result of negligence by providers of medical services.[1]

Partly as a consequence of these developments, the issue of medical malpractice and especially of the cost of malpractice insurance coverage has become a far more significant determinant of the behavior of medical care providers than was the case as recently as five years ago. Until quite recently, professional liability insurance could be treated, by most physicians, as a relatively minor component of the fixed costs of medical practice—comparable, roughly, to the cost of utilities or rent.

Ironically, the increased risk of suit for malpractice has paralleled improvements in the physician's ability to treat his patients' problems. Brook, Brutoco, and Williams have pointed out that the same developments in medical technology which have enhanced the effectiveness of medical services also may have increased the likelihood of injury to the patient:

> Forty years ago, the primary function of the medical care system was the compassionate caring for patients. Malprac-

---

[1] In most cases three elements are necessary to show that malpractice has taken place: injury, negligence, and proximate cause (that is, that the injury was the result of negligence). See Ronald E. Gots, *The Truth about Medical Malpractice* (New York: Stein and Day, 1975). According to Brian Forst, about 85 percent of malpractice cases revolve around the issue of injury due to negligence. Another 10 percent relate to the issue of informed consent. See Brian E. Forst, "Decision Analysis and Medical Malpractice," *Operations Research*, vol. 22 (January-February 1974), pp. 1-12.

tice resulting from an injury caused by improper therapy was almost an impossibility, since most therapies were place- bos. . . . Today, due to advances in the biomedical sciences, another function of medical care must also be considered: efficient delivery to the entire population of efficacious medical services that result in cure or control of disease and main- tenance or improvement of health. Unfortunately, new thera- pies . . . are also capable of producing serious iatrogenic [doctor caused] disease.[2]

This increased probability of injury makes malpractice insurance costs loom ever larger among the fixed costs of medical practice.[3] The dollar amount of insurance costs is rising significantly and noticeably, the probability of being sued is increasing for the individual physician,[4] and the issues surrounding malpractice are growing in general visibility.

Economists have worried about the implications of the malpractice problem for the allocation of scarce resources in the production of medical services.[5] In particular, the incentives and disincentives em- bodied in the growing threat of a malpractice suit may influence the behavior of medical care providers with respect to the geographical and specialty distributions of physicians, the employment of (and degree of delegation to) allied health personnel,[6] the financial viability of part-

---

[2] Robert H. Brook, Rudolf L. Brutoco, and Kathleen N. Williams, "The Relation- ship between Medical Malpractice and Quality of Care," *Duke Law Journal*, vol. 1975 (January 1976), p. 1209.

[3] An American Medical Association survey of office-based physicians providing direct patient care showed that malpractice insurance expenses were 6.3 percent of total professional expenses (excluding physician remuneration) in 1973. See Barry S. Eisenberg, "A Profile of Professional Liability Premiums in Physicians' Office Practices," *Reference Data on Profile of Medical Practice*, 1975-76 Edition, James R. Cantwell, ed. (Chicago: American Medical Association, 1976), pp. 53-60.

[4] According to a recent prediction, every physician engaged in patient care is likely to be sued for malpractice at least once during his career. See Charlotte L. Rosenberg, "Liability vs. Protection," *Medical Economics,* vol. 50 (October 29, 1973), pp. 92-126. This estimate may, in fact, be too low, judging, for example, by the extent of malpractice activity in California, which tends to lead the nation.

[5] For example, see Simon Rottenberg, "Some Economics of Medical Malpractice" (Paper presented to the annual meetings of the Health Economics Research Organization, New York, December 1973). Brook, Brutoco, and Williams, "Medical Malpractice and Quality of Care," also discuss the probability of various deleterious effects ensuing from continuation in the growth of the malpractice problem.

[6] For a discussion of the relationship between employment of allied health personnel and physicians' malpractice insurance expenses, see Barbara H. Kehrer and Michael D. Intriligator, "Malpractice and Employment of Allied Health Personnel," *Medical Care,* vol. 13 (October 1975), pp. 876-83. On the delegation to allied health personnel in physicians' offices, see Barbara H. Kehrer and Michael D. Intriligator, "Task Delegation in Physician Office Practice," *Inquiry,* vol. 11 (December 1974), pp. 292-99.

time medical practice,[7] the willingness of physicians to accept new patients, the degree to which innovative medical techniques and therapies are employed in treatment, and, more generally, the practice of defensive medicine, defined as "the alteration of modes of medical practice, induced by the threat of liability, for the principal purpose of forestalling the possibility of lawsuits by patients as well as providing a good legal defense in the event such lawsuits are instituted." [8]

The purpose of this paper is to address some of the issues involved in the growth of the medical malpractice problem by developing both a theoretical analysis of medical malpractice activity (in the second section) and a related econometric model (in the third section). The theoretical analysis implies that certain behavioral changes will occur among all parties involved—physicians, patients, attorneys, and insurance companies—in response to a changed malpractice environment. When estimated, the econometric model may be useful as a tool for analyzing the relationships among various elements of the system determining malpractice outcomes, for forecasting future levels of malpractice activity (claims and awards, for example), and for assisting in the formulation and evaluation of policy in this area, including policies to cope with future crises. The model may also assist insurance carriers in setting their rates.

A Theoretical Analysis of Malpractice Activity

A theoretical analysis of medical malpractice activity must take explicit account of three considerations. First, such an analysis must recognize that malpractice outcomes are the result of decisions taken by four parties—physicians, patients, attorneys, and insurance companies. Physicians must decide upon the level of malpractice insurance coverage they will carry, the kinds of patients they will treat, and the types of care they will provide (including the degree of delegation of care to allied health personnel, the extent to which they will use diagnostic tests, and their willingness to employ innovative treatment regimens). Patients must decide whether to bring suit, the amount of the suit (if they decide to bring one), and the amount for which they would agree to settle the suit. Attorneys must decide whether to participate in bringing

---

[7] A physician's malpractice insurance premiums are determined mainly by geographical location, specialty, and how much surgery the physician does. They do not reflect the size of the physician's practice. Hence, higher malpractice premiums may discourage part-time practice.

[8] U.S. Department of Health, Education, and Welfare, *Medical Malpractice: Report of the Secretary's Commission on Medical Malpractice*, DHEW pub. no. (OS) 73-88 (1973), p. 14.

a malpractice suit, and they may advise their clients (the patients) on the amount of the suit to be brought. Insurance companies must decide whether to sell malpractice insurance coverage, and those who do offer it must make decisions on the price structure of the coverage they offer; in addition, at various points during the course of a malpractice suit, the companies must decide whether to offer a settlement to the plaintiff and, if so, the size of the settlement to be offered. It should be noted that, just as in the financing of health care, third parties play a highly significant role in medical malpractice activity, though in this area it is the attorneys and the insurance companies—not the government—that are the significant third parties. Government entities, which have traditionally been little more than bystanders and regulators of insurance activities, may of course become an additional important third party in the future.

A second consideration that must enter into a theoretical analysis of medical malpractice activity is the underlying stochastic nature of the components of malpractice outcomes.[9] For the patient, there is a probability of receiving negligent medical treatment that will result in injury, and there are probabilities attached to the various possible outcomes of a suit. For the physician, there is a probability that a given treatment of a given patient will result in injury, a probability that a malpractice suit will be initiated, and there are probabilities attached to the outcomes. These probabilities are generally conditional probabilities: for example, for the physician, the probability that suit will be brought is conditional on the kind of patient treated and the kind of care provided, reflecting decisions made by the physician.

A third consideration that must enter a theoretical analysis is the substantial cost of the medical malpractice system to all parties. Physicians bear the cost of malpractice insurance and the risk of a substantial loss in time and reputation (not even counting possible monetary loss) in the event of a malpractice suit. All patients incur the increased cost of medical care as physicians pass on some or all of the monetary costs of malpractice insurance or settlements. For those patients who choose to litigate there are various costs, both direct and indirect, resulting from the litigation process. For the attorney there is the cost in time and money for a malpractice suit which fails. Finally, insurance carriers must bear the cost of litigation as well as the risk of substantial loss.

A general theoretical treatment of decision making when outcomes are stochastic—a treatment which provides a useful tool for analyzing medical malpractice issues—is Clifford Hildreth's, set forth in his 1973

---

[9] See K. J. Arrow, "Uncertainty and the Welfare Economics of Medical Care," *American Economic Review,* vol. 53 (December 1963), pp. 941-73.

presidential address to the American Statistical Association.[10] Hildreth developed a model of economic decision making under uncertainty and applied it to several hypothetical decision problems, such as betting situations and economic problems in which endowments of initial wealth are random rather than fixed and the current prospect may or may not be independent of the random ventures contemplated. The formal problem Hildreth treated is

$$\max_{\alpha} \eta(\alpha) = E \phi(X + \alpha Y). \tag{1}$$

Here, X is a random variable, representing the decision maker's current prospect, that is, the future wealth assuming no new ventures are undertaken. Y, also a random variable, represents the returns from a potential new venture, such as the purchase or sale of securities, the purchase of insurance, or a new business contract. Most new ventures can be undertaken in various amounts, and α is a measure of the amount of the new venture chosen by the decision maker. Thus $(X + \alpha Y)$ is the future wealth given that the decision maker has chosen α of the new venture. The $\phi(\cdot)$ function is the von Neumann-Morgenstern utility-of-wealth function, and $E(\cdot)$ is the expectation operator, based on a set of personal subjective probabilities for relevant future events. The problem is thus one of maximizing the expected utility of future wealth, written $\eta(\alpha)$, by choice of the level of the new venture to be undertaken, α. Under reasonable assumptions, the unique solution to this problem is that α which satisfies

$$\eta'(\alpha) = E Y \phi'(X + \alpha Y) = 0, \tag{2}$$

yielding that level of the new venture which maximizes expected utility.

To apply this general decision-theoretic structure to the problem of medical malpractice, let us consider the decision facing the physician regarding the choice of a level of malpractice insurance coverage. If X is the physician's net wealth in the absence of malpractice insurance, and Y is a random variable representing premiums for a standard level of coverage, then α may be considered a choice variable representing the level of coverage purchased. With this framework of analysis, the decision-theoretic and stochastic nature of malpractice activity is explicit. Thus the first two of the three general considerations noted above are taken directly into account. The third consideration—the substantial cost of malpractice insurance—is taken into account by noting that the random variable Y is negative and large, on average, relative to X. Indeed, as noted in the introduction, malpractice insurance costs have

---

[10] Clifford Hildreth, "Expected Utility of Uncertain Ventures," *Journal of the American Statistical Association,* vol. 69 (March 1974), pp. 9-17.

become far more significant in recent years than they ever were before, a fact represented in the theoretical analysis by an increase in (the average value of) Y relative to X. Some years ago malpractice insurance could be relegated to secondary importance simply because Y was so small relative to X. The same theoretical analysis was applicable then, but the issues were much less significant because of the relative unimportance of malpractice insurance costs.

Within this Hildreth framework, condition (2) requires the purchase of malpractice insurance up to the point at which the net addition to expected utility obtained by increased coverage, weighted by the level of coverage, is zero. An implication of the comparative static analysis of the model is that, as premiums increase, physicians tend to buy less malpractice insurance, possibly substituting self-insurance.[11] However, self-insurance, holding all other factors constant, is only one possible response to increases in malpractice insurance premiums. Another possible response to increased premium charges for a given quantity of malpractice insurance coverage might be for the physician to change the style of practice engaged in to avoid adverse legal outcomes. For example, the physician might increase the amount of time spent with patients, perform more diagnostic tests, delegate care less frequently, or perform less surgery, thereby reducing the risk of being sued.[12] In a sense, changes of this sort may be viewed as a form of self-insurance. Such changes, however, might well be reflected in changes in the value of X—that is, the level of future wealth that would have been achieved in the absence of malpractice considerations. We might therefore extend the Hildreth approach by making X an endogenous variable in a system of equations, such that X is a function of Y, among other things.

The same type of decision-theoretic structure can be applied to the patient, for whom a major choice involves the decision to litigate and the amount of the suit.[13] Again, the decision making and stochastic

---

[11] Letting $\hat{\alpha}$ be the optimum level of α and reducing Y to the new lower level of $(Y - h)$, it follows that $\dfrac{\partial \hat{\alpha}}{\partial h} < 0$. This result is basic to all the comparative static results reported here (pp. 89-94).

[12] A New York City physician reported recently that the malpractice situation in his area has encouraged doctors to "[grade] down their practices to bring themselves to a lower premium level and at the same time make themselves less susceptible to suit. General practitioners are eliminating minor surgical procedures, and even surgeons are becoming more selective in the procedures they'll perform." Norman S. Blackman, "How the Malpractice Squeeze is Redistributing Doctors," *Medical Economics,* vol. 53 (April 5, 1976), pp. 71-4.

[13] For a discussion of the propensity to litigate, see Jerry Green, "Medical Malpractice and the Propensity to Litigate," in this volume.

nature of malpractice activity is explicit. The cost to patients of malpractice is reflected in a large Y relative to X, on average. Again the optimal level involves balancing expected gains and expected losses, and comparative static analysis of the model suggests that higher probabilities of increased settlements encourage larger suits. Hildreth provides the following example, which suggests that, from the patient's point of view, a malpractice suit may function as a form of insurance against a bad result of medical care:

> A handicapped person contemplates an operation which, if successful, will greatly increase his earning power. If it fails, his physical circumstances are about as before. Suppose he bets the operation fails. If he loses the bet, he pays out of increased earnings. If he wins the bet and it covers the cost of the operation, he has not lost financially. The doctor and the hospital might be good prospects to take his bet. Any effect on their incentives would certainly be in the right direction. The same final prospect could be achieved if the doctor and/or hospital charged more for successful operations than for unsuccessful ones.[14]

The threat of bringing a malpractice suit provides a result similar to that of Hildreth's bet between patient and physician. It is also similar to charging more for successful operations than for unsuccessful ones. In particular, malpractice suits provide a mechanism for recouping financially on grossly unsuccessful medical treatment. Unlike Hildreth's bet, however, the malpractice system involves third parties—attorneys and insurance companies—at a substantial cost.

The decision-theoretic framework may also be applied to the malpractice attorney. In particular, the institutional factors that characterize the process of bringing a malpractice suit—the contingency fee system, for example, whereby the legal cost to the patient of an unsuccessful suit is minimal, while a percentage of the award is paid to the attorney in the event of a successful suit—act to reduce the patient's expected loss in initiating action. Indeed, the patient's attorney may well suffer a greater loss than the patient from an unsuccessful suit. The burden of decision then may be transferred to the attorney.[15] However, the same basic considerations set forth by Hildreth still apply. For example, higher settlements or higher probabilities of such settlements should make attorneys more willing to undertake malpractice suits.

[14] Hildreth, "Expected Utility of Uncertain Ventures," p. 16.
[15] See the discussion of the malpractice attorney in Melvin Reder, "Contingent Fees in Litigation with Special Reference to Medical Malpractice," in this volume. Because of the contingency fee system the relation between client and attorney is similar to that in Hildreth's bet between patient and physician.

Finally, the malpractice insurance company also must make decisions in a state of uncertainty. An insuror must decide whether to offer coverage for professional liability, and it must determine a rate structure for the coverage it offers. During the course of a malpractice suit, the insuror must weigh the likelihood of the plaintiff's success in court: a greater probability that the plaintiff might win should encourage a greater willingness by the insurance company to offer a certain but smaller settlement out of court. Again, Hildreth's model is pertinent. The model is also applicable to the decision by the insurance company to offer malpractice coverage and the rates set for such coverage: a greater probability of a suit or larger awards should lead either to higher rates or to withdrawal from the market.

An Econometric Model of Malpractice Activity

The general decision-theoretic structure of the previous section provides a foundation for an empirical econometric analysis of the volume of malpractice activity. Such an analysis could have significant value for understanding basic mechanisms connecting determinants of malpractice outcomes as well as for forecasting and policy evaluation in this area.

A simple prototype econometric model of malpractice activity within a given geographical area could explain the following, which constitute the endogenous variables of the model:[16]

C = number (or value) of claims per capita,

A = total awards or settlements per capita, and

P = average premium levels (expenditures on malpractice insurance).

The other variables of the model, which are largely determined by other mechanisms, and hence are exogenous, include the following:

D = physicians per capita,

$\underset{\sim}{S}$ = a vector of patient characteristics which contribute to the propensity to bring suit (as, for example, age, income, education, mobility),

$\underset{\sim}{M}$ = a vector of characteristics of the medical care system and the delivery of services which affect the probability of injury and suit (as, for example, specialty distribution, training, and experience of physicians; presence of sophisticated hospital facilities; PSRO; degree of delegation),

---

[16] For a related model, see Marnie Mueller, "The Economics of Medical Malpractice: Claims, Awards, and Defensive Medicine" (Paper presented at the American Economic Association meeting, September 1976).

F = a vector of characteristics of the medical care system which, given M, affect the likelihood that a given suit will be successful—that is to say, elements of defensive medicine (as, for example, ordering of X-rays or lab tests, consultations), and

L = a vector of characteristics of the legal system which affect the likelihood of bringing suit (as, for example, the statute of limitations or the presence of no-fault automobile insurance).

In an expanded model, however, a number of the characteristics that are treated as exogenous in the prototype model would be explained by the system itself and hence would be endogenous. In addition, dynamic factors could be taken into account. For example, in the long run, the number of physicians per capita in an area may change in response to the malpractice climate of the area.[17] Doctors, particularly those about to establish new practices, may tend to flow toward areas where malpractice activity is relatively light and away from areas characterized by malpractice crises. Many characteristics of the medical care system and the delivery of medical services also may show changes in response to malpractice activity. Physicians may tend to limit their practices with respect to the range of services they perform (for example, a general practitioner may stop doing minor surgery) and they may become more cautious than they have been about employing new modes of treatment. New physicians may choose their specialties on the basis of relative malpractice risk, which means that, on the margin, there may be a shift away from high-risk specialties and toward low-risk fields. Finally, the practice of defensive medicine is by definition likely to be a sensitive reflector of the various dimensions of malpractice activity in an area.

The equations of the prototype model are:

$$C = f_c (A_{-1}, D, L, M, S) \tag{3}$$

$$A = f_a (C_{-1}, F, L) \tag{4}$$

$$P = f_p (C_{-1}, A_{-1}, M, F). \tag{5}$$

In (3) current claims depend on five variables. First, they depend on past awards (information on such awards may encourage or discourage current claims). Second, they depend on physicians per capita, a variable which serves as a proxy for the degree of (im)personal care provided and a measure of the demand pressure on physicians—which

---

[17] See, however, the paper by Bruce Greenwald and Marnie Mueller entitled "Medical Malpractice and Medical Costs" in this volume.

may influence the amount of time a physician can spend with each patient. D is also a scale measure, however, since the more physicians there are per capita in any area, the more medical treatments there are likely to be and the greater the likelihood that malpractice will take place; hence the expected effect of D on C, current claims, is ambiguous. Third, current claims depend on characteristics of the legal system which may affect the probability of bringing suit. Fourth, they depend on characteristics of the medical services delivery system that may be associated with variations in the incidence of medical negligence. Fifth, they depend on characteristics of the patient population that may be associated with a greater or lesser propensity to sue (other things being equal).

In equation (4), current awards depend upon past claims (from which they arise), characteristics of the medical system reflecting the extent to which providers practice defensive medicine (which would reduce the likelihood that a given suit will be successful), and characteristics of the legal system, indicating attitudes of courts and juries regarding proper levels of settlement.

In equation (5), current premium levels depend on past claims (which give rise to necessary expenses on the part of insurance carriers, apart from the awards or settlements reached) and past awards (which must, on an actuarial basis, influence current levels of premiums), on characteristics of the medical care system (since premium rates for constant levels of coverage vary with physician specialty and whether the practice is solo or group), and the extent to which physicians practice defensive medicine (since such practices may function as substitutes for higher levels of malpractice insurance coverage).

Once the four vectors of characteristics are defined in terms of operational measures, the econometric model in these three equations could be estimated on the basis of pooled cross-section (say, statewide) time-series (say, annual) data. Numerous efforts are currently underway to develop a data base on malpractice activity, but available statistics are not complete.[18] If we could find the requisite data for estimating the econometric model specified above, the resulting estimates could be used to forecast all three endogenous variables over the short-term and medium-term periods—over the next one to five years. They also could be used to determine the extent to which the recent dramatic changes in malpractice activity have been generated internally—through the effects of lagged endogenous variables—rather than being generated exter-

---

[18] For example, the series, *Malpractice Claims,* published by the National Association of Insurance Commissioners, has begun to tabulate current measures of malpractice activity. Its first volume relates to fiscal 1976. The Greenwald-Mueller paper in this volume uses a data base developed by the authors.

nally—through the effects of exogenous variables. This question whether changes in malpractice activity are generated internally or externally is important in determining whether recent trends can be expected to continue or whether they represent a temporary disturbance to the equilibrium of the system. In particular, if the processes have been internally generated, large increases in malpractice activity may continue, while if they have been based on exogenous shocks they may, in the absence of further shocks, be expected to diminish.

A potential further development of the econometric approach to the analysis of medical malpractice issues would be the conceptualization and implementation of a microeconometric model.[19] Such a model would analyze the interactions among certain relatively homogeneous groups of agents. For example, in the context of medical malpractice, physicians might be classified according to specialty, years in practice, and location, while patients might be classified according to age, sex, race, education, and income. With sufficient data keyed to these classifications it would be possible to estimate the relationships between certain kinds of physicians and certain kinds of patients. One possible use of such a model would be to determine the probabilities of a particular kind of patient bringing suit and of a particular kind of physician being sued. These probabilities could be useful in analyzing potential inconsistencies in malpractice insurance premium rate setting for different types of physicians. They could also be used to make predictions, based on demographic, economic, medical, and other changes, of future levels of malpractice activity.

Conclusion

This paper represents a preliminary effort to contribute to informed discussion on issues relating to the "crisis" in medical malpractice. It has set forth a theoretical analysis of malpractice activity and a related econometric model. Both formulations provide promising vehicles for understanding, forecasting, and controlling aspects of this problem. The lack of the necessary data precludes estimation of this econometric model at present, however, and the development of an appropriate data base is the important next step for this line of research into issues relating to

---

[19] See Donald E. Yett, Leonard J. Drabek, Michael D. Intriligator, and Larry J. Kimbell, "A Microeconometric Model of the Health Care System in the United States," *Annals of Economic and Social Measurement*, vol. 4 (July 1975), pp. 407-33; and idem, *A Forecasting and Policy Simulation Model of the Health Care Sector: the HRRC Prototype Microeconometric Model* (Lexington, Mass.: Lexington Books, 1977) for the development of a microeconomic model of the health care system as a whole.

medical malpractice. (For data relating to malpractice premiums in 1974 and 1975, approximating one of the endogenous variables of the model, see the Appendix.[20]) Nevertheless, the conceptualizations of the theoretical analysis and the econometric model provide useful approaches to studying the complex issues of medical malpractice.

[20] This data set describes insurance premium *prices* for a given level of coverage. In contrast, the dependent variable in equation (5), the third equation in the prototype model, is average premiums paid, which has both price and quantity (level of coverage) components. While prices are set by insurance companies on the basis of past and expected future malpractice activity in an area, medical providers determine the level of coverage purchased. In the current malpractice "crisis," prices have exhibited considerable short-run volatility. It is not clear how physicians have responded with respect to levels of coverage, and the authors have not seen any data (other than anecdotal reports, such as Charles E. Lewis and Howard Freeman, "The Opinions and Actions of Physicians during a Malpractice Crisis," unpublished paper, 1976) describing that response.

Appendix
"AVERAGE" MALPRACTICE PREMIUMS PAID BY CLASS I AND CLASS V PHYSICIANS BY STATE, 1974 AND 1975

State	Year	Class I MD Pre-mium	Class I MD Average annual per-centage increase	Class V MD Pre-mium	Class V MD Average annual per-centage increase	Notes
Alabama	1974	$ 192	40	$1,209	40	Rates are for Employers of Wausau, which insures about half the physicians in the state. St. Paul and Aetna, which cover most of the rest of the state's MDs, charge about 20% more.
	1975	269		1,692		
Alaska	1974	400–500	100	3,000–4,000	100	
	1975	1,000		8,000–9,000		
Arizona	1972	612	54	3,700	49	
	1975	1,595		9,119		
Arkansas	1975	488		3,130		
California						Rates in California have gone up about 600% from 1965 to February 1975. The numerous programs and rate changes in the state make state-wide averages impossible to compile.
Colorado	1971	374	5	2,473	15	Rates are for $1 million-limit coverage.
	1974	430		3,590		
Connecticut	1971	445	17	2,549	39	Figures are for the Aetna program covering 80% of the MDs in the state.
	1974	678		5,258		
Delaware	1971	395	33	2,283	59	
	1974	783		6,297		
DC	(see note)					
Florida	1975	Dade and Broward Counties 1,113		8,243		
	1975	Elsewhere in Florida 814		5,148		
Georgia	1975	285		1,530		
Hawaii	1975	431		2,700		

State	Year	Class I MD Pre-mium	Class I MD Average annual per-centage increase	Class V MD Pre-mium	Class V MD Average annual per-centage increase	Notes
Idaho	1973			1,743		Rates given are for
	1974	272	266		130	$250,000/$500,000
	1975	995		6,264		coverage.
Illinois		Chicago				Illinois State Medical
	1972	185		3,595		Society group policy
	1974	288		3,988		rates. 1974 and 1975
	1975	516		7,116		premiums are for
						$1 million coverage.
Indiana	(see note)					
Iowa	(see note)					
Kansas	1975	340		2,750		
Kentucky	1971	158		1,281		Premiums charged
	1973	237	47	1,519	14	by Medical Protec-
	1974	381		1,832		tive.
	1974	721		3,662		Aetna, which insures 25% of the state MDs, charges considerably higher rates.
Louisiana	1974	260	77	1,612	76	St. Paul rates.
	1975	460		2,840		
	1974	197	15	1,240	15	Hartford rates.
	1975	227		1,426		
Maine	1970			832		Rates for orthopedic
	1973			2,600	97	surgeons only.
	1974			4,080		
Maryland	1971	245	16	1,550	16	
	1974	360		2,273		
Massachusetts	(see note)					
Michigan	1974	194	278	2,676	107	Medical Protective Co. rates, covering about half of state MDs.
	1975	735		4,551		
	1974	194	658	2,676	348	Shelby Mutual rates, covering 22% of state MDs.
	1975	1,471		12,002		
Minnesota	1974	347		2,196		
Mississippi	1970	116	6.3	739	6.3	
	1974	145		924		
Missouri	1974	150		2,400		

Appendix (continued)

State	Year	Class I MD Premium	Class I MD Average annual percentage increase	Class V MD Premium	Class V MD Average annual percentage increase	Notes
Montana	1975	918				
Nebraska	1975	410		2,586		
Nevada	1974	750	384	3,571	384	Argonaut rates (1975) raise was not yet approved by the State Insurance Commission.
	1975	3,630		17,284		
New Hampshire	(see note)					
New Jersey	1975	901				For $1 million/$3 million coverage.
New Mexico	1975	511		3,350		
New York	(see note)					
North Carolina	1974	96	82	474	84	
	1975	175		872		
North Dakota	1975	225		1,800		
Ohio	1969	176	85	889	86	
	1974	922		4,707		
Oklahoma	1972	153	5	769	14	Rates based on coverage for $100,000 per claim.
	1974	169		984		
Oregon	1975	1,116				Class VI, the highest risk class, MDs paid $7,240 in 1975.
Pennsylvania		Philadelphia				
	1971	185	12	2,427	13	Philadelphia rates are the highest in the state.
	1974	250		3,385		
Rhode Island	1970	85	116	215	116	
	1974	479		1,209		
South Carolina	1975	160		1,010		
South Dakota	1975	788		5,000		
Tennessee	1974	402		2,052		
Texas	(see note)					
Utah	1973	582	32			
	1974	769				
Vermont	1973	323	76			Premiums for $1 million coverage.
	1974	567				

Appendix (continued)

State	Year	Class I MD Pre-mium	Class I MD Average annual per-centage increase	Class V MD Pre-mium	Class V MD Average annual per-centage increase	Notes
Virginia	1971	135		824		
	1972	179	73	1,134	77	
	1973	270		1,705		
	1974	432		2,728		
Washington	1975	788		3,212–6,356		
West Virginia	1974	358	72			
	1975	615				
Wisconsin	1970	194	45	1,229	64	Rates are for
	1975	629		5,133		St. Paul.
Wyoming	1973	247				Rates are for
	1974	348	99			$100,000/$300,000
	1975	738				with $1 million um-
						brella coverage.

Note: Unless otherwise indicated, rates are for $100,000/$300,000 coverage. Physicians are classified (for example, Class I, Class V) according to specialty and the extent of surgery performed (see footnote 7). The information for each state apparently was obtained from the state medical society. Some state societies surveyed their membership, and the reported premium levels are statewide means. In other instances the reported premiums are the rates charged by the major carrier in the state. In yet other cases no statewide data are available, and the entry in the table has been left blank.

Source: "State-by-State Analysis of Physicians Medical Malpractice," *American Medical News,* February 24, 1975. Reprinted in: U.S. Congress, House Committee on Interstate and Foreign Commerce, *An Overview of Medical Malpractice* (Washington, D.C., 1975), pp. 205-18.

MEDICAL MALPRACTICE AND THE SUPPLY OF PHYSICIANS

Galen Burghardt, Jr.

Introduction

The main purpose of the present paper is to examine the relationships between medical malpractice and the quantity and quality of services physicians are willing to provide at any given price. Serious study of the problem is bound to be hampered at least in part because the available data cannot be exactly tailored to fit the relevant economic concepts. For example, it is far easier to obtain information on the quantity than on the quality of medical services. One can examine changes in the numbers of physicians, hours worked, and number of patients treated, but not get a full empirical grip on changes in the quality of care.

In the market for medical care, as in markets for other kinds of expertise, inputs are more easily measured than outputs. It is widely recognized that medical care in general and physicians' services in particular make up only one of several resources which an individual can use to change his general level of health. Such factors as education, nutrition, occupation, location, and dissipation also affect one's health— as, of course, does medical care. In this setting, the quality of medical care should be defined by the incremental effect it has on an individual's level of health. But even if the relationship between medical inputs and changes in health were free of random elements, the task of estimating quality would be difficult. If allowance is made for the presence of a random element in the effect of medical care on health as well, the task becomes truly formidable. The empirical content of this paper is limited, therefore, to fairly rudimentary comparisons of hours, visits, and similar data.

The main text is divided into three main sections. The first of these deals with the supply of hours of work. The second is devoted to the

The author is an economist, Division of Research and Statistics, Board of Governors of the Federal Reserve System. The opinions expressed here are his own and do not necessarily represent the opinions of the Board of Governors.

103

problem of specialization. The third reviews recent developments in the distribution of practicing and new physicians. A brief final section contains concluding remarks. The major findings are reviewed briefly here.

In the second section, it is argued that, analytically, the cost of malpractice insurance is better treated as a lump-sum payment or tax, whose size is largely unaffected by the size of the physician's practice, rather than as an excise tax, where the payment would be directly related to size of practice. As a lump-sum tax it would not affect the extra monetary gain from treating an additional patient, nor would it affect the monetary loss from reducing the scale of patient care. In the short run, two effects dominate. First, by decreasing the physician's wealth, the cost of malpractice insurance encourages those physicians continuing in practice to work longer hours. Offsetting this so-called wealth effect is the fugitive effect. That is, some physicians can be expected to abandon their practice and flee to another location or specialty, or perhaps into early retirement. The relative sizes of the two effects are empirical questions; hence the effect of an increase in malpractice insurance rates on the short-run supply of hours cannot be predicted from logic alone.

If malpractice insurance costs more closely resemble short-run fixed costs, two important conclusions follow. The first is that the cost of malpractice insurance, except in the long run, cannot be treated analytically as an excise tax. It is not a cost that can be "added on" to the previously existing price, and it is therefore not passed through to the consumer, at least in the short run. The second is that at present it is far too early for us to assess the ultimate effect of a change in liability rules on the market for physicians and their services. Only after some time has passed, and the existing stock of physicians has either retired or had a chance to adjust to a new set of rules, will such an assessment be possible.

In the third section, the effect of a change in liability rules on the degree of specialization is taken up in two different settings. The settings differ in patient awareness of physician quality, in the presence of uninsurable costs, in the degree of sophistication used in insurance rate setting, and in the ability of physicians to discriminate in price between high-risk and low-risk patients. The leading result of our exploration of the matter is a discovery that in neither of these settings is it reasonable to suppose or expect that the quality of medical practice will rise, and under one set of plausible assumptions, the quality of medical practice could uniformly fall.

The fourth section is a review of recent trends in the distribution of new and existing physicians. The finding that stands out in this section is that, while the rates of growth in the number of practicing physicians per capita tend to be lower in states that appear to have medical malpractice problems than in states without such problems, the absolute number of physicians per capita tends to be higher in the problem states than elsewhere. The higher malpractice rates and lower growth rates may result from the larger number of physicians per capita in the problem states, and the inverse relationship between the higher insurance rates and lower growth rates may be spurious.

The Supply of Hours

In determining the effect of shifting liability from the patient to the physician, one must distinguish carefully between the short run and the long run, and control for potential changes in the quality of medical care. Also, one must correctly specify the way in which insurance costs affect the physician's opportunities and hence his decisions.

Any response to a change in environment or rules requires time, and the size of the response depends in part on how much time has passed. The long run is that amount of time which permits all adjustment that is going to take place, to take place. During the short run, only limited adjustment is possible. In the case of the medical industry's response to a change in liability rules, the short run may be quite long. Some adjustments, such as selling a practice and either moving, taking up teaching, or retiring, can be made within a year or so. Others, such as learning a new specialty, take considerably longer. Still others, such as replacing the existing physician stock with physicians who have worked only in an environment of physician liability, can take several decades. In any case, adjustment to a change is slower, the more costly the adjustment process. It is safe to suppose that the adjustment costs are large for all but new and fairly young physicians and for fairly old physicians.

In dealing with the cost of malpractice insurance, two plausible economic propositions are applicable. The first is that someone faced with a pecuniary loss will attempt to make up a portion of the loss by working a few more hours, allowing some of the loss to be absorbed by a reduction of time spent outside of work. In other words, someone faced with a $100 tax typically will not allow net income to fall by the full $100, but will earn back some of the loss by working longer. The second proposition is that if the price of something is reduced, a person will want more of it. For example, a reduction in the cost of nonpatient activities such as leisure, research, or teaching will encourage a physician to spend more time on these and less time in active patient care. The two forces work in opposite directions. The first would cause the physician to work more hours, the second fewer. Which force dominates is an empirical issue. The effect on hours worked of a change which affects both the physician's wealth and the relative monetary rewards of competing activities cannot be determined by logic alone, or without some evidence.

In the short run, the dilemma does not exist since no relationship exists between insurance costs and hours worked. If the physician purchased a policy for each patient seen, both propositions would apply. As it is, the purchase of an insurance policy simply makes the physician worse off without affecting the relative monetary rewards of patient and nonpatient activities. Hence, those physicians who choose to buy insurance and to remain in active practice will also tend to work longer hours to make up some of the cost of insurance.

As shown in Table 1, changes in the allocation of time by physicians are not inconsistent with the notion that only the first of the two effects is at work. Notice that while there was some tendency for the length of the average work week to fall between 1969 and 1973, the average number of hours spent in active patient care rose. Moreover, it seems that the number of hours spent in patient care was more likely to rise if the physician was in surgery (where the length of the work week actually increased), radiology (where the increase was rather substantial), or anesthesiology. Each of these specialties has been particularly vulnerable to malpractice litigation. In the less beleaguered specialties, both the average work week and hours spent in patient care declined.

The effect of an increase in insurance costs on the length of the work week applies only to those physicians who continue to practice actively in the same specialty and the same location. What may be called the fugitive effect is missing, since the physician's choice was limited to deciding whether to spend more or less time in active patient care. In fact, the range of choices is much wider. A physician can vote with his feet, and walk away from his current practice, although the time required to relocate practice would be different for different people. Included in the wider range of choices are a less hostile specialty (or, perhaps, teaching and research in the same specialty), a less hostile environment, and retirement.

Whether a physician decides to stay or go will depend on his personal circumstances. A physician's age should prove to be an important determinant of whether the benefits of a less hostile practicing environment warrant the costs of the change, or whether retirement is a preferred alternative. Every practicing physician has invested time and resources in developing a set of skills; some of those skills are

Table 1

ALLOCATION OF PHYSICIAN TIME, 1969 AND 1973

Specialty	1969			1973		
	Hours per week in practice (1)	Hours per week in patient care (2)	Ratio (3) = (2) ÷ (1)	Hours per week in prac- tice (4)	Hours per week in patient care (5)	Ratio (6) = (5) ÷ (4)
General practice	52.0	47.8	.919	51.1	47.6	.932
Internal medicine	52.8	47.7	.903	52.7	47.5	.901
Surgery	51.5	45.5	.883	52.4	47.8	.912
Ob/Gyn.	54.3	48.8	.899	52.3	48.8	.933
Pediatrics	52.9	46.9	.887	49.3	44.5	.903
Psychiatry	47.3	39.3	.831	46.7	40.3	.863
Radiology	47.7	32.8	.688	47.3	41.8	.884
Anesthesiology	52.4	47.0	.897	52.1	48.0	.921
Other	47.5	35.5	.747	45.8	39.5	.862
Total	51.3	44.7	.871	50.8	46.1	.907

Source: Center for Health Services Research and Development, American Medical Association, *Profile of Medical Practice* (Chicago: American Medical Association, 1974).

peculiar to his present specialty while others can be applied in different kinds of medical practice. Also, every practicing physician (at least every physician in office-based practice) has built up a practice which is unique in certain respects to that physician.

Even for a well-trained and experienced physician, choosing a new specialty requires a period of investment in new skills which he believes will be repaid by an increased flow of future benefits, either pecuniary or nonpecuniary. Since the expected flow of future benefits diminishes with age, younger physicians are more likely to change specialties than are older physicians. Also, there is the problem of building up a new practice, a task which would be faced more willingly by a young physician.

The value of the existing practice is another matter. The medical records, office personnel and equipment, location, and so forth all have asset values derived from their use in a particular practice. The asset value of each will tend to be higher for the physician who assembled

107

the practice than for anyone else. The difference between their value to the practicing physician and their value to the next highest bidder in the rest of society would be a measure of the "quasi-rents" earned by a particular physician in a particular practice.

The distinction between a pure economic rent and a quasi-rent is useful here. The former is a payment greater than is required to entice someone into a voluntary exchange and is not affected in any way by the individual's past choices. A quasi-rent is also a payment in excess of that necessary to elicit voluntary exchange, but it results from previous actions which cannot now be undone. The income from rental property is a good example. A portion of the payment typically will be for improvements which have been undertaken by someone expecting a rate of return sufficiently large to compensate him for not having invested in something else. Once the improvements are in place, a payment which is less than was expected often will serve to keep the improvements in place—hence, there is a quasi-rent. Should the income be less than could be earned elsewhere, however, no further improvements will be undertaken. Existing apartments, for example, may not be razed, but neither will new ones be built if the rate of return falls below the competitive level.

In the case of physicians, those who have already acquired their skills and have built up their practices, along with valued professional contracts, may earn substantial quasi-rents, but not pure economic rents.[1] Therefore, the effect a change in the malpractice environment will have on existing physicians is not the same as the effect of the same change on new physicians. Existing physicians, while they may not be especially pleased by the change in environment, may also find it unprofitable to do anything but continue their practice. Incoming physicians, on the other hand, are not saddled by the consequences of such decisions and can be expected to respond differently from existing physicians.

The first conclusion to be drawn from this discussion is that the short-run effect of a change in liability regimes on the supply of physicians' services is indeterminate. Because the cost of malpractice insurance is more like a short-run flat cost than like an addition to variable costs, those who remain in a specialty will tend to devote more hours to patient care. Some physicians, however, will prefer to leave the specialty—or at least the location. The fugitive effect will tend to grow with time, as more physicians complete the adjustment, and the hours effect will tend to diminish. Nonetheless, whether the hours effect or

[1] See K. B. Leffler, "Physician Licensure: Compensation and Monopoly in American Medicine," Working Paper Series No. 7620 (Rochester: University of Rochester, Graduate School of Management), for a good discussion of the economic rents among physicians.

the fugitive effect is greater in the short run is an empirical matter which cannot be resolved here.

Note that because the effect on total hours supplied cannot be determined, neither can the effect on the price of services. If, for example, the total number of hours supplied increases in the short run, the market will only absorb those hours at a lower price. If the supply of hours decreases, the price of services will rise. As a result, the cost of malpractice insurance is not something which is simply "passed through" to the patient in the short run. Hence, it is incorrect to state that thus-and-so percent of the price of a physician visit is due to the cost of malpractice insurance.

The second conclusion is that the long run may be very long. The malpractice issue did not become empirically interesting until recently. Only as existing physicians adjust (that is, retire, change location, change specialty or type of practice) and new physicians enter the market, will its long-run consequences be observed. Because of the age structure of the medical profession, such an adjustment could take as long as several decades. Certainly, the present structure of medical practice cannot serve as an adequate description of a long-run equilibrium in a setting of physician liability.

Malpractice, Specialization, and Quality

The degree of specialization in medical practice is determined by a wide variety of market and technical considerations. There is a large and still growing number of diagnostic, therapeutic, and surgical techniques. Even if all of these could be mastered by a single individual, it would probably not be economic for that individual to dispense a little bit of each kind of service. At the same time, physicians do not limit themselves to a single well-defined activity. Rather, given the size of the market for medical services and the prevailing prices for inputs and outputs, a physician's desire for income and for variety of work will cause him to provide a variety of services.

The effect of a change in liability rules on the physician's willingness to provide any one of these various services, and therefore its effect upon the general quality of medical care, depends largely (1) on whether patients can discern quality differences among physicians, (2) on available risk-pooling or insurance arrangements, and (3) on the extra costs of providing high-quality rather than low-quality care. In what follows, the effect of a rules change is considered in two distinct settings, involving important differences in perceptions, abilities, and insurance schemes. Neither setting is meant to be a first-rate

109

representation of the truth, but the reader may find one or more aspects of each case appealing. If so, the main theme of this section will be appealing also. That is, one should not be surprised if a change in liability rules does not cause the quality of care to increase all around, but instead causes the quality of some kinds of care to fall.

The First Setting. In the first setting, it is assumed that patients find the task of discerning quality differences among physicians difficult in the extreme. The differences in quality, which are measured here as differences in the likelihood of success of treatment, are assumed to be due to immutable physician characteristics. Also, it is assumed that insurance rates are not experience-rated by individual physicians—that is, malpractice insurance rates do not reflect the actual probabilities that one physician or another will be successful in his ministrations. Finally, it is assumed that in the event of malpractice litigation there are some losses against which physicians cannot insure.

Before we go on with this case, each of the assumptions deserves some attention. Patients are not entirely incapable of discovering true quality differences among physicians, but the task can hardly be thought an easy one. For one thing, the professional ban on physician advertising has served as an effective barrier to the production and use of reliable information about physicians' abilities.[2] Under the present circumstances, the truth is not badly served by assuming that patients select physicians according to a random process.

Next there is the problem of physician quality. Each physician is equipped with a unique set of intellectual and physical characteristics which, when combined with a unique training experience, serve to make him better than some physicians and worse than others. Once a physician has begun active practice, these parts of his background are beyond his control and are the cause of what may be called ascriptive quality differences between him and any other physician. Beyond this, physicians can practice better or worse medicine by devoting more or less time (both in practice and in study) and more or less costly medical resources to their practice. The result could be discretionary quality differences. What is assumed here is that the discretionary quality differences are sufficiently small to make them empirically uninteresting.

To assume that insurance premiums are not based on experience ratings for physicians (who differ both in quality and in difficulty of practice) seems altogether reasonable, at least over broad classes of

---

[2] The obvious difficulties in measuring or describing physician quality cannot be ignored, but the presence of measurement problems does not imply that no information is better than some.

physicians and patients. There are some departures from this rule, such as the raising of insurance rates for physicians with demonstrable losses, but not many. In particular, rates do not seem to vary with the size of practice, age, experience, and training of the physician, or with any of the many other physician and practice characteristics that could reasonably be supposed to affect the likelihood and frequency of success or failure and the resulting costs.

Last, under any reasonable set of circumstances, a physician is not likely to be insured fully against the costs of being sued for malpractice. Typically, there are some expected out-of-pocket costs associated with exceptionally large damage awards. Income from practice is lost while the physician is dealing with the suit itself. There are psychic costs when there is insult and lost prestige. Also, it is difficult to insure against lost future income resulting from a diminished practice or a change to a less attractive specialty.

Under these circumstances, shifting the liability for damages from the patient to the physician can have interesting and unpredictable effects on the price and quality of medical care. For purposes of illustration, it is assumed here that there are two quality classes of physicians and that there are two types of patient, each suffering from its own distinct malady or disorder. Each class of physician is assumed at the outset (under the patient liability regime) to treat whatever patients show up in the office. That is, quality differences notwithstanding, every physician feels competent enough to treat either of the two disorders. In the following discussion, one physician from the first group will be compared with one physician from the second group.

The main distinction between the two liability regimes is that the physician is not sued under the former, but may be sued under the latter. When the physician is liable, uninsured costs are important to him, but when the patient is liable, they are not. The relative attractiveness to physicians of caring for the two disorders depends on which regime prevails. Where the patients are liable, the relative monetary rewards are determined by the prevailing prices for the two services. If we do not count the cost of treatment (including time) then, if the price for treating the first malady is P_1 and the price for treating the second is P_2, the relative rewards for treating the two maladies will be the same for each physician, or P_1/P_2.

Where physicians are liable, however, the relative attractiveness of treating the disorders will depend on the physician as well as on the market prices for treatment. In particular, the relative pecuniary rewards as seen by any one physician may be written as

$$\frac{P^*_{1i}}{P^*_{2i}} = \frac{P'_1 - q_{1i}\,C_{1i}}{P'_2 - q_{2i}\,C_{2i}} \qquad (i = 1,2) \qquad (1)$$

where in the numerator P^*_{1i} is a risk-adjusted price to a physician in the ith quality class for treating the first malady, q_{1i} is the likelihood that a physician in the ith quality class will fail, and C_{1i} represents the uninsured costs if failure occurs. P'_1 may be different from the original P_1.

Under a patient liability regime, the relative pecuniary rewards are the same for the two physicians. Under a physician liability scheme, they differ because of differences in physician quality and in the uninsured costs faced by each physician. Although there is no way of telling how the relative rewards will change for each physician, suppose the final result is

$$\frac{P^*_{11}}{P^*_{12}} > \frac{P^*_{21}}{P^*_{22}} \qquad (2)$$

so that the first physician perceives the first disorder to be relatively more lucrative than does the second physician. Ignoring the various market adjustments that the liability change would require, we may still be confident that, given time, the first physician now will tend to see fewer patients suffering from the second disorder than before—referring them perhaps to the second physician. The second physician for his part will prefer to treat more patients suffering from the second malady than before. Hence, a change in liability rules may cause an increase in specialization, but the direction of quality changes cannot be determined.

What effect will the resulting specialization have on the quality of treatment for each disorder? There is no unambiguous answer. The relative monetary rewards are determined both by the physicians' skills and the physicians' perceptions of the uninsurable costs. The physician who specializes in treating the first disorder may do so not because he is better than the other physician, but rather because he sees the costs of being sued for failure in treating the first disorder to be markedly lower than the costs of being sued for failure in treating the second.

In the absence of any good information about the uninsured costs associated with malpractice litigation, it is impossible to say what will happen to the quality of medical practice except perhaps that the quality of care for some disorders will improve, while for others the quality of care will worsen. As a consequence, patients suffering from one type of disorder may expect to gain at the expense of those suffering from other disorders.

The Second Setting. The major drawbacks to the preceding section are the assumptions regarding patient knowledge about the quality of medical care, the inability to affect the quality of care by using more or less costly therapies, and the absence of any discussion of the patients themselves. These are remedied in part here.

Patients are not a homogeneous lot. Instead, they differ in education, income, attitude toward risk, vulnerability to disabling injuries, and a variety of other characteristics which would tend to cause one patient to be more concerned than another about the quality of health care received. To the extent that concern is revealed by more intensive search for quality and by a willingness to pay for better medical care, different qualities of health care will be produced at prices reflecting the time and resources employed.

Patients who are especially vulnerable to harm, or for whom the costs which result in the event of harm are especially great, will tend to seek out higher-quality medical care.[3] Those whose physical or psychic characteristics make them relatively impervious to harm, or for whom harm is not very costly, will be satisfied with lower-quality medical care at a correspondingly lower price, in terms of either search or physician fees. To simplify the following discussion, suppose that patients are of two types, high-cost and low-cost. Further, suppose that each quality of medical care can be produced—where quality is measured in terms of the likelihood of success or failure—at a flat cost per unit of care.

The decision to purchase high-quality medical care hinges on whether the value of the incremental improvement in the quality of care warrants the additional expense. If we write the cost of harm, in the event it occurs, as A, the likelihood of harm as q, and the cost of treatment as C, a patient will purchase the higher-quality care if

$$(q_2 - q_1)A > C_1 - C_2, \tag{3}$$

where q_2 is the likelihood of harm with the lower-quality care, C_1 is the cost of higher-quality care, and so on. On the left-hand side is the expected incremental damage of purchasing lower-quality care as perceived by the patient. On the right-hand side is the incremental resource cost of avoiding that damage through higher-quality care.

In this setting, patients will be self-selected into two distinct groups, according to the size of damage in the event of harm. The critical value that will separate one group from the other is simply

$$A^* = \frac{C_1 - C_2}{q_2 - q_1}. \tag{4}$$

---

[3] For an excellent and more complete discussion of this aspect of product quality, see W. Y. Oi, "The Economics of Product Safety," *Bell Journal of Economics and Management Science*, Spring 1973, pp. 3-28.

If a patient sees the value of A as greater than the value of $A*$, he will choose the more costly care. If the value of A is less than the value of $A*$, the patient will choose lower-quality care. Suppose, in what follows, that the mean cost in the former group is A_1, and in the latter group A_2.

In this setting, what is the effect of making physicians liable for damages in the event of harm? The answer depends on the nature of the risk-pooling or insurance arrangements and upon the ability of physicians to charge different prices to different customers—to discriminate by price on the basis of high-cost and low-cost care and patients. (This is not price discrimination for the purpose of exercising monopoly discretion.) As will be shown, the ability to discriminate by price is the only thing that will permit both qualities of medicine to be practiced after the change in liability regimes.

The importance of producing two (or more) qualities of medicine should not be underestimated. Given the distributions of such things as income and education among individual members of society, the patient liability arrangement described here would be economically efficient. In contrast, to provide higher-quality care at the correspondingly higher cost for someone in the low-cost patient group causes some members of society to lose more than is gained by others. That is, if the patient were required to compensate other members of society for the increased expense of better care, he would be worse off. than if he had had lower-cost care to begin with. Otherwise, someone else would be worse off. A change in rules that would cause high-quality medical care to be given to patients who do not place a high cost on damage would not be an efficient way to redistribute social well-being.

To highlight the effect of the ability to discriminate by price, let us suppose that physicians cannot distinguish between the two groups. If physicians are liable for damages, the incentive for patients to distinguish between high-quality and low-quality care is removed.[4] Patients would be largely indifferent between high-quality and low-quality care and so would seek out physicians on the basis of price. In such a market, the prices for both types of care would come to be the same.

If the prices of high- and low-quality care are forced by competitive pressures to be the same, only one quality of medical care can survive. Which survives depends on the way insurance rates are set. The two possibilities considered here include one under which the same premiums are paid irrespective of the cost class of the patient treated, and one under which the insurance premiums paid by the physician are determined by the relative volume of care given to each type of patient.

---

[4] Under a less restrictive assumption, the incentive would only be diminished. The conclusions still hold.

The first of these arrangements automatically drives out high-quality care, at least in the absence of any side arrangements made between patient and physician. Since the cost of insurance is the same irrespective of the quality of care provided, only the lower-quality care can survive the competitive pressures. Those physicians providing higher-quality care can only lose money, and so will go out of business. (Whether this is an empirically interesting possibility depends on the nature of the insurance industry. In its present state, the industry seems capable of providing only very primitive rate structures, and so it would not be surprising if the quality of care fell for these reasons.)

If we permit a bit more actuarial sophistication in rate setting, we may conclude that a physician will pay a premium reflecting the expected costs in his own practice. The insurance premium paid by a physician providing high-quality care will, by actuarial principles, be

$$I_1 = a_1(q_1A_1) + a_2(q_1A_2) , \tag{5}$$

while the premium paid by a physician providing lower-quality care will be

$$I_2 = a_1(q_2A_1) + a_2(q_2A_2) , \tag{6}$$

where a_1 is the fraction of total patient load drawn from the high-cost patient group, and a_2 the fraction from the low-cost group.

Since physicians cannot discriminate by price, and since patients are indifferent between high- and low-quality care, only one of the two qualities of care will survive. The quality of care that survives is the one with the price advantage under this arrangement. High-quality care will be forced out, or will survive, depending on whether

$$P_1 = C_1 + I_1 \gtrless C_2 + I_2 = P_2 , \tag{7}$$

which in turn depends on whether

$$C_1 - C_2 \gtrless (q_2 - q_1)(a_1A_1 + a_2A_2). \tag{8}$$

On the left-hand side of this expression is the extra resource cost of providing better care. On the right-hand side is the insurance cost advantage that the higher-quality physician has over the lower-quality physician. Both face the same average cost in the event of harm, but the expected cost is lower for the better physician.

It is not possible to predict which quality will survive. If the additional resource cost of providing better care exceeded the insurance cost advantage, high-quality care could not compete with low-quality care. If, in contrast, the resource-cost difference were less than the insurance advantage, low-quality medicine would be driven out. Either way, patients will be able to purchase only one quality of medicine, except in the unlikely instance that the two cost differences are just offsetting.

The implications of this analysis for the way a physician allocates his time should not go unnoticed. It is rightly supposed that a physician can diminish the likelihood of malpractice costs by devoting more time to each patient visit, thereby diminishing the likelihood of failure or harm. Also, it is rightly supposed that the physician will devote additional time to a visit up to the point where the incremental gain (in the form of either higher fees or reduced malpractice costs) is just equal to the incremental cost of the physician's time. The foregoing analysis has not shown, however, that a physician liability regime will change the incremental gains and losses in such a way that more rather than less care is warranted. Rather, because a physician who had been treating only high-cost patients must now treat a mixture of high- and low-cost patients, the incremental rewards to caution may be reduced, and with them the warranted level of caution or care.

Some Evidence. One thing an economist should learn is that if output is an important characteristic of a process, it deserves more attention than input. If it is the quality of medical care in which one is interested, one should find objective measures of quality of care and look at those. Failing that, however, one may look at the inputs to medical care to see if anything unusual is going on. With the use of physician time in patient care, something is.

One would not be surprised if, in the face of an increased liability for damages, the amount of time spent by physicians in each patient visit increased. By increasing the average time of consultations, a physician could decrease the likelihood of harm by using his time instead of his assistants' time, or perhaps more of his time in addition to his assistants' time. Such a response would be consistent with a defensive stance.

For most specialties, however, such a defensive response does not show up in the data. As Table 2 indicates, the average time spent per patient visit fell rather than rose between 1969 and 1973. The only exceptions were in anesthesiology and radiology. In both of those cases, the time spent in direct patient care rose, while the number of patient visits fell. Both of these specialties have been more susceptible to malpractice litigation than most. On the other hand, the time spent per treatment or visit fell more than 10 percent for general surgery, a specialty which harbors a large number of vulnerable subspecialties.

To look at average time spent per visit, rather than at the composition and quality of output, may be misleading. Any number of factors—

Table 2
PHYSICIAN TIME PER PATIENT VISIT, 1969 AND 1973

Specialty	1969			1973		
	Hours per week in direct patient care (1)	Patient visits per week (2)	Hours per patient visit (3) = (1) ÷ (2)	Hours per week in direct patient care (4)	Patient visits per week (5)	Hours per patient visit (6) = (4) ÷ (5)
General practice	47.8	167.0	.29	47.6	189.9	.25
Internal medicine	47.7	127.2	.38	47.5	127.2	.37
Surgery	45.5	109.5	.42	47.8	129.5	.37
Ob/Gyn.	48.8	124.2	.39	48.8	132.4	.37
Pediatrics	46.9	146.5	.32	44.5	158.1	.28
Psychiatry	39.2	49.6	.79	40.3	52.2	.77
Radiology	32.8	197.7	.17	41.8	166.8	.25
Anesthesiology	47.0	49.8	.94	48.0	42.6	1.13
All	44.7	126.9	.35	46.1	137.7	.33

Source: Center for Health Services Research and Development, American Medical Association, *Profile of Medical Practice* (Chicago: American Medical Association, 1974).

technological change, change in the mix of patients and ailments dealt with, and faulty reporting—may have been responsible for the general decline in time per visit. Given the data available, for example, one cannot even tell if the decline was statistically significant. Nonetheless, the observed decline is surprising. Given the apparent decline in the use of physician time for any given treatment, however (and especially if the decline holds up in more recent data), one should not be surprised to find that objective measures of medical care quality also show declines.[5]

---

[5] The decline in time spent per patient visit may also be due to what can be called the Medicaid effect. Until very recently, and perhaps even now, the Medicaid and Medicare programs were "ripe for plucking." By compensating physicians on the basis of something as ill defined as a "visit," the programs may have established incentives to turn what might have been one visit into two or more. The recent New York experience with so-called Medicaid scandals is a case in point. Under these circumstances, of course, the inferences about declines in quality would not necessarily hold, but the misuse of patients' time might cause some concern.

Recent Trends in Medical Markets

To organize and compare available evidence on medical practice, we have divided the fifty states into two groups. The first part is comprised of those states in which the malpractice situation was considered to have reached crisis proportions in 1975.[6] These are Alaska, California, Florida, Maine, New York, Ohio, South Carolina, South Dakota, Tennessee, and Texas. California and New York are shown separately, for two reasons: developments in those states seem to have dominated the press coverage; and California and New York account for the bulk of practicing physicians in the so-called crisis states. The second group comprises the remaining forty "noncrisis" states.

To capture the flavor of events, 1966 was chosen as a base year, and 1974 as the end year. Medical malpractice was not an empirically important issue ten years ago, and so 1966 provides a base year comparatively free of disruptions. The latest available information on numbers and locations of physicians is for 1974. The data yield some interesting comparisons.

The Supply of Physicians. The number of physicians in active patient care has grown relative to the number of people served. To be sure, there has been a decline in general practice, but the growth in the various specialties has more than outweighed it. In all, the number of practicing physicians per capita grew from 1,247 per million in 1966 to 1,321 in 1974, or by nearly 6 percent. General practitioners per capita fell by 28 percent. The number of doctors in specialized practice grew by 28 percent. The number of miscellaneous specialists grew by 20 percent, and the number of surgical specialists by 11 percent.

If one compares the figures for the crisis states with those for the rest of the country, two findings stand out. First, the rate of growth of physicians per capita has been lower in the so-called crisis states than in the rest of the country, and (as part of this growth) the rate of decline in general practice was greater. Just the same, the crisis states had, and continue to have, more physicians of every kind, per capita. The actual figures vary from specialty to specialty, but the number of practicing physicians per capita was 29 percent greater than elsewhere in the crisis states in 1966 and 27 percent greater in 1974.

---

[6] See C. Brierly and J. McDonald, eds., *Malpractice in Focus: A National Problem the States Must Solve* (Chicago: American Medical Association, 1975). The criteria vary from state to state, but the absolute level of insurance rates and the availabiliy of insurance—or lack of it—dominate the Brierly-McDonald classification scheme.

The data suggest that physicians are not fleeing hostile litigative environments en masse. What seems to be at issue is the size of the growth rate in sensitive or vulnerable specialties, rather than the prospect of actual decreases in the relative numbers of practicing physicians. Also, it is worth noting that the growth rates with crisis states are not uniformly lower than in the rest of the country. There is considerable dispersion. This would suggest that while medical malpractice may be an important consideration in determining the location of physicians, there are a great many others that also have some influence. If one cannot disentangle these various effects empirically, one is hard put to attribute any one change in the medical services industry to the growth of malpractice litigation and insurance costs.

Consider the changes in surgical specialties, an especially vulnerable field. For the United States, the number of surgeons per capita grew by 11 percent between 1966 and 1974. In the crisis states, the figure was 9 percent, and just over 11 percent in the rest of the country. In California, however, the growth rate was 11.6 percent, greater than for the comparatively safe states. In New York, the growth rate was only 3 percent. In New York, however, there were 563 surgeons per million residents, while in California the figure was 489. These figures compare with an average of 400 for the nation, and 373 in the noncrisis states. In other words, New York in 1974 had half again as many practicing surgeons per capita as the noncrisis states. The comparisons for other specialties yield similar results (see Tables 3 and 4).

The increased intensity of litigation in the crisis states may not be responsible for the diminished growth rates. Rather, it may be that both are the result of a much higher concentration of physicians per capita in those states that appear to have developed malpractice problems. Unless there were very marked differences in the patient populations being served, physicians in the crisis states were likely to have been dispensing a greater flow of services per capita than was true in the noncrisis states. In order for this greater flow to be dispensed, it would be necessary to undertake a larger number of risky procedures on a larger number of risky patients. The larger damages and insurance rates observed in New York, California, and the other crisis states may be due to a greater incidence of harm in those states, rather than to any differences in those communities' taste for litigation.

The Location of New Physicians. It is not enough to confine one's attention to the distribution of physicians already in active patient care. It is the decisions of new physicians that will determine the long-run distribution of physicians. If there is a tendency to escape from high-risk

119

environments, the tendency is more likely to show up in the decisions of new physicians than in the decisions of established physicians.

If one looks at the number of newly licensed physicians, however, the states with malpractice crises seem to be attracting more new doctors than one would expect. It is not unreasonable to suppose that a physician who is given a new license is interested in actively practicing medicine. (The exception is the new physician who is merely hedging his position.) Comparing the number of newly licensed physicians per capita, one finds that the crisis states enjoyed an average inflow of 198 new physicians per million people in 1974. The average in the noncrisis states was only 151. In New York, the figure was 335, although 1974 was an unusually big year. In California, the figure was 185.

Table 3

PRACTICING PHYSICIANS BY SPECIALTY, 1966 AND 1974

(in physicians per million people)

	United States	Crisis States	Rest of U.S.	California	New York
Active patient care					
1966	1,247	1,399	1,157	1,553	1,958
1974	1,321	1,476	1,228	1,690	1,965
Percent change	5.9	5.5	6.1	8.8	0.4
General practice					
1966	338	353	329	413	396
1974	242	250	236	314	227
Percent change	−28.4	−29.2	−28.3	−24.0	−42.7
Medical specialties					
1966	271	319	243	340	507
1974	347	399	317	433	619
Percent change	28.0	25.1	30.5	27.4	22.1
Surgical specialties					
1966	361	405	335	438	545
1974	400	445	373	489	563
Percent change	10.8	9.9	11.3	11.6	3.3
Miscellaneous specialties					
1966	276	322	245	363	510
1974	332	382	298	454	556
Percent change	20.3	18.6	21.6	25.1	9.0

Source: Center for Health Services Research and Development, American Medical Association, *Distribution of Physicians in the United States* (Chicago: American Medical Association, 1966 and 1974). See also, Bureau of the Census, *Statistical Abstract of the United States 1976* (Washington, D.C., 1977), p. 11.

Table 4
PRACTICING PHYSICIANS IN SELECTED
VULNERABLE SPECIALTIES, 1966 AND 1974
(in physicians per million people)

	United States	Crisis States	Rest of U.S.	California	New York
Anesthesiology					
1966	42	53	35	67	68
1974	53	63	46	78	78
Percent change	26.2	18.9	31.4	16.4	14.7
Neurosurgery					
1966	10	11	9	13	12
1974	12	13	11	17	13
Percent change	27.4	19.8	29.9	27.6	6.9
Ob/Gyn.					
1966	81	92	75	98	131
1974	90	100	84	109	137
Percent change	10.9	8.7	12.0	11.5	4.6
Orthopedic surgery					
1966	36	42	32	56	46
1974	47	54	43	72	54
Percent change	30.4	27.7	33.0	27.7	17.9

Source: Center for Health Services Research and Development, American Medical Association, *Distribution of Physicians in the United States* (Chicago: American Medical Association, 1966 and 1974). See also, Bureau of the Census, *Statistical Abstract of the United States 1976* (Washington, D.C., 1977), p. 11.

The number of new licenses issued tends to overstate the true or net inflow because there is no accommodation for emigration or retirement. The number of newly licensed physicians sheds some light on why the rate of growth of physicians is smaller in the crisis states than elsewhere. In 1974, the number of actively practicing physicians per capita in the crisis states was 20 percent greater than in the other states. At the same time, the number of newly licensed physicians per capita was 31 percent greater in the crisis states than elsewhere. It is not new physicians' being repulsed by hostile communities, but rather the disappearance of existing physicians that must account for the smaller growth rate of practicing physicians per capita in the crisis states. Again, it is not possible to disentangle the effect of malpractice on the decisions of new physicians from the effects of education opportunities, demographic changes, and a great variety of

121

other things. One should conclude nothing from the information presented here except that new physicians do not appear to have been driven away from the crisis states. It would be interesting to know why.

Conclusions

It is far too early to know what effect the increase in malpractice litigation and malpractice insurance rates will have on the work habits and location decisions of physicians, or upon the quality and price of services they dispense. Any effects of medical malpractice on the practice of medicine that one observes now, to the extent that anything at all can be observed, are short-run effects only. A complete adjustment to a new liability regime may require as much as several decades, if a complete adjustment is permitted—that is, if the rules are not changed again.

It is not possible to predict what effect physician liability will have on the quality of medicine. The most likely outcome is that in some cases quality will rise, while in others quality will fall. Moreover, because of the difficulty consumers face in discovering quality differences among physicians, because of the relatively primitive methods used to set insurance rates in this market, and because of the presence of uninsurable costs, it is also not possible to predict whether the resulting change in the allocation of scarce medical resources will represent an improvement in economic efficiency. Some participants in this market are certain to gain, while others are certain to lose. There is no assurance, however, that those who gain would be willing to compensate those who lose.

In those states where the American Medical Association has identified a medical malpractice crisis, one observes a somewhat slower rate of growth in the numbers of physicians per capita than in those states where the situation is not yet thought to be critical. At the same time, however, one also observes much larger numbers of physicians per capita in the crisis states than elsewhere. It is not inconceivable that the higher malpractice insurance rates and the slower rates of per capita physician growth in the crisis states are due jointly to the presence of larger numbers of physicians doing relatively more damage. If so, it would not be necessary to rely on the ad hoc notion of differences among communities in the taste for litigation to explain differences in the incidence of malpractice litigation.

It is worth noting, in closing, that the existence of a malpractice crisis is not evident in the data. Only very recently have malpractice insurance costs become large enough to be interesting. Even now a physician is likely to be almost as concerned about a 5 percent increase in labor costs as about a 50 percent increase in the malpractice premium.[7] Also, the expansion of Medicare and Medicaid expenditures has increased the demand for physicians' services dramatically. Finally, the rate of output of medical schools appears still to be increasing, and the quality of medical school admissions has also been rising (if quality can be measured by aptitude scores), perhaps because of a sharp rise in the number of women applying for admission. Taken together, these things may dwarf the quantitative importance of medical malpractice.

It is altogether possible that the malpractice situation is seen to be a crisis not so much because of the money and time involved, but because there seems to have been a fundamental change in the demand for expertise. If this is true, it would account also for the extreme sympathy which other professionals may feel for physicians. After all, if physicians can be sued, so can lawyers and teachers and even, heaven help us, government bureaucrats.

---

[7] See Arthur Owens, "Holding Down Professional Costs: Latest Figures on Nine Specialities," *Medical Economics,* vol. 52 (December 8, 1975), p. 144-48. For self-employed solo physicians, malpractice insurance averaged 1.6 percent of gross receipts in 1974 while office salaries and bonuses accounted for 14.2 percent. For a physician with this expenditure pattern, and ignoring possible input substitution (for example, capital for labor), a 5 percent increase in the level of wages would cost the same amount of money as would a 45 percent increase in malpractice expenses. It appears that even recently, salaries have been a greater source of cost increases than have malpractice premiums.

CAUSES OF THE MEDICAL MALPRACTICE INSURANCE CRISIS: RISKS AND REGULATION

Patricia Munch

The purpose of this paper is to review the causes of the crisis in medical malpractice insurance that erupted in 1975 in order to assess the viability of the solutions that have been adopted and the alleged need for more drastic alternatives, such as government subsidy. We will be concerned not with the causes of the increase in malpractice claims per se, but with the alleged inability of the insurance industry to handle this increase in claims, as manifested by premium increases of over 300 percent in a single year in some states and the withdrawal of carriers from the market in others.

First we will examine the changes that have occurred in the nature of the malpractice risk and their impact on the supply and demand for insurance through traditional institutions. In particular, the frequency and severity of claims, the rate of return on reserves, and the depletion of net worth of the insurance industry due to the decline in the value of financial assets in 1974 will be considered. Institutional responses, such as the growth of physician-owned mutuals and the shift from an occurrence to a claims-made policy form will be evaluated in the light of the changed nature of the risk.[1] The objective is to determine to what extent these institutional changes are an efficient response to the changed environment. Those developments that cannot be rationalized in terms of economic efficiency must be attributed to regulatory constraints.[2]

The research documented here is based in part on work done for the California Citizens Commission on Tort Reform and was in part funded by the Rand Corporation under its program of public service. It does not necessarily reflect the opinions or policies of the sponsors.

[1] A claims-made policy covers all claims filed in the year the policy is purchased, arising from practice in that or any prior year in which the insured was covered by the same company. The availability, but not the price, of coverage for claims reported in later years is guaranteed. An occurrence policy covers all claims arising out of practice in the year the policy is purchased, regardless of when the claims are filed.

[2] The term "efficient" is used here in the strictly nonnormative sense of standard welfare economics. An efficient institution is one which would be chosen voluntarily in a free-market context, given the endowments of wealth (including potential liability) and information of the parties involved. Thus "efficient" does not necessarily imply "desirable."

It is argued that a large part of the premium increase that occurred in 1975–1976 appears to be explicable in terms of the lag of premiums behind increases in claims costs over the previous six years, at least in California, the only area that has been studied in detail. Some of the institutional changes, in particular the shift to the claims-made policy form, represent an efficient and viable response to the changed environment. However, the total collapse of the traditional market in some areas can only be explained by regulatory intervention, exacerbated by the resistance of medical societies to selective underwriting, deductibles, and experience rating.

Background

The past decade has witnessed a great increase in both the frequency and severity of medical malpractice claims. Accurate statistics on a national basis are unavailable. The evidence for Southern California indicates an average rate of increase in both the frequency and the severity of claims of roughly 10 percent per annum since the early sixties, with some acceleration towards the end of the decade and into the seventies.[3] Although the level of claims in California is higher than elsewhere, the rate of change there is probably not atypical.[4]

The cost of malpractice insurance has increased dramatically. Data on the premium rates actually charged are unavailable. In the absence of a superior alternative, Table 1 shows the movements of an index of the cost of a constant level of malpractice coverage calculated by Steves and McWhorter in 1975, using a technique developed by Kendall and Haldi. This index is a weighted average of rates recommended by the Insurance Services Office (ISO), which may exceed those actually charged.[5] It is at most a rough indicator of trends. It suggests that

---

[3] This will be discussed in more detail below.

[4] From 1963 to 1974 the level of malpractice premiums in California relative to the national average has remained roughly constant. See Buddy Steves and Archer McWhorter, Jr., "Notes on the Malpractice Insurance Market," *CPCU Annals*, vol. 28, no. 4, pp. 229-30.

[5] A "constant level of coverage" is defined as coverage of a constant percentage of the distribution of expected losses. The estimated policy limits required to provide this constant level rose from $100,000/$300,000 in 1955 to $738,000/$2,214,000 in 1976. Given this estimate of the level of coverage physicians are assumed to buy in each year, the ISO rates for this policy, by medical specialty and territory, are weighted by the percentage of physicians in each specialty/territory category. The index is thus a weighted national average, with weights corresponding to the actual distribution of physicians by specialty and locality. Movements in the index reflect changes in the policy limits demanded and changes in the distribution of the physician population, in addition to changes in the price of a policy of specified limits, which is what we are concerned with.

Table 1
PRICE INDEX FOR MALPRACTICE COVERAGE, SELECTED GROUPS AND U.S. AVERAGE, SELECTED YEARS
(1966 = 100)

Year	Group I	Group III	Group VII	Group IX	U.S. Average
1955	90.7	58.4	39.0	37.9	57.9
1960	81.5	84.0	55.6	55.1	67.8
1962	93.1	93.9	62.7	62.6	76.8
1964	87.0	87.2	87.4	87.1	87.1
1966	100.0	100.0	100.0	100.0	100.0
1967	100.1	125.2	111.9	110.9	114.0
1968	103.4	129.3	144.4	114.8	126.9
1969	189.6	230.7	259.5	210.7	230.2
1970	289.9	475.5	533.3	423.2	435.4
1971	327.7	538.0	602.2	478.2	491.5
1972	359.5	590.3	662.2	524.9	538.8
1973	372.5	754.8	844.9	669.6	655.7
1974	483.9	772.1	1388.0	894.1	809.8
1975	954.3	1221.5	2146.5	1379.4	1329.2
1976	3171.8	4039.1	7133.3	4482.7	4414.7

Note: Group I: physicians, no surgery; Group III: physicians who perform major surgery, for example, ophthalmologists and proctologists; Group VII: orthopedists and neurosurgeons; Group IX: general and cardiac surgeons. See text and footnote 5 for explanation of how the index is calculated.

Source: Buddy Steves and Archer McWhorter, Jr., "Notes on the Malpractice Insurance Market," *CPCU Annals*, vol. 28, no. 4, pp. 229-30.

premiums were relatively stable through the sixties until increases of over 80 percent occurred in 1969 and 1970. Thereafter annual increases were of the order of 10 to 25 percent, until the 64 percent increase in 1975 and the 300 percent proposed increase of 1976. In fact, actual increases in 1976 have been, on average, much less than the increase implied by the ISO rates.[6] In some areas, however, including Southern California, premium increases of over 300 percent have been realized.

Aside from huge but erratic premium increases, the major characteristic of the malpractice insurance crisis has been the contraction of availability. In 1974, the majority of physicians in all but a few

[6] Steves and McWhorter, "Malpractice Insurance," p. 231.

midwestern states obtained coverage through programs sponsored by state or local medical associations.[7] Since 1975 commercial carriers have withdrawn from medical-society-sponsored programs in Arizona, California (Bay Area Counties), Florida, Hawaii, Idaho, Massachusetts, Maryland, Pennsylvania, Nevada, and New York. As of January 1976, a significant number of physicians in approximately twenty-five states had difficulty obtaining coverage, according to an AMA survey.[8]

Several states have attempted to halt the contraction of the medical malpractice insurance market by establishing a Joint Underwriting Association (JUA) or assigned-risk pool. All companies writing personal liability insurance in the state are required to participate in the JUA as a condition of their continuing to write other, more profitable lines of insurance. Thus a JUA is a device for making insurance available to high-risk physicians by mandating a subsidy from the policyholders of other lines of insurance, such as automobile and homeowners. As of May 1976, JUAs were in operation in nine states, and a further sixteen had enacted standby arrangements, empowering the insurance commissioner to activate a JUA if insurance were not readily available in the private market.[9] This is intended as a temporary solution to the problem of availability, pending legislation to achieve a more permanent solution. A JUA is typically established for two years.

Two solutions that have emerged in the voluntary market are the formation of physician-owned mutuals in twelve states[10] and the switch by some carriers from the traditional occurrence policy form to a claims-made policy form. Since a claims-made policy does not guarantee in advance the price of coverage for claims reported in later years, it essentially shifts from the insurer to the insured the risk associated with estimating and providing for claims incurred but not reported in the policy year.

Insurance is a means of spreading risk. The demand for insurance by a typical risk-averse individual is expected to increase if there is an increase in the expected loss he faces.[11] Yet the withdrawal of carriers,

---

[7] Ibid., p. 225.

[8] *American Medical News,* January 1976.

[9] States with JUAs: Arizona, Florida, Maryland, Massachusetts, New York, Ohio, Pennsylvania, Texas, Wisconsin. States with standby JUAs: Alabama, California, Hawaii, Idaho, Illinois, Iowa, Kentucky, Maine, Michigan, Nevada, New Hampshire, New Mexico, Rhode Island, South Carolina, Tennessee, Virginia. National Association of Blue Shield Plans, *Medical Liability Update* (Chicago, May 1976).

[10] New York, Maryland, North Carolina, California, Michigan, Tennessee, Florida, Alabama, New York, Illinois, Massachusetts, Arizona.

[11] See, for example, Isaac Ehrlich and Gary S. Becker, "Market Insurance, Self-insurance, and Self-protection," *Journal of Political Economy,* vol. 80 (1972), pp. 623-48.

the formation of mutuals, and the switch to the claims-made policy form represent varying degrees of contraction of the market in risk spreading. This contraction of the market for risk is prima facie paradoxical, occurring as it does at a time when the risk faced by physicians, and presumably the demand for some means to reduce this risk, have increased.

This paper therefore addresses the question, To what extent can the contraction in the market for risk spreading be explained as an efficient (cost-effective) response to the changed nature of that risk, and to what extent can it only be explained by regulatory and other constraints? The underlying objective of the analysis is to bring some evidence to bear on the allegation that the recent crisis demonstrates that medical malpractice is becoming uninsurable through traditional channels and that some form of subsidy, either an indirect one through a JUA or a direct one from government revenues, is required in order to guarantee the availability of insurance—and ultimately of medical care, if physicians are unwilling to practice without insurance. Before turning to institutional adjustments, however, let me examine the factors that have contributed to an increase in the supply price of insurance through traditional institutions.

The Increase in Premiums

Frequency and Severity of Claims: The Case of Southern California.
This analysis of the 1975–1976 increase in premiums focuses on the experience of the insurance program sponsored by the Southern California Physicians Council (SOCAP).[12] This narrow focus, dictated by the availability of time and data, suggests some conclusions from which it may be possible to generalize about other states. The history of the turnover of carriers for the program will be briefly described first, as evidence of the competitive environment in which rates have been set in this market.

From 1944 to 1970 the professional liability program sponsored by SOCAP was brokered and administered by the Nettleship Company. After a succession of three different carriers, the program was taken on by Pacific Indemnity in 1963, which put together a pool of carriers to share the risk on a percentage basis. During the sixties, a total of twenty carriers participated in the pool with Pacific Indemnity for varying periods of time. Nettleship performed the individual underwriting, claims handling, and reserving functions. Following premium increases

---

[12] The SOCAP program covers seven counties in Southern California: Los Angeles, Orange, Santa Barbara, Ventura, Kern, San Bernardino, and San Luis Obispo.

of over 100 percent in 1968 and 1969, with comparable increases in Northern California, the California Medical Association commissioned an independent actuarial report on the insurance situation in the state. The resulting Linder Report was critical of the Nettleship program.[13] In 1970 SOCAP retained the brokerage firm of Johnson and Higgins and switched from Pacific Indemnity to the Hartford as the carrier.

Nettleship responded by offering individual policies at lower rates for preferred-risk physicians, that is, those who had no open file and had had no claim settled against them during the preceding five years. The carriers for this preferred-risk program were Pacific Indemnity and the Imperial Insurance Company. In 1974, however, Pacific Indemnity withdrew, and in September 1975 Imperial was put into conservatorship by the insurance commissioner on the grounds of inadequate reserves.[14]

The Hartford wrote the SOCAP program until 1974, with less than a 10 percent rate increase over the period, although the frequency and the severity of claims were both increasing at rates in excess of 15 percent per annum (see below); the Hartford's experience was probably worse than the average because of the loss of low-risk physicians to Pacific Indemnity and Imperial. Premium data for the three companies are not available, but data on enrollment in the SOCAP program suggest that the Hartford was engaged in aggressive price competition to attract the low risks back into the group program. Enrollment in the group plan fell from 10,082 in 1969, the last year with Pacific Indemnity, to 1,444 in 1970, the first year with the Hartford, while 5,365 stayed with Pacific Indemnity. By 1974, the group program had recovered the largest share of the market, with 8,024 physicians enrolled. Pacific Indemnity withdrew, but Imperial was still writing for preferred risks.

When the Hartford requested a 75 percent rate increase for 1974, SOCAP solicited bids from several other carriers, making available to them the data on the past experience of the program on which to base their bids. The contract was awarded to the Travelers, which took on the program with an initial 55 percent rate increase over the level previously charged by the Hartford. Under a five-year contract, it guaranteed the initial rate for one year and an increase of no more than 15 percent for the second year. No restrictions were set on subsequent rate increases, except that they should not occur more than once a year. At the termination of the second year in December 1975, a 486 percent rate increase was proposed, which was reduced to 327 percent through

---

[13] Joseph Linder, *A Study of Professional Liability Coverage in Southern California* (New York: A. S. Hansen, Inc., February 1970).

[14] Imperial's reserves were judged inadequate on the assumption that its loss experience would be similar to that of the SOCAP program as a whole, although it was writing for preferred-risk physicians only.

the intervention of the insurance commissioner. SOCAP attempted to find other carriers but none volunteered.

In summary, during the six years between the time the Hartford took on the SOCAP program in January 1970 to January 1976 when the Travelers proposed the 486 percent rate increase, premiums had not kept pace with the rate of increase in claims cost. It is impossible at this point to determine whether the rates established in 1976 are actuarially correct (after allowing for expenses and a competitive rate of profit). However, given the rates charged in 1970 when the Hartford took over the program and given the increase in claims costs in the subsequent six years and the actual increase in premiums from 1970 to 1975, one can calculate the premium increase necessary in 1976 to restore the loss ratio that prevailed in 1970, assuming all other factors constant.[15]

Any calculation of the increase in claims cost per physician over the period 1970–1976 is at best a crude estimate. With the occurrence form of policy, the ultimate cost of claims arising from a particular policy year may not be known for up to ten years, because of the lag in reporting and adjudicating claims. In reporting claims costs for recent policy years, insurance companies usually report "incurred cost," which is their estimate of what the policy year will ultimately cost. Obviously, it can be charged that these estimates can be adjusted to justify any level of premium increase. The estimates reported here are therefore based on rates of change in the frequency of claims filed and the severity of claims settled, the only objective data available. The rates of change are calculated over the calendar period we are concerned with. They therefore apply to claims against earlier policy years. Using these estimates to predict the change in the ultimate costs of policy year 1976, relative to 1970, requires the assumptions that frequency and severity will continue to increase at the same average rate over the next decade and that the distribution of payments on claims over the policy year does not change.

Table 2 shows the incidence of reported claims per 100 physicians for Southern California, by policy year, as of December 1975. Through 1969, the data are for the group program written by Pacific Indemnity. After 1970, the Pacific Indemnity experience with the preferred-risk physicians written on an individual basis is shown in parentheses. The numbers without parentheses are for the physicians who stayed with the SOCAP program. Table 3 shows the average cost per settled claim for the SOCAP program physicians. Again the data for policy years 1970–

---

[15] The loss ratio is the ratio of claims cost to premiums. The assumption made here, that other factors affecting the desired loss ratio remained constant over the period 1970–1976, is dropped later.

Table 2
REPORTED MALPRACTICE CLAIMS PER 100 PHYSICIANS FOR POLICY YEARS 1963–1974, SOUTHERN CALIFORNIA

Policy Year	Number of Doctors	Claims Accumulated to End of										
		24 Mos.	36 Mos.	48 Mos.	60 Mos.	72 Mos.	84 Mos.	96 Mos.	108 Mos.	120 Mos.	132 Mos.	144 Mos.
1963	6,028	3.68	6.32	7.03	7.37	7.81	7.86	8.10	8.31	8.94	9.11	9.17
1964	6,764	3.53	6.12	6.90	7.35	7.50	7.70	7.88	8.01	8.13	8.18	
1965	7,224	3.64	6.41	7.71	8.39	8.79	8.90	9.08	9.18	9.19		
1966	8,136	3.82	7.88	9.11	9.76	10.19	10.56	10.82	10.96			
1967	9,491	4.32	8.14	9.46	10.22	10.82	11.40	11.64				
1968	10,388	4.25	8.14	9.83	10.91	11.64	12.01					
1969	10,082	4.80	8.87	11.50	13.01	14.11						
1970	(5,365) 1,444	(6.88)	(12.02)	(14.45)	(16.42)	29.02						
1971	(1,373) 6,942	(6.41)	(10.85)	(13.26)	24.83							
1972	(1,182) 7,883	(7.61)	(16.33)	26.91								
1973	8,357	16.55	24.92									
1974	8,024											

Note: The numbers without parentheses show claims under the SOCAP Program; those in parentheses are for Pacific Indemnity preferred-risk physicians.

Source: For SOCAP, 1963-1969, Joseph Linder, "A Study of Professional Liability Coverage in Southern California" (New York: A. S. Hansen, Inc., February 1970), and California Department of Insurance, unpublished memorandum, May 28, 1975. For SOCAP, 1970-1974, Johnson and Higgins, unpublished memorandum, 1976; for Pacific Indemnity, 1970-1974, California Department of Insurance, unpublished memorandum, May 28, 1975.

Table 3

AVERAGE COST PER SETTLED CLAIM, SOCAP PROGRAM

Policy Year	Claims Accumulated to End of					
	24 Mos.	36 Mos.	48 Mos.	60 Mos.	72 Mos.	84 Mos.
1963	$ 758	$1,299	$2,650	$3,203	$ 4,540	$4,532
1964	1,078	4,379	3,916	5,523	6,525	
1965	3,610	3,186	3,764	5,029		
1966	1,286	1,986	4,388			
1967	997	3,122				
1968	907					
1970					11,865	
1971				9,471		
1972			8,678			
1973		8,216				
1974	5,256					

Note: Average cost includes payment to the plaintiff and the allocated and unallocated claims expenses of the insurance company incurred in defense.

Source: For 1963-1968, Linder, "Professional Liability"; for 1970-1974, Johnson and Higgins.

1974 exclude the preferred-risk physicians written by Pacific Indemnity and Signal.

Reading down a column in Table 2, one observes the increase in the number of claims reported within a specified maturity period, for successive policy years. Estimates of the rate of increase of filings vary with the time span, the maturity period, and the type of trend (linear or exponential) calculated. For the policy years 1963–1969, frequency increased at an average annual rate of 5.8 percent, measured at three years' maturity. After 1970, the rate of increase accelerated, even for the supposedly preferred-risk physicians who stayed with Pacific Indemnity. For policy year 1972, frequency for this group was 84 percent higher than it had been for the total SOCAP program for 1969. (Note that this implies an increase in filings over the calendar period 1972–1974.) However, the experience of the physicians who remained with the SOCAP program was much worse. The comparable figure for 1972 is not available, but for 1973 the frequency for SOCAP physicians was

133

180 percent higher than that for 1969.[16] For the calendar period December 1969–December 1975, the average annual rate of increase in frequency for the SOCAP program was 20.5 percent.[17]

Reading down the columns of Table 3 one can see the change in the average value per settled claim within the specified maturity period. The upward trend is highly erratic; it is impossible to calculate a unique, correct trend in severity. Taking the three-year maturity, the average annual rate of increase between December 1969 and December 1975 was 17.5 percent.

These estimates—a 20.5 percent per annum trend in frequency and a 17.5 percent trend in severity—imply that by December 1975 claims costs would have been 705 percent higher than in 1969. During this six-year period, there had been one premium increase of 55 percent on average and one of 15 percent.[18] Therefore, by 1976 an increase of 352 percent was required to place premiums in the same ratio to claims costs that they had had at the inception of the Hartford program in January 1970.[19] The objection may be raised that the 1970 rates and, by this calculation, the 1976 rates, were excessive. The only evidence on this issue is circumstantial: the Hartford's 1970 rate was set with a view to bidding away the SOCAP business from Pacific Indemnity and in the face of competitive pressure from Pacific Indemnity and Imperial for preferred-risk physicians. It seems unlikely that this rate was much above the best estimate of the competitive cost of writing this business available at the time. If anything, this rate probably proved inadequate, being based on the experience of the sixties, before the acceleration of both frequency and severity that occurred in the seventies.

---

[16] It is tempting to draw conclusions from this data on the potential for greater use of experience-rating among individuals within premium classes. The infrequent use of experience-rating is often rationalized on the grounds that suits tend to be random, so it is impossible ex ante to distinguish between high- and low-risk individuals. Pacific Indemnity attempted to separate lower-risk individuals, using past claims history as a selection criterion. These data suggest that its insureds were subject to fewer claims than individuals who either did not submit themselves to or did not pass the selection tests. However, the conclusion cannot be drawn that past claims history is a valid predictor of future claims and provides information additional to medical specialty (which is the only information currently used by the SOCAP program to rate physicians) because this "experiment" does not control for medical specialty. In other words, one needs to compare the claims experience of physicians in the same medical specialty who did and did not pass the Pacific Indemnity screen in order to conclude that suits are not random among individuals within a specialty. The necessary data are not available.

[17] This is obtained by comparing the experience at three years' maturity of policy years 1967 and 1973.

[18] Actual premium increases differed for different rating classes, the percentage increase being less for low- than for high-risk classes.

[19] $(1.205 \times 1.175)^6 = 8.05$; $(8.05)(1.55)^{-1}(1.15)^{-1} = 4.52$.

The question arises whether the Southern California experience was unique or whether similar circumstances explain similar large increases in 1976 in other parts of the country. The only other area I have examined in detail is a group of county medical societies in Northern California. The pattern is very similar: the Travelers obtained the business by underbidding the established carrier, American Mutual, in May 1973. From the last year with American Mutual (May 1972– April 1973) through October 1975, rates increased by only 5 percent. In November 1975, a 341 percent rate increase was announced.

This crude analysis suggests that, if viewed over a longer perspective, a large part of the huge premium increase in 1976 can be accounted for by the increase in claims cost over the period 1970–1975 and by the lag in premiums over that period. It is not clear how far this volatility of premiums can be attributed to the inadequacy of the data available at the time premiums are set. The problem in California was not one of data collection, as is often alleged, since the group programs had maintained data for over a decade and made this available to carriers invited to bid for the business. However, as Tables 2 and 3 demonstrate, the volatility of claims makes estimating trends a risky business. Even small differences in the estimated rates of change in the cost of claims project to a wide range of estimates of an adequate premium level when compounded over the ten-year life of an occurrence policy. In addition to the increase in claims cost, however, other changes occurred which tended to increase the competitive cost of malpractice insurance. These are discussed next.

Rate of Return on Reserves. With an occurrence form of policy, the insurance carrier sets rates and collects premiums at the start of the policy year and pays claims arising out of that year of practice over the subsequent ten years. Table 4 shows the distribution of payments on claims for California in 1975. The exact distribution of payments varies by carrier and over time, but it is not atypical for 50 percent of loss payments to occur more than five years after the collection of the premium. The income from invested premium is therefore substantial. If insurance rates are set competitively, which appears to be the case, the expected value of this investment income will be passed on to policyholders in the form of lower premiums. Therefore, any change in the rate of return on premium reserves[20] implies a change in the price of insurance.

---

[20] The term premium reserves is used to refer to all assets purchased with premium dollars. This includes the accounting items Unearned Premium Reserves, Loss Reserves, and Reserves on Losses Incurred but not Reported.

Table 4

DELAY IN REPORTING AND PAYMENT OF
MALPRACTICE CLAIMS

Years from Incident	Percent of Total Claims Reported	Percent of Total Dollars Paid
0	15	Less than 5
1	35	5
2	20	10
3	10	10
4		10
5		10
6	20	10
7		10
8 +		30

Source: Office of the Auditor General, California Legislature, *Doctors' Malpractice Insurance* (Sacramento, December 1975).

Using the distribution of payments on claims shown in Table 4, it is possible to calculate the effect on premium levels of a change in the expected rate of return on reserves. For example, if losses are $100, a premium of $72.50 is adequate when the expected rate of return is 10 percent; with a 5 percent rate of return on reserves, a premium of $81 is necessary.[21] Therefore, if premiums have been set on the basis of an expected rate of return of 10 percent and this falls to 5 percent, a 12 percent increase in premium is implied; if the expected rate of return falls from 10 percent to zero, a 38 percent increase in premium is implied. Given the decline of the stock market in 1974, its very hesitant recovery through 1975, and an average annual rate of inflation of 12 percent in 1974 and 7 percent in 1975 which severely reduced the real rate of return on fixed-interest assets, a conservative actuary might conceivably use a zero expected real rate of return in setting premiums for 1976. Thus, an increase of premiums in the range of 10 percent to 40 percent might be explained by a decrease in the expected rate of return on reserves.[22]

[21] This example omits administrative expenses and hence may overstate the leverage potential of the rate of return if administrative expenses are concentrated in the early years.

[22] This assumes no change in the distribution over time of disbursements or claims. If the rate of return on reserves exceeds the rate of interest built into awards to compensate the victim for delay in receiving compensation, then claims adjusters will accelerate the rate of disposition of claims in the event of a decline in the rate of return on reserves. A decrease in the length of time funds are on reserve will decrease investment income and hence further increase premiums.

PATRICIA MUNCH

Risk and the Supply Price of Capital. The insurance industry is in the business of assuming risk of economic loss from individuals. However, economic analysis of the supply of insurance usually assumes that the risk faced by the owners of capital in the insurance firm is zero, because pooling and diversification eliminate uncertainty as to the losses for policyholders in the aggregate, despite uncertainty as to the loss for any individual policyholder.[23] It will be argued here that in medical malpractice the nature of the risk insured against has changed in ways that undermine the basic principles on which risk-free insurance is usually based. In addition, recent events in the capital markets make it unrealistic to focus exclusively on the underwriting side and to ignore the investment side of the insurance business. Increased uncertainty with respect to both the underwriting and investment functions of insurance firms have increased uncertainty with respect to the rate of return on capital invested in the insurance industry. In other words, the variance around the expected rate of return on equity has increased. To the extent this risk is not diversifiable by shareholders, the supply price of capital to the insurance firm and hence the price of insurance will increase.

The various factors which have tended to increase the underwriting and financial risk will be discussed in turn. A more rigorous statement may be found in the Appendix.

Dispersion of the distribution of awards. There appears to have been an increase in the dispersion and positive skewness of the distribution of awards.[24] Table 5 compares some simple statistics derived from the survey of claims closed in 1974 conducted by the American Insurance Association (AIA) and the survey of claims closed between July 1975 and July 1976 conducted by the National Association of Insurance Commissioners (NAIC).[25]

[23] This follows from two basic statistical principles underlying insurance: (1) the variance of the estimate of the mean of a sample of n independent drawings from a population of homogeneous stochastic events, distributed with mean μ and variance σ^2, is equal to the variance of the underlying distribution, divided by the number in the sample, σ^2/n; and (2) the variance of the outcome on a portfolio of n independently distributed random variables is given by:

$$\sigma_M^2 = \sum_{i=1}^{n} \sigma_i^2 + 2\sum_{i \neq j} \rho_{ij}\sigma_i\sigma_j.$$

Thus, in principle the portfolio may be composed of items with sufficiently negatively correlated outcomes that the variance on the portfolio overall, σ^2_M, is reduced to zero.

[24] "Awards" here include both trial verdicts and out-of-court settlements.

[25] Conclusions based on a comparison of two surveys are tentative because some carriers did not report to the AIA; so some states, including New York and Florida, are seriously underrepresented in the 1974 data base. The NAIC survey comprises all claims closed by major carriers, nationwide.

137

Table 5

DISPERSION OF MALPRACTICE AWARDS, 1974 AND 1975–1976

	1974 (AIA)	1975– 1976 (NAIC)
Percentage of claims closed without payment to plaintiff	54	65
Mean award per claim, including cases with no payment	$ 6,610	$ 5,830
Mean award per claim for claims with positive payment	$14,330	$16,490
Percentage of total claim dollars accounted for by top 12 percent of cases	84	90

Source: *Special Malpractice Review: 1974 Closed Claim Survey—Preliminary Analysis* (New York: American Insurance Association, December 1975); *NAIC Malpractice Claims*, vol. 1, no. 3 (Milwaukee: National Association of Insurance Commissioners, September 1976).

The outstanding feature of Table 5 is the extreme positive skewness of the distribution of awards and the increase in this skewness between these two surveys.[26] The percentage of total claim dollars accounted for by the top 12 percent of cases increased from 84 percent in 1974 to 90 percent in 1975–1976. This increase is due largely to the increase in the percentage of claims closed with no payment to the plaintiff, from 54 percent in 1974 to 65 percent in 1975–1976. As a result, the mean award for all claims fell, although the mean award on cases where some payment was made increased.

If the conclusion implied by Table 5 is correct—that the variance and positive skewness of the distribution of awards have increased—the best estimate of the actuarially fair price of insurance is less certain than was previously the case, and has a higher probability of being inadequate.[27] This implies greater risk of underwriting loss for a given level of premium relative to expected claims cost.

Changes in the sociolegal environment: positive correlation among insureds. A second factor that has increased the underwriting risk associated with medical malpractice insurance is the volatility of the sociolegal environment. The growth in malpractice claims costs presumably reflects to a large extent not an increase in the frequency of

---

[26] A distribution is said to be positively skewed if less than 50 percent of the cases account for over 50 percent of the dollars paid out.

[27] This assumes no decrease in uncertainty with respect to frequency.

severity of injuries, but an increase in the frequency of suit by injured
patients and an increase in the sums awarded for given injuries. Changes
in tort law which have reduced the cost of proving negligence and hence
have stimulated the frequency of claims include the introduction of the
doctrines of *res ipsa loquitur* and informed consent, the demise of the
locality rule, and the admission of medical texts as evidence. It may be
argued that uncertainty with respect to the sociolegal environment, which
determines the probability that a claim will be filed for a given injury
and the size of the claim, constitutes an increasingly large component
of the uncertainty with respect to the actuarially fair premium for an
individual physician.[28] This component of uncertainty is common to
all physicians. To the extent that outcomes for individuals in the
insurance pool are positively correlated, the basic principles of insurance—elimination of risk by pooling and diversification—are under-
mined. The relative importance of this common component of variance
is greater with an occurrence than a claims-made policy because the
ultimate cost of an occurrence policy is affected by changes in the
sociolegal environment ten years after the policy is written. The effect
is more severe with a long statute of limitations or a discovery rule.[29]

Depletion of surplus. The third factor increasing the risk to capital
in the medical malpractice insurance industry is the reduction in the net
worth or "surplus" of insurance firms that resulted from the 1974 decline
in the value of the stock market. The point here is not that premiums
were increased in order to replenish depleted surplus. That argument
ignores the market forces within which an insurance firm operates. The
effect of depletion of surplus on the price and availability of insurance
operates through its effect on the risk facing the owners of that surplus.

The purpose of surplus is to provide a cushion of reserves out of

---

[28] Assume that, for physician i, the expected cost of claims arising out of policy
year t is:

$$E(\widetilde{C}_{it}) = E[\widetilde{A}_t(\widetilde{L}_t, \widetilde{L}_{t+1}, ..., \widetilde{L}_{t+10}) + \widetilde{X}_{it}]$$

where A_t is an environmental variable common to all physicians,
  L_t is vector of variables determining the sociolegal environment,
  X_{it} is a vector of individual characteristics of the ith physician, and
  a tilde denotes a random variable.
Then the variance around the expected claims cost is:

$$\sigma^2_{C_{it}} = \sigma^2_{A_t} + \beta^2 \sigma^2_{X_{it}} + 2\text{COV.}_{A_t, X_{it}}$$

The hypothesis is that $\sigma^2_{A_t}$, the component of variance common to all insureds,
has grown relative to $\sigma^2_{X_{it}}$.

[29] With a discovery rule, the statute of limitations does not begin to run until
the injury is, or should have been, discovered. It has the effect of lengthening
the period during which claims may be filed and hence increases the potential for
changes in the sociolegal environment to affect outcomes.

139

which to pay underwriting losses, should premiums prove inadequate. The ratio of premium to surplus is a commonly used indicator of the financial strength of an insurance firm. It is probably a useless test of solvency if applied rigidly, across different companies and different lines of insurance.[30] But when applied to a single group of companies over a period short enough that changes in the composition of policyholders and assets can be ignored, the premium/surplus ratio gives an indication of the risk faced by the owners of the surplus in the event of underwriting losses. If the ratio of premiums to surplus is two to one, as it was in the 1960s, a 10 percent error in setting premiums results in a 20 percent reduction in surplus. At a premium/surplus ratio of four to one, which was the case by December 1974 for the seven companies writing malpractice in California, a 10 percent error in premium results in a 40 percent reduction in surplus.

Variance of the rate of return on reserves. The importance of investment income with an occurrence form of policy has already been discussed. The effect of a change in the mean or expected rate of return on the cost of an occurrence policy was illustrated. Here we are concerned with the effect of uncertainty, as measured by the variance around the expected rate of return on reserves. The experience of financial markets in the 1970s and a volatile rate of inflation of the general price level no doubt increased the variance around the expectation of the real rate of return on reserves. This has a multiplied effect on the variance of the rate of return on equity in the insurance firm, where the multiplier is a postive function of the premium/surplus ratio.[31]

It has been argued that the risk to equity capital in the insurance industry has increased because of the conjunction of events affecting the underwriting and financial aspects of the business. Assuming the investing public is risk averse, this implies an increase in the supply price of capital to the insurance industry.[32] Crude evidence to support

[30] A given premium volume may entail a very different risk of underwriting loss depending on the line of insurance, the markup over expected claims cost built into premium rates, and so on. Similarly, a given book value of surplus may imply different degrees of ability to meet unexpected underwriting losses depending on the liquidity of the assets being held.

[31] This is described in the Appendix.

[32] Theory and evidence from the finance literature show that the extent to which industry-specific risk affects the price of capital to that industry depends on the correlation between the outcome for the industry and for other assets in the market. Two factors suggest that the insurance industry risk is not fully diversifiable: (1) because the insurance firm is like a leveraged investment trust the variance of the rate of return on insurance stock is a multiple of the variance of the market return; (2) on the basis of recent experience, underwriting and financial losses are positively correlated, through their common dependence on the rate of inflation.

this thesis is that in August 1975, A. M. Best Company downgraded 24 percent of the 1,000 liability insurance companies it lists.[33]

The effect on the price and quantity of insurance of an increase in the supply price of capital to the industry is illustrated in Figure 1. The vertical axis measures the price charged for a given level of coverage (say $100,000/$300,000) and the horizontal axis measures the number of policyholders.[34] Assume S_1 is the supply of insurance at the original (1973) price of capital, D_1 is the demand, P_1 the initial premium, and Q_1 the number of policies written. (D_2 should be ignored for the present.) An increase in the risk of loss to equity owners that raises the supply price of capital to the firm implies an upward shift in the supply of insurance to S_2. The increase in premiums is greater and contraction of policyholders is less, the less elastic the demand for insurance. If premiums can be maintained above actuarial cost for some time, surplus can be replenished from underwriting profit. To the extent this reduces risk to equity owners, the supply curve gradually shifts back towards the original positive. Note that if policyholders are not homogeneous, a flat increase in premiums will tend to result in adverse selection, with lower-risk individuals being the first to drop their coverage. This raises the average loss cost to the company. Thus, a premium increase designed to replenish surplus may be counterproductive unless applied flexibly, by offering deductibles, or accompanied by selective underwriting.

Effect of the Changed Structure of Risk on the Market for Insurance

It has been argued that the risk associated with writing medical malpractice insurance has increased. One cannot infer from greater risk, however, the withdrawal of all carriers from the market. The argument that insurance companies are unwilling to write malpractice insurance because of the risk involved implies that there is no price which physicians are prepared to pay at which others can be induced to bear any part of the risk. This is highly implausible. Many of the factors that have increased the riskiness of writing malpractice insurance impinge on the physician if he is not insured. They are intrinsic to the practice of medicine in the current environment and therefore affect the demand for, as well as the supply of, insurance. The division of the risk between the physician and the insurance company depends, in a free market, on which party is the lowest-cost risk bearer. Because of the advantages

---

[33] A. M. Best performs a rating function for the insurance industry similar to Moody's or Standard and Poor's.

[34] The analysis is similar if the unit of measurement is dollars of coverage, rather than number of policies with a fixed dollar level of coverage.

141

Figure 1

DEMAND AND SUPPLY OF COVERAGE UP TO FIXED LIMITS OF LIABILITY

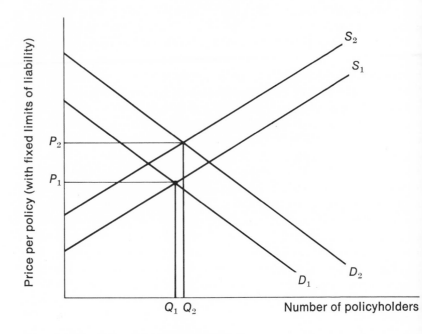

Note: The example used is $100,000/$300,000.

of pooling and diversification, this is likely to be the insurance company. The effect of changes in the malpractice environment on the demand for insurance will therefore be briefly discussed before we evaluate the changes that have occurred in the insurance market, in the light of shifts in both supply and demand.

If physicians are risk-averse—as most appear to be—they will devote some resources to reducing the risk of loss implied by liability for malpractice. The alternatives available to reduce this risk include self-insurance and various methods of loss prevention, in addition to the purchase of market insurance. Economic theory predicts that the total amount of resources a typical person will devote to loss reduction or insurance is positively related to the expected size of the potential loss. Thus an increase in the size of malpractice awards is predicted to increase the amount of resources physicians will devote to insurance or loss prevention in some form. While total expenditure will increase, expenditure on each of the various alternatives individually need not increase, because to some extent they are substitutes. Thus, it is conceivable that, given the costs and benefits of the various alternatives, loss prevention by such means as practicing with more care, avoiding high-risk patients or procedures, or practicing "defensive medicine" may be a relatively more efficient means of risk reduction, such that the demand for market insurance actually falls. But if the alternatives are ineffective relative to their cost to the physician, the demand for market insurance may rise. The effect of an increase in demand is shown in Figure 1 as a shift in the demand schedule to D_2. This results in a higher price per policy and partially or totally offsets the reduction in the number of policies written caused by the shift of the supply schedule.

Thus, it is unlikely that, because of the availability of alternatives, the demand for insurance has fallen to a level where a market cannot exist at a price mutually acceptable to physicians and carriers. The basic principle that makes insurance a viable institution—that certain types of risk can be borne more cheaply by pooling or diversification—stands, if less firmly than in the past. Moreover, to the extent that physicians adopt loss-reduction measures, the risk of loss to carriers is reduced simultaneously with the risk of loss to physicians. This implies a downward shift of both the supply and the demand for insurance, so a contraction of the market is not necessarily implied. Loss prevention and insurance may thus be complements, rather than substitutes.[35]

Let us, therefore, review the changes that have taken place in the structure of the malpractice risk and evaluate the changes that have taken place in institutional arrangements to bear this risk, in the light of effects on both demand and supply.

The most significant change is obviously the increase in the frequency and severity of claims and consequent increase in the size of the expected loss faced by the physician. Any form or method of loss prevention which involves fixed costs, regardless of the size of the loss prevented, becomes relatively more cost effective at higher levels of expected loss. Examples of such loss-prevention measures which involve fixed costs are selective underwriting and experience-rating, which entail administrative costs. An increase in this practice is therefore to be expected and may explain why mutuals have developed for the first time in this line of insurance. If small, physician-owned mutuals have an advantage over large-stock insurers in performing the investigations and monitoring necessary to practice selective underwriting and experience-rating, then the withdrawal of the commercial carriers and their

---

[35] Ehrlich and Becker, "Market Insurance."

replacement by physician-owned mutuals in several states may be an efficient response to the changed structure of risk. However, in most cases, the mutuals have replaced programs sponsored by medical societies; usually the peer review committee of the medical society was actively involved in underwriting, premium setting, and claims management and therefore was presumably in possession of the information available to the physician managers of a mutual. Unless the incentives to use this information have increased, the growth of mutuals cannot readily be explained by a cost advantage in underwriting that compensates for their relative disadvantage as risk bearers, because of their small, undiversified portfolios. Whether they will prove viable in the absence of a subsidy remains an empirical question.

The second change in the nature of the malpractice risk discussed above is the increase in the variance and positive skewness of the distribution of awards. This creates an uncertainty that is borne by the physician if he does not shift it to the insurance carrier. The net effect on the amount of insurance purchased cannot be predicted without a more rigorous parameterization of the supply and demand for insurance. However, to the extent that the increased variance is attributable to a greater proportion of zero awards because plaintiffs are naming a larger number of defendants in connection with any suit, there are economies of scale in providing insurance to the several defendants. If each defendant is either self-insured or insured with a different company, then uncertainty as to how the award will be apportioned among the several defendants named is likely to result in a higher level, and hence a higher cost, of reserves, in the aggregate, than if all are covered by a single insurer. This effect, therefore, increases the optimum size of the insurance pool, other things equal.

The third source of increased risk is the increase in the relative importance of the component of variance common to all insureds, that is, the risk attributable to changes in the sociolegal environment. This is a factor that reduces the gains from pooling through market insurance but does not affect the alternatives available to the physician, such as self-insurance. Thus, this factor might be expected to result in a contraction of the insurance market. However, given the possibility of rearranging portfolios within the insurance industry, the conclusion does not necessarily follow. The increase in the covariance of outcomes on individuals in the malpractice pool implies a reduction in the optimum share of an insurer's total underwriting portfolio that should be assigned to medical malpractice.[36] In other words, for a portfolio of a given size,

---

[36] The optimum underwriting portfolio for the firm depends on the costs of diversifying the risk within the firm, relative to the costs of diversification by shareholders.

144

the optimum amount of diversification has increased. A company can reduce its malpractice exposure by two routes: either by reducing the number of policyholders or by increasing the percentage of its exposure which it passes on to other insurers through reinsurance. The choice between these two alternatives depends on their relative costs and advantages.

Even if some companies opt for the former solution, reducing the number of malpractice policies written, other companies with smaller shares of malpractice business should be willing to assume the cancelled policyholders, assuming diversification were the sole reason for the cancellations. Since the property casualty industry consists of over 1,000 firms, only roughly 50 of which are now engaged in writing medical malpractice, and in 1975 the medical malpractice premium volume accounted for only 2 percent of the industry total, there must be firms which could expand into this line without substantially increasing the overall riskiness of their portfolios. The prime candidates for entry would be large, diversified companies not previously specialized in other lines of liability insurance, since experience in these lines is positively correlated with experience in medical malpractice because of their common dependence on the evolution of legal doctrine. In fact, as noted previously, the companies that have entered areas where previous carriers have withdrawn are for the most part small and undiversified, which suggests that the increase in covariance is not a major source of the problems in this market.

To the extent that increased covariance among malpractice insureds and across all lines of tort liability has significantly affected the risk inherent in writing these lines, reinsuring a larger percentage of the exposure is probably a more efficient means of reducing exposure for a primary carrier than reducing the number of policyholders. This is because the risk that arises from adverse legal precedents may be reduced by investment of resources in defending cases and establishing precedents favorable to the defense. Because of the public-good aspects of precedents, the optimum expenditure on precedent setting, from the viewpoint of the defense, is more likely to be undertaken if a single insurer insures all individuals that are affected by the precedent. There are certainly other factors at work that prevent tort liability insurance from being a natural monopoly. The point here is simply that the increased importance of legal doctrine tends not only to reduce optimal portfolio share, because of its effect on covariance, but also to lower the cost of defending cases through economies of scale. The net effect is that reduction in exposure is probably more efficiently obtained by reinsuring than by reducing the number of policyholders.

Finally, the increase in risk attributable to uncertainty about the rate of return on reserves set aside to pay future claims is a risk common to insured and insurance carrier so could not explain a reduction in the shifting of risk between them if the only issue were which party should maintain the reserves. However, there has been an increase in the relative price of insurance that depends on financial reserves, and this may explain the shift of risk to the physician inherent in the switch from a claims-made to an occurrence form of policy.

A claims-made policy covers all claims filed in the policy year, arising out of practice in that or any preceding year during which the insured was covered by the same company.[37] An occurrence policy covers all claims arising out of practice in the policy year, regardless of how long thereafter they are filed. Thus, with an occurrence policy, the insurer assumes the risk of estimating the cost of claims that will be filed in subsequent years and of maintaining the necessary financial reserves. A claims-made policy shifts to the insured the risk of covering claims in subsequent years. Typically, the insurer guarantees the availability but not the price of a policy to cover future liability.

If the switch to claims-made merely resulted in the insured physician rather than the insurance company assuming the financial risk of setting up and maintaining reserves to pay for future installments of coverage, it would be hard to rationalize as an efficient change, since an insurance company presumably has lower costs of information for estimating the optimal level of reserves than the individual physician and is the more efficient investor of funds for reasons of portfolio size. However, claims-made creates the option of simply not setting aside financial reserves to pay for future liability arising out of current practice, but paying out of future income. Liability for claims arising out of current practice but filed in the future will be covered by a claims-made policy bought in the future. This policy can be purchased out of future income. The physician who adopts this strategy retains more uncertainty as to his future income, net of insurance premium, than the physician who sets up a reserve, either himself or through an insurance company, by buying an occurrence policy. But the extent of this uncertainty with respect to his future net income depends on the elasticity of demand for his services. The more inelastic the demand, the greater his ability to pass on to consumers fluctuations in his insurance premium and the less the variability in his net income. The cost to him of this level of uncertainty may be less than the cost of paying an insurance company

---

[37] This restriction on retroactive coverage to incidents occurring in years covered by the same company does not exist in the claims-made forms used in other lines of professional liability and will probably disappear for medical malpractice if claims-made is more widely adopted.

to bear the risk of estimating the cost of future claims and maintaining adequate reserves. Thus, in the current environment it may be more efficient to write insurance on a claims-made than an occurrence basis, at least for some physicians.[38]

A second efficiency rationalization for the growth of claims-made relates to its effect on loss prevention. As the cost of providing insurance through the establishment of reserves rises, the alternative of loss prevention becomes relatively more cost effective. If an individual is insured, the incentive to prevent losses depends on whether his insurance premium is adjusted to reflect his claims record. With an occurrence policy, the premium is set once and for all, prior to the insured year of practice. With a claims-made policy, only the price of the first installment is set prior to the year of practice. The price of subsequent installments may be experience-rated on the basis of two sources of information: first, claims experience in the first year; second, the information the physician reveals, through his choice of coverage limits for subsequent installments, about his own anticipation of a claim's arising out of the year of practice completed. If he is aware of having made a mistake, he is more likely to select higher limits of coverage. The insurer can set the price of higher limits of coverage to account for this adverse selection and therefore achieve some degree of experience-rating. The claims-made system of charging for coverage in installments effectively reduces the cost to the insurer of obtaining information about the individual's probability of suit, thereby increasing the potential for experience-rating and increasing the individual practitioner's incentive to prevent losses.

Thus, the switch from the occurrence to the claims-made form of policy is a means of shifting risk from the insurer to the insured that appears consistent with an efficient response to the changed structure of risk because it reduces dependence on financial reserves and encourages loss prevention. This conclusion is confirmed by the fact that claims-made has become the dominant form of policy in other lines of professional liability insurance which have experienced an increase in level and volatility of claims similar to that experienced by the medical profession. Claims-made is now the only type of coverage available to architects, engineers, accountants, and corporate directors and officers and accounts for roughly half the market in malpractice insurance for attorneys. Indeed, it is puzzling that the occurrence form has survived for so long for the medical profession. The prevalence of the occurrence form has probably contributed to the greater volatility of

---

[38] This conclusion ignores the interests of future consumers of health care to whom some of the risk is shifted.

premiums and the greater difficulty of procuring coverage for physicians than for other professionals.

In conclusion, it has been argued that the recent changes in the nature of the medical malpractice risk have affected both the demand and the supply of insurance through traditional channels. Some of the changes in the institutions for bearing this risk are consistent with an efficient response to the changed nature of the risk. In particular, shifts in risk from the insurer to the insured that encourage loss prevention and decrease dependence on financial reserves have become relatively more cost effective. Changes in this category include more frequent use of deductibles and experience-rating, perhaps the growth of mutuals (to the extent that they exploit a comparative advantage in encouraging loss prevention), and the replacement of the occurrence form of policy with the claims-made form. However, the wholesale withdrawal of commercial carriers from some areas, their refusal to write any level of malpractice insurance for any individual, cannot readily be explained in terms of an unconstrained market response because the changed nature of risk has increased the demand price simultaneously with the supply price. It is implausible that, in the absence of constraints, a voluntary market in this risk would not exist, although at a higher price. To explain this situation, we must turn to regulation and other institutional constraints.

Regulation

The direct intervention of insurance commissioners in the medical malpractice insurance market is a recent phenomenon, although the regulation of the insurance industry is not. Under the McCarran-Ferguson Act of 1945, the insurance industry is immune from prosecution under federal antitrust law, provided it is regulated at the state level. Following the passage of this act, some form of regulation was instituted in all states. The details of the regulatory statutes differ but they have two common goals: to ensure that rates are neither "excessive, inadequate, nor unfairly discriminatory" and to maintain the solvency and stability of the insurance enterprise. These goals are pursued by regulation of rates and of the ratio of net worth, or surplus, to the volume of premium.

Until the 1970s, medical malpractice insurance was too insignificant for regulators to become actively involved in determining rates. Following the huge premium increases requested by carriers in 1975, however, insurance commissioners intervened to hold down rates, often at the request of local medical societies. This occurred in New York, Maryland, and California, for example. If, in an attempt to prevent excessive rates, regulators impose rates that are inadequate to compensate the owners of equity for the risk perceived, the supply of capital to this line of insurance will contract and, as in any case of price control, a discrepancy will arise between the quantity demanded and the quantity supplied at the controlled price.

In most lines of insurance, regulation of rates to levels that are inadequate to cover all individuals in a rating class tends to result in selective underwriting by insurers. Only the lower-risk individuals, for whom the rates are adequate, are able to obtain insurance in the voluntary market. This phenomenon is common in automobile insurance. Total withdrawal from the line is less common. Another device for circumventing rate regulation is to increase deductibles. In medical malpractice, however, the use of both selective underwriting and deductibles as devices for circumventing rate regulation is limited by the medical societies that sponsor the group plans through which most malpractice insurance is provided. Medical societies have generally opposed selective underwriting, individual experience-rating, and the use of deductibles. In addition to discouraging loss prevention and hence increasing risk to the carrier, this deprives the insurer of his flexibility to adjust either the availability or the price of insurance so that some market is maintained.

I have not yet undertaken a survey of all the states where medical society programs have been cancelled to see in how many instances the withdrawal followed the denial of a requested rate increase. This was the case in New York. In Nevada, Pennsylvania, and the Bay Area of California, Argonaut refused to continue to write the society program, but agreed to continue to write on an individual, hence presumably selective, basis. Thus, the institutional constraints of rate regulation and medical society sponsorship have aggravated the availability problem, although how much remains to be determined. If it is true that an increase in risk cannot explain the total collapse of the market, then the role of these institutional constraints is probably large.

A second form of regulation that has contributed to the availability problem is the regulation of the ratio of premium volume to surplus. The precise ratio preferred by regulators varies from state to state and is usually applied with some flexibility. For example, a ratio of three dollars of premium to one dollar of surplus is considered acceptable in California, but this was allowed to rise to 4.4:1 in December 1974 for the composite of companies studied in the Auditor General's Report. It is difficult to assess the impact of the regulation of this ratio on the availability of insurance without a measure of the ratio that would be adopted in the absence of constraints by a firm selecting the optimum trade-off between mean and variance of return for its shareholders. The unconstrained ratio would certainly vary according to the line of insurance, type of asset, and so on. If the regulated ratio is a binding constraint, the company is in a paradoxical situation. If it raises premiums in order to increase expected underwriting profit and raise the rate of return on capital, thereby replenishing surplus, the initial premium increase raises the ratio of premium volume to surplus[39] and makes the company appear more, not less, risky in the eyes of the regulator.[40] Premium/surplus regulation, then, operates like rate regulation.

Another effect of premium/surplus regulation has been to establish a barrier to the entry of new firms by holding new entrants to a more rigid rule than established firms. For example, in California, while the ratio for established firms writing occurrence policies has been allowed to rise above four to one, new companies have been held to a ratio of three to one for occurrence policies and one to one for claims-made.[41] By raising the capital costs of entry for new firms, this reduces the competitive pressure faced by established firms and may result in higher prices for consumers, depending on the strength of other competitive forces in the industry.

Premium/surplus regulation may advance its stated purpose, reducing the risk of insurer insolvency. Insolvency imposes costs on policyholders and, in the case of liability insurance, on claimants against the policyholders, who might be unable to collect a judgment in the event of default by the defendant's insurer. A case might be made that some form of insolvency regulation is potentially efficient, based on economies of scale in information or externalities imposed on the claimants of liability actions. This issue cannot be analyzed here, and in the absence of such an analysis, no conclusion can be drawn on the overall efficiency of this form of regulation. The point being made here is that it will tend to add to the cost and decrease the availability of malpractice insurance. The surplus reserve is like any form of insurance: it reduces the risk of a large loss at the price of a smaller but certain cost, which is paid by policyholders either indirectly as part of their premium or, in the case of a mutual, as a direct contribution to capital.

---

[39] This assumes an inelastic demand.

[40] This is most likely to be the case for small firms for which a change in malpractice premium volume constitutes a large percentage change in total premium volume.

[41] The reason for this difference is unclear since the probability of error in setting premiums is surely greater with an occurrence than with a claims-made policy.

Whether regulators have adopted the optimum trade-off between risk of insolvency and cost of reducing this risk remains unanswered.[42]

Conclusion

It has been argued that the increased frequency and severity of malpractice claims, the instability of the sociolegal environment and its effect on claims, the decline of the stock market, and lower and less certain rates of return on financial assets have affected both the demand and the supply of insurance through traditional channels. Some of the institutional changes that have occurred appear consistent with an efficient market in risk spreading, given the changed nature of various components of the risk of writing malpractice insurance. Devices that encourage loss prevention and decrease dependence on financial reserves have become relatively more cost effective. Such changes include more frequent use of deductibles and experience-rating, the growth of mutuals, and the switch to the claims-made policy form. However, the total withdrawal of commercial carriers from some states cannot be attributed simply to the fact that the business has become more risky because most of the factors increasing the risk to the insurance firm similarly increase the risk faced by the physician if he is not insured. It seems highly probable that an insurance firm is still the most efficient bearer of this risk. If so, the collapse of the market can only be explained by regulation. This paper has outlined the potential impact of rate regulation (in conjunction with constraints on selective underwriting by medical societies) and regulation of capital requirements on the price and availability of insurance. However, the contribution of these various forms of regulation to the crisis of availability remains to be quantified.

Appendix

An insurance firm is like a levered investment trust.[43] Shareholders put up equity capital, K, which is invested by the insurance company. Denote the rate of return on this investment trust side of the business, r_m. The insurance company then writes Q insurance policies at premium rate P, on which it pays out underwriting costs of $\sum_{i=1}^{Q} C_i$, where C_i is the

---

[42] Solvency regulation of the insurance industry is examined in detail in Patricia Munch and Dennis Smallwood, "Solvency Regulation in the Property/Casualty Insurance Industry" (Paper presented at the National Bureau of Economic Research Conference on Regulation, December 1977).

[43] For a more complete model of the insurance firm, see Munch and Smallwood, "Solvency Regulation."

cost for policyholder i (including claims cost, administrative expenses, and so on). Assume that these costs occur at the end of one period. The expected rate of return on shareholder equity is then:[44]

$$E(r_I) = E(r_m) + \frac{PQ}{K} [1 + E(r_m)] - \frac{1}{K} E[\sum_{i=1}^{Q} C_i] \qquad (1)$$

where: r_I = rate of return on equity of the insurance firm,
r_m = rate of return on funds invested by the insurance firm,
E = expectations operator,
P = insurance premium,
Q = number of policyholders,
C_i = cost for policyholder i, and
K = equity of the insurance firm.

The variance of this expectation is:

$$(2)$$

$$\sigma_{r_I}^2 = \sigma_{r_m}^2 (1 + \frac{PQ^2}{K}) + \frac{1}{K^2} \sigma_{\Sigma_i C_i}^2 - \frac{2}{K} (1 + \frac{PQ}{K}) COVAR (r_m, \Sigma_i C_i)$$

where:

$$\sigma_{\Sigma_i C_i}^2 = \Sigma_i \sigma_{C_i}^2 + 2 \underset{i \neq 1}{\Sigma} COVAR(C_i, C_j). \qquad (3)$$

Assuming competitive capital markets, the expected rate of return, $E(r_I)$ must equal the risk-free market rate of return, plus a premium for undiversifiable risk. The following conclusions may be drawn:

(1) The extent to which expected investment income on premium reserves is passed on to policyholders in the form of lower rates depends on the rate of return that can be earned on the investment trust side of the business, r_m, and on the degree of undiversifiable risk. At the limit, if there are no constraints on the type of asset in which the firm may invest its surplus, so r_m is the risk-free market rate, and if all underwriting risk is diversifiable, then competition in the capital and insurance markets would ensure that all expected investment income on premium reserves was passed on to policyholders:

$$P = \frac{E(C)}{1 + E(r_m)}. \qquad (4)$$

Note that if none of the expected investment income on premium reserve is passed on to policyholders, $P = E(C)$, and the equation for the expected rate of return on equity in the firm reduces to:

$$E(r_I) = E(r_m) (1 + \frac{PQ}{K}). \qquad (5)$$

Since the ratio of premium volume to surplus is typically at least three, this implies an expected rate of return to equity in the insurance

---

[44] This formulation ignores differences in the types of assets in which unearned premium reserves, loss reserves, and net worth may be held.

firm equal to four times the expected rate of return on its investment trust business, which is highly implausible.

(2) The variance of the rate of return on equity in the insurance firm, $\sigma^2_{r_I}$, is a multiple of the variance of the return on the market portfolio, $\sigma^2_{r_m}$, where the multiplier is determined by the ratio of insurance premium to capital, $\frac{PQ}{K}$. This is because the equity owners bear the risk both of the investment trust side of the business and of the underwriting side, underwriting losses being paid out of surplus.[45] Thus, a simultaneous increase in $\sigma^2_{r_m}$ and in $\frac{PQ}{K}$ in 1974–1975 interacted to increase $\sigma^2_{r_I}$.

(3) The overall variance, $\sigma^2_{r_I}$, is positively related to the variance of claims cost per policyholder, positively related to the covariance of claims costs among policyholders, and negatively related to the covariance between the underwriting and investment sides of the business. If the firm can diversify internally by investing in assets whose return is positively correlated with claims cost, the negative covariance term can offset the positive variance terms and reduce the overall variance. It is often argued that one reason for the severity of the recent crisis was the atypical coincidence of a surge in claims costs and severe investment losses in 1974–1975. Historically, the covariance of claims cost and investment income has been positive. To the extent investors have revised previously held expectations on the basis of this recent experience, an increase in $\sigma^2_{r_I}$ is implied and, to the extent this risk is undiversifiable by shareholders, an increase in the supply price of capital to the firm is implied.

Thus, the hypothesis is that three factors have coincided recently to increase the supply price of capital to the insurance industry: an increase in $\sigma^2_{r_m}$, in $\sigma^2_{\Sigma_i C_i}$, and in the absolute value of $COVAR(r_m, \Sigma_i C_i)$. An increase in the leverage ratio, $\frac{PQ}{K}$, tends to increase both $\sigma^2_{r_I}$ and $E(r_I)$, so its net effect on the supply price of capital cannot be determined without a more complex model.

---

[45] Note that although the ex post loss falls on the owners of equity, the ultimate incidence of this "tax" among policyholders and owners of capital depends on demand and supply elasticities. Since the long-run supply elasticity is surely very high, policyholders ultimately bear the ex ante cost of this risk.

FACTORS AFFECTING THE SUPPLY PRICE OF MEDICAL MALPRACTICE INSURANCE

Judith K. Mann

Despite the withdrawal of many major underwriters from the physician malpractice insurance market, and possibly because of substantial premium increases on the part of those willing to remain, the notion that coverage is excessively priced remains current in many of the debates surrounding the malpractice crisis. Explicit expressions of this belief, such as the regularly reappearing allegation that underwriters raise premiums artificially in order to offset stock market losses on "mismanaged" funds,[1] may be overplayed by the press, but implicit acceptance of the assumption is both more widespread and of potentially greater impact.

Proposals for, and establishment of, physician self-insurance pools and government-managed malpractice funds are based largely on the tacit premise that underwriters overcharge and on the attendant conclusion that insurance *can* be provided efficiently at lower prices. If that conclusion is false, low-priced physician pools will fail, and government funds which charge lower-than-prevailing rates will simply transfer the cost of malpractice liability from physicians to taxpayers.

It is widely conceded, by even the severest critics of commercial insurers, that both the number of claims filed and the dollar settlement on the typical claim have increased substantially in recent years. That this is not accepted as prima facie justification for actual premium adjustments derives from the traditional practice of rate makers and regulating authorities of relying on experiential (empirical) actuarial

The author is assistant professor of economics at the University of California, San Diego. This research was supported in part by a grant from the Economics-Carthage Fund of the University of California at Los Angeles Foundation. I wish to express gratitude to Allan Andersen, Daniel Orr, and Allan Mitchem for valuable comments on an earlier draft. Any errors which remain are mine.

[1] The president of the American Trial Lawyers' Association, for example, expressed this view recently, charging insurance companies with raising premiums and withholding coverage "with all the conscience of a barracuda," claiming that insurers lost $10 billion in the stock market in eighteen months, and warning that "we're not going to stand for your picking up $10 billion in the next eighteen months." Quoted in *Malpractice Lifeline,* vol. 1, no. 26 (November 8, 1976), p. 2.

data from closed claims to justify rates. Because of the long "tail," or time lag, between the filing and disposition of malpractice claims, experiential data on the closure of claims arising today will not be available in statistically useful quantities for several years. This paucity of what is traditionally regarded as the only relevant evidence has led both to suspicion of the validity of actual premium increases and to some confusion concerning the effect on rate making of the so-called long tail.

The common view of the long-tail effect is summarized by the following passage from a government report published in 1972:[2]

> ... the most vexing problem for the rate-maker is the protracted period of time that passes before he can know with any degree of certainty what his past experience has been. . . . It can be seen that if it takes more than five years before an average cost per claim can be computed and if the number of claims filed per year and the amount paid per claim is increasing rapidly, then base data . . . that is more than five years old is of little value.

Two points in this passage deserve closer analysis. The first sentence is simply invalid: no period of time, much less a protracted one, passes before the rate maker can know what past experience has been. Indeed, the only thing he—or any other economic agent—knows with perfect certainty is the past. The rate maker's problem is *extrapolating* from the certainty of the past experience to the uncertainty of future events. And, in a stable environment where the past is a mirror of the future, that extrapolation problem is a simple one regardless of the length of time between a malpractice incident and the final disposition of an associated claim. In fact, in a stationary environment, the only effect of the long tail is a favorable one: because payouts occur far into the future, their present-value cost, and hence insurance premiums, are lower than they otherwise would be. It is important to emphasize that the instability of the malpractice claims-making environment creates an extrapolation problem, not that the long tail makes rate making difficult.

A second point which deserves scrutiny in the paragraph cited above is more subtle but equally important. When the number of claims filed per year and the amount paid per claim are increasing rapidly,

[2] U.S. Department of Health, Education, and Welfare, *Medical Malpractice: Report of the Secretary's Commission on Medical Malpractice*, DHEW pub. no. (OS) 73-88 (1973), p. 42.

there is no doubt that the simple extrapolation rule "the future will be the same as the past" is no longer valid. Moreover, a long tail on open claims does increase the probability that when the number of filings increases, past premiums will fail to cover current and future payouts on open claims. However, it is not true that base data which are more than five years old are of little value in setting current rates to cover future expected payouts.

Although the computed average cost on recently closed claims arising five years ago cannot be assumed to be *equal* to the average future cost on claims arising today, data on recent closures can be extremely valuable in discovering and estimating trends in dollar payout per case. More important, the base data used to set rates need not be closure data: because of the mathematical relationship between the filing and closing of claims, data on the number of cases filed are just as valid for predicting the number of future settlements, and this is equally true for a changing environment and a stationary one. Although one may be tempted to argue that the long tail makes it more difficult for the insurer to adjust, the model presented in this paper demonstrates that ease of adjustment is unaffected by the length of the tail. The very fact that future payouts derive from present filings permits an insurer to adjust as rapidly to a change in the environment evidenced by increased filings as to one evidenced by increased closings. It is the insistence on experiential closing data as the only justification of premium rates that creates the problem, not the long tail.

This paper presents a first-approximation model of rate making primarily for the purpose of explaining the relationship between current filings and future payouts. However, the model also serves to generate estimates of the percentage adjustment in premium rates required to compensate for an increase in the filing rate under simplified conditions. As we will argue in the concluding section of the paper, relaxation of the assumptions of the model to conform more closely to the realities of malpractice claims experience will tend to increase estimated premiums. That is, our simplified model gives downward-biased estimates of required premium adjustment.

Using data from San Diego County and from published sources, we then show that premium adjustments actually instituted conform closely to the model's estimates. Our research concludes that, rather than over-pricing malpractice insurance, commercial carriers are more likely to be under-pricing their coverage. It follows that the crisis in premiums cannot be solved merely by transferring the underwriting of liability from commercial specialists to physician-owned or government-managed insurance pools.

The Model

The minimum price at which any insurance can be supplied is determined by the expected dollar payout on claims filed plus the marginal cost of administering the insurance fund. The former cost is simply the mean of the payout distribution, while the latter is a function of its variance. The lower the variance in payouts—that is, the more predictable they are—the less frequent the need to transfer funds into and out of noncash assets.[3] This reduces administrative costs. While the impact on administrative costs of recent trends in malpractice claims filing has been anything but trivial, our focus in this paper is only on the expected payout portion of the supply price.[4] This is the major source of the downward bias alluded to above.

In a stationary environment, in which the parameters of the filing, time-to-disposition, and dollar-payout distributions remain constant over time, actual payout on claims arising in a given period is the stochastic variable

$$P = \sum_{i=o}^{n} D_{i,w} e^{-\alpha w} \tag{1}$$

where P is the present-value payout; n is the number of claims arising during the period; $D_{i,w}$ is the dollar payout, including claims-processing costs, on the ith claim reaching disposition w periods into the future; and α is the rate of return to the insurer on invested funds.

The variables n, D, and w are governed by probability distributions. The expected value of P therefore depends on each of those underlying densities. It is conventionally assumed that the number of claims arising in a given period is Poisson-distributed with mean λ. That is, taking the total number of doctor-patient contacts in a given period as the number of "trials," and a malpractice incident as a "success" (in statistical terminology), it is reasonable to regard the number of incidents arising in a given period as the outcome of an experiment consisting of a large number of trials where the probability of success on a single trial is very small. These are the classic characteristics of a Poisson variable.

Realistically, the probability distribution governing the dollar payout on a given claim depends on the type of claim made. Complaints

---

[3] In other words, the lower the variance in payout, the smaller the dollar loss from failure to transfer in and out of noncash assets.

[4] The effects of changing payout variance are considered in Judith K. Mann, "The Queueing of Malpractice Claims: Implications for Actuarial Insurance Values," University of California at San Diego Discussion Paper 76-14 (revised, December 1976).

that negligence resulted in the loss of life or limb carry a higher probability of large payout and impose higher investigation costs than those alleging that negligence resulted in additional medical bills or a few months' loss of income. For this reason, payout P is accurately expressed as the weighted sum of various discounted payout distributions by type of case. Unfortunately, data on payouts by type of claim are not available. We will therefore make the simplifying assumption that the payout distribution is identical over claims: that is, a given claim represents a random drawing from an overall settlement distribution with mean (in current dollars) δ.

Given the foregoing assumptions, and the additional assumption that D and w are independent, the expected value of the periodic payout is[5]

$$p = E(P) = \lambda E(D)E(e^{-\alpha w}) = \lambda \delta E(y) \qquad (2)$$

where $y = e^{-\alpha w}$ is the stochastic discount factor.[6] Note that the longer the time to disposition, the lower the present-value cost of covering the settlement on a claim arising today. It is for this reason that the long tail on malpractice insurance makes it cheaper to supply than if claims were settled instantly at the same cost.

The distribution of w and, hence, y are related to the rate at which claims arise, the rate at which open claims are "serviced," and the likelihood that an open claim will remain in the "service system" until it is closed. Because we have time series data only for litigated claims, our derivation of the distribution of time-to-disposition is couched in terms of litigation service. This does not mean that time to pretrial settlement is ignored. In fact, as we explain below, pretrial settlements dominate the estimate of mean time to disposition. We simply describe the "service mechanism" for processing claims as if all claims represented legal suits. Published data indicate that only half of all claims filed are in fact litigated;[7] but if the litigation process reflects the general characteristics of overall claims filing, our estimates of changes in the litigation environment can be taken as representative of changes in the general claims-filing process.

---

[5] See, for example, William Feller, *An Introduction to Probability Theory and Its Applications,* 3rd ed., (New York: John Wiley & Sons, 1968), chap. 12.

[6] It must be acknowledged that the costs of settling a claim and the time to settlement are probably not mutually independent. Difficult cases consume time and resources and insurers are more likely to undertake costly defense on cases which are time consuming and represent high potential losses than on others. We are currently working to incorporate these factors into a more refined model of rate making, but the general conclusions of this paper are not likely to be affected in a major way by such refinements.

[7] U.S. Department of Health, Education, and Welfare, *Medical Malpractice,* p. 10.

The litigation system is a standard example of a general queueing system, described as a system designed to provide some service, over a stochastic time interval, to "customers" or "arrivals" entering the system at random points in time. In this context, the length of time between filing and final disposition of any claim is the claim's waiting time in the litigation queue. Much of queueing theory focuses on the derivation of waiting-time distributions for various assumptions concerning the behavior of queue members. The process of litigation can be characterized in a number of ways within a general queueing context, but for purposes of tractability and ease of exposition we make the following assumptions.

Basically, we treat the litigation system as one consisting of a queue of claims waiting for judicial service plus a service mechanism consisting of formal trial. In reality, of course, the queue of malpractice suits is only part of a much larger general litigation queue served by a number of channels (courtrooms and judges). By assuming a single server, we are taking the simplifying view that one courtroom is reserved for malpractice suits. While this will lead to an underestimate of the mean waiting time to trial, the effect on mean waiting time to disposition will be slight: most malpractice suits filed do not, in fact, reach the trial stage. Our data from San Diego County show that of 655 cases reaching known dispositions between 1966 and 1976, only sixty-three (less than 10 percent) reached the trial stage. While the percentage varied from year to year, the maximum was 21 percent, recorded in 1970.[8] These data suggest that the distribution of waiting time for the typical case is governed primarily by the time elapsed until "reneging" (that is, leaving the queue before entering service). Therefore any underestimate of time to trial resulting from our simplifications will be of secondary importance in deriving estimates of the time to final disposition of a suit.

Gnedenko has studied the problem of waiting time in a single-server system with reneging which closely parallels the litigation process.[9] A special case of his general approach can be characterized in the following way. Suppose that a suit chosen at random will remain in the litigation queue for up to τ periods before reaching pretrial disposition (out-of-court settlement or dismissal). If the probability that a suit will reach such disposition in any period is given by a Poisson distribution with parameter γ (a reasonable assumption), the distribution of τ is a negative exponential with mean $\frac{1}{\gamma}$. If we further assume that trial service is

---

[8] For that same year, the secretary's commission reports a nationwide figure of 23 percent for suits reaching the trial stage. Ibid.

[9] See, for example, Thomas Saaty, *Elements of Queueing Theory* (New York: McGraw-Hill, 1960), pp. 206-209.

Poisson-distributed, the time to disposition of a claim chosen at random is a weighted average, w, of time to pretrial disposition and time to trial verdict, where the weights are the probabilities that the suit will renege and will not renege, respectively. It can be shown that under these conditions, the expected value of the random discount factor $y = e^{-\alpha w}$ is closely approximated by [10]

$$E(y) = \frac{\alpha}{\alpha+\gamma}\left(\frac{\gamma}{\lambda}\right)^{\frac{\alpha}{\gamma}+1} + \frac{\gamma}{\alpha+\gamma}. \tag{3}$$

Note that the larger the filing rate, λ, the smaller the expected value of the discount factor: a given litigation system, and Poisson-distributed claims processing which does not change in response to a greater filing rate, will lead to an increase in the time to disposition of the typical claim. Therefore, while an increase in the filing rate will *increase* the expected dollar payout on settled claims through the effect of λ, it *reduces* the present value of those payouts through the effect of w. The net change in the periodic price at which insurance can be supplied depends upon the relative magnitudes of the two effects.

Specifically, the percentage change in expected present-value payout resulting from a given percentage change in the number of suits filed per period (the elasticity of payout with respect to filing) is

$$\epsilon(p,\lambda) = \frac{\partial p}{\partial \lambda}\frac{\lambda}{p} = \left[\frac{p}{\lambda} - \frac{\alpha\delta}{\lambda}\left(\frac{\gamma}{\lambda}\right)^{\frac{\alpha}{\gamma}}\right]\frac{\lambda}{p} = 1 - \frac{\alpha\delta}{p}\left(\frac{\gamma}{\lambda}\right)^{\frac{\alpha}{\gamma}}. \tag{4}$$

Because the term $\dfrac{\alpha\delta}{p}\left(\dfrac{\gamma}{\lambda}\right)^{\frac{\alpha}{\gamma}}$ is strictly nonnegative, it follows that payout elasticity is less than one: a given percentage change in the filing rate leads to a smaller percentage change in expected payout. However, the larger the filing rate relative to γ, the closer elasticity approaches unity. This statement implies that the relative *change* in expected payouts is higher the longer the tail. In other words, although the long tail makes the supply price of malpractice insurance lower than it otherwise would be, it also makes relative changes in supply price more responsive to increased filing rates.

The Evidence

Using data on litigated malpractice cases in San Diego County over the ten-year period 1966 through 1975, we have been able to derive

---

[10] The derivation of this expression can be found in Mann, "Queueing."

estimates for expected payout elasticities for alternative filing rates. Over the four-year period 1966 through 1969, the filing process was extremely stable. Linear and exponential trend estimates resulted in time coefficients of —.018 and —.006, respectively, with corresponding t-values of —.64 and —.84. If anything, these estimates suggest a slight downward trend in filing, but the t-values are too low to reject the hypothesis that the number of filings was stationary.

The stability of the period 1966 through 1969 is serendipitous for our purposes because the secretary's commission reports data on claims closed in 1970. Approximately 62 percent of claims closed in that year derived from incidents occurring during our base period.[11] If the time between incident and filing is relatively stable, we can assume that the typical claim closed in 1970 originated in the 1966–1969 period. As further support, the average time to pretrial disposition exhibited by our data is 29.54 months, or two and one-half years. Hence the typical claim filed between July 1967 and July 1968—precisely the middle interval of our base period—would have reached disposition in 1970. This correspondence permits us to augment our data with those reported by the secretary's commission.

The mean filing rate estimated from our data for 1966 through 1969 was 2.538 cases per month. Using 29.54 months as an estimate of the reciprocal of γ, and assuming a monthly discount rate of .01, the elasticity of expected payout with respect to the filing rate is .9985— very nearly unity. The correct interpretation of this estimate compares the expected payout in two different stationary claims-filing settings: if one stationary setting exhibits a filing rate exactly twice as large as another, expected payouts in that setting will be very nearly twice as great. It would be an error, however, to conclude that a doubling of the filing rate in one setting would instantaneously result in a doubling of expected payout, for the following reason.

In a changing environment, it is the payout on the queue of claims which is of primary significance for pricing. The expected closure rate in any period is, roughly, γQ_t, where Q_t is the number of claims in the queue during that period. While a rise in the filing rate will immediately enlarge Q_t, resulting in an immediate increase in expected total dollar payout, the bulk of the queue in the first period following a filing change consists of claims against which premiums have already been collected. Thus, premiums in that period must rise only enough to cover the new queue members. Nevertheless, as the "old queue" dissipates over time and the "new queue" comes to dominate, premiums must eventually

---

[11] U.S. Department of Health, Education, and Welfare, *Medical Malpractice,* p. 11.

rise to the level implied by expected payouts in the new stationary setting. The time lapse to full adjustment depends upon the new filing rate and the rate of processing claims.

Beginning in the first half of 1970, the number of suits filed per month in San Diego County rose from an average of 2.538 to an eventual average of 5.821. From the second half of 1970 through the first half of 1972, the increased filing rate remained stable, suggesting a new stationary environment. By the beginning of 1973, approximately 88 percent of the old queue had been dissipated: only 14 of the 116 suits filed between 1966 and 1969 remained open as of January 1973. Expected payouts were then dominated by the new stationary mean filing rate of 5.821, an increase of slightly less than 130 percent. Had the queue of open suits consisted solely of new filings (those occurring between 1969 and 1973), premiums would have risen by the full 130 percent; but because 12 percent of the queue consisted of old claims, the premium increase required by the new filing rate, as of January 1973, was in the neighborhood of .88 $\times$ 130 percent, or 114 percent.

If litigated claims were perfectly representative of the typical claim, and if neither the dollar awards nor the tendency to settle out of court had changed, 1973 premiums would have had to be approximately 114 percent higher than they were in 1969 merely to cover increased expected payout. Because a larger filing rate also implies a larger variance in present-value payout and concomitantly higher administrative costs, the 114 percent increase reflects the minimum upward adjustment in the supply price of insurance needed in the absence of other changes. The actual increase reported by the secretary's commission over that period was 90 percent for physicians in the moderate-risk class and 106 percent for surgeons.[12] These upward adjustments would appear, if anything, to be insufficient to cover the actual increase in cost.

There are, of course, a number of qualifying factors which must be considered in the interpretation of our findings. First, our litigation data apply only to San Diego County, while the premium figures reported by the secretary's commission are nationwide averages. There is some evidence that California not only exhibits a higher than average propensity to file malpractice claims but has also experienced a higher than average increase in this propensity.[13] Thus, our data are likely to overstate the percentage increase in claims filed nationwide. But this may simply explain why national premium increases were actually in

---

[12] This estimate is based on interpolated figures of $1226.00 for class four premiums and $435.00 for class two premiums in 1969, and extrapolated figures (based on the immediately preceding trend) of $2520 for class four premiums and $822.90 for class two premiums in 1973. Ibid, p. 13.

[13] Ibid, pp. 7-8.

the neighborhood of 100 percent, while our figures suggest something in excess of 114 percent.

A second factor to be considered is the impact of other changes which have, in fact, taken place but were not reflected in our model. Although there are no published data on the trend in jury awards during the period from 1966 through 1973, it is widely conceded that they rose perhaps as dramatically as the filing rate. Indeed, the economic theory of demand would suggest that a major cause of increased suit filings would be an increase in the expected return to claimants. If the average dollar award did in fact rise over the period in question, it follows that the 114 percent estimate we derived further understates required premium increases.

Possibly mitigating this effect to some degree is a probable change in the pattern of out-of-court settlements. The most plausible a priori argument, however, is two-sided. On the one hand, the typical claimant, faced with an ever-lengthening time to jury trial, has greater incentive to accept a sure, smaller settlement now than a larger uncertain settlement pushed further and further into the future. Hence overall settlements may be expected to be smaller in the future than past trends indicate. On the other hand, the very fact that those smaller settlements are made now rather than later raises their present-value cost to the insurer. The net impact on premiums from these countervailing factors obviously requires correct identification of the supply of and demand for out-of-court settlements; but we are inclined to the view that, at best, they mitigate required premium increases only slightly.

A final change which should be noted is the probable increase in the legal merit (not necessarily equivalent to the moral or medical merit) of the typical suit filed. An increased tendency of patients to litigate (as evidenced by increased suit filing) is met by an increased supply of suit filing services: not only does the number of attorneys willing to press malpractice cases increase, but so also does the degree of specialization.[14] With the increased knowledge associated with specialization, attorneys are more able to screen suits for legal merit before filing. Moreover, with the increased demand for litigation, they have a greater incentive to do so: by incurring relatively low costs in acquiring prefiling information, they can effectively discriminate among the large number of demanders according to their informed perceptions of the probability of successful suit. This increase in the legal merit of the

---

[14] In our conversations with plaintiff attorneys in the San Diego area, this point was revealed again and again. In a typical interview, a senior partner would explain that whereas a few years ago he was able to meet the demand for malpractice suits with a small fraction of his own time, he now employs a full-time specialist in the field.

typical suit filed raises the probability of positive and large future pay-outs on the part of insurers, requiring a still larger upward adjustment in premiums than our study indicates.

A number of points raised above suggest that our data on litigated claims are not, in fact, representative of the general claims-filing experience, at least not in the current malpractice environment. This offers the only major possibility that our litigation data may reflect an upward, rather than a downward, bias in required premium increases. It is not unreasonable to conjecture that current litigated cases are those with larger than average expected payouts. Highly meritorious claims involving small awards are likely to be revealed to insurers by plaintiff attorneys at the presuit stage. Because of their high probability of success and their low payout, it does not pay the insurer to incur the defense costs of litigation. If the payout is sufficiently small, even less meritorious claims will be adjusted before litigation.

Expensive claims, on the other hand, will tend to be litigated. Even if they are of relatively high legal merit, the length of the litigation process makes them relatively less costly to defend, precisely because the payout, however probable, is pushed significantly into the future.[15] Moreover, expensive claims tend to be those with high emotional impact, which the plaintiff attorney may pursue in the anticipation of jury sympathy, but which the insurer may consider defensible in terms of strict legal merit. Thus, compared with typical claims, litigated cases may have a bias toward higher potential dollar settlements. This would not, in itself, affect our conclusions concerning premium adjustment, as our mean payout figure was derived from an average of overall claims. To the extent that the high payout on litigated claims has encouraged an increase in suit filing relative to out-of-court settlements, however, our estimate of the change in the mean filing rate may be too high. If so, the 114 percent estimated rise in expected payout is overstated.

Conclusion

We have attempted to show, through the use of a simplified queueing model, that recent changes in the mean filing rate for malpractice suits increased the expected payout on claims by approximately 114 percent. If premium adjustments were confined to covering expected payout alone, they would have had to rise by 114 percent. Although some arguments can be advanced that our estimated adjustment is over-stated—most notably the argument that increased suit filing over-

---

[15] This "advantage" to insurers is, of course, completely eliminated if jurors and/or attorneys consider loss of interest in determining awards.

estimates increased claims filing—other arguments suggest that our estimate is understated. For example, dollar settlement amounts and risk to insurers, treated as constant in our model, have both increased. Without additional data we cannot determine which of these arguments carries the heavier impact; but there is clearly no evidence that the approximate 100 percent premium increases actually introduced by commercial underwriters were instances of irresponsible or unwarranted price adjustment.

The outlook for the future path of expected payouts is not bright. In the second half of 1972 the number of suits filed per month began another substantial increase. The average monthly frequency over the two-year period 1973 through 1975 is 12.777. More important, the data exhibit a significant upward trend. Even if we could depend on the 12.777 figure's remaining stationary, premiums in 1977–1978 would have to be, at a minimum, two and a half times what they were in 1973. But the upward trend indicates that it may be some time before a new stationary setting is achieved—at a mean filing rate well above 12.777 per month. Expected payouts, and therefore required premiums, will continue to rise at a substantial rate unless the number of claims filed reverses its trend or there is an absolute decline in dollar settlement amounts.

EXPECTATIONS, IMPERFECT MARKETS, AND MEDICAL MALPRACTICE INSURANCE

Mark C. Kendall

It could be easy to infer from the Senate hearings on medical malpractice insurance that the major cause of the medical malpractice insurance crisis is the insurer.[1] The best that can be said for the testimony of the representatives of the Insurance Services Organization (ISO)—"a leading insurance statistical organization" [2]—is that it is enlightening as to what the insurers do *not* know. The exchange between the representatives of ISO and the committee chairman began with the ISO actuary presenting a figure of $36,400 as "the average cost per insured claim." [3]

The committee chairman pointed out, correctly, that the average claim payment was approximately $8,500 in 1973. A representative of the American Mutual Insurance Alliance speculated that the reason for the difference was that the ISO figure "represents claimants that were in fact paid" whereas the chairman's figure was for all claims. The ISO actuary indicated (with more than a little help from the committee chairman) that the $36,500 figure was the average cost of claims to be ultimately paid; that this figure was a projection; and that he did not know the average for claims actually paid.

It should be noted that ISO was able, at a later date, to respond with the average claim paid to date for the 1973 policy year—$10,857. The difference between the final projection of $36,400 and the average for claims actually paid to date indicates ISO's expectations concerning the future costs of claims made but not settled and claims to be filed against malpractice insurance policies expiring in policy year 1973.

The views expressed are not those of the National Planning Association or its trustees. The comments and assistance of Jacqueline Ru.̣ ̣l and Leslie Smith are appreciated.

1. U.S. Congress, Senate, Subcommittee on Health of the Committee on Labor and Public Welfare, *Continuing Medical Malpractice Insurance Crisis, 1975,* 94th Congress, 1st session, April and December 1975.

2. Robert Gilmore, Senior Vice President of Legal Affairs, American Insurance Association, in Senate, Subcommittee on Health of the Committee on Labor and Public Welfare, *Medical Malpractice Insurance, 1975,* p. 448.

3. Ibid., p. 463.

Note that this average does not reflect the other major component of expected total malpractice loss payments—the total *number* of claims that will eventually be paid. It is the expectation concerning the future number of claims and payments for claims that determines the present and presumably "correct," malpractice insurance rates. For a significant portion of the market, these expectations are being defined by ISO. Yet an ISO actuary (and vice president) appearing before the Senate subcommittee was unable or unwilling even to estimate the average cost for claims paid to date for the most recently available policy year.

This exchange exemplifies the limited information and associated uncertainty characteristic of the medical malpractice insurance market at the time of its "crisis" in 1975. Changes in the imperfect, noncompetitive market for medical services; significant changes in society's attitudes as reflected by changes in legal rules and doctrine; and the inauspicious timing of the recession combined with limited information to make impossible the specification of a "correct" price for medical malpractice insurance.

The Market for Medical Care

It has been argued that the medical profession constitutes a monopoly. An argument in this vein was made by Reuben Kessel in 1958.[5] Kessel applied a discriminating monopoly model in an attempt to understand various characteristics of the market for medical services. He argued that the reason physicians behaved in a way inconsistent with the maximization of individual income was not that physicians were leading servants of the public interest but that their behavior was consistent with the maintenance of a medical monopoly. Included in his applications was an explanation of physician reactions to medical malpractice claims against their colleagues. This analysis will be examined later.

Kessel attempted to explain most of the social institutions governing the delivery of medical care as mechanisms to maintain a monopoly. A different explanation for the existence of these social institutions was offered by Arrow in 1963. He argued "that the failure of the (medical) market to insure against uncertainty has created many social institutions in which the usual assumptions of the market are to some extent con-

---

[4] ISO estimates that approximately 50 percent of the total premium volume written for medical professional liability insurance is being reported to ISO as a detail required by the ISO statistical plan. See ibid, p. 607.

[5] Reuben A. Kessel, "Price Discrimination in Medicine," *Journal of Law and Economics,* vol. 1 (January/February 1958) pp. 20-53.

radicted." [6] Arrow argued that the gaps in knowledge between the physician and his patient, combined with the uncertainty associated with the outcome of a physician's treatment, required the existence of a market that did not fulfill the usual competitive assumptions. However, he warned: "The economic importance of personal and especially family relationships, though declining, is by no means trivial in the most advanced economies. It is based on nonmarket relations that create guarantees of behavior which would otherwise be afflicted with excessive uncertainty." [7] The contributions of Kessel and Arrow define a fairly wide range for investigating the medical care market. They will be used in the next section, which describes the evolution of the medical care market, and in a later section, which attempts to isolate the components of the medical malpractice insurance crisis.

The Medical Care Provider.[8] At one time, almost anyone who wanted to practice medicine was free to declare his practice open. Medical education was varied and open to anyone willing to pay the price and devote the time. Until the formation of the American Medical Association in 1847, there seems to have been no popular dissatisfaction with this relatively free market for medical services. For example, Benjamin Franklin wrote Joseph Priestley that "all diseases may by sheer means be prevented or cured, not excepting that of old age, and our lives lengthened at pleasure even beyond the antediluvian standard." [9]

From its beginning, the AMA committed itself to two propositions: (1) that medical students should have acquired a suitable preliminary education and (2) that a uniform elevated standard of requirements for the degree of M.D. should be adopted by all medical schools in the United States.[10] The adoption of these goals by the AMA and their eventual acceptance by the public can be explained either as an effort to monopolize the market for medical services or as a recognition of the uncertainty in the delivery of medical services that required the development of suitable social institutions to decrease this uncertainty.

The plausibility of a monopolization argument is obvious. These two goals were met through licensing of physicians and accreditation of medical schools. During the last half of the nineteenth century, state

Kenneth J. Arrow, *Essays in the Theory of Risk-Bearing* (Chicago: Markham Publishing Company, 1971), pp. 177-219.

Ibid., p. 210.

This brief historical summary is based on Kessel, "Price Discrimination in Medicine," pp. 25-29.

Rene DuBos, "Medical Utopias," *Daedalus*, vol. 88 (Summer 1959), p. 413.

Abraham Flexner, *Medical Education in the U.S. and Canada*, Bulletin no. 4 (Pittsburgh: Carnegie Foundation for the Advancement of Teaching, 1910).

legislatures instituted licensing requirements for the practice of medicine During the first quarter of the twentieth century, licensing requirements were used to impose minimum standards upon medical schools. Licensing permitted medical societies to determine who was qualified to practice medicine. By making these qualifications contingent upon completion of studies at an accredited medical school (where accreditation was determined by the AMA) the AMA was effectively given the power to limit entry into the medical profession by limiting the number of places at medical schools and discouraging expansion by accredited schools

The AMA has long argued that this control is necessary to ensure the quality of medical services. Many economists, on the other hand have argued that this control is necessary to the existence of a medical monopoly. For example, Friedman and Kuznetz found that during the period before World War II the cost of producing doctors was 17 percent greater than the cost of producing dentists, while the average income of doctors was 32 percent greater.[11] Although most of us would be willing to concede that the AMA has tried, and continues to try, to maintain monopoly control of the delivery of medical services, it does not necessarily follow that "the delegation by the state legislatures to the AMA of the power to regulate the medical industry in the public interest is on a par with giving the American Iron and Steel Institute the power to determine the output of steel."[12] It is just as reasonable to conclude that every state legislature's acceptance of the AMA's argument for control of "the quality of medicine" implies (in the absence of other evidence) that the public demanded the creation of social institutions that would decrease the uncertainty induced by what they perceived to be a gap in knowledge between them and the providers of medical services. The short-term benefits bestowed on the public by not having to worry, in some sense, about the quality of their medical services might be worth the costs imposed by removing the delivery of medical services from the free market. However, the long-term dynamics associated with this change might be socially undesirable.[13]

Whether one adopts the argument of Kessel or of Arrow, the market for medical services was imperfect. Further, whether one argues that medical societies were social and economic clubs with legally defined enforcement mechanisms or that the market for medical services was imbedded in the social institutions that rely on defined social

---

[11] Milton Friedman and Simon Kuznetz, *Income from Independent Professional Practice* (New York: National Bureau of Economic Research, 1945), p. 133.

[12] Kessel, "Price Discrimination in Medicine," p. 29.

[13] James Buchanan, *The Limits of Liberty: Between Anarchy and Leviathan* (Chicago: University of Chicago Press, 1975).

roles, the continued existence of the medical service market, as it was known in the first half of this century, required continued fulfillment of certain social roles and the continued enforcement of certain legal doctrines. In the absence of these, either market—Kessel's or Arrow's—was unstable in the traditional economic sense.

Doubts Concerning the Effect of Medical Care. Bad health is unpleasant. One is out of sorts when stricken by an illness. When a child is sick, the parents' typical (although not invariable) reaction is to hustle it off to the doctor because "he will make you well." Whether we can do anything about the illness or not—which is problematic in the case of a large number of diseases that afflict us—we feel compelled to try. Usually we consult a physician. As was confirmed in a recent poll by the Roper organization, we believe and expect our physician to be motivated by the public interests.[14]

It seems fair to say that most of us continue to believe in the altruism of our doctor and in his ability to cure our diseases.[15] The past twenty years have nonetheless seen increasing doubt concerning the benefits of medical care in general and the effectiveness of the provider. This is a significant change in the attitude of a proportion of the population toward physicians. Medieval Christianity had little faith in the possibility of creating a medical paradise on earth, but the Renaissance followed with its imaginary utopias where medical needs could be foreseen and provided for with certainty.[16] This idea made it to the United States, as attested by the passage quoted from Ben Franklin. This faith has stayed with us, as our rising propensity to visit the doctor, our rising medical expenditures, and our acceptance of the proposition that medical care is a right all share. Whether feasible or not, Medicare, Medicaid, and the recent proposals for national health insurance represent the legislative effort to ensure that no individual will be denied needed health care because of inability to pay. The Hill-Burton program, begun in 1964, the Regional Medical Program, enacted in 1965, and the Comprehensive Health Planning Program, enacted in 1966, all are legislative efforts to ensure the availability of health care services when individuals require them. All of these legislative efforts and the acceptance of AMA definitions of quality medical training and licensing requirements am-

---

14 *Wall Street Journal,* October 27, 1976, p. 1.

15 Office visits to physicians increased from 4.5 per person per year in 1963-64 to 5.0 per person per year in 1972. Source for 1963-64 is U.S. Department of Health, Education, and Welfare, Public Health Service, *Vital and Health Statistics,* series 10, no. 9. Source for 1972 is U.S. National Center for Health Statistics, *Vital and Health Statistics,* series 10, no. 85.

16 DuBos, "Medical Utopias," pp. 412-13.

171

plify the belief that, in the words of a New York state commissioner of health, ". . . public health is purchasable. Within natural limitations any community can determine its own death rate." [17]

One of the first writers to question the proposition that better health is obtainable through more health care delivery was Rene DuBos in 1959. His article, unlike Ivan Illich's recent book,[18] could hardly be construed as a condemnation of the medical profession. It did, however, raise some serious questions concerning the possibility that medical care would, in some sense, deliver us to a health utopia. Much like Victor Fuchs in his recent book,[19] DuBos argued that many significant health advances were due not to changes in the quality or quantity of medical care but to changes in nutrition and living habits. Although Illich's book, *Medical Nemesis,* is inferior to either DuBos's or Fuchs's work, its popularity does seem to indicate that many people are willing to doubt the efficacy of the typical medical care provider.

While these doubts have been growing, physicians as an economic class have been raised to a level second only to that of successful entertainers and professional basketball players. Reliable estimates of physician income are difficult to obtain. According to the 1970 census, experienced male medical and osteopathic physicians, who were heads of a family, had a median total family income of $32,152, or nearly three times the median for all male family heads in the experienced civilian labor force.[20] In addition, increased medical knowledge and economic and personal incentives have resulted in a marked increase in the level of specialization. In 1963, 26.7 percent of the practicing physicians were general practitioners; by 1970 this percentage had fallen to 17.3.[21]

All of these occurrences—increased contact with physicians through increased visits, the physician's rapidly escalating economic status, and the impersonality of increased specialization—tend to give the patient the feeling that he is a consumer more than a patient. Each change tends to knock down those social and family constraints associated with the institutions governing the delivery of medical care.

[17] Ibid., p. 413.

[18] Ivan Illich, *Medical Nemesis* (New York: Pantheon Books, 1975).

[19] Victor Fuchs, *The Economics of Medical Care* (New York: Basic Books 1974).

[20] U.S. Department of Commerce, Bureau of the Census, *Census of Population, 1970: Occupational Characteristics,* Final Report PC(2)-7A (Washington, D.C. 1973), p. 521.

[21] American Medical Association Center for Health Services Research and Development, *Distribution of Physicians in the United States,* Table A, 1963 volume Table 1, 1973 volume, Chicago.

whether the institutions were developed to handle uncertainty or to institute and maintain a monopoly. The weakening of these social institutions leaves an unstable situation and this instability manifests itself in a variety of ways. The medical malpractice insurance crisis is one of these manifestations.

The Medical Malpractice Insurance Market

Until the relaxation of the locality rule, medical societies could and did play a crucial role in protecting their members against malpractice suits. The essence of the locality rule was that a physician's performance was to be compared with "the degree of ability or skill possessed by other physicians in the same or similar community, neighborhood, or locality."[22] Where the rule was strictly enforced, the only admissible expert testimony was from physicians in the same locality or community. Thus, in order to bring a malpractice suit it was necessary to obtain the testimony of a physician who lived in the same community where the alleged malpractice had occurred and who was likely to be a member of the same local medical society as the defendant physician. It was claimed that the ability of organized medicine to expel doctors from hospital staffs gave the societies the power to prevent their members from testifying against other members.[23] For example, a practitioner who acted as an expert witness in a 1950s malpractice suit was subsequently barred from the staff of every hospital in California.[24]

Until the relaxation of the locality rule, the force of law coupled with the power of county medical societies to determine who was qualified for local hospital staffs significantly diminished the threat of a successful malpractice suit. In addition, many state and county medical societies controlled access to malpractice insurance through group-sponsored plans. The medical society designs a model plan that is used as a basis for shopping and negotiating with carriers.[25] Although these group plans seldom automatically entitle any member to malpractice insurance, the societies do intervene formally and informally in the

---

[22] Steven K. Dietz, C. Bruce Baird, and Lawrence Berul, "The Medical Malpractice Legal System," in U.S. Department of Health, Education, and Welfare, *Report of the Secretary's Commission on Medical Malpractice* (Washington, D.C., 1973), Appendix, p. 123.

[23] Kessel, "Price Discrimination in Medicine," p. 45.

[24] Melvin Belli, "The California Medical Malpractice Controversy," *Stanford Law Review*, vol. 9 (1957), p. 98.

[25] For a more complete discussion of group malpractice insurance plans see Mark Kendall and John Haldi, "Medical Malpractice Insurance Market," *Report of the Secretary's Commission*, Appendix, pp. 512-21.

underwriting decision. Thus, an acceptable medical society member obtains the benefits of having the weight of his medical society behind him when the insurer decides on whether to issue him a policy or not. In addition, the medical society performs a variety of administrative and other tasks that may lower the total price of medical malpractice insurance to its members.

One of the nasty long-term implications of the creation of a group plan is that it eventually dominates the market because of its ability to offer malpractice insurance at lower rates with surer coverage. This monopoly-monopsony market within a state effectively precludes the writing of malpractice insurance by many other firms. One of the primary determinants of malpractice rates is the state's law, and a dominant group plan prevents any other insurer from obtaining a number of cases sufficient to determine an appropriate price for malpractice insurance in that state. The advantages of group plans to an insurer are also substantial. Particularly before the abolition of the locality rule, an insurer could rely implicitly upon the medical society's reluctance to prosecute one of its own members for malpractice since a successful prosecution would be reflected in higher malpractice insurance rates for all society members. The uncertainty, in selling malpractice insurance, concerning the probable number of claims and of awards, was thus decreased by the combination of a group plan with the locality rule.

One quirk of group policies was that premiums were not necessarily lower than those for individual policies. It seems that one reason premiums did not decrease was that "under the generally easier underwriting screen of (the) groups, high-risk physicians may obtain medical malpractice coverage at the same (or similar) rate as low-risks." [26] The subsidy arrangement also tended to increase the medical society's power to control its members. Underwriting practices implied that any physician with a successful malpractice claim against him became a less desirable risk. Since those physicians who were able to find lower rates outside the group plans were "usually 'good-risk' types," [27] the subsidy to high-risk positions would induce a risk-averting, low-risk physician to opt for the group plan, given the assurance of continued coverage even if a successful malpractice suit were brought against him.

Thus, enforcement of the locality rule, group malpractice insurance plans, and the medical society's ability to certify doctors for hospital privileges all combined to help decrease the probability of a successful malpractice claim. The effect of these practices on the average value of a successful malpractice claim is not certain. However, the effect on

---

[26] Ibid., p. 514.
[27] Ibid.

successful claim frequency is unambiguous. Moreover, the insurer assumes the cost of defending a malpractice claim. A group plan, regardless of the effectiveness of the locality rule, implies the ready availability of expert witnesses for the defense.

The Insurer. Before 1970, there were occasional jumps in medical malpractice insurance premiums as well as occasional problems with its availability. For example, in one study of medical malpractice insurance all six group insurance plans examined had as one of their motivating forces either a recent increase in malpractice insurance rates or a problem of insuring some of their members.[28] However, the first national crisis in medical malpractice insurance occurred during and shortly after 1970, when malpractice insurance rates increased dramatically. This significant increase is reflected in Table 1, which displays malpractice insurance premium volume between 1960 and 1974. There are admitted uncertainties concerning these estimates, but it is clear that malpractice insurance rates jumped significantly during and immediately before 1970. This jump, coupled with some isolated problems of availability, was one of the major motivating factors in the formation of the (HEW) Secretary's Commission on Medical Malpractice.

Until 1970, the insurer faced what he thought was a relatively well-defined market. Moreover, until 1970 the premium volume on medical malpractice insurance was less than 0.5 percent of total property and liability premium volume.[29] Since malpractice insurance was a relatively small proportion of total property and liability insurance, and since the social institutions governing the delivery of medical care and the adjudication of medical malpractice suits were long established, the insurer made a rational business decision to ignore the malpractice insurance market.

For example, it was not possible reliably to estimate historical malpractice insurance premium volume, since the practice of the industry was not to keep separate accounts on medical malpractice insurance premium volume for more than five years.[30] Consider an insurer who is deciding whether to write malpractice insurance in the early 1960s. If the insurer is like most individuals, he considers physicians to be motivated by the public interest. Second, he observes a large number of social and legal constraints against "suing the doctor." Third, he knows that the social institutions that regulate the delivery of medical care also make the pursuit of a medical malpractice claim difficult.

---

[28] Ibid., pp. 562-98.
[29] Ibid., p. 510.
[30] Ibid., p. 508.

Table 1
MEDICAL MALPRACTICE INSURANCE PREMIUMS PAID BY DENTISTS, PHYSICIANS, SURGEONS, AND HOSPITALS, 1960–1974
(in millions of dollars)

Year	Dentists	Physicians	Surgeons	Hospitals	Total
1960	5.1	7.6	19.7	28.7	61.1
1961	5.3	7.9	22.4	30.3	65.9
1962	5.4	8.1	25.2	31.1	69.8
1963	5.6	8.9	30.3	32.2	77.0
1964	5.8	9.6	35.5	33.2	84.1
1965	6.4	10.5	38.5	35.1	90.5
1966	7.0	11.4	43.7	33.2	95.3
1967	7.4	15.2	51.7	35.7	110.0
1968	7.7	19.0	59.7	38.1	124.5
1969	8.9	30.2	110.5	63.0	212.6
1970	11.0	48.7	206.7	104.2	370.6
1971	11.7	272.7		113.3	397.7
1972	12.5	291.2		123.1	426.8
1973	13.4	310.9		133.8	458.1
1974	14.3	332.0		145.5	491.8

Source: 1960-1970 from Mark Kendall and John Haldi, "Medical Malpractice Insurance Market," *Report of the Secretary's Commission on Medical Malpractice*, Department of Health, Education, and Welfare (Washington, D.C., 1973), Appendix, p. 509. The 1974 figures for physicians, surgeons, and hospitals are estimates by the Insurance Services Organization based on a survey of member firms, in U.S. Congress, Senate, Subcommittee on Health of the Committee on Labor and Public Welfare, *Continuing Medical Malpractice Insurance Crisis, 1975*, 94th Congress, 1st session, April and December 1975, p. 603. The 1971-1973 figures are interpolations. The 1971-1974 figures for dentists are estimated as a constant share (based on 1970) of the figures for physicians and surgeons.

Fourth, the volume of medical malpractice insurance premiums is trivial in proportion to that of total property and liability insurance. Fifth, even if he has some doubts as to whether the rates will cover his losses, he knows that the period of payout for any one policy year is in excess of ten years and that 10 percent or less of the total claims to be paid will be paid during the first two years. Thus, he faces a reasonably certain market with a long payoff period (and the associated bonus of investment income that is not included in the regulatory process of determining insurance rates).

Given this perceived stability and the assured coverage of possible excessive payouts that is provided by the earnings on investment income, an insurer would make the rational decision that if he writes medical malpractice insurance it is not worth the effort to collect, maintain, and analyze a large volume of medical malpractice insurance data. Resources for this data collection effort would be better devoted to automobile insurance, which accounted for nearly 20 percent of his property and liability premium volume. Moreover, the growth of automobile losses during the 1960s would reinforce the insurer's inclination.

The Crisis in Medical Malpractice Insurance

By the late 1960s, the forthcoming crisis in medical malpractice insurance should have been obvious—if anyone had been paying any attention. Admittedly, the medical malpractice insurance problem is trivial compared to the other problems plaguing the delivery of medical services. However, the Senate has chosen to label it a crisis, and it seems pointless to argue with that august body. The indicators of this impending crisis were a weakening in the social institutions that governed delivery of medical care and inhibited pursuit of valid or invalid medical malpractice claims, coupled with a significant change in society's attitude toward receiving compensation, reflected in changes in legal rules and doctrine. These social changes and the monopoly-monopsony arrangements in the malpractice insurance market combined with a rapid increase in the number of lawyers, a dearth of medical malpractice insurance data, and heightened risk aversion on the part of insurers (due to their portfolio losses in the recent recession) to create a severe medical malpractice insurance problem in 1975. The problem is the great uncertainty concerning the "correct" medical malpractice insurance price. This uncertainty is revealed by the rapidly escalating quoted rates for malpractice insurance and by its unavailability, at a quoted price, for some practitioners.

The Physician. In 1960, 65.7 percent of all physicians belonged to the American Medical Association. By 1970, the figure had fallen to 62.8 percent. This reflects a weakening of the control of the American Medical Association in the delivery of medical services, once a physician is out of medical school. In addition, the AMA's control over the accreditation of medical schools has become less significant than it was in the past. For example, 17.7 percent of the physicians licensed in the U.S. in 1960 were graduates of foreign medical schools. By 1972, this percentage had grown to 46.0.[31] Thus, there are a large number of newly-licensed physicians who are not highly susceptible to being forced into in-group relationships with one another.

Legal Rules and Doctrine. Historically, the legal rules and doctrine had the effect of discouraging or barring medical malpractice claims. Particularly well-known examples of changes in this historical pattern include *res ipsa loquitur,* fraudulent concealment, abolition of charitable immunity, and relaxation of the locality rule.

The application of *res ipsa loquitur*—the thing speaks for itself—to medical malpractice cases was, in some sense, an implied acceptance of Kessel's argument that members of county medical societies protect each other from malpractice claims. Dietz, Baird, and Berul state that courts applied this doctrine because of the judicially perceived "conspiracy of silence which some allege exists on the part of the medical community insofar as expert testimony is involved." [32] Roughly, if the plaintiff can prove that whatever occurred to him would not ordinarily occur in the absence of negligence, that he was under the exclusive control of the defendant doctor or institution, and that the plaintiff did nothing to contribute to the event, then the burden of proof is on the defendant to show that medical malpractice did not occur or that the defendant was not responsible for it. Note that successful application of this doctrine removes the requirement to *prove* negligence did occur as well as requiring the defendant physician to produce expert testimony on his own behalf. This doctrine lessens the requirements on the plaintiff in pursuing a valid or invalid malpractice claim. It also tends to mitigate the medical society's control of expert witnesses. By 1972, this doctrine had been successfully applied and upheld in appellate cases in thirty-four states.[33]

Historically, some states have had special statutes of limitation that apply only to malpractice actions. In the absence of these special statutes, general statutes of limitation were applicable. Application of these rules has been, in general, that the period of limitation commenced when the wrong act was committed. Two modifications of this general rule have extended the period in which a valid medical claim can be brought. The discovery rule modified the commencement date of the statute of limitation to the time when the wrong act was discovered or, with reasonable diligence, should have been discovered. In addition,

---

[31] American Medical Association, *Medical Licensure Statistics, 1960,* and *1972* (Chicago).

[32] Dietz, et al., "Legal System," p. 124.

[33] Ibid., p. 132.

a particular application of fraudulent concealment has extended the statutes of limitations for malpractice cases. In some states, it has been held that the special relationship of trust between the physician and his patient imposes a duty of disclosure upon the physician. Thus, failure to inform a patient of a possible injury may be construed as "fraudulent concealment." By 1972, thirty-six states had used the discovery rule or the doctrine of fraudulent concealment to relax the statute of limitation.[34]

As was indicated earlier, the locality rule established the standard of care as the standard prevailing in the locality or community. In order to prove malpractice, it was necessary for the patient to prove that the physician did not use "that degree of care, skill, diligence used by physicians, generally, in the same locality or community." [35] Strictly applied, the locality rule made control over local physicians through a county medical society an effective barrier to the pursuit of malpractice cases. Recently, the locality rule has been weakened by broadening the definition of locality. For example, the locality for specialists may be the United States. By 1972, the locality rule had been weakened in twenty-two states.[36]

The doctrine of informed consent had been applied in twenty-three states by 1972.[37] It holds that the physician has an affirmative duty to disclose enough information to allow the patient to give his informed consent. Whether the patient inquires as to specific risks or not, the physician is obliged to inform the patient of these risks. This application modifies the historical assumption that the gap in knowledge between physician and patient was so large that the patient could not form an informed opinion.

The majority of hospitals have been operated by government or other non-profit institutions. Until the late 1950s, the doctrines of charitable immunity and governmental immunity effectively protected these hospitals against malpractice claims. By 1972, forty states had rejected the absurd concept of charitable immunity and twenty-seven states had rejected governmental immunity. Removal of immunity has been coupled with the application of *respondeat superior* to hospitals. Under *respondeat superior*, an employer is held liable for the wrongful acts of an employee acting within the scope of his employment, even where the employer's conduct has in practice been without fault. *Respondeat superior* was applied in thirty-three states by 1972.[38]

---

[34] Ibid.
[35] Ibid., p. 124.
[36] Ibid., p. 132.
[37] Ibid., p. 134.
[38] Ibid.

All of these changes in legal rules and doctrine made it easier for a patient to pursue a claim. Many of these changes also had the effect of weakening the controls against malpractice claims that were exercised by social institutions other than the legal system. These changes directly increased the frequency of successful claims. Indirectly, they increased the average value of a successful claim, since all of these changes increased the probability of success once a malpractice claim was tried, thus encouraging the defendant to settle. Further, it seems reasonable to believe that increased frequency of malpractice claims and increased awards would induce others to pursue malpractice claims, since they would perceive a higher probability of success.

Accompanying these changes in the legal system was a marked increase in the number of lawyers. In 1954, there were some 242,000, or 1.5 lawyers for every 1,000 individuals in the United States.[39] This ratio increased to 1.6 in 1960 and 1.7 in 1970. Furthermore, the number of law school graduates increased from 9,240 in 1960 to 21,760 in 1972.[40] This significant increase in the number of lawyers must be associated with increased medical malpractice litigation. The increase in the number of lawyers, the prospect—though risky—of obtaining a fee of some 30 percent of the award, and the changes in legal rules and doctrine, must result in a marked increase in malpractice claims. This should not be construed as a criticism of the contingent fee system. The inequities induced by a contingent fee system are probably more than offset by the increased probability that a valid malpractice claim will be pursued.

The Recession. Investment income on loss reserves was not reflected in the standard rate-making procedures for medical professional liability insurance. However, expected investment income on loss reserves can be substantial and provides an inducement for insurers to write medical insurance. That is, although an insurer might not know whether his premium charges would cover his costs and loss payments, these uncertainties would be offset by the earnings on loss reserves.

These earnings are not inconsequential. With a 5 percent rate of return on investment, investment income on the loss reserves produces an average return of 22.9 percent of earned premiums.[41] If the insurer believes that his actuarial estimates of the "correct" premium are accu-

---

[39] U.S. Department of Commerce, Bureau of the Census, *Statistical Abstract of the United States, 1975* (Washington, D.C., 1976), p. 163.

[40] U.S. National Center for Education Statistics, *Digest of Educational Statistics, 1973* (Washington, D.C., 1974).

[41] These calculations are by the ISO in Senate, Subcommittee on Health of the Committee on Labor and Public Welfare, *Medical Malpractice Insurance*, p. 523.

rate (if he does not, he should fire his actuary) and if he expects a reasonable rate of return on investment, he should have no reluctance to sell malpractice insurance.

At the onset of the 1974–1975 recession and the roughly 30 percent decline in the stock market, insurers had begun to recognize that the rules had changed for medical malpractice insurance. Their participation in the Secretary's Commission on Medical Malpractice reflects this recognition, and the obvious changes in legal rules and doctrine would, at a minimum, make them question their rates. However, before the recession they were willing to continue offering malpractice insurance while rates were increased to the new equilibrium value dictated by the changed environment.

The 1974–1975 recession had to change their expectations as well as their willingness to take the risks associated with the long time lag, or "tail," between medical malpractice claims and payoffs. The recession decreased the average value of insurers' portfolios by roughly one-third. In the absence of any other changes, this alone increased their risk aversion. This increased risk aversion implied that they would be less anxious to offer malpractice insurance. However, the recession was associated with recognition of substantial price inflation continuing over the midterm. Since there was no reason to expect that medical malpractice claims should be more immune to inflation than any other item, this expectation meant that they were required to increase, by some amount, their projections of the cost of an average claim.

The insurer was then faced with the need to adjust his expectations to account for a perceived increase in claim frequency due to changing social institutions and laws, the associated increase in the value and cost of a claim, and inflation. The problem is that the insurer must establish a rate that reflects all these changes and offer malpractice insurance when he is prone to be much more risk averse. In addition, the investment income from loss reserves would be expected to fall with the recession and its effect on expectations of productivity growth. Moreover, since the insurer has ignored the medical malpractice insurance market, he has an inadequate data base on which to form his future expectations.

Medical Malpractice Insurance Rates

In order to isolate the cause of the medical malpractice insurance crisis, it is necessary to determine how the insurer revised his expectations. Determining how any firm or individual forms expectations is difficult at best.[42] Since many components of the process by which an individual firm generates its expectations are unobservable—for example, its level of knowledge and ignorance and its own particular interpretation of recent events—it is difficult to associate changes in the environment with explicit changes in expectations. However, the "correct" price for medical malpractice insurance is determined almost completely by future expected values—the average cost of future claims and the number of claims. Given the long tail on medical malpractice claims (see Table 2) the "correct" price for medical malpractice insurance is primarily dependent upon events expected to occur five or more years after the policy has lapsed.

The uncertainty associated with the development of these expectations is exemplified by the actuarial practices used by the industry. Between 10 and 50 percent of every premium dollar is allocated to selling cost, administrative expenses, fees, and so on. It is easy to question the validity of some of these charges. However, almost all of them are incurred within the year the policy is in effect, and the insurer's problem of estimating these costs is relatively trivial compared to that of developing estimates of future claim costs. The remainder of this discussion will avoid entering into these problems and will consider only the determination of the actuarially fair price for malpractice insurance, where actuarially fair is defined as the present price required to cover the cost of future expected malpractice claims. The long tail on malpractice claims requires that this actuarially fair price take into consideration returns from investment of loss reserves. Similarly, the actuarially fair price should include a risk premium, since neither the probability of a claim's being made nor its expected cost can be independent of the probability on the expected cost of other claims.

The probability that any one individual will file a mapractice claim depends, in part, on whether other individuals file malpractice claims. If an individual hears of a claim—particularly a successful claim—being filed against his doctor, then the probability of that individual's filing a claim may increase, since he would perceive a higher probability of success. Moreover, the expected cost of a claim will not be independent of the cost of every other claim. There are two components to the cost of a claim—the payment to the claimant and the cost associated with

---

[42] Shackle has argued that specification of a well-defined expectations generator is impossible since an individual's expectations are formed, at any one time, upon the basis of his knowledge and lack of knowledge, which are partially unobservable, and as operated on by the unobserved processes of his mind. See G. L. Shackle, *Epistometics in Economics: A Critique of Economic Doctrines* (Cambridge, Massachusetts: Cambridge University Press, 1972).

Table 2
AVERAGE DISTRIBUTION OF INSURANCE PAYMENTS ON SUCCESSFUL MALPRACTICE CLAIMS OVER TEN YEARS

Year	Percentage of Claims Paid (cumulative)
1	3
2	8
3	22
4	43
5	61
6	77
7	84
8	88
9	94
10	98

Source: Kendall and Haldi, "Medical Malpractice Insurance Market," *Report of the Secretary's Commission*, Appendix, p. 523.

defending the claim. For example, a jury determines that a claimant should receive a level of compensation that differs significantly from the levels of compensation awarded or settled historically for similar claims. The new award level tends to redefine the range within which the claimant and insurer will settle.

Furthermore, the cost of defending any one claim is not independent of the cost of defending every other claim. For example, defense costs are affected by legal rules and doctrine as applied to malpractice claims. If these legal rules and doctrine change in their application to any one claim, they change in their application to future claims. Thus, the costs of any one claim are not independent of the cost of other claims, and it cannot be argued that either the strong or weak law of large numbers removes the requirement that the insurer receive a risk premium for insuring against medical malpractice claims. The position of the insurance industry, that investment income should not be included in the determination of the appropriate premium, is in some sense defensible only if insurance commissions do not permit an appropriate risk premium.

The relative scarcity of malpractice insurance data and the reliance on actuarial techniques based on the law of large numbers leave a great deal of uncertainty in any estimate of the correct malpractice insurance rate. The first problem in developing medical malpractice insurance rates is the establishment of a historical data base that is, in some sense, consistent. The adjustment to premium volume is trivial. In order to follow this adjustment, it is first necessary to understand the meaning of a policy year. The policy year ending December 31, 1970, is defined to include all of the policies that expired in the previous twelve months, that is, all the policies—with an assumed one year duration—written between January 1, 1969, and December 31, 1969. Adjusted premium volume for the policy year ending December 31, 1970, is calculated by multiplying the number of insured, by category, by the rates in effect for the 1970 policy year. As a first step, these rates reflect the rate for the coverage within basic limits specified by the policy. For example, basic limits of $25,000 and $75,000 (typically written $25,000/ $75,000) mean that the insurer will pay up to $25,000 on any one claim made against the policy and up to $75,000 on the total number of claims made against the policy. The rates for insurance in excess of basic limits are calculated separately.

Since the calculation of losses is also based upon losses against the basic limits, the remainder of this discussion will concern policies with a basic limit of $25,000/$75,000. At any one point in time for any policy year, the insurer knows the total number of claims paid to date for that policy year and the claim costs for each. He also knows of a number of claims made but not yet paid. He does not know the number of claims that will arise from that particular policy year unless ten or more years have passed. Table 3 summarizes the adjustments necessary for a policy year twenty-seven months after the first day of coverage for that policy year. The values for the three categories displayed in the table are those presented by the Insurance Services Office for Massachusetts for the policy year ended December 31, 1973.[43] For example, as of March 31, 1974, the insurer estimates the average claims made but not yet paid against the policy year at $191 per insured or nearly five times the value of claims made against that policy year and paid. There is no standard formula for estimating the eventual cost of claims made but not paid. Generally, these estimates are made individually for each claim based upon the insurer's assessment of its validity and strength and the associated defense costs.

In Massachusetts the average claims cost for a year is estimated at $698 per insured. However, claims made and paid and claims made and not paid account for only $231 per insured or only one-third of the estimated claims cost for the policy year. The major component of the

[43] Senate, Subcommittee on Labor and Public Welfare, *Medical Malpractice Insurance*, pp. 555, 605.

Table 3
EXPECTED LOSSES FOR THE POLICY YEAR ENDING DECEMBER 31, 1973, 27 MONTHS AFTER ITS CLOSE
(in dollars)

Category	Cost (average per insured)
Claims made and paid	40
Claims made, but not paid	191
Claims to be made	467
Total claims cost	698

Source: *Continuing Medical Malpractice Insurance Crisis*, pp. 555, 605.

claims cost is the cost of claims to be made—the claims the insurer has not yet seen. For the policy year ending December 31, 1973, ISO estimated the cost of these claims as a multiple (2.019) of the sum of claims made and paid and claims made but not yet paid. The multiple is termed a loss development factor.

The loss development factors actually used by ISO over the last ten years are given in Table 4. Estimates of these loss development factors are based on an analysis of the development of losses for the policy years since 1960. This multiple is intended to capture the value of claims to be made against the policy year 1973 and reflects the expectation that future claims will cost more because of general inflation as well as other factors. It also reflects an increasing claims frequency. For example, an individual who is a victim of malpractice in 1970 and discovers this fact in 1970 is less likely to lodge a claim against a physician than if he discovers the injury in 1975. Although application of the discovery rule implies that the claim is not voided by the statute of limitation, changing legal rules and doctrine coupled with increasing claim frequency between 1970 and 1975 would imply that any individual who discovered a 1970 act of malpractice in 1975 would be more likely to file a malpractice claim than if he had discovered the act in 1970. The loss development factor also reflects the expectation that our hypothetical individual would receive a larger settlement if he filed in 1975 than in 1970. Inflation as well as the perceived willingness of juries to offer higher settlements would imply a higher claim value. In addition, the loss development factor captures the fact that larger claims generally take longer to settle or adjudicate.

Once these adjustments are made, the insurer presumably has a consistent set of premium and loss data for all previous policy years.

Table 4
PHYSICIANS' AND SURGEONS' BASIC LIMITS LOSS DEVELOPMENT FACTORS, 1966–1975

Loss Development From	1966[a]	1967[a]	1968[a]	1969[a]	1970[a]	1971	1972	1973	1974	1975
75 to 123 Months	1.000	1.000	1.000	1.000	1.000	1.039	1.066	1.091	1.093	1.086
63 to 123 Months	1.024	.997	1.014	1.032	1.050	1.098	1.135	1.159	1.133	1.124
51 to 123 Months	1.040	.966	1.054	1.109	1.138	1.197	1.249	1.307	1.270	1.248
39 to 123 Months	1.188	1.107	1.222	1.320	1.420	1.488	1.536	1.758	1.692	1.633
27 to 123 Months	1.747	1.556	1.721	1.927	2.106	2.408	2.251	3.236	3.112	3.019

Note: 1966-1971 factors based on $5,000/$15,000 basic limits experience. 1972 factors based on total limits experience. 1973-1975 factors based on $25,000/$75,000 basic limits experience.

[a] Losses developed to 75 months from 1966-1970.

Source: U.S. Congress, Senate, Subcommittee on Health of the Committee on Labor and Public Welfare, *Medical Malpractice Insurance*, p. 606.

The results of these adjustments for the average number of claims per 100 insured physicians are given in Table 5. Given that the data for the later years are primarily determined by the loss development factors and that those for the earlier years reflect a significantly different environment, the reliability of the series for determining future expectations is not particularly high.

Two other factors are estimated in order to derive the correct set of rates for basic limits malpractice insurance. One factor is an estimate that is supposed to reflect the increasing claims frequency per 100 insured exhibited in Table 5. To do this, ISO fits an exponential curve to the observed claims frequency data. Using this exponential curve, ISO estimates the growth rate in claims frequency per 100 insured at 12.7 percent per policy year. In other words, there will be 12.7 percent more claims per 100 insured for policy year 1976 than for policy year 1975.

A second trend factor is estimated to reflect the increasing average award per claim. An exponential curve fitted to the data in Table 6 implies that the average cost of a claim paid is growing at an annual rate of 10.2 percent. In other words, the average cost of a claim paid in 1976 is 10.2 percent higher than the average cost of a claim paid in 1975.

These factors and the data for the policy years ending December 31, 1972 and December 31, 1973 were used to determine the rates for the policy year ending December 31, 1976—the policies first written in the crisis year 1975. Note that the policy year data for 1972 and 1973 were the latest available for the 1976 policy year. In order to estimate the average claim cost per insured for the 1976 policy year, ISO inflated the average claim cost per insured from the 1973 policy year by the two trend factors.[44] The resulting estimate of expected claim loss per insured was then divided by the average premium to get an average multiple that was applied to all existing malpractice insurance rates. In practice, the ratios for the two most recently available policy years, 1972 and 1973, were weighted by 30 percent and 70 percent, respectively.

What is interesting about these trend and inflation factors is that for Massachusetts—with per insured averages of $40 in claims made and paid and $191 in claims made but not paid for the 1973 policy year—a $1,333 loss per insured is implied for policy year 1976.[45] Needless to

---

[44] The value of this inflation factor for 1973 is 1.910. For policy year 1972, the factor is 2.379.

[45] Although the example is for Massachusetts, the inflation factors are the same for each state since ISO estimates them from national data.

Table 5

ANNUAL CLAIM FREQUENCY FOR PHYSICIANS' AND SURGEONS' PROFESSIONAL LIABILITY INSURANCE

Policy Year Ending	Number of Insured Doctors	Number of Incurred Claims[a]	Claim Frequency[b]
12/31/66	87,131	1,517	1.741
12/31/67	92,657	1,784	1.925
12/31/68	101,716	1,866	1.835
12/31/69	97,425	2,051	2.105
12/31/70	106,412	2,261	2.125
12/31/71	104,126	2,571	2.469
12/31/72	105,993	3,423	3.229
12/31/73	104,609	4,340	4.149

[a] Developed to 123 months of maturity.
[b] Per 100 doctors (column 2 divided by column 1).
Source: *Continuing Medical Malpractice Insurance Crisis*, p. 568.

Table 6

NUMBER AND COST OF CLAIMS PAID ON BASIC LIMITS COVERAGE, UNITED STATES, 1969–1973

Year Ended	Paid Losses with $25,000 Basic Limits[a] (total)	Paid Claims (number)	Cost of Paid Claim (average)
6/30/69	$21,911,932	6,444	$3,400
12/31/69	24,009,583	6,606	3,635
6/30/70	26,132,901	6,780	3,854
12/31/70	29,271,828	7,067	4,142
6/30/71	31,650,272	7,537	4,199
12/31/71	32,746,397	7,354	4,453
6/30/72	34,684,486	7,367	4,708
12/31/72	38,736,177	8,135	4,762
6/30/73	47,526,239	9,321	5,099
12/31/73	54,882,269	10,151	5,407

[a] Excluding all loss adjustment expense.
Source: *Continuing Medical Malpractice Insurance Crisis*, p. 567.

say, if the trend factors or the loss development factors are significantly misstated, the resulting medical malpractice insurance rates will not be near the correct level. In addition, the previous arguments imply that these various factors are not independent. If any one of these factors happens to be incorrect, all of the other factors would tend to be incorrect and in the same direction.

For example, the discovery rule has lengthened the tail on medical malpractice insurance claims. This implies that there is a longer period in which a valid medical malpractice insurance claim may be brought. Thus, imposing the discovery rule would tend to increase the loss development factors. It would also tend to increase claim frequency per doctor. In addition, since the defense of older malpractice insurance claims is more difficult, it would tend to increase average claim cost.

The present techniques for estimating malpractice insurance rates are subject to a host of criticisms. First, the lack of interest by the insurance industry before 1970 means that there is not a large volume of data relating to medical malpractice insurance. Second, the procedures for estimating loss development factors are obscured. Third, the claim frequency trend factor is estimated on data that are estimates subject to dispute. Fourth, the trend factor for average cost per claim may include only an indirect allowance for the fact that a basic limits policy requires a claim not exceeding $25,000. The validity of estimating the trend factor, with no upper bound, on data based on basic limits policies is suspect.

Alternatives to Solving the Medical Malpractice Insurance Crisis

The natural predilection of anyone who believes in the efficiency of the free market is to seek the reasons for "nonavailability" of medical malpractice insurance in artificial constraints on the market. However, insurers' response to uncertainty may have created a "pure availability" problem, even if there were no artificial constraints on the market.

Recognition that the appearance of malpractice claims depends upon a variety of factors implies that a risk-averting insurer would not offer malpractice insurance at an actuarially fair price. This natural reluctance, coupled with the one-third decrease in the value of their portfolios experienced in 1975, would imply that some insurers would withdraw from the malpractice insurance market simply because they were uncertain about the magnitude of the risk involved and their level of risk aversion was heightened by the decrease in their net worth. Thus, one of the availability problems will be alleviated by a recovery of stock market prices.

189

There are other availability-related problems that reflect imperfections in the market. The time required by state insurance regulators and their hesitancy in accepting 80 to 500 percent increases in malpractice insurance rates induced insurers to threaten to withdraw, or actually to withdraw, from the malpractice insurance market. For example, in 1972, researchers warned that the monopoly-monopsony arrangement in group-sponsored practitioner malpractice insurance plans could very well generate short-term problems in availability, since no other insurer would have sufficient experience in that state to formulate rates quickly.[46] This problem seems to have contributed to the claims of unavailability that occurred in Maryland, New York, and Northern California. The doctors' strikes can be interpreted as efforts by medical societies to maintain the power they obtained through their monopsony arrangement in the purchase of malpractice insurance.

Since the delivery of medical care has historically been regulated—for better or worse—by the states and their agencies and since the states have also attempted to regulate insurance rates, it is not surprising that there has been a proliferation of proposed state legislation to attack the medical malpractice problem. These approaches have included peer review, special statute of limitation laws, attorney fee regulation, liability limits, creation of standby insurance pools, and mandatory and voluntary arbitration.[47] It is far beyond the scope of this paper to discuss separately each of these various proposals.

Some of the proposals would alter the regulatory structure for physicians. Physicians have long claimed that they are the ones who should regulate the quality of medical care. Their record—twelve license suspensions in 1972 [48]—is indefensible. It is not obvious that delivery of medical services should be regulated. But if society decides that regulation is desirable, states should not abdicate their responsibility to physician groups.

Another line of legislative attack has been special modifications to legal rules and doctrine as applied to medical malpractice claims. Both physician groups and insurers support this type of legislation for obvious reasons. The effect of these proposals would be to make the trial of medical malpractice insurance claims a special case. It can be plausibly argued that legal rules and doctrine governing the adjudication of liability claims are not appropriate, either economically or morally. How-

[46] Kendall and Haldi, "Medical Malpractice Insurance," p. 530.

[47] A summary of recent legislation related to medical malpractice appears in Senate, Subcommittee on Labor and Public Welfare, *Medical Malpractice Insurance*, pp. 236-45.

[48] Senate, Subcommittee on Labor and Public Welfare, *Medical Malpractice Insurance*, p. 132.

ever, making a special case for a particular profession is, at best, repugnant. There is no overwhelming reason for exempting physicians from large portions of our liability laws. The problems of malpractice insurance claims are no more or less overwhelming than the problems of product liability, for example. That the American Medical Association can honestly claim that it should be excluded from chunks of our liability laws is particularly strong support for Kessel's description of the market for medical services. The primary problem with almost all of the suggested reforms is that they do not focus upon the victims of malpractice or upon disabling medical accidents, which should be the focus of any "reform." [49]

One federal legislative remedy is Senate Bill 188. This bill would establish a federal reinsurance mechanism for medical malpractice insurance. The crisis in the medical malpractice insurance market was primarily the result of the weakening of the social institutions governing the delivery of medical care coupled with changes in the legal rules and doctrine as applied to malpractice claims. It does seem unfair to force individual physicians and individual insurers to bear the burden of these changes. As a short-term solution, federal reinsurance makes sense. By offering a comprehensive reinsurance mechanism, the government could reduce the necessity for insurers to charge a risk premium for selling malpractice policies. The federal government would also be in a position to amass significant amounts of data, permitting more accurate determination of the appropriate price for malpractice insurance.

The problems with this proposal lie in its long-term implications. Relieving the physician of the burden of increased malpractice insurance rates can only decrease his sense of urgency concerning the level and frequency of medical malpractice. Moreover, past history indicates that the federal government's involvement would probably result in some arbitrary limitation on the highest price paid for malpractice insurance. At present, the only effective cost imposed upon a physician for committing malpractice is an increase in his medical malpractice insurance rates. Physician groups refuse to regulate their members; state-designated regulatory agencies refuse to police their licensees. Apart from increased premiums, the only present weapon available against medical malpractice is a refusal by insurers to underwrite a physician.

The effect on patient incentives would also be perverse. Most or all of the malpractice premium increase is shifted to the patient in

---

[49] Marc A. Franklin, "Replacing the Negligence Lottery," *Virginia Law Review,* vol. 53 (1967) pp. 795-814. Franklin suggests that the primary focus for articulating alternative reparations systems should be the victims of disabling accidents.

higher medical bills [50] and health insurance rates. If this burden is relieved, patients may be less prone to question the quality of their medical services. They may also be less prone to question the equity and morality of our liability laws. There is good reason to question both.

In summary, problems do exist in the medical malpractice insurance market. Any insurer faces the need to develop an estimate of the correct rates for medical malpractice insurance based upon a dearth of historical data and to formulate these expectations in a changing environment. However, medical malpractice insurance rate changes have been caused by the changing environment in delivery of medical services and in the adjudication of liability suits. Actuarial and statistical techniques are simply insufficient to determine, at this time, the correct price for medical malpractice insurance. Moreover, the remedies offered for curing the medical malpractice insurance crisis are improper. There is no proof that the present level and frequency of claims and the legal rules and doctrine governing their adjudication are more or less socially desirable than the previous state of affairs.

Once questions concerning the form and functions of social institutions governing the delivery of medical care are resolved, and once the legal rules and doctrine governing the adjudication of medical malpractice claims are stabilized, it will be possible to determine the correct price for malpractice insurance. Until then, the uncertainties associated with the appropriate price for medical malpractice insurance will simply have to be tolerated.

---

[50] Bruce C. N. Greenwald, Marnie N. Mueller, and Alan Marcus, "Medical Malpractice and the Cost of Doctors' Services," unpublished paper, Wesleyan University, August 1976, pp. 25-26.

MEDICAL MALPRACTICE AND THE PROPENSITY TO LITIGATE

Jerry R. Green

Introduction

The right of patients to sue their physicians for negligence has several complex implications. On one level, it provides a way for a victim of injury to be compensated, just as automobile accident liability does. At the same time, it acts as an indirect system of control on physicians, obliging them to take precautions to avoid adverse legal findings. The difficulty of adequately monitoring the quality of medical care requires that some indirect methods of this type be employed to increase the incentives for better services.

However, the rapid increase in the number of cases and the increasingly large awards being granted have given rise to concern about the reliability and practicality of the present malpractice system. The real cost of administering the necessary system of checks and balances is enormous. The burden of malpractice payments falls only partially on the physician. It may be passed on to the public through the mechanism of increased premiums for malpractice insurance, rising fees for medical and surgical services and finally, higher medical insurance premiums. To be sure, some of the costs of incentives for better care rest with the physician even if he is insured for malpractice. The widespread concern about defensive, as opposed to best-practice, medicine is sufficient evidence that physicians feel the impact of these imposed risks in a real way. If the potential burden of malpractice suits does not induce a significant increase in the quality of care, the extra expenses incurred in litigation will have been wasted. But if medical care for everyone can be improved by the advocacy system, then the net benefit to society may far exceed the higher costs that this system entails.

In this paper, I will focus on the desirability of using an adversary system of justice as an indirect way of exerting influence on the quality of medical care. Special attention will be paid to the costs of the legal system itself. Its efficiency depends upon the frequency with which litigation is undertaken, as well as on the care level it can produce. I will contrast this system with a peer review procedure. It will be argued that the latter has advantages over litigation in that it is a more flexible policy. Under peer review, the standards for nonnegligent care can be raised without inducing a rise in the cost of administering the process. On the other hand, peer review, or investigation by any third party, has two adverse effects. It dulls the incentives for exceeding any fixed negligence standard, and it results in a somewhat lower accuracy in the selection of cases for investigation. I will try to delineate the circumstances under which one or the other system will appear more favorable on balance.

Throughout the analysis I will neglect the function of malpractice as a provider of a type of insurance for the patient. Presumably this kind of insurance could be arranged by other means. Coverage for adverse physical and economic outcomes need not be linked to the cause of the event.[1] It is, therefore, not impossible to arrange for such insurance in other ways, and it may even be preferable to do so. At any rate, this paper will concentrate entirely on the other role of malpractice claims, that is, as a regulator of care.

There is one salient difference between litigation for medical malpractice and other forms of accident liability. It is this: the complexity of modern medicine, and its inaccessibility to the layman, prevent a patient whose outcome has been worse than expected from knowing whether his unfortunate circumstance is the result of malpractice or whether it is a chance event not under the control of his physician. In automobile cases, quite the opposite is true. The transparency of the matter usually leaves little doubt whether an accident in fact occurred. Placing the fault, however, may be a highly contested issue, not easily resolvable by the parties at the time of the incident.

The implication of this rather simple observation is that while virtually all serious automobile liability cases are contested and ultimately settled, it is quite likely that some equally serious incidents of malpractice will escape the system, disguised as bad luck. More specifically, the decision to undertake a malpractice suit on the part of the patient and his attorney will be influenced by their perceptions of the probability of winning the case. This has a very strong bearing on the efficiency of the current malpractice system. Suppose courts increase the care standard used for negligence, making doctors responsible for damages in some situations in which they would previously have escaped liability. There is a large body of evidence indicating that this has

---

[1] This is forcefully argued in Steven Shavell's paper "Theoretical Issues in Medical Malpractice" in this volume.

occurred during the last ten years.[2] Such a change would increase the propensity to undertake litigation. The risks faced by physicians are thus increased in two ways: stricter standards for care will be applied, and physicians are more likely to be sued than previously. A similar shift in the automobile fault standards would not induce an increase in the litigation rate; instead, only the direct effect of higher standards would be operative.

There is also some indirect evidence that the decision to undertake litigation is endogenous—that is, it will vary with changes in the other aspects of the system. If the propensity to litigate were not endogenous, the higher standards applied would lead to a higher proportion of successful suits than previously. In fact, exactly the opposite has been the case. Over half the malpractice actions initiated now result in no award. This is a substantially higher proportion than in recent years.[3] Although, as I shall argue, the increase in this zero-award rate is not a necessary consequence of higher standards for negligence, it is consistent with the hypotheses I assume, and it would be incompatible if one were to use a more standard framework for studying this type of liability.

In the following sections I will attempt to describe how the optimal negligence standard should be set under the present system and to contrast this with the workings of an optimal negligence rule for accidents in which the propensity to litigate is not endogenous. Let me preface this by analyzing the simpler case in which the occurrence of an accident can be immediately recognized by the party who bears the direct costs. In such circumstances, the optimal rule for negligence is simply to hold the injurer liable in all such circumstances, regardless of the precautions he may be able to prove had been taken. Operating in this way is simple—litigation is reduced to the question of whether an accident did or did not occur—and with the full incentives on potential injurers, they will choose their care level so as to minimize the sum of the expected cost of accidents and the cost of care, which is precisely the social objective.

---

[2] Some of this is documented by Richard Epstein's paper "Medical Malpractice: Its Cause and Cure" in this volume.

[3] Data from the American Insurance Association's Special Malpractice Review: 1974 Closed Claim Survey indicate that somewhat under 50 percent of claims closed in that year received no award. Comparable data in U.S. Department of Health, Education, and Welfare, *Report of the Secretary's Commission on Medical Malpractice* (Washington, D.C., 1973), Appendix, indicates a 40 percent zero-award rate in the 1965-1971 period. A precise comparison cannot be made because of differences in the inclusion of claims against hospitals and testing laboratories.

Such a method would clearly not work in the medical context.[4] If physicians had to compensate all patients whose outcomes were unfortunate, the entire health care delivery system would break down. Therefore, a real standard for measuring care taken must be instituted. It must be set so as to make litigation sufficiently likely that physicians have real incentives to take care, but it must also reflect the real costs of the induced litigation imposed on both defendants and plaintiffs.

Complexities of the Medical Setting for Adversary Proceedings

There are many other differences between ordinary accident law as an incentive system and the malpractice situation. These differences, though they will not be discussed directly here, complicate the malpractice problem. One of the most interesting features of medical injuries is the extraordinarily long lag between the actual incident and the date at which injury is perceived and litigation ensues. The American Insurance Association's recent closed claim survey reveals that although 91 percent of medical cases involved a lag of less than one month from incident to perception of injury, over 60 percent had a lag of over six months until the date they were reported. Weighting claims by the dollar value of the resulting settlement, over 70 percent of medical litigation had a report lag of over six months, indicating that the more serious cases may involve a longer lag than the average. The delay in bringing suit has implications for the nature and accuracy of evidence that can be gathered and brought to bear on such cases. By the time legal action is initiated, the opportunity may have been missed to perform some of the medical tests or observations which could have indicated whether prior negligence played a role in creating the patient's condition. Further, the extent of the injury suffered might be greatly magnified by the delay.

A second difference is related to the multifaceted nature of medical care. The least-cost method of reducing the probability of an adverse medical outcome might not be readily observable to the court. An

---

[4] There are two special points that should be made in this connection. The first is that if the standard or benchmark is too unfavorable to physicians, they will respond simply by refusing to take on the riskier patients and cases presented to them. Since it would be virtually inconceivable to avoid this problem while maintaining an adversary malpractice system, the benchmark necessarily is set so that malpractice, defined as a shortfall from the standard, is a rare event. In this way the problem of a patient-selection bias is largely circumvented for most specialties.

Second, the benchmark is actually arbitrary, but its level will affect the identity of the plaintiff in an adversary proceeding. Differential treatment of plaintiffs and defendants will then have an impact on the choice of the benchmark.

example would be the time taken during a physical examination and the thoroughness with which it was performed. The attributes of care readily observable in court typically would be those procedures for which records are kept: tests ordered, X-rays, frequency of reexamination, length of hospital stay. Focusing on these aspects of care when others that would be more efficient are bypassed is defensive medicine. The problem of defensive medicine is a serious one, but, unfortunately, one which cannot be dealt with except by redirecting the attention of our courts or monitoring agencies. It obviously would be working at cross-purposes to improve the incentive structure for physicians to take precautions that we do not really want to encourage. Throughout this paper, I will be speaking of care as an entity that can be measured at least in a rough way. By care we shall mean simply whatever mixture of activities for accident reduction is encouraged by the system. If these activities are not the most appropriate for this purpose, costs considered, a restructuring of the measured attributes of care is called for. To the extent that this is impossible, the resulting inefficiencies are a reflection of the costs of imperfect information—which are real economic costs to be reckoned with.

Finally, and most to the point, the highly technical nature of medicine makes the litigation process very costly—in fact, more so relative to claims and insurance coverage than litigation in other areas of tort law. Using data from the American Insurance Association's recent closed claims survey, I have calculated that over one-fifth of the dollar settlements made were payments of plaintiffs' legal fees. This omits the legal fees paid in losing cases and all of the direct legal costs of the insurance carriers themselves. To include these costs would probably bring court costs to around one-half of the settlement costs. These must be regarded as real economic costs to the system. The analysis below will discuss the ways in which these costs affect the propensity to undertake litigation and, through this, the overall structure and performance of the medical system.

A Model of the Effects of the Endogenous Propensity to Sue on the Efficiency of Malpractice Litigation

If we accept these stylized facts as an accurate reflection of the structure underlying medical malpractice, the following describes the workings of the system of litigation in detail. In particular, we will try to analyze the ways in which the policies implicitly followed by the courts shape the behavior and performance of the medical sector.

197

The most important aspect of the system, and the characteristic that distinguishes it from the application of liability rules in other areas, is the way in which information becomes known and its accuracy as a representation of the true circumstances concerning the accident is determined. Unlike other accident problems, the long lags surrounding medical claims often preclude knowing whether malpractice was really involved.

It is natural to presume that whatever the inaccuracies of the final determination may be, the grounds on which the legal action is initiated are even less precise. We shall view the patient's ex ante estimate of the extent of care taken by the physician as a random variable which is positively correlated with the court's ex post estimate. Because of the difficulty of assessing the strength of the evidence that could be brought to bear by the defense, and because of the highly variable time to settlement, the plaintiff and his lawyer have to make the decision to press suit on the basis of the limited information available to them.

Although in actuality information on a case continually accrues through the process of litigation, and in principle the litigation can be terminated by the plaintiff at any date if the evidence starts to accumulate adversely, it will be simpler if we view the process in two discrete stages. First, the patient establishes a cutoff ex ante perceived care standard below which he will undertake the suit and pay the costs of litigation. Second, the outcome is determined by the court on the basis of the observations available at the end of the litigation. The court sets a cutoff level such that if the ex post indications are below this, the case is decided in the plaintiff's favor.

It may be, of course, because of the large amount of random variation inherent in the system, that some cases which could have been pressed successfully will not be tried because the ex ante indications were too unfavorable. Many cases may be tried unsuccessfully. But the vast majority of cases are probably ones where there is little or no a priori indication of malpractice and which, if tried, would uncover none because the level of care given was, in fact, entirely satisfactory.

The court system, in executing this role as a regulator of care provided, causes substantial resource costs to be incurred in the process. Some of these are the direct costs of legal fees. Assuming that there are many lawyers whose services can substitute quite closely for each other's, we would not make a great error if we identified the social costs of malpractice lawyers' time with the private costs borne by plaintiffs and defendants or their insurance companies. In addition, the vast number of cases litigated crowds court calendars and induces massive bottlenecks for other types of cases as well. In 1974, the average length of time from the reporting of a malpractice claim to its closing was over one year.[5] Even if only part of this interval represents the actual settlement process (part of it is the waiting period due to claims previously filed), the costs of delay would be a significant portion of total litigation costs. These time costs are difficult to measure, but they are likely to be very heavy. Consider the fact that every new case brought to trial delays every case whose position in the queue is later by the full amount of the time taken to settle it. Since the queues are very long, a short trial period will still impose costs on many others, so that its total social costs will be very large.

I will ignore the time costs because of the difficulty of measuring them even approximately. Moreover, until the current malpractice crisis results in a change in procedures and a return to normality, the court system will not be able to assess the demands that will be made on it and adjust its capacity to meet the flow of cases without imposing such delays. In the long run, the real costs of excessive and frequent litigation of malpractice claims is the required expansion of the judicial system.

How will the two principal groups of decision making individuals, potential plaintiffs and defendants, react to the system in which they are embedded? The usual economist's view, probably a correct one in this case, is that they will each decide in their own best interest using the available information, under the assumption that the behavior patterns of the opposition will remain unaffected.

The individual patient will undertake a suit if the expected gain from this action exceeds his expected costs of litigation. The patient's calculations of these two critical parameters depend on the information available to him relevant to his case, on his perception of the general level of medical care being offered, and on the extent to which his legal costs depend on the settlement. The impact of the contingent fee system is most strongly felt in this last area. But the relationship between the legal fee and the settlement received is important only if considerations of risks weigh more heavily in the decision to sue than normal returns. If expected net return is the relevant decision variable, it is the expected costs of litigation that enter into the individual's calculations, not realized fees and awards.

The physician is assumed to know how his care level would affect the probability of losing a suit. He chooses a care level that maximizes the difference between the profitability that is associated with it, in the absence of malpractice claims, and the expected costs of losing malprac-

---

[5] Data from the American Insurance Association survey cited above imply an average time from filing to closing of 12.2 months on all claims closed with positive awards in 1974; weighted by the dollar value of settlements, this lag is 14.7 months.

tice litigation. These costs are compounded from two factors: the probability of being sued, and the probability of losing a suit given that it has been initiated.

Putting these patterns of behavior together, we can see that the standard set by the court gives rise to both a prevailing level of care taken by physicians and a propensity to sue by patients, with the property that each is an optimal pattern of behavior given the actions of the other. By varying the negligence standard these actions will be shifted. Our problem is to evaluate how they will respond and thus to characterize and evaluate the optimal standard for this type of liability system. Finally, we will compare it with other possible systems.

The care level of physicians is of direct and central importance to the issue at hand. Ideally, as mentioned above, we would seek a balance between the costs and benefits of additional care. The problem is that attaining such an optimum is precluded by the costs of litigation. In order to evaluate the litigation costs it is necessary to relate the ex ante cutoff level used by patients to the actual care level, the probability of litigation going up with the latter and down with the former.

In our search for the optimal negligence standard, we note, therefore, that as long as higher standards can induce higher care levels and lower cutoff values, they will be superior. Trade-offs will come when, in order to induce higher care levels, progressively higher negligence standards must be used, and the latter increase so rapidly that the propensity to litigate increases.

Choosing the Best Care Standard

We begin the analysis of the negligence standard by looking at the way in which each of the two types of individuals will respond to an upward shift in its level. The patients respond by choosing a higher cutoff level for ex ante indications of malpractice at each underlying level of care. The reason for this is clear. If it becomes easier to win malpractice cases, it is profitable to press some suits which previously would not have been worthwhile. Similarly, if the physician is facing a higher probability of loss given that the suit is undertaken, he will endeavor to protect himself against this. He does so by taking more care. This actually has two effects when the cutoff level for filing claims is viewed as fixed. It lowers both the likelihood of being sued and the likelihood of losing a case once legal action has been undertaken.

In order to trace the effects of these responses on the equilibrium of this system, it is necessary to know how the actions of each group depend on the other, given a fixed negligence standard. More care by physicians will lower the cutoff level for filing suits. The suits previously

JERRY R. GREEN

iled will be less successful, on average, when the care level has increased, and therefore those in the marginal category will not be pressed.

A higher ex ante cutoff by patients will lead to more care by physicians. They are at greater risk of being sued and, since some of the
cases added will involve adverse decisions for them, (even though they
will have a lower success rate than all those currently being tried), the
total level of successful suits will increase.

Thus the situation can be depicted by the diagram in Figure 1.

The upward-sloping curves (*a* and *a'*) represent the care level chosen
in response to each cutoff level for suits to be filed at two different
levels for the negligence standard. In accordance with the discussion
above, the line farther to the right (*a'*) corresponds to the higher negligence standard: a larger probability of loss giving rise to more care
taken for each ex ante cutoff level for suits to be initiated. The down-
ward-sloping lines (*b* and *b'*) describe the reactions of the patients to
increasing care levels. The higher curve (*b'*) is associated with the higher
negligence standard because if it is easier to win a suit, cases that are
increasingly less clear-cut on an ex ante basis will be pressed.

It is clear from this analysis that an increase in the negligence

Figure 1

DETERMINATION OF EQUILIBRIUM FOR EACH
NEGLIGENCE STANDARD

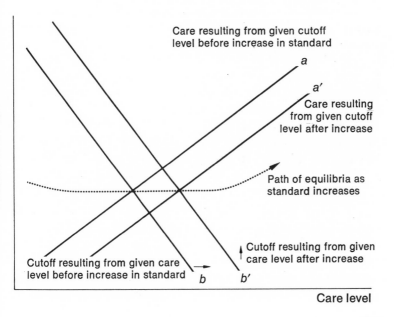

201

standard will raise the level of care taken and that the effect on the cutoff level of ex ante indications for a suit to be pressed could go either way. The reason for this ambiguity is clear. A higher care standard induces more suits because it makes it more profitable to sue at the margin. But on the other hand, the induced increase in care makes suing less likely to be profitable, on the average, because the conditional distribution of ex post evidence will have improved for every ex ante indication that might have been realized. Without knowing how much extra care will be taken in response to an increase in the standard, it is impossible to predict which of these effects will predominate.

What is the effect of these shifts on the efficiency of the system as a whole? The care level is a central focus of this analysis, but the cutoff level for suits is only indirectly relevant. What really matters is the frequency with which litigation is undertaken. Broadly speaking it is this that determines the level of resources expended in the legal process through which medical practice is, at least partially, regulated

This frequency is itself dependent on the care level and the cutoff for suits. If the cutoff level for suits is rising when care is rising, the resulting change in frequency will be in doubt. If the cutoff level is falling while care is rising, then the frequency of suits will be decreasing as the negligence standard is rising.

Although either case is possible, in principle, the recent evidence would surely indicate that we currently are in a regime of rising negligence standards and propensity to undertake suits. This means, necessarily, that cutoff standards have been rising as well—the public a consumers of medical services have become more litigation-minded, in the words of the Secretary's Commission on Medical Malpractice.

If we graph the path of the relevant objectives—frequency of suit and care taken—as the negligence standard increases, we are likely to see a pattern similar to that in Figure 2.

How well can this system do in attaining a socially superior situation even when the optimal negligence standard is being used? It is clear that the overall optimum is not attainable. The incentives of all parties involved preclude it. It would be to set the care level so as to balance the costs and benefits of increased care and to avoid all litigation. The best attainable situation is illustrated in the diagram above It involves some litigation and a somewhat lower level of care than the optimum. Note that in order to attain it, we must be in a situation in which higher negligence standards are associated with higher litigation frequencies and hence with increasingly less severe requirements for the ex ante indications required for patients to undertake legal action.

Figure 2
DETERMINATION OF THE OPTIMAL NEGLIGENCE STANDARD

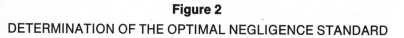
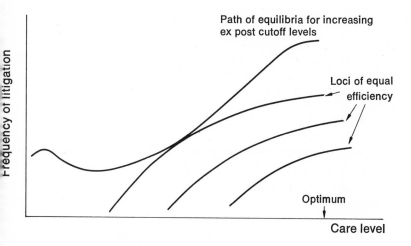

Alternatives to the Negligence Standard System

The method outlined above, which describes our current practice in its broadest outlines, is not capable of attaining an optimal situation. Resources will have to be used up in the litigation process. We may therefore justifiably inquire whether there are other systems through which control over the care of physicians may be exercised, without adversely impinging upon the practice of medicine.

Under one such system, review of a certain proportion of cases would be undertaken by a medical review board, or a governmental health care monitoring agency, rather than relying on the patient's own perceptions of his care to determine whether or not a review should be undertaken. Such a board might function in the same way as a court, exacting penalty fees from negligent physicians as a way of establishing the appropriate incentives for better medical care. Whether these fees would be rebated directly to the injured party or used to subsidize health insurance schemes in general is irrelevant to the matter at hand, since no one's actions would be affected by the use of the funds collected. The dual roles of litigation as a form of insurance and as an instrument of regulation would have to be treated separately, but this facet of the problem is outside the scope of the present study.

There is one clear advantage to such a system and one clear disadvantage, in comparison with the litigation system. It is superior in that the proportion of cases investigated may be selected independently from the negligence standard employed, rather than being set endogenously as a result of interactions between the two sides. But the system loses efficiency to the extent that it cannot hope to be as selective in its undertaking of investigations as the negligence litigation method can be. The information in the hands of the patient, his family, and his attorney is much more accurate and detailed than that available to an outside agency. Unless patients have an incentive to put their own cases under review, this information is not likely to be transmitted in sufficient depth. If cases are not undertaken selectively, the administering agency is forced to investigate a much higher proportion of them in order to find the same number below the negligence standard. To keep the analysis simple, we presume that the administering agency's information does not help it select the cases in which a negligence finding is at all more likely.

Let us consider how the care level of physicians would respond to the rate of investigation, holding the negligence standard fixed. The physicians would choose care to minimize both the direct costs of taking care and expected losses due to adverse investigation findings. Additional care is beneficial in avoiding the latter only insofar as it reduces the frequency with which the ex post observed value falls short of the standard. It does not decrease the probability that a given case is examined more closely, as it would under a negligence system. Therefore, for a given negligence standard, if the rate of investigation is set at the same level as would be induced by patients bringing suits under the litigation system, the corresponding level of care would be lower. However, the extra flexibility of the review method allows it to have higher rates of investigation at a fixed negligence standard, or alternatively, higher negligence standards without incurring more costs of investigations. For each frequency of investigation, it is therefore natural to ask what the optimal, or care-maximizing, negligence standard is under this system. The answer depends, in general, on the nature of the statistical dependence between the care taken and the result of the investigation. In qualitative terms, the negligence standard will have its strongest impact if it is set at the level where the results of investigations most commonly occur. In this way, the effort to avoid adverse findings by raising the care level taken will be strongest. If the correlation between the investigations' findings and the care taken is strong, the care level can be made quite high by raising the standard for negligence while keeping the frequency of investigation quite low. In these cases, a sufficiently high standard could induce more care than the negligence rule with a comparable rate of litigation. When the relationship between care and the

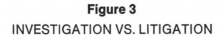

Figure 3

INVESTIGATION VS. LITIGATION

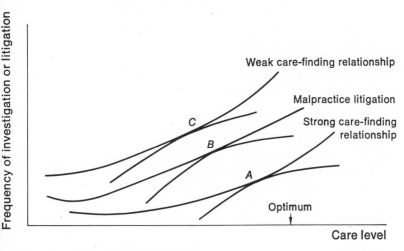

Note: *A, B,* and *C* are conditional optima.

findings is weaker, the potential gain to the physician from an increased care level is much lower since he will have little chance of affecting the result of the investigations by taking more care. Here the added impetus to avoid litigation would be an important factor in sustaining care levels above those which could be attained through investigations initiated on a random basis.

Conclusions

I have tried to present a model of medical malpractice litigation that is consistent with the broad qualitative aspects of our real experience that have become increasingly apparent in recent years. Viewing the present environment in this context, it is possible to contrast the efficiency of the system of litigation with alternatives such as peer review or medical-legal panels. Litigation has the advantage of inducing a higher degree of selectivity than the investigation method. The incidence of malpractice observed among cases pressed to suit would be higher in the former than in the latter. In this way litigation economizes on costs of administration relative to a nonlitigation alternative. Moreover, it provides a double-edged incentive in that it causes care to be taken both to avoid litigation and to reduce the risk of losing those suits that are brought. The alternative scheme provides only the latter incentive. However,

205

litigation links together the care standard used and the frequency of litigation. It is inherently unable to treat these as separate policy tools, without at the same time destroying the natural advantages just discussed. For this reason, the alternative schemes will prove more flexible. Which method is best depends on the adequacy of the information in the hands of plaintiffs and courts. This question is an empirical one. The existence of a variety of such procedures in different states should serve as a natural laboratory in which their relevant attributes highlighted herein can be measured and evaluated.

Appendix: An Analytical Model of the Propensity to Litigate

The care level being taken by physicians is expressed by a real number, x, that represents the cost of this care. When a level of x prevails in the medical sector, a frequency distribution of outcomes results. Outcomes are described by three variables:

$a\epsilon\{0,1\}$ indicates the occurrence $(a = 1)$ or nonoccurrence $(a = 0)$ of an adverse medical outcome.

$y\epsilon R$ indicates the ex post care level that would be indicated by the investigation of a court or other outside agency.

$z\epsilon R$ indicates the ex ante care level as perceived by the patient and his attorney.

All adverse medical outcomes cost C. Only those cases in which an adverse outcome occurs can lead to suits. The values of y and z when $a = 0$ are therefore really irrelevant.

Let $f(y,z|x)$ be the conditional density of y and z given x and given that $a = 1$. Let $p(x)$ be the probability that $a = 1$. Let $f(y|x,z)$ be the conditional density of y given x and z.

The cost of filing suit to a potential plaintiff is S. If successful, he recovers the cost C.

Let:

$\bar{y} = $ court's cutoff level for finding in plaintiff's favor, when $y \leq \bar{y}$.

$\bar{z} = $ patient's cutoff for pressing suit, when $z \leq \bar{z}$.

It is natural to assume that:

$$\frac{\partial f(y|x,z)}{\partial x} < 0$$

and

$$\int_{y \leq \bar{y}} \frac{\partial f(y|x,z)}{\partial x} dx < 0$$

206

whenever y and z are on the lower tail of their respective distributions. Since malpractice is still a rare event in the realm of all medical treatment, these assumptions are valid throughout the range in which such a claim might be made—namely when $z \leq \bar{z}$.

The frequency of litigation, given a bad outcome, is given by:

$$L(x,\bar{y},\bar{z}) = Pr(a = 1, z \leq \bar{z}) = p(x) \cdot \int\limits_{z \leq \bar{z}} \int f(y,z|x) \, dy \, dz$$

L is the frequency of litigation and $p(x)$ is the frequency of adverse outcomes. Let $p'(x) = {dp}/{dx}$.

The social objective is to minimize

$$p(x) \, (S \cdot L \, (x,\bar{y},\bar{z}) + C) + x$$

Of course, x, $\bar{y}$, and $\bar{z}$ are not all policy variables. The only policy variable is $\bar{y}$. The others are determined by the equilibrium of the system.

The Malpractice Litigation Equilibrium

Patient's Decision. Choose $\bar{z}$ to satisfy

$$C \int\limits_{y \leq \bar{y}} f(y|\bar{z},x) \, dy = S \tag{1}$$

The result is $\bar{z}(\bar{y},x)$.

We want to find the signs of $\dfrac{d\bar{z}}{dx}$ and $\dfrac{d\bar{z}}{dy}$. Totally differentiating (1) with respect to x and $\bar{z}$:

$$C \int\limits_{y \leq \bar{y}} \frac{\partial f(y|x,\bar{z})}{\partial \bar{z}} \, dy d\bar{z} + C \int\limits_{y \leq \bar{y}} \frac{\partial f(y|x,\bar{z})}{\partial x} \, dy dx = 0$$

we have

$$\frac{d\bar{z}}{dx} = \frac{\displaystyle\int\limits_{y \leq \bar{y}} \frac{\partial f(y|x,\bar{z})}{\partial x} \, dy}{\displaystyle\int\limits_{y \leq \bar{y}} \frac{\partial f(y|x,\bar{z})}{\partial \bar{z}} \, dy} < 0$$

under the assumptions that

$$\frac{\partial f(y|x,\bar{z})}{dx} < 0 \quad \text{and} \quad \int\limits_{y \leq \bar{y}} \frac{\partial f(y|x,\bar{z})}{\partial \bar{z}} \, dy$$

over this range of integration.

207

Totally differentiating (1) with respect to $\bar{y}$ and $\bar{z}$:

$$C \int\limits_{y \leq \bar{y}} \frac{\partial f(y|x,\bar{z})}{\partial \bar{z}} \, dy d\bar{z} + C f(\bar{y}|x,\bar{z}) \, d\bar{y} = 0$$

and thus,

$$\frac{d\bar{z}}{d\bar{y}} = \frac{- f(\bar{y}|x,\bar{z})}{\displaystyle\int\limits_{y \leq \bar{y}} \frac{\partial f(y|x,\bar{z})}{\partial \bar{z}} \, dy} > 0$$

under the assumption that y and z are positively related given x.

Doctor's Decision. Choose x to minimize

$$x + Cp\,(x) \int\limits_{z \leq \bar{z}} \int\limits_{y \leq \bar{y}} f(y,z|x) \, dy \, dz \qquad (2)$$

The optimal care level is denoted $x(\bar{y},\bar{z})$. Thus, the first-order condition is

$$0 = 1 + Cp'(x) \int\limits_{z \leq \bar{z}} \int\limits_{y \leq \bar{y}} f(y,z|x) \, dy \, dz \qquad (3)$$

$$+ Cp(x) \int\limits_{z \leq \bar{z}} \int\limits_{y \leq \bar{y}} \frac{\partial f(y,z|x)}{\partial x} \, dy \, dz$$

Totally differentiating (3) with respect to x and $\bar{y}$ we find,

$$\frac{\partial x(\bar{y},\bar{z})}{\partial \bar{y}} = - \frac{p'(x) \displaystyle\int\limits_{z \leq \bar{z}} f(\bar{y},z|x) \, dz + p(x) \displaystyle\int\limits_{z \leq \bar{z}} \frac{\partial f(\bar{y},z|x)}{\partial x} \, dz}{\triangle}$$

where $\triangle$, the second derivative of (2) with respect to x, is positive by the second-order condition. The numerator is negative since $p'(x) < 0$ and $\dfrac{\partial f(y,z|x)}{dx} < 0$ in this range of integration. Thus

$$\frac{\partial x(\bar{y},\bar{z})}{\partial \bar{y}} > 0$$

Similarly we find that

$$\frac{\partial x(\bar{y},\bar{z})}{\partial \bar{z}} = - \frac{p'(x) \displaystyle\int\limits_{y \leq \bar{y}} f(y,\bar{z}|x) \, dy + p(x) \displaystyle\int\limits_{y \leq \bar{y}} \frac{\partial f(\bar{y},z|x)}{dx} \, dy}{\triangle} > 0$$

The properties of these response functions assumed in the text are therefore verified.

Equilibrium. Let the functions $x^*(\bar{y})$ and $\bar{z}^*(\bar{y})$ satisfy

$$x^*(\bar{y}) = x(\bar{y}, \bar{z}(\bar{y}, x^*(\bar{y})))$$

and

$$\bar{z}^*(\bar{y}) = \bar{z}(\bar{y}, x(\bar{y}, \bar{z}^*(\bar{y})))$$

These define the outcome for every fixed $\bar{y}$. The outcome is clearly unique because $\dfrac{d\bar{z}(\bar{y}, x)}{dx} < 0$ and $\dfrac{dx(\bar{y}, \bar{z})}{d\bar{z}} > 0$.

It is straightforward to derive that $\dfrac{dx^*(\bar{y})}{d\bar{y}} > 0$ and that $\dfrac{d\bar{z}^*(\bar{y})}{d\bar{y}}$ is ambiguous in sign. Clearly the frequency of litigation, L, can also respond in either direction.

The Peer Review Equilibrium

In the peer review equilibrium, $\bar{z}$ does not play any role since investigations are done at random among all cases experiencing adverse outcome. Let ρ be the proportion of such cases investigated.

Physicians set x to respond to ρ and $\bar{y}$, which are now independent controls of the regulatory agency. They minimize

$$x + Cp(x)\rho \iint\limits_{y \leq \bar{y}} f(y,z|x) \, dz \, dy \qquad (4)$$

This gives the first order condition:

$$0 = 1 + Cp'(x)\rho \iint\limits_{y \leq \bar{y}} f(y,z|x) \, dz \, dy \qquad (5)$$

$$+ Cp(x)\rho \iint\limits_{y \leq \bar{y}} \frac{\partial f(y,z|x)}{\partial x} \, dz \, dy$$

If ρ is fixed at the level of the propensity to litigate in a malpractice equilibrium with care standard $\bar{y}$, a comparison of (5) and (3) leads to the conclusion that litigation will induce a higher equilibrium care level than peer review. However, since peer review can raise $\bar{y}$ without changing ρ, it can be the case that a higher care level would be attainable at this ρ, and hence that a superior outcome would be attained.

209

CONTINGENT FEES IN LITIGATION WITH SPECIAL REFERENCE TO MEDICAL MALPRACTICE

Melvin W. Reder

In the past several years, the rapid rise in insurer losses on medical malpractice claims has led to a wave of legislative reforms designed to halt or reverse this trend.[1] These reforms include, *inter alia,* modification of the prevailing method of compensating plaintiff attorneys, in which the fee is made contingent upon recovery by the plaintiff.[2] In this paper I shall be concerned primarily with the economic consequences of alternative methods of compensating attorneys. Although the analysis stems from a study of medical malpractice, it is applicable to all types of litigation where pecuniary compensation is sought for injury to person or property.

Before embarking upon the main part of the discussion it is necessary briefly to describe the set of interrelated activities that generates acts of medical malpractice and related attempts to obtain compensation for the victims. After this, I attempt to explain the economic rationale for paying plaintiff attorneys by contingent fee. The third section discusses the economic consequences of preventing lawyers from buying clients' equities in damage claims, and the fourth analyzes a conflict of interest between plaintiffs and their attorneys that results from their different wealth and portfolio positions.

A preliminary version of this paper was presented at a joint meeting of the Labor Economics and Law and Economics Workshops of the University of Chicago. The discussion greatly helped me at a number of points. I am also indebted for written suggestions to my colleagues John Burton and J. T. Reid. Support of the Charles R. Walgreen Foundation is gratefully acknowledged.

[1] In 1975 alone twenty-five states enacted such legislation. See M. W. Reder, "Medical Malpractice: An Economist's View," *American Bar Foundation Research Journal,* no. 2 (1976), pp. 511-63; p. 512, n. 2.

[2] In 1975, nine states enacted legislation to this effect; Steven A. Grossman, "An Analysis of 1975 Legislation Relating to Medical Malpractice," in David G. Warren and Richard Merritt, eds., *A Legislator's Guide to the Malpractice Issue,* (Washington, D.C.: Health Policy Center, Georgetown University, 1976), p. 10. In addition, New Jersey has restricted contingent fees in malpractice cases for a number of years.

The Place of the Plaintiff Malpractice Attorney in the Production of Medical Care

Malpractice Claims and the Quality of Medical Care. The title of this section is not an attempt at humor. Economic analysis of the problem considered here requires that we treat the purchaser of medical care as the buyer of a probability distribution of outcomes, some of which may be extremely adverse. The purchaser tries to influence this distribution by hiring a good doctor, but given limited resources his optimal solution is to settle for a combination of (1) doctor-hospital (care) quality with an associated probability of an adverse outcome, and (2) other things to which his resources may be devoted.[3]

Given his selection of care quality, the purchaser of medical care might hedge his implicit risk of injury-in-treatment by purchasing accident insurance, though few do so. Instead, most individuals rely on the availability of a contingent asset that is jointly produced with units of medical care that have an adverse outcome; namely, the opportunity to make a malpractice claim.[4] For simplicity's sake, assume that such claim opportunities cannot be used alone, but require a joint input, lawyer service, to produce yet a further asset—a "recovery."[5] Other things being equal, the expected value of a claim opportunity to the plaintiff will vary inversely with the cost of lawyer service. That is, any exogenous variable that raises the cost of lawyer service will thereby reduce the expected value of any given claim opportunity, assuming that jury attitudes toward compensating malpractice victims and the state of the law regarding negligence remain unchanged. Reducing the value

---

[3] The discussion in this section is very compressed because its purpose is only to provide background for the argument that follows. In this spirit, I offer the following definitions: (1) quality of care is an inverse function of the probability of an adverse outcome of treatment; (2) adverse outcome of treatment is a dichotomous variable such that an acceptable (nonadverse) outcome is associated with a zero probability of a malpractice claim; (3) quantity of care is any conventionally acceptable increasing function of the amount of time used by a provider of medical care with a given technology. For convenience, I assume quantity and quality of care to be capable of independent variation.

I attempt a fuller conceptual development and analysis in M. W. Reder, "An Economic Analysis of Medical Malpractice," *Journal of Legal Studies,* vol. 5 (June 1976), pp. 267-92.

[4] A claim opportunity arises whenever there is an adverse outcome of treatment. Obviously, not all claim opportunities result in claims.

[5] Lawyer service has the dimensions of both quality and quantity; assume that the expenditure for lawyer service associated with a given claim opportunity increases both with quality and quantity of lawyer service used. To avoid irrelevant complications, further assume that hours of service of different quality lawyers can be measured in efficiency units, so that the cost per "efficiency hour" of lawyer time is the same for all lawyers.

of claim opportunities will reduce the number of claims prosecuted and the aggregate cost of settling them resulting from the production of any given quantity of care provided at any level of care quality.

To avoid irrelevant complications, I shall not analyze the supply response of health care providers to exogenous changes in the expected cost of settling malpractice claims that arise from a given quantity and quality of medical service.[6] However, the direction of such response is clear: an exogenous increase in the expected cost to an insurer of settling a typical malpractice claim will cause rational producers to devote more resources to avoiding adverse outcomes. This means that for each dollar of patient expenditure they will offer a service mix of more quality and less quantity. To accomplish this, doctors will invest more in their training, become more specialized, and confine their practice more narrowly to their area of greatest competence. Since this involves using more human capital per hour (quantum) of service, it will lead to higher fees per hour.

A caveat on the term "quality of care" is in order. The bland assumption that better quality care is uniquely related to the inverse of the expected value of the claim opportunities generated in its production is simplistic and would be bitterly resisted by the medical profession. Having discussed the matter elsewhere, I shall not repeat my defense of this assumption here.[7] The essential point is that, given equal cost, it is in the patient's interest for his doctor to take any action that will reduce the risk of a claim opportunity's arising.[8] However, the cost required to accomplish any specified reduction in this risk may be in excess of the value of the resulting improvement in care quality as quality would be judged by a doctor, by an informed patient, or even by an uninformed patient.[9]

The crux of the issue of defensive medicine[10] is not whether such practice is physically injurious to a patient—it rarely is—but whether

---

[6] This is discussed in Reder, "Economic Analysis," pp. 272-75.

[7] Ibid., pp. 270-72, 275-78.

[8] A qualification is in order: the statement in the text holds if (but only if) the expected compensation for a malpractice claim is less than the expected utility loss from injury-in-treatment. This would appear to be the actual situation: few if any individuals shop around for an inept doctor in the hope of a big malpractice settlement. However, if expected compensation were sufficient, such behavior would be common.

[9] It is also possible that malpractice risk avoidance by doctors causes failure to utilize procedures even where the expected gain to the patient would warrant use, but where the doctor cannot obtain sufficient compensation (or adequate protection from malpractice risk through pretreatment agreements; see below) to induce him to act in the patient's best interest.

[10] See Reder, "Economist's View," pp. 541-43.

it is worth its additional cost to him. But if an improvement in care quality is not worth the associated increase in cost, why do patients bear this cost? To answer that rational doctors will not provide care—at acceptable fees—without resorting to the self-protection of defensive medicine is only to push the question one step back. Why do patients and doctors not exchange lower fees for waivers of the right to sue for malpractice, inducing doctors to provide care without engaging in cost-inefficient methods of practice or in the purchase of very expensive malpractice insurance?

The answer to this fundamental question is that under ordinary circumstances the courts would not honor such waivers.[11] Presumably this is why interested parties have not utilized this potentially advantageous mode of barter. The indirect effects of this barrier to individual negotiation between doctors and patients is an increase in the minimum quality of medical care that the market will offer, and a corresponding increase in the minimum price at which care of any quality will be available.

The Number of Malpractice Claims and the Percentage of Recovery Paid to the Plaintiff Attorney. Before turning to explicit consideration of the contingent fee, let me discuss briefly the determinants of the share of gross recovery that goes to the plaintiff lawyer. This is a sketch of the problem, not, obviously, an attempt to solve it. At the outset, let me note that the cost of lawyers' services is a substantial fraction of the gross recovery from malpractice claims.[12] I have estimated elsewhere that in 1970 the cost of litigation, to plaintiffs and insurers combined, averaged between 53 and 58 percent of the gross recovery from medical malpractice claims; plaintiffs (victims) paid, on average, between 38 and 45 percent of their settlements for lawyers' fees and court costs.[13] Accordingly, I shall assume that lawyers' fees are an important component of the cost of obtaining a malpractice recovery.

In most analyses of the behavior of a single industry under competitive conditions, cost minimization is assumed to determine the combination of input quantities of various kinds, but the methods by which

---

[11] See ibid., pp. 535-36.

[12] By "gross recovery" I mean the amount paid to the plaintiff-victim before deduction of attorney fees, court costs, and other costs of preparing his claim.

[13] See Reder, "Economist's View," p. 546. Thus far the reaction of experts to these admittedly crude guesses is that they underestimate the lawyers' share of recoveries.

214

their suppliers are compensated is not discussed.[14] Implicitly, it is assumed that inputs are service streams hired at market determined prices and with no risk of contract default by either party; all risks are assumed to be shifted without cost to the supplier of equity capital.

Such an assumption precludes consideration of the problem at hand. Accordingly we generalize the single industry model slightly, classifying input units both by their technical properties and by the method of payment; input units paid on an incentive basis are considered to be different factors from those paid on a time basis even though they are technically identical. Cost minimization by each firm is assumed to occur over the augmented set of factors, and the supply function of the industry becomes dependent, *inter alia,* upon the effort response of labor inputs to incentive payments.

In the case of the malpractice recovery "industry," competitive equilibrium requires selection of the least cost combination of lawyer hours and hours used per claim opportunity. It also requires selection of the least cost combination of lawyer hours paid by time and paid by contingency fee, a percentage of gross recovery.[15] As it happens, on the plaintiff side, payment by contingent fee is so much more efficient as a method of compensation that, with negligible exceptions, it is the only method of payment used. Its superiority is so marked that hampering or prohibiting its use is correctly considered an effective means of discouraging malpractice suits.

The marked superiority of the contingent fee method of payment is closely related to the uncertainty that attends recovery from a malpractice claim. To avoid irrelevant complications due to risk aversion, assume that all lawyers are risk neutral and that the supply price of attorney time to the industry depends only upon expected earnings. Further to simplify, assume that lawyer hours can be measured in efficiency units and (since the medical malpractice recovery industry is very small) that the supply price of attorney hours in efficiency units

---

[14] An important exception to this statement is in the study of agriculture where there is a long tradition of explicit consideration of the determinants and consequences of the legal form of the contractual relation between landlords and tenants. For a good recent discussion of sharecropping, see J. T. Reid, Jr., "Sharecropping and Agricultural Uncertainty," *Economic Development and Cultural Change,* vol. 24, no. 3 (April 1976), pp. 549-76; this article contains extensive references to the earlier literature. Two other important references are S. N. S. Cheung, "The Theory of Share Tenancy," (Chicago: University of Chicago Press, 1969), and J. E. Stiglitz, "Incentives and Risk Sharing in Sharecropping," *Review of Economic Studies,* vol. 41 (April 1974), pp. 219-56.

[15] Lawyers with different schedules of percentage of recovery as related to amount of recovery would be treated as different inputs in this model. For simplicity's sake I shall assume that all lawyers have the same schedule.

is independent of the number of hours used in prosecuting malpractice claims. Given these assumptions, expected hourly earnings of plaintiff lawyers will be independent of the number or character of claim opportunities arising. Demand can affect only the number of efficiency hours of attorney time employed.[16]

Assume that as of the moment of acceptance by a plaintiff attorney, or at any time thereafter, a given malpractice claim opportunity can be described by a frequency distribution of pecuniary payoffs (gross recoveries) characterized by two parameters: (1) the probability of a zero recovery due to inability to establish the required combination of negligence and liability of the health care provider, and (2) the expected gross recovery in the event it is not zero. Assume that the circumstances attending claim opportunities can be ranked from those least likely to those most likely to generate a zero recovery under a given state of the law regarding liability and negligence. Further assume that (2) depends upon the injuries sustained and some frequency distribution of payoffs conditional upon the injuries sustained.[17] Let this distribution have an expected value that varies with the state of juror attitudes toward rewarding malpractice victims. Finally, assume that (1) and (2) are independent of one another.[18]

Now assume an exogenous shift in jury attitudes such that the expected gross recovery from any claim opportunity (with a nonzero payoff) increases. The effect will be to raise some previously submarginal claims above the threshold of expected gross recovery at which it pays to prosecute them. That is, the rise in expected recovery in the event that the recovery is not zero induces the prosecution of claims with a higher probability of a zero recovery by lawyers whose time has a given supply price. It is this interrelation of expected recovery in the event of success with the number of claims prosecuted and with the relative frequency of zero recoveries that has given rise to the charge that

---

[16] The assumption that the supply of lawyer time to the medical malpractice recovery industry is infinitely elastic reflects the judgment that the elasticity of substitution of lawyer time between this industry and the personal injury industry is very high and that the former industry is of negligible size relative to the latter.

[17] For an example of how malpractice injuries may be classified by severity, see A. Mirabella et al., "Medical Malpractice Insurance Claim Files Closed in 1970," in U.S. Department of Health, Education, and Welfare, *Report of the Secretary's Commission on Medical Malpractice* (Washington, D.C., 1973), appendix, especially pp. 9-12.

[18] The assumption that (1) and (2) are independent is unnecessarily restrictive, but it facilitates exposition and does not affect the argument in any essential way.

the contingent fee has stimulated the filing and prosecution of large numbers of what are sometimes called frivolous claims.

The available evidence indicates that malpractice claim recovery is an activity in which a substantial probability of zero recovery (especially at the trial stage) is associated with the expectation of high payoff in the event of success.[19] In equilibrium, the large percentage of zero recoveries is the theoretically implied counterpart of high expected recoveries in the event of success and is in no way indicative of lack of serious intent by the plaintiff attorney.

Put differently, prosecution of a malpractice claim is analogous to an investment activity in which there is a small probability of a large reward and a high probability of zero payoff. A lottery is the paradigm of such activities; oil exploration is also an excellent example. An increase in the expected value of a barrel of oil leads to more drilling of new wells, especially in places where drilling and extraction costs are high or where there is a high probability of "dry holes." Similarly, an increase in the expected damage awards for successful malpractice claims will increase the number of claims prosecuted (per comparable doctor-patient contact) and increase the proportion of claims earning zero recoveries.

Therefore to reduce the expected gross recovery in the event of success (for example, through a legislated limit on the maximum size of the recovery) would reduce both the number of malpractice claims prosecuted for a given amount of doctor-patient contact and the proportion of claims yielding a zero recovery. Restricting the percentage of the gross recovery that the plaintiff attorney can obtain as a contingent fee would have a similar effect, since it is this percentage that determines the attorney-entrepreneur's reward.[20] Thus, limiting the percentage of gross recovery that can be paid as a contingent fee to the attorney would be an efficacious means of reducing the fraction of claim opportunities prosecuted.

The assumptions of risk neutrality and constant supply price per efficiency hour of attorney time ensure that the malpractice recovery activity is a fair game in the actuarial sense for the plaintiff lawyers; that is, in equilibrium the expected return for an hour's time will equal

---

[19] Mirabella, "Files Closed," p. 14, table 2 indicates that among claims settled after trial, payment of $1 or more was made in only 29 percent of the cases. Also see S. K. Dietz et al., "The Medical Malpractice Legal System," in HEW, *Secretary's Report*, appendix, p. 116.

[20] This statement ignores the possibility that the claimant may exercise his right to act as his own attorney.

what that hour would earn in an alternative activity.[21] This does not, however, tell us anything about the equilibrium share of expected gross recovery that goes to the plaintiff attorney. This share depends upon the expected cost of prosecuting a claim.

The cost of prosecuting a claim consists mainly of the attorney time required. (For simplicity's sake, assume that all other elements of cost bear a fixed ratio to attorney time.) The fees earned on "winners" must cover the value of the time wasted on "losers." How much time an attorney wastes on losers depends upon how readily he can identify a claim as a loser (not worthy of *further* investment of time).[22]

To indicate the essence of the problem, simplify drastically and assume that the settlement strategy of the defendant (insurance company) is a known datum. The expected cost (to the plaintiff lawyer) of preparing a claim increases with the rate of interest, given the time shape of input of lawyer hours, and with the price per hour of lawyer service. But most important, expected cost depends upon the time shape of the relationship between lawyer hours invested and the information acquired by the plaintiff attorney about the expected value of a claim. In other words, the greater the information generated as a byproduct of the first few hours invested in preparing a claim, the smaller the quantity of hours wasted in ventures whose yield is less than their cost and the lower the (equilibrium) cost per successful venture.

Given the necessary simplifications, the plaintiff attorney's problem becomes similar to that of the oil prospector. Search cost per barrel depends critically upon how much the oil man must invest before ascertaining whether the drilling project is good enough to warrant the investment initially projected. Similarly, if a plaintiff lawyer, after investing only a few hours of time, could determine with great precision whether a claim opportunity would yield a substantial recovery, his optimum investment strategy would not entail as many sizable investments in claims that eventuate in zero recoveries as he must apparently make

---

[21] The recovery procedure, however, is biased in favor of losing claimants and their lawyers (claimants obtaining zero recovery) since they do not have to pay the costs they impose on defendants. (See R. A. Epstein, "Medical Malpractice: The Case for Contract," *American Bar Foundation Research Journal*, vol. 1 (1976), pp. 135-36, for a discussion of this point.) This state of affairs causes a de facto transfer from defendants to claimants, and especially to those whose claims have low probabilities of success. It increases both the fraction of claim opportunities that are prosecuted and the fraction of those prosecuted that have zero payoff.

[22] Mirabella, "Files Closed," p. 14, table 2, indicates that of all claims closed in 1970, about 55 percent were closed without payment before trial (abandoned). Dietz, "Legal System," p. 116, table III-48, reports that among the specialized plaintiff malpractice lawyers responding to a questionnaire, the mean number of hours spent on cases with zero recovery was 440; the median was 220.

under present circumstances. This would reduce expected lawyer hours per dollar recovered and, under competitive conditions, the percentage of gross recovery going for plaintiff attorney fees in the long run.[23]

In short, the equilibrium share of the gross recovery that goes to the plaintiff lawyer depends upon (1) the expected amount of time required in the event of a "success" and (2) the expected amount of time that must be invested in losers before they can be recognized as such and abandoned. I have emphasized (2) for reasons of exposition, though (1) is also important.

The Comparative Advantage of Payment by Contingent Fees

As already remarked, in malpractice cases the plaintiff attorney is almost always paid by contingent fee. It would, of course, be possible to compensate the plaintiff attorney on the basis of a fixed hourly rate of pay, but this does not often occur for reasons set forth in the next section of this paper. Given that the contingent fee is the most efficient method of compensating the plaintiff attorney under present legal arrangements, imposing a limit (either of absolute dollar amount or of percentage taken) is de facto a tax upon the activity of prosecuting a malpractice claim.[24] Without leaving the industry, it is difficult to avoid such taxes when lawyer time is (1) an essential input (that is, has a low elasticity of substitution with all other inputs), (2) is paid a large fraction of the total cost of prosecuting a claim, and (3) has a high long-run elasticity of supply to the industry. Given these conditions, the effect of limiting attorney fees is, quite intentionally, to discourage use of attorney time in prosecuting malpractice claims.[25]

---

[23] This assertion is conjectural, though I am confident that it is substantially correct. I had intended to provide a brief "simple" proof of it as an appendix to this paper. The major problem is so to model the interaction of plaintiff and defendant lawyers that their resulting behavior is qualitatively similar to that of an oil prospector "playing against nature." I found this problem harder than I had expected and, given the constraints of time and talent, I have decided to leave the assertion illustrated but not demonstrated—at least for the present. I take this occasion to draw the attention of theorists to this problem in the hope that they can determine more readily than I the precise conditions under which this conjecture holds.

[24] For example, a flat limit on contingent fees per claim is analytically equivalent to a 100 percent marginal tax on earnings above that limit. Similarly, a limit on the percentage that a lawyer may retain of a gross recovery is a 100 percent marginal tax on earnings per dollar of gross recovery.

[25] For a previous discussion of contingent fees, see Murray L. Schwartz and Daniel J. B. Mitchell, "An Economic Analysis of the Contingent Fee in Personal-Injury Litigation," *Stanford Law Review*, vol. 22 (1970), pp. 1125-62.

In principle, a malpractice claimant could assume the entrepreneurial role rather than delegating it to his lawyer. To do this would involve compensating the lawyer for his services on an hourly basis— or using some other arrangement such that compensation was not dependent upon recovery—paying court costs, bearing the expenses of preparing the case, and capturing the entire recovery.[26] A few, but very few, malpractice claimants may actually have done this. At least one state, Wisconsin, now requires that an attorney offer at the time of engagement to work on a per diem or per hour basis as an alternative to a contingency arrangement.[27] However, with very few exceptions, the fees of *plaintiff* malpractice lawyers are contingent upon recovery.[28] By contrast, the compensation of malpractice defense lawyers, typically, is on the basis of time spent. The reasons for this striking dissimilarity call for explanation.

Cost of Monitoring. One reason for the aforementioned contrast is that an insurance company can monitor the effort of an attorney with greater facility and at lower cost than an individual could. An insurance company employs salaried lawyers who can, *inter alia,* oversee and appraise the performance of hired outside attorneys at low marginal cost. Most individual litigants do not have the expertise for such monitoring and would have to engage a second lawyer to monitor the "operating" attorney.

The difference in cost of monitoring between an individual and an insurance company results essentially from economies of scale and joint production. An insurance company hires staff counsel for many purposes. Intermittent monitoring of outside defense specialists can be done during slack periods when forgone marginal product is low. (For individuals who retain a lawyer on a regular basis, monitoring cost would not explain the use of a contingent fee in a malpractice matter.)

In my opinion, the relative cost of monitoring lawyer performance is not the major factor in explaining the different methods of compensating plaintiff and defense attorneys. I mention it only because monitoring cost is (properly) emphasized as an important factor bearing upon the choice of payment method used in compensating wage earners.[29]

---

[26] I ignore intermediate possibilities in which the client would assume the entrepreneurial role but would relate the attorney's fee to the results obtained. For the moment, I shall avoid fundamental questions on the nature of entrepreneurship. However, see below, pp. 224 ff.

[27] Grossman, "1975 Legislation," p. 10.

[28] See Dietz, "Legal System," pp. 113-16.

[29] See, for example, J. H. Pencavel, "Work Effort, On-the-Job Screening, and Alternative Methods of Remuneration," in Ronald Ehrenberg, ed., *Research in Labor Economics,* vol. I (Greenwich, Conn.: Johnson Associates, 1977).

Briefly, let me summarize the advantages and disadvantages of incentive methods of payment. A worker with any positive degree of risk aversion will prefer the prospect of a sure payment to the expectation of an equal payment with a nonzero dispersion. Therefore, to induce a risk-averse worker of given characteristics to bear the risk associated with payment contingent upon results, it is necessary that such payment result in greater expected compensation in an equivalent time period than payment on a fixed-time basis. Assuming realistically that employers are not more risk-averse than workers, the only reason for them to offer workers piece rates that result in a higher expected hourly return in exchange for accepting a greater variance in hourly earnings is that the value of the expected performance would increase commensurately, presumably because of reduced shirking.[30] The greater the shirking that would occur under time payment, the greater the opportunity for the employer to gain through reduced shirking. Shirking under time payment is usually assumed to increase with the difficulty and consequent cost of monitoring worker performance.[31]

But this argument has one missing step; we have not specified the penalty suffered by a worker who is found to shirk excessively.[32] Assume that the probability of being detected in excessive shirking is an increasing function of the utility gained by the associated reduction in effort. (Roughly, the probability of being caught in excessive shirking increases with the grossness of the excess.) Then, a rational worker will determine his degree of shirking so as to balance the expected marginal gain in utility from reduced effort against the expected marginal loss from being punished if detected.

The expected loss from punishment in the event of detection is equal to the probability of detection times the expected loss of utility from punishment in the event of detection. But what is the punishment? By hypothesis, if the worker is paid per unit of time, his compensation is certain and cannot be withheld; this is also the practically relevant assumption. All that the employer can do to punish the time-compen-

---

[30] J. Stiglitz, "Incentives, Risk, and Information: Notes Towards a Theory of Hierarchy," *Bell Journal of Economics*, vol. 6, no. 2 (Autumn 1975), pp. 552-79.

[31] Pencavel, "Alternative Remuneration."

[32] Presumably, everyone paid on a time basis shirks somewhat. For simplicity's sake, posit a degree of shirking beyond which the employer takes action. Shirking beyond the degree the employer will tolerate is "excessive." For the present purpose, I treat the margin between acceptable and "excessive" shirking as exogenously determined. However, in a more complete discussion the location of this margin would be determined by the employer's optimization conditions.

sated shirker is to dismiss him.[33] But the loss of utility from dismissal depends upon the search cost of finding new employment, "reputational capital" given, and upon the effect of dismissal (and diffusion of information about its cause) upon the worker's reputation.[34]

Reputational Capital. Reputational capital is the labor market analogue of good will in the product market. The reputational capital of an individual or a firm is the expectation of potential transactors in the market(s) in which he operates that he will fulfill the letter and spirit of the contracts into which he enters. The reputational capital of an individual may be conveniently thought of as the ratio of his own reputational capital to that of the average individual with observable characteristics similar to his own, who sells labor services in the same labor market. These ratios, across individuals, may be arrayed ordinally or, if there is a convenient scale, measured cardinally.

The capital value of a superior reputation arises from the lower search cost required to obtain a given labor contract, or from the higher expected wage rate obtainable at given search cost, or from some combination of both. A superior reputation itself arises from a history of superior on-the-job performance and has a present value dependent upon the rate of interest, the rate at which reputation decays, the expected length of work life, and so on.

Obviously, this is not a very detailed exposition of the concept of reputational capital. However, this is not the place for such a discussion; moreover, the concept itself is not novel. It is simply the simultaneous application of two familiar propositions: (1) during part of an individual's working life up to (but not including) the date on which he retires from the labor force,[35] optimization requires that he so behave that at the end of the period he retains some (nonzero) amount of human capital,

---

[33] Of course, an employer might demote (or refrain from promoting) a shirking worker, fine him, or warn him. However, if fines or demotions are possible, the worker's reward per time period *is not certain*; in other words, in such cases, a disguised incentive system is operating. (Thus, incentive systems are far more prevalent than they are often thought to be; the incentive pay is the variation in the rate of promotion associated with superior performance.) If warnings have any effect, they operate to raise the expected penalty in the event of further excessive shirking; ultimately, they must be backed by a penalty.

[34] In a world where job search cost was zero, and there was no possibility of accelerated promotion, under a system of pure time payment workers would have no pecuniary incentive to do anything other than what pleased them. Hence, except in populations with a strong work ethic, such a system of compensation could not survive.

[35] This suggests that immediately before retirement, or just before going out of business, individuals and firms may perform less well than previously because they are no longer concerned with their reputations. Illustrations of such behavior are not hard to find.

and (2) that part of an individual's human capital is his reputation as a good worker.

The relevance of this concept to the problem at hand arises from the distinct possibility that concern for reputation may serve as a substitute for an incentive payment in inducing effort from a hired agent. Consider: if a particular lawsuit is attended with a great deal of publicity, within or without the legal fraternity, a contending attorney's reputation can be made or broken by his performance on that suit. The fee on the case becomes a secondary consideration in motivating his effort, so that making payment independent of results might not entail appreciable risk of shirking. Under these circumstances, the increment in expected hourly wage cost required to induce a lawyer of given quality to accept a contingent fee, rather than a specified fee per hour, would be greater than the expected gain in productivity that would result. But the net advantage of one method of compensation over the other will vary with the lawyer's concern for his reputation and with the effect that performance on the given case will have upon it.

Insurance companies have longstanding relations with their defense attorneys and make frequent use of them. Moreover, they observe and discuss attorney performance. Thus the reputation of a defense lawyer is at stake in almost every case he handles, and there is little to be gained by relating payment to results, case by case. But the plaintiff attorney may be in a different position, depending upon the importance of the particular case and the attendant publicity. As many attorneys obtain a substantial part of their business from referrals from other attorneys, concern for the effect of performance upon reputation is always present. But the degree of this concern and its effect upon performance will vary with the importance of the claim.

Where the potential value of a claim is high, it is likely to attract considerable attention and put the plaintiff attorney on his mettle, lessening the need for a contingent fee to serve as a performance incentive.[36] Furthermore, relatively large claims tend to be handled by a small fraternity of malpractice specialists who would take immediate note of unusual shirking of professional responsibility. In claims with small potential the risk of shirking is greater. A lawyer in need of business may accept a claim of small potential, but give it only such attention as its financial prospects warrant. Economic theory suggests that in such cases a contingent fee would increase the expected recovery.

---

[36] By the potential value of a case I refer to the rough judgment that a plaintiff lawyer makes when he decides whether the claim opportunity presented him is worth the time involved in handling it. The potential value of a claim opportunity is roughly equal to the expected gross recovery, assuming liability; this is obviously greater than the unconditional expected gross recovery.

Risk of Nonpayment. The principal reason why malpractice plaintiffs and their lawyers contract for a contingent fee is the risk that the former will not have sufficient funds to pay in the event of zero or small recovery. The limited evidence available indicates that malpractice plaintiffs have about the same distributions of age, income, and occupation as the general population of persons undergoing short-stay hospitalization in 1969.[37] That is, they had these distributions before their injuries-in-treatment. Therefore the victim, if his injury is at all serious, is likely to be below the community average in ability to bear legal expenses. Indeed, a major part of the wealth of many malpractice claimants is the value of their claim. If a case is lost, the plaintiff lawyer has little chance of collecting a noncontingent fee for his services. Consequently he cannot avoid much of the risk of failure.

If he contracts for a specific (noncontingent) fee, he risks an uncollectable bill.[38] Given risk neutrality of plaintiff attorneys, the expected fee under contingent and noncontingent contracts must be equal, if both are to be in use. This implies that for small and even intermediate gross recoveries, the fee paid would be greater under the noncontingent arrangement. For zero and near-zero gross recoveries, which are numerous, the noncontingent fee would surely exceed the total recovery. In such cases, the costs and difficulties of collecting a specific (noncontingent) fee are obvious; these costs would include substantial disapproval by the public, the bar, and the courts, which might even refuse to enforce the contract. Suffice it to say that the difficulties of collecting fees in excess of a "reasonable" share of the gross recovery, and especially in excess of the whole of the amount recovered, are a substantial deterrent to use of the noncontingent contract for rewarding plaintiff attorneys. Obviously such considerations are of negligible weight in determining the contractual mode between insurance companies and their lawyers.

Legal Impediments to the Optimal Allocation of Claim Ownership

The ubiquity of the contingent fee on the plaintiff side of malpractice cases can be better appreciated if we consider a malpractice claim opportunity as a risky asset, ownership of which is fully transferable. (That

---

[37] Mirabella, "Files Closed," pp. 11-12.

[38] The principal difference between the negotiating situation of plaintiff attorneys and their clients in malpractice and personal injury cases and that of workers and their employers lies in the virtual certainty of a worker that he will be able to collect what his employer has agreed to pay. Because the excellent discussions of Pencavel and Stiglitz do not consider risk of employer wage default, they are of only limited relevance to this situation.

this is contrary to fact will be considered in a moment.) As we have already seen, the process by which a claim opportunity is produced implies that its initial owner is the patient-victim. But a claim opportunity is a very risky asset which individuals who are normally risk-averse would wish to exchange for a more diversified portfolio. This is especially so in view of the wealth position of the typical claimant (see above).

In other words, the typical malpractice claimant has been "endowed" with an injury and a risky claim.[39] Prior to any exchange of assets he has a serious problem of portfolio imbalance, which he could rectify by selling part or all of his malpractice claim. Because such claims are not worth much unless prosecuted by a lawyer, anyone contemplating purchase would be well advised to make prior arrangements with one. Better still, because lawyers are likely to hear of such claims and have a situational advantage as appraisers of their value (they can make an appraisal as a byproduct of deciding whether to handle the claim) it would be efficient for the buyer to be a lawyer, or a consortium of lawyers, who might retail shares to third parties if law and legal ethics were to permit.

An obvious buyer of a malpractice claim is the lawyer who is to handle it. De facto, to accept a case on the basis of a contingent fee is to trade a promise of legal services for a share of the claim. However, it is unethical and/or illegal for a plaintiff attorney to make an outright purchase of a client's claim, with a cash payment for the claimant's equity.[40] The legal impediments to transacting in this type of contingent claim obviously hamper attainment of an efficient allocation of risk.

[39] This assumption implies that malpractice claimants make no appreciable attempts to include in their portfolios hedges against risk of malpractice injury. As of the present, it is likely that this assumption is descriptively accurate. However, this could and quite possibly should change. For example, personal accident insurance (including accidents in medical treatment) could serve as a hedge against risk of malpractice injury. In the presence of such insurance, a claim for injury-in-treatment would generate a contest between insurers both of whose portfolios were well diversified.

[40] The questions of law and legal ethics involved in this problem are quite complicated, and it is unnecessary to embark upon them here beyond noting that they act as a serious impediment to transactions in claims between lawyers and clients. The impropriety of an attorney's acquiring a financial interest in a case in which he is involved is an old doctrine of common law (Maintenance and Champerty) which continues in effect, albeit with modifications, to the present. However, it may be legally and ethically permissible in some states for attorneys to join consortia that purchase claims, provided they are not professionally involved in the ensuing actions at law. But such consortia have so far been infrequent, suggesting that the cost of organizing and operating them exceeds the prospective returns. I am indebted for some instruction on this point to Professor Spencer H. Kimball and the members of the University of Chicago Workshop in Law and Economics.

But even if there were no legal impediments to doing so, often it would be inefficient to eliminate all interest of a claimant in the settlement of his claim. Where he must be available as a witness, or as an exhibit, in the event of a trial; or where his public conduct, prior to settlement, might influence the outcome by providing evidence as to the extent of his injuries, the victim's performance will tend to be more conducive to a successful outcome if he retains a financial stake in the matter.[41]

From the viewpoint of portfolio diversification, the plaintiff attorney has a clear advantage over the claimant as claim owner. This is partly because the lawyer handles many claims, which gives him "automatic" portfolio diversification, while the claimant normally has only one claim per lifetime. In addition, the lawyer is usually richer than the claimant, which further enhances his comparative advantage as claim owner.[42]

In other words, the contingent fee is a contractual arrangement that partially circumvents the legal impediments to the attorney's outright purchase of his client's claim. Depending upon the out-of-pocket expense of preparing the case and the amount advanced to the claimant for living and/or medical expenses, the plaintiff attorney may become the de facto owner of more than 50 percent of the expected value of the claim.[43]

Where the cost of prosecuting a claim is large, a plaintiff attorney may invest a sizable fraction of a year's income in preparing the claim for trial.[44] Normal risk aversion, or desire for portfolio diversification, would suggest the sale or exchange of shares in large claims, at least among lawyers. And it is quite possible that this actually occurs; the practice of engaging a referring attorney as co-counsel is one method by which attorneys may pool their risks; partnerships are another.[45] In view of the secrecy involved, it is impossible to judge the extent to which risk-pooling among attorneys takes place.

---

[41] The importance of this consideration will vary from case to case with the importance of the client's role as a witness. The optimal sharing arrangement as between attorney and claimant obviously varies with the moral hazard (to the attorney) of assuming the claimant's risk. Throughout the subsequent discussion I ignore this hazard.

[42] This statement assumes that risk aversion decreases with wealth.

[43] See Reder, "Economist's View," pp. 511-63.

[44] Detailed information on this point is scanty. However, among malpractice specialists, the mean fee per case was reported at about $20,000 (Dietz, "Legal System," pp. 105-106, table III-29), which suggests an appreciable amount of time expended per case.

[45] For a discussion of referral practices and fee arrangements in malpractice cases, see Dietz, "Legal System," pp. 101-102.

But however much risk-pooling there is among lawyers, there is a strong possibility, especially for claims of large potential value, that there remains an appreciable misallocation of risk as between claimants and their attorneys. Most malpractice claims that go to trial are large, and, of these, about 60 percent obtain zero gross recovery.[46] Assuming that both the insurance companies and the plaintiff lawyers who are involved in prosecuting large claims are experienced appraisers of the value of claims and approximately risk-neutral, and assuming that each is aware of the other side's expertise and risk neutrality, it is plausible to infer that offers to settle will approximate the expected value of the claims.

Given the asset position of most malpractice claimants, and especially of those injured seriously enough to have a claim with a large potential, it is unlikely that they would wish to wager most of their wealth on a game—assumed to be fair—in which the probability of losing the entire stake is greater than one-half. Barring an unusual and unsuspected appetite for risk, it seems likely that most plaintiffs would accept the pretrial settlement offer that insurance companies would make provided that (1) they were fully informed of the risks of going to trial and (2) the transaction costs of changing or dismissing their attorneys were negligible.[47]

In offering this speculation, I assume that plaintiffs and their attorneys have identical attitudes toward risk but are in different wealth positions and have greatly different costs of portfolio diversification (risk-pooling). Both attorney and plaintiff are maximizers of expected utility, but the situation of the former leads him to take many fair gambles at rather long odds in order to maximize expected utility, while the situation of the latter leads him to shun such gambles and accept less than their expected value in order to avoid the risk of gambler's ruin.

Let us assume that, as of the inception of the damage-recovery process, the normal terms of agreement between attorney and plaintiff

---

[46] Mirabella, "Files Closed," p. 14, table 2.

[47] The meaning of "fully informed" is the nub of the matter. The odds in a particular case are hard to calculate and a plaintiff lawyer's honest opinion reflects, *inter alia*, his confidence in his own skill. The lawyer's opinion, obviously, will color the client's.

The transactions cost of changing plaintiff lawyers near the point of trial is surely very high. The original lawyer's claim to compensation for the value of time already expended and for costs incurred is unassailable and represents a substantial fraction of the expected gross recovery. These costs become an obligation of a new attorney and constitute a substantial obstacle to a switch by a plaintiff.

are efficient.[48] However, as information about the extent of the injuries suffered and the liability of the doctor or hospital accumulates, the situation changes. Most claims are abandoned or settled for small amounts; these are not considered here. The remainder have a substantial expected value, but high risk if taken to trial. It is on these claims that there is a potential conflict of interest between the plaintiff and his attorney; the former "should" accept an offer of settlement appreciably below the expected value of the claim, but the latter probably will not wish to do so.

It is a matter of dispute whether this potential conflict of interest between the plaintiff and his lawyer is often realized in practice. Some readers of previous drafts (especially Richard Posner) have stressed the importance that an attorney attaches to his reputation and his consequent concern to avoid giving the impression that he inflicts "excessive" risk upon his clients. If this concern were controlling we should expect to find that, among comparable claims, pretrial settlements averaged less than jury awards minus costs of trial. This would reflect the tendency of plaintiff attorneys to settle claims for less than their expected value in deference to their clients' risk aversion. Conversely, if average jury awards (less costs of going to trial) were equal to average pretrial settlements, one would infer that plaintiff attorneys were rejecting pretrial settlements offering less than the expected value of claims, and somehow inducing the plaintiffs to bear the entailed risk.

Data bearing on these alternative possibilities are contained in the files of Jury Verdict Research, Inc. For cases going to trial, these data consist of final offers made before trial by both plaintiffs and defendants and of the amounts awarded by the jury; for cases settled before trial, the amount of the settlement is reported. Baird et al. report on these data for medical malpractice cases.[49] They offer no tabular presentations, but only charts; moreover, they do not give explicit consideration to the cost of going to trial. Accordingly it is difficult to make use of their brief report on this body of data. However, these data provide information of great value in testing the hypothesis discussed in the preceding paragraph and merit careful analysis.

In concluding this section, it is useful to compare the distribution of risk on the plaintiff and defense sides of a malpractice case: on the defense side the principals are, with few exceptions, insured; and the

---

48 This statement may not apply to the small number of cases where both liability and the fact of considerable injury is apparent from the outset. Interpreting the failure to settle such cases early in the adjudication process presents difficulties which I have not resolved.

49 C. B. Baird et al., "Alternatives to Litigation, I: Technical Analysis," in HEW, *Secretary's Report,* appendix, pp. 259-62.

insurers are legally free to reinsure or otherwise engage in mutually advantageous exchanges of risks.[50] On the plaintiff side, the aforementioned impediments to assignment of a malpractice claim lock plaintiffs and their attorneys, especially the former, into portfolios that are less diversified than those they would otherwise hold. Use of the contingent fee is one way of preventing this portfolio imbalance from becoming even worse.

Conflict of Interest Between Plaintiffs and Their Lawyers

As already argued, there is the possibility of a divergence of interest between a malpractice plaintiff and his lawyer because of the difference in their wealth and portfolio positions. This creates the possibility that, close to the point of trial, an informed plaintiff might wish to settle his claim on terms that are obtainable but unacceptable to a risk-neutral attorney.

In addition to the divergence of interest, there is also a difference in the information available to the plaintiff and to his lawyer. Presumably the lawyer has a good idea of the probability distribution of gross recoveries. But it is in his interest to overestimate the expected recovery in order to encourage his client to reject settlement offers. While a client may be aware of this bias, he will find it difficult to correct for it. Of course, the defending insurance company would be happy to offer advice to the plaintiff, but its expressed opinion would be at least as suspect as that of his own attorney.

Clearly the plaintiff needs a disinterested expert to appraise his claim. But it would not be easy to find one, or to identify him if by chance he were found. What is needed is a *certified* competent and disinterested appraiser. But who is to serve as a certifier? The state has a long and erratic history as certifier of weights and measures, coinage, qualifications of members of various occupations, and so forth. Substitute certifiers are not lacking—clubs of livestock breeders, leagues of civic improvers, and professional associations of all kinds have filled this need. To note their limitations is not to preclude their utilization, but merely to suggest that the problem of certifying the certifier is not trivial.

The need for an independent claim appraiser may sometimes be filled by the informal activity of judges in pretrial conferences.[51] In such

---

[50] M. Kendall and J. Haldi, "The Medical Malpractice Insurance Market," HEW, *Secretary's Report,* appendix, pp. 546-47, gives a brief description of the market for medical malpractice reinsurance; this is one obvious method for risk-pooling among insurance companies.

[51] This possibility was suggested to the author by both Edward Kitch and John Burton.

conferences, the judge may give the attorneys, the principals to the lawsuit, or both, his view of the value of a claim, usually with an eye to inducing pretrial settlement. While the frequency and effectiveness of such judicial intervention is not known, it may function as part of the institutional framework that resolves or limits the impact of this potential conflict of interest.

But suppose, for the sake of argument, that upon investigation it is found that judicial intervention is insufficient and that certified appraisers are needed. Such appraisers would presumably be expert lawyers; obviously their time would be valuable. Enter the cost-benefit question: would the combined gain from the appraisal to plaintiff and insurance company equal the fees of the appraisers?

To facilitate an affirmative answer to this question, assume that the law were amended so that, on request of a plaintiff, the records and other relevant information of all attorneys involved would be made available to a certified appraiser of the plaintiff's designation. (This should reduce the time needed by an appraiser to become familiar with the case.) The report of the appraiser(s) as to the expected gross recovery of the claim, probability of zero recovery, and so on would be made available to all interested parties; and negotiation about the terms of settlement would proceed as at present, save for the significant difference that the plaintiff would have an appraisal of the prospects and attendant risks of his claim by an independent expert.

The defending insurance companies would stand to gain from such an institutional innovation. This is because the smaller wealth and greater portfolio imbalance of the plaintiff, relative to his attorney, would probably lead him to settle for a smaller fraction of the expected gross recovery at trial than the attorney would accept. If the credibility gap caused by the fact of their involvement could be overcome through the certification process, it might pay insurance carriers to bear the cost of the appraisals. Obviously, such an institutional innovation could be of use throughout the entire field of personal injury litigation.

However, this would be but a second-best solution: a more efficient arrangement would be attained if injury claims were made assignable without restraint and lawyers were permitted to buy them. If such were the case, claim appraisers would become superfluous, as the market for claims would provide an independent appraisal of their value.

Of course, any institutional change that altered lawyer-claimant relations so that the latter could more effectively press for pretrial settlement (on less favorable terms than the attorney desired) would cause adjustments in the contingent fees demanded by plaintiff lawyers. The reasoning is as follows: Whatever increases the probability of a lawyer's being compelled to accept settlement terms he would prefer to reject reduces his estimate of the expected gross recovery from a given claim. Assuming the supply price of the plaintiff attorney services is unchanged, the reduction in the expected gross recovery must be offset either by (1) a rise in the plaintiff lawyer's share of the gross recovery, to hold his expected hourly earnings constant, or (2) an improvement in the "quality" of claim opportunities prosecuted, so as to reduce the expected investment of lawyer time per dollar of gross recovery.[52]

Conclusion

The contingent fee is used to pay plaintiff attorneys in malpractice cases because the plaintiff's resources are usually too limited for him to pay the attorney in the event of a small or zero recovery. Obviously, this situation does not obtain on the defense side, where payment by time prevails. Moreover, insurance company defendants are far better situated than the typical plaintiff to monitor the performance of their attorneys and to punish unsatisfactory performance.

However, the problem of how to compensate the plaintiff attorney is more a matter of portfolio composition than of establishing incentives for performance. Considerations of efficiency in the allocation of risk suggest strongly that malpractice claims should be sold outright by their plaintiffs to a lawyer or syndicate of lawyers. At present, this is impeded by law and legal ethics.[53] The contingent fee, combined with the practice of the plaintiff lawyer of assuming the cost of preparing and trying the case, is an attempt to circumvent these impediments by transferring part of the claimant's equity to his lawyer in exchange for legal services.

While efficiency in risk allocation would be increased by eliminating restrictions upon the right of attorneys to own and traffic in unsettled claims for damages, it does not follow that legislative action should proceed in this direction. To permit lawyers to buy damage claims outright would increase their value to claimants by reducing the transaction cost in disposing of them. This would transfer wealth from whoever it is that bears the cost of malpractice settlements at present to the victims of malpractice; it would also tend to increase the fraction of claim opportunities that are prosecuted. Whether the gain from the greater efficiency in the allocation of risk would warrant the associated redistribution of wealth is moot.

---

[52] There might be still further repercussions: plaintiffs seeking to avoid the increase in the lawyer's share of gross recovery might negotiate partial or total waivers of their rights to settle claims without their lawyer's agreement.

[53] See Epstein, "The Case for Contract," pp. 87-149.

THE PROBLEM OF MALPRACTICE—TRYING TO ROUND OUT THE CIRCLE

Guido Calabresi

The problem of medical malpractice is difficult only if one believes that liability rules are important tools for achieving the minimization of the sum of medical accident costs and medical safety costs. Elsewhere I have called this primary accident cost reduction.[1] In the medical context this "economic efficiency" motive is no different from the knotty problem of achieving the highest quality of medical care, where highest quality implies *considering the price.*

I have not said that the desire to reduce the sum of medical accident costs and medical accident avoidance costs by *itself* makes medical malpractice a difficult problem. If one believes that collective, regulatory approaches suffice to limit medical maloccurrences to those, and only those, which would be too costly to avoid, then medical malpractice as we know it today, or generally discuss it in reform proposals, becomes unimportant.

Approaches Outside Tort Law

If governmental rules, which are roughly akin to building codes, or peer-group controls, such as PSROs, can discriminate between what medical care is worthwhile and is to be mandated and what is noxious or simply too costly and is to be proscribed (this exaggerates the ideological purity of the approach, of course), then efficient medical care can be achieved without the dubious benefits of tort law.[2]

This paper is a preliminary version of the C. A. Wright Memorial Lecture delivered at the University of Toronto on February 9, 1977. The final version of that lecture will be published in the *University of Toronto Law Journal.*

[1] For a definition of liability rules see, Guido Calabresi and A. Douglas Melamed, "Property Rules, Liability Rules, and Inalienability: One View of the Cathedral," *Harvard Law Review,* vol. 85, no. 6 (April 1972), pp. 1089-1128; "Primary accident cost reduction" is defined and analyzed in Guido Calabresi, *The Cost of Accidents* (New Haven: Yale University Press, 1970).

[2] PSROs (Professional Standards Review Organizations) were authorized by Congress in 1972 to monitor the appropriateness of health services financed by Medicare, Medicaid, and other health programs. U.S. Congress, House of Representatives, *Social Security Amendments of 1972,* Pub. Law 92-603, 92d Congress, 2d session, 1972, H.R. 1. See also Institute of Medicine, *Assessing Quality in Health Care: An Evaluation,* Final Report (Washington, D.C.: National Academy of Sciences, 1976).

Similarly, though conversely, medical malpractice has no role to play if one believes that doctors and patients have substantially equal knowledge of risks and negotiate as to appropriate treatment. In such a case also, tort law would not be needed because patients would choose those and just those treatments whose risks and costs they desire, and just those doctors whose abilities they find optimal for the price.[3]

The first non-tort-law approach to achieving optimal quality of medical care that I described is a parody of a collectivist ideologue's search for utilitarian efficiency in medical care. That this regulatory or criminal law model is not infrequently suggested will frighten some and amuse others, but, from my point of view, what is important is that most thoughtful people are likely to recognize that it is not a very promising way of assuring optimal medical care. It can work to control extreme abuses: the butcher can be deterred; the obviously unnecessary treatment can be forbidden. But this approach, which is so rigid that it fails even in relatively stable technological areas (such as the building trades), is apt to be a very poor guide indeed in an area where the issue (what care is worth risking) changes as rapidly as it does in modern medicine.

The second non-tort-law approach that I mentioned is a parody of the market ideologue's dream of utilitarian efficiency in medical care. This contractual model is, at first glance, particularly appealing because transactions costs seem absent. (These costs frequently make the pure market a poor road to a utilitarian's heaven.) The victim does not, as in automobile-pedestrian cases, have to seek out every possible injurer and bribe him to employ better brakes—he is staring at his potential injurer across the examining room. Unfortunately parity of knowledge of risks is needed for contractual arrangements to lead to Professor Coase's optimum,[4] and the cost of giving that knowledge may be very high indeed. Extreme cases of bad treatment and bad doctors may well ultimately be controlled by the unfettered market—but those cases could also be controlled by regulation and are not the key to our problem. Consequently, as many despair of the contractual approach as do of the regulatory, criminal-law approach.

---

[3] Cf. Richard A. Epstein, "Medical Malpractice: The Case for Contract," *American Bar Foundation Research Journal*, vol. 1 (January 1976), pp. 96-107. For a very different contractual approach, one that assumes medical malpractice law as a starting point but allows persons to contract out of that fault-based liability by electing a system of no-fault liability and compensation, see Jeffrey O'Connell, "An Elective No-Fault Liability Statute," *The Insurance Law Journal*, no. 628 (May 1975), pp. 261-93.

[4] For the classic description of how contractual approaches can, in the absence of transaction costs, lead to efficiency, see Ronald Coase, "The Problem of Social Cost," *Journal of Law and Economics*, vol. 3 (1960), pp. 1-44.

This situation is in no way unique to medical malpractice. It applies as well to most areas where there is a trade-off between safety costs and accident costs. In those areas too, regulation or criminal law is occasionally deemed effective and employed, while at other times contractual negotiations are allowed to establish the desired level of safety. The major difference between those areas and medical malpractice is that in those areas the tort law approach—whatever its flaws, and be it fault or no-fault based—seems to be a reasonably effective supplement when regulation and contract do not suffice to minimize the sum of accident and safety costs. What is so troublesome about medical malpractice is that neither the fault-based approach, which so far has been dominant, nor any proposed no-fault substitute, has seemed to be a satisfactory means of medical care assurance in that apparently broad set of situations in which neither regulation nor contract seems likely to work.[5]

It may, of course, be that our society is not interested in reducing the sum of medical maloccurrence costs and the costs of avoiding them, or—what is the same thing—that the cost of any system which would do so beyond what can be done by regulation and contract is so high as to be not worth undertaking. It may even be that the fuss about malpractice has little to do with the quality of medical care. It could, instead, have to do with a desire to compel the spreading of the costs of certain catastrophic medical maloccurrences. Or it could have to do with a desire to remove the cost of such maloccurrences (whether spread or not) from victims and doctors and have them be borne—purely for reasons of wealth distribution—by taxpayers at large. If either of these goals is what we are seeking, then, once again, the malpractice problem becomes relatively simple. We will require people to insure against those losses which we would have spread. The premiums can be borne by patients and by doctors—if, like good monopolists, doctors are already charging the most the traffic will bear.[6] Or they can be removed and paid out of the general fisc—that is, assessed to whomever, for reasons of wealth distribution, society wishes to assess. If they are removed, of course, all financial incentives for optimal quality of medical care are also removed, but by the hypothesis that I stated, the society either would not care or could achieve what it sought by other means, such as regulation.

---

[5] Cf. Robert Keeton, "Compensation for Medical Accidents," *University of Pennsylvania Law Review*, vol. 121 (1973), pp. 590-617.
[6] Cf. Reuben Kessel, "Price Discrimination in Medicine," *Journal of Law & Economics*, vol. 1 (1958), pp. 20-53.

THE PROBLEM OF MALPRACTICE

Unfortunately, however, we cannot ignore the possibility that financial incentives established through the allocation of liability are important to the achievement of that level of medical care our society desires. It may be that after considering the miserable job that current malpractice law does in this regard, and after examining the difficulties with possible reforms, we are reduced to saying: Let us rely on the internal pressures for good care that the profession develops; let us deal with extreme cases through regulation or criminal law; let us spread losses or redistribute burdens to our (ideological) heart's desire, and let us, since we can do no better, accept that what we have (without financial incentives) is efficient, indeed optimal, even if pretty dreadful.[7] We may be reduced to this, yet we cannot begin with that gloomy conclusion.

The Fault-Based Approach

I cannot spend much time here on the problems, real and fancied, with the existing system of malpractice law. The theory of that branch of law is simple enough and not totally unsound; the reasons it does not work adequately are real and have been sufficiently written about. Like most fault-based approaches to liability, medical malpractice begins with the assumption that the costs of any medical maloccur-rences which cannot be judged (by a jury, court, administrative agency, or legislature) to be worth avoiding should rest on the victim. If, instead, a governmental agency of the kind just listed is prepared to say that the cost of avoiding the maloccurrence is less than the dis-counted cost of the untoward event, and that the doctor should have known this, then the doctor is at fault and must pay for the maloccur-rence. In theory the same fault approach would charge doctors with unnecessary avoidance costs, costs the doctors should have known were not worth the maloccurrences they avoided.

In the malpractice area the governmental-utilitarian (or cost-benefit) analysis just described has been influenced to an extent unknown in other areas by the custom of the trade (medical practice as shown by expert testimony). This is not crucial, however, since if that aspect is considered undesirable it could be cured relatively easily. Similarly, one need not worry unduly about the fact that this traditional approach leaves on the hapless victim all the medical maloccurrence losses which are not deemed worth avoiding. One need not worry about that since, if we wish, insurance against such losses, or some particularly cata-

---

[7] Such an approach also retains whatever incentives would be imposed through patient-doctor negotiations. See Epstein, "The Case for Contract."

strophic set of such losses, could be required, and the burden of the losses could thereby be spread among all users, or even removed to distributionally preferred payers. All this could be done without substantially altering the incentive element on doctors to avoid just those medical maloccurrences the governmental agency deems, after the fact, to have been worth avoiding before the fact. (Spreading losses or removing losses from victims might, in theory, reduce victim care. But it seems most unlikely that these losses—by hypothesis deemed not worth avoiding by doctors—would be subject to significant reduction through victim care.)

Similarly, the basic problem with fault-based malpractice as a vehicle for assuring optimal quality of medical care does not lie in the very real inadequacies of the insurance market. Since the law in this area is changing rapidly, though perhaps not more rapidly than tort law generally, and since malpractice cases do not get decided until many years after the alleged tort, it may well be true that insurance companies are incapable of approximating the actuarial risk they undertake in insuring doctors against distant future losses arising out of today's events. Insurance companies cannot be sure that they will be able to charge future generations of doctors premiums high enough to cover old liabilities which are just coming to judgment. New entrants in the insurance market could undersell old companies in insuring such future doctors since these new insurers would not bear the liability backlog. The result is that present insurance rates tend to be "gambling" rather than actuarial rates. They are designed to cover an unknown future risk. Insurance companies are most unwilling to take on a gamble—they are actuaries, not entrepreneurs. As a result there are few insurers, and they offer rates that may, in retrospect, turn out to have been exorbitant but that cannot ex ante be shown to be wrong.[8] The rate of return demanded for bearing an entrepreneur's risk has always been high, even when sought by those less risk-averse than insurance companies. Still, this problem could be alleviated by systems designed to assure insurers that they will be able to compel future generations of doctors to bear a share of the past risk backlog. Indeed, that is what reforms like medical association malpractice insurance often come down to. If the medical society can compel future doctors to insure with it, it need not worry if past rates turn out to be inadequate and can compute those rates without a gambling premuim.

No, the basic problems in fault-based malpractice law do not lie in these real but on the whole correctable problems. Nor do they lie in

---

[8] Compare, Richard S. L. Roddis and Richard E. Stewart, "The Insurance of Medical Losses," *Duke Law Journal*, vol. 1975 (January 1975), pp. 1281-1303.

that much maligned (but nevertheless admirable) lawyer's fee, mutual-insurance scheme that we call the contingent fee system. They stem, rather, from the fact that we have little or no faith in courts, juries, administrative agencies, and even peer-group tribunals when they purport to tell us which medical maloccurrences are worth avoiding, which are not, and, perhaps more important, which maloccurrence-avoidance costs are too expensive and should themselves be avoided. I again except the easy cases of butchery, because those, as I have said, probably can be dealt with adequately under any approach. Short of those cases, however, we have virtually no assurance that the approach we use, which is administratively highly expensive and which irresponsibly stigmatizes doctors, creates those incentives to good medical care which, ultimately, are its only reason for being. And if it does not, then we would be justified, it would seem, in abandoning it and substituting for it whatever systems would give us the spreading of losses or redistribution of burdens we desire, regardless of incentives.

Why does not the fault-based system give us the incentives which are needed to justify it? In theory, as I have said, there is no reason why it should not. As a practical matter, however, it is clear that the governmental or peer-group decision maker will consistently find only certain categories of maloccurrences to be avoidable. In almost every instance, for every treatment which if it goes wrong would give rise to a compensable loss, there exists a substitute treatment or nontreatment whose harm in practice would not be recognized as a compensable loss. This defect in the decision makers is compounded by the fact that the victim is equally biased in what he recognizes as a compensable cost. In other words, almost inevitably, the fault-malpractice system penalizes some medical maloccurrences and some avoidance costs while systematically failing to penalize the medical maloccurrence and avoidance costs of substitute approaches. One need not be an economist to realize that any approach which so biases incentives is unlikely to lead to an efficient result. Defensive medicine is an apt term for what unfortunately is only the tip of this iceberg. Unless we can round out the circle and create roughly equivalent incentives for avoiding medical maloccurrence costs and safety costs in substitute forms of treatment and nontreatment, we will not do what alone can justify the existence of this cumbersome and expensive area of the law. But if the unsolved problem of creating unbiased incentives is the source of our fundamental dissatisfaction with existing malpractice law, it equally bedevils proposals for its reform, to which I now turn.

Suggested Reforms

The most promising attempt at reform, I think, is that tried by
Havighurst and Tancredi.[9] They recognize the need to establish incentives for providing good medical care that will affect treatment and nontreatment alike, as well as substitute forms of treatment. Their solution is
to single out areas of medical care in which all significant maloccurrence
costs of substitute treatments can either be compensated for on a no-
fault basis or can be prevented by regulation. That is, if nontreatment
in a particular circumstance is so grotesque as to be readily proscribed
(or even without proscription, to be avoided by doctors regardless of
financial incentives)—say, a failure to operate or to use anesthesia in an
operation—then that nontreatment need not be worried about in establishing an incentive scheme for medical care. Nontreatment is not a
meaningful substitute. This fact permits us to charge—on a no-fault
basis—for any harm arising out of the treatment (the clearly justified
operation and anesthesia), thereby creating appropriate incentives for
choosing among all meaningful substitutes.

Unfortunately, the number of situations in which such a circle of
possible substitute treatment either is complete or can satisfactorily be
completed by regulation is quite limited. Much remains out of Havighurst and Tancredi's control. More important, their approach tends
to create a series of borderline situations in which victim compensation
depends on whether the injury occurred within the scheme or without.
Whenever that is the case administrative costs multiply, because the victims have a strong incentive to describe the facts so that they fall within
the scheme, and the injurers have the opposite incentive. One major
source of the high cost of workmen's compensation plans is the litigation expense of fighting out the often crucial issue of whether an injury
arose out of and in the course of employment, and therefore is covered
by the scheme, or did not, and therefore is covered by the riskier (but
occasionally more liberal) general law of torts. Unless we are prepared
to compensate victims to the same extent, whatever the source of their
injury, treatment, or nontreatment (if in one area of medicine, then
in all others), we will have created precisely the borderline costs which
have so bedevilled other reform schemes.

What would be a complete system of financial incentives for providing good medical care? What would round out the circle so that on

[9] Clark C. Havighurst and Laurence Tancredi, "Medical Adversity Insurance—
A No-Fault Approach to Medical Malpractice and Quality Assurance," *The
Insurance Law Journal*, vol. 613 (1974), p. 69; Clark C. Havighurst, " 'Medical
Adversity Insurance'—Has Its Time Come?," *Duke Law Journal*, vol. 1975
(January 1975), pp. 1233-80.

a no-fault basis the appropriate incentives would operate and we would be free to abandon both fault and regulatory approaches? It is not difficult to state such a complete circle—in one context. But to state it is immediately to suggest the problems—the costs, if you will—of rounding out the circle.

Because of this and because there are a number of other, equally flawed, ways of rounding out the circle, I do not describe my complete circle as a proposed reform, but rather as a "joke," or way of raising the question of whether it is worth pursuing any reform which proposes to take seriously the goal of achieving optimal quality of medical care through financial incentives.

Let us posit a system of health maintenance organizations (HMOs) with sufficient competition to enable a consumer to have a substantial choice among them.[10] Let us posit also that the choice of HMO will be made in the employment context through union-management negotiations, so that costs of treatment and nontreatment become available as understandable statistics to those who are to opt for more avoidance (at more expense) or the converse. (The costs of all this in terms of individual choice, even if we posit representative unions, are so obvious that they need not be dwelt upon.)

Such an approach would immediately internalize to each HMO some costs of "bad" medical care and cause these to be reflected in the rates each HMO would charge. This would not round out the circle, however.

Specifically, the costs of the subsequent medical care resulting from either inadequate or excessive treatment would be internalized to the HMOs, and this would create an incentive to treat initially in such a way as to reduce subsequent costs appropriately. But there would be no incentive linked to the HMO to avoid treatment which, if it failed, would produce an untreatable, but perhaps unemployed and unemployable, victim.

Again, if individual consumers could adequately know this risk, without insurance, and therefore make it a part of the HMO negotiation, there would be no problem. But this is no more than saying that, in theory, pure contract law could cope with the problem of adequate

---

[10] "HMOs' [Health Maintenance Organizations'] distinguishing characteristic is that they undertake to provide all the medical care their enrollees need in exchange for fixed, advance capitation payments." R. Bovbjerg, "The Medical Malpractice Standard of Care: HMOs and Customary Practice," *Duke Law Journal*, vol. 1975 (January 1975), p. 1376. The same article, pp. 1375-1414, contains a careful description of HMOs and of how malpractice law would affect and be affected by them.

medical care. If that were so, this conference would have been brief.[11] No, to convert this unemployment risk into a statistical figure which could be meaningfully assimilated in the HMO-employment contract, some sort of wage maintenance insurance would be required. And, since it would be hard to define when wage maintenance was needed because of treatment and nontreatment errors and when it was needed for non-medical reasons, the most likely form such insurance would take would be universal wage maintenance. (The "moral hazard" costs involved in such an approach should be readily apparent.) With such insurance any given employer-union combination, in any given industry, could readily compare the cost of competing HMOs, not only in terms of their present and future treatment costs, but also in terms of their "absenteeism" costs.

The circle would still not be complete, however. The HMO which either cured or killed could underbid the HMO which preserved life at a higher present or future medical and absenteeism cost. The same would be true for the HMO which reduced safety and accident costs by increasing chances of pain which could not be alleviated by treatment and which did not bring on absenteeism. The second is perhaps too fanciful to be worried about. The first may well not be. In order to deal with the first, we would have to require that life insurance for a substantial amount be made part of the union-employer package, along with wage maintenance and insurance against future medical care needs. Then the circle would be complete, the buyer would know that virtu-ally all treatment and nontreatment costs were reflected in the price of any HMO and that, therefore, incentives to reduce such costs appro-priately would lie on the HMO and its employees, the doctors.

Reduction in HMO price by reducing amenities of care would, of course, remain possible, as would an increased price for increased com-fort. But as to these, I become a pure contractarian. I think the con-sumer has adequate knowledge to decide whether standing in line is worth what it saves and whether having an HMO which permits rela-tives to visit the hospitalized patient comfortably and easily is worth what it costs. As a result, such comparisons among competing HMOs would not, in my view, require any intervention to maximize satisfac-

11 To the extent that HMOs, by working in an employment context, generate greater knowledge of such risks than would otherwise be available to individual patients, some of the impediments to a pure contractual solution would be removed, as H. E. Frech points out in his disscusion of this paper. One may well doubt, however, that the union-employer-HMO nexus will, without specific incentives, do an adequate job of internalizing the costs of those injuries which would make a patient unemployable and untreatable (that is, injuries which make the patient not only no longer a charge on the HMO, but possibly no longer the responsibility of either the employer or the union).

tion. I hope not, for rounding out the circle would be exceedingly costly even without further intervention.

It may be worthwhile to consider for a moment why it is so complex and costly. That may best be done by thinking about what it is that we did when we completed the circle. In effect, we made any death which occurs sooner than the appropriate life expectancy for individuals in that industry a part of the medical care cost. We also made any absenteeism, whether treatable or not, part of the same cost. And, of course, we began by making subsequent medical care part of the cost as well. To the extent that an HMO does an average job on any of these counts (as presumably it would if death or absenteeism were genuinely unrelated to treatment or nontreatment), the HMO and its competitors would be affected equally. A superior or inferior job—however seemingly unrelated to medicine—would instead be reflected in the costs of the competing HMOs. Financial incentives would now be present because any medical maloccurrence and any costs of avoiding that maloccurrence would now be part of the scheme and be compensable. But to create the scheme all sorts of nonmedical costs were included in it and made subject to compulsory insurance. Insurance is, obviously, not cost free. The rounded circle comes anything but cheap—in terms of incentives to avoid harm, in terms of costs of administration, and in terms of permitting individuals the option to choose risks rather than coverage and to spend the money saved elsewhere.

If one believes that except for extreme cases of butchery anything short of a complete circle of incentives is worse than no incentives, what are the alternatives? The fault approach, by trying to concentrate on those treatments and nontreatments which, ex post, we can say were worth avoiding ex ante, was one solution. It is plausible—unfortunately it has failed. We could try a Havighurst-Tancredi (medical adversity insurance) approach, but it does not, ultimately, promise enough of an answer. We could go to regulation. In my judgment this could create a system which does nothing but may give people at large the feeling that something is being done—at least until they wake up and realize they have been fooled. Worse, we might create a system which applies real standards that will be quickly out of date and lead to poor medical care. Finally, we could give up on any incentives to good medical care—except in the extreme cases—and concentrate solely on cost spreading and wealth distribution goals. This would entail the abolition of malpractice law, the establishment of medical catastrophe insurance, and the creation of peer or criminal law bodies to punish the occasional scoundrel.

I have been told that this last approach would prove unacceptable to the mass of people, especially the more our society moves toward universal medical care plans. In such circumstances people demand the appearance of controls, even if the controls are ineffective and costly. And certainly, our tendency to look for scapegoats or for what appear to be solutions (even when they do not exist) in other areas of law supports this cynical view. Perhaps the old, old, rarely successful malpractice suit, ineffective as a source of both incentives and disincentives, served this very function of creating a useful illusion of control where no control was feasible. It is, nonetheless, dead and cannot be resurrected. Old subterfuges, once exposed, can almost never regain credibility. Maybe if no-fault compensation for medical catastrophes, paid for out of the general fisc, had been established, we might not have felt the pressure to enlarge (and ultimately to expose as a sham incentive system) the liability of doctors for malpractice. But whatever one may think about that question today, the option it represented is probably no longer open to us.

As a result we are faced with an uncomfortable problem. We can try to round out the circle of incentives, all the while being deeply uncertain as to whether such schemes will be worth their costs. We can openly abandon incentives in this area (except for those that either pure contract or regulation can give at the extremes) and concentrate on spreading and redistributing some medical burdens, knowing all the while that perhaps a more sophisticated incentive scheme might have been worth it. We can try to control by regulation what in easier areas has proved very hard to regulate intelligently. Or finally, we can create new subterfuges—less adequate than the old, precisely because chosen rather than found—which only give the semblance of ensuring quality medical care while freeing us to spend or redistribute to the extent we wish. I, it should be obvious, would opt for either of the first two. I strongly suspect, however, that both will be rejected in favor of regulation or subterfuge, or most likely a mixture of regulation and subterfuge like PSROs.

MEDICAL MALPRACTICE:
ITS CAUSE AND CURE

Richard A. Epstein

I want to accomplish two distinct, but closely related tasks in this paper. First, I hope to give some explanation of the origin of the current medical malpractice problem, by showing how the traditional negligence standard of reasonable care has been transformed and expanded by courts in recent years. Second, I want to evaluate two possible responses to the current situation, one that would place greater reliance upon the traditional devices of private contract, and one—the various no-fault medical plans, including so-called medical adversity insurance—that would use direct administrative controls to provide, if anything, expanded protection to the victims of medical injury.

The Changing Concept of Negligence

Harry Kalven once remarked to me that the term negligence in the law of tort covers much too much of the legal terrain. In no other area of substantive law, he noted, is any single concept pressed into service to discharge so many distinct tasks. Instead, concepts with a narrower gauge—think only of the detailed rules of contract law governing offer and acceptance by post—are used to give fairly precise legal solutions to problems within well-defined limits. One of the consequences of the broadness of the negligence concept is that it alone does not determine particular outcomes in specific cases. The real business of sorting out the rights and duties of parties in physical-injury cases is left to particular subrules. While these might appear to be simple deductions from the basic negligence premise, in reality they turn out to be independent judgments about the standard of liability applicable to particular contexts.

The transformation of the negligence subrules has had much to do with the emergence of the current problems in the law of medical malpractice. Few of the recent cases repudiate the basic negligence standard, which requires a physician to exercise only such skill and judgment as are possessed by similar physicians engaged in the same area of practice. But through these cases the courts have consciously developed

245

special subrules which create liability where none existed before. Perhaps the most dramatic instance of this kind of interstitial change is *Tarasoff* v. *Board of Regents*.[1] In that case the California Supreme Court imposed a revolutionary change in tort law by holding that, if a psychiatric patient expresses threats against a third party and subsequently commits crimes against that party, his psychiatrist is liable unless he has warned the third person of the threats against him, where it is reasonable under the circumstances for him to do so. In writing the majority opinion, Justice Matthew Tobriner glossed over the portions of the ruling that created a new duty of physicians to nonpatients, concluding that his decision was hardly revolutionary. Citing one case dealing with informed consent and another dealing with *res ipsa loquitur,* he observed:

> We recognize the difficulty that a therapist encounters in attempting to forecast whether a patient presents a serious danger of violence. Obviously we do not require that the therapist, in making that determination, render a perfect performance; the therapist need only exercise "that reasonable degree of skill, knowledge, and care ordinarily possessed and exercised by members of [that professional specialty] under similar circumstances."[2]

Many of the extensions of the law of negligence that have taken place in the last fifteen or twenty years are less dramatic than the step taken in *Tarasoff.* Yet their cumulative effect has been to transform the negligence concept from within and to impose, but without explicit recognition, a wholly new set of obligations upon physicians. One convenient way to show the plasticity of the negligence concept is to compare some English and American cases that illustrate particular points of medical malpractice law. While the English and American cases both use the same basic negligence test, the potential exposure to suit is vastly greater in this country, largely because of the different subrules that fill out the two systems.

Take first the doctrine of informed consent. In the English case of *Hatcher* v. *Black,* the patient underwent a throat operation which carried a slight risk of permanently impairing her ability to speak.[3]

---

[1] 17 Cal. 3d 425, 551 P.2d 334, 131 Cal. Rptr. 14 (1976).

[2] Ibid., p. 438, P.2d at 345, and Cal. Rptr. at 25.

[3] I have not found the case in the English reports, a point of interest in itself. The relevant portions of the opinion are reproduced in Addison and Bayles, "The Malpractice Problem in Great Britain," found in a United States government staff report, *An Overview of Medical Malpractice,* 94th Congress 1st session, pp. 259, 267-68 (March 1975). I have reproduced portions of the opinion in C. Gregory, H. Kalven, Jr., and R. Epstein, *Cases and Materials in the Law of Torts* (Boston: Little, Brown, 1977), pp. 174-75.

The defendant, knowing of this risk beforehand, deliberately decided not to mention it to the plaintiff for fear that it would so upset her as to reduce the operation's chances of success. After the operation, the plaintiff indeed suffered from the disability. Her action, essentially under a theory of informed consent, however, was rejected by the court as a matter of law. Lord Denning, who has long been one of the most activist members of the English bench, held that all decisions on disclosure rested with the physician and that any judicial effort to superintend medical judgments in individual cases could only place a "dagger" over a physician's head. If, he argued, no physician was prepared to say that the conduct of the defendant amounted to bad medical practice, then there was no reason why the jury should be allowed to say it. In effect the English courts decided with that one ruling that the doctrine of informed consent had no place in the law of medical malpractice and that the physician's duty of reasonable care was discharged as a matter of law by any physician who used his own best judgment on disclosure.

The history of informed consent in American jurisdictions is quite different. Originally the doctrine grew up as an exception to the defense of consent available to physicians charged with a technical assault and battery. In more recent years, disclosure has been treated as one of the duties which the doctrine of negligence, with its concept of reasonable care, imposes upon the physician. While the exact contours of the duty to disclose and the exceptions to it are subject to some dispute in the current cases, there seem in general to be two distinct lines of authority.[4] Some states allow the physician to invoke the standards of "customary practice" to decide, first, which disclosures are material, and, second, whether the circumstances (emergency, incapacity, and so on) warrant non-disclosure in any given case. The stricter view of the subject is that the customs on disclosure, if any, may be disregarded, leaving the jury free to decide both the questions of materiality and of possible privilege as it sees fit.

Whatever one may think of either of these variations of the informed-consent doctrine, it is quite clear that they embrace a very

---

[4] For a collection of the cases, see *81 Annotated Law Reports 1028* (Rochester: Lawyers Co-operative Publishing Co., 1961) and the supplementary updates thereto. Note that the recent developments in the area are so great that both of the standard references on the subject, William L. Prosser, *Handbook on the Law of Torts* (Minneapolis: West Publishing Company, 1971) and Fowler Harper and Fleming James, Jr., *The Law of Torts*, 2 vols. (Boston: Little, Brown, 1956) are totally inadequate on the question. For my extensive criticism of the doctrine, see Richard A. Epstein, "Medical Malpractice: The Case for Contract," *American Bar Foundation Research Journal*, vol. 1, no. 1 (January 1976), pp. 119-28.

different conception of medical malpractice from the English view announced by Lord Denning in *Hatcher* v. *Black*. The English rule of good faith eliminates the need to elaborate the contours of all variations of the informed-consent doctrines. The American law, in either of its forms, requires us to develop much learning about the questions of materiality of disclosure, the privilege of nondisclosure, the burdens of proof on causation, the appropriate statute of limitations for the action, the need for expert evidence, and the like. We might wish to say that both the English and the American laws of medical malpractice are based on negligence principles, but given the difference in particular rules on informed consent, it seems quite clear that little is gained by that categorization. And when we remember that informed consent did not emerge as a definite legal doctrine until somewhere between 1955 and 1960, we can appreciate the magnitude of the transformation that has taken place in the American law.

A second point on which it is instructive to compare the English and American cases is on the doctrine of *res ipsa loquitur*. The origins of *res ipsa loquitur* can be traced to Baron Pollock's casual use of the words while questioning counsel in the case of *Byrne* v. *Boadle* in England in 1863.[5] There the defendant was sued for the injuries that resulted when the plaintiff, while walking on the street, was struck by a barrel falling out of the defendant's loft. The plaintiff could offer no direct evidence as to why the barrel had fallen, but the court allowed the case to go to the jury on the ground of *res ipsa loquitur*. The entire affair "spoke for itself," and it was up to the defendant to show how the barrel could have fallen out of the loft other than through negligence on his part or on the part of his servants—for example, by showing that a stranger had broken into the shop and had thrown the barrel out of the window.

There is a very real question of how far the doctrine of *res ipsa loquitur* should apply to medical malpractice cases. In one sense the argument for its application is quite simple: cases of falling barrels and cases of medical malpractice are both cases of negligence, and the principles of proof that are applicable to one branch of the subject should be equally available in the other. In one sense this is a truism; yet it is an error to treat barrel cases and malpractice cases as part of a single unified class. The justifications for applying the doctrine in barrel cases may well not apply in medical malpractice cases.

The doctrine of *res ipsa loquitur* is one of circumstantial evidence designed to allow the plaintiff to show that the harm he has suffered is attributable to some conduct for which the defendant is legally respon-

---

[5] 2 H. & C. 722, 159 English Reprints 299 (1863).

sible. The possible explanations for the barrel's falling out the window fall into two convenient groups: in the first, the defendant or his servants were in charge of the management of the barrel, and in the second, the barrel was in the control of the plaintiff or a third party. On the evidence, the plaintiff's control of the barrel is quite out of the question, and the probability of a third party's control is, though not utterly disproved, quite remote. Unless one thinks that barrels just happen to fall out of windows (as by leaping onto ledges), it is quite proper to hold that more likely than not the harm was attributable to the negligence of the defendant or his servants. The plaintiff quite properly rests on the doctrine, particularly since the plaintiff is entitled to a verdict in his favor upon a bare preponderance of the evidence.

Turning to medical malpractice cases we must ask what is the distribution of causal agents between responsible and nonresponsible causes. When the English court considered this problem in *Mahon* v. *Osborne*, it was quite troubled by the fact that medical injuries are easily attributable to disease or other nonresponsible causes.[6] On the facts of that case the plaintiff sued for damages caused by the presence of a sponge that had been left inside him upon completion of an operation. The court had to decide whether failure to remove the sponge was evidence upon which a verdict of negligence could be sustained. There was a sharp division of opinion on the question, with Lord Justice Scott taking the position that the doctrine has no application at all because everyone knows that all sorts of complications can arise during surgery without the negligence of anyone, and Lord Justice Goddard taking the opposite opinion, that the existence of recognized procedures for removing sponges upon the completion of operations was sufficient to allow the jury—absent an explanation from the defendant—to find negligence. It seems that Goddard's position has prevailed in the case, although the opinion of the third justice was so obscure that the matter is somewhat doubtful. In any event, it is still true that since that case was decided in 1939 there has been little effort to use *res ipsa loquitur* in medical malpractice cases in England, and none whatsoever to extend it to more complex situations.

American courts have adopted by and large the basic doctrine of *res ipsa loquitur*, and *Byrne* v. *Boadle* is the leading case in both countries. The doctrine has been used very differently in medical cases in England and the United States, however—so much so that it is quite mistaken to think that on this point English and American courts apply the same legal principle. American courts universally hold that the doctrine applies to sponge and instrument cases. In addition, they

---

[6] *Mahon* v. *Osborne*, [1939] 2 K.B. 14, 1 All. Eng. Rep. 535 (1939).

249

extend it to more complicated situations. In the leading case of *Ybarra* v. *Spangard*, the plaintiff suffered traumatic injury to his shoulder when he fell off the operating table during an appendectomy.[7] The court, noting the "conspiracy of silence" among physicians in malpractice suits, held that *res ipsa loquitur* could be invoked for the benefit of the plaintiff, who was unconscious at the time of the accident, and himself in no way responsible for it. At the time the decision was handed down, some commentators took strong exception to it, regarding it as an unacceptable departure from principle, largely because it implicitly held several independent defendants responsible for the actions of each other.[8] Yet given that it is likely that someone (we do not know who) let the plaintiff fall off the operating table, the case looks like a straightforward extension of *Byrne* v. *Boadle* and does not seem to raise any of the mysteries of medical causation.

The further extensions of *res ipsa loquitur*, however, are much more difficult to justify because they have applied the doctrine when it was at least likely that natural causes were responsible for the patient's injury. In *ZeBarth* v. *Swedish Hospital Medical Center*, the court upheld the use of *res ipsa loquitur* when a patient who was being treated for Hodgkin's disease suffered partial paralysis after being exposed to allegedly excessive dosages of radiation.[9] Here there was no adequate causal explanation of how the radiation could possibly have had this effect, and several possible biological explanations were offered of how the paralysis could have occurred. The application of the doctrine, therefore, appears to have led to the wrong result. The case also shows the extent to which some courts have extended the doctrine beyond its original function in *Byrne* v. *Boadle*, allowing it, at least in part, to shift the basis of responsibility in medical malpractice cases as to make a physician accountable not for his own negligence, but for the patient's physical condition.

The *ZeBarth* decision, which holds physicians responsible for what are in essence acts of God, is in striking contrast with the California opinion of some fifteen years earlier in *Salgo* v. *Leland Stanford Hospital*, once but perhaps no longer a leading authority on *res ipsa loquitur*.[10] There the plaintiff had suffered paralysis after being given an aortogram and wished to use *res ipsa loquitur* (it appears) to establish both the negligence of the defendant physician and the causal

---

[7] 25 Cal. 2d 486, 154 P.2d 687 (1944).

[8] See, for example, Warren A. Seavey, "Res Ipsa Loquitur: Tabula in Naufragio," *Harvard Law Review*, vol. 63 (February 1950), pp. 643-48.

[9] 81 Wash. 2d 12, 499 P.2d 1 (1972).

[10] 154 Cal. App. 2d 560, 317 P.2d 170 (1957).

connection between that negligence and his own subsequent paralysis. The court, rightly in my view, refused to admit this use of the doctrine because it was not shown that the injection of contrast material had been made in an incorrect location and, further, the paralysis could well have been attributable to a stroke brought on by the plaintiff's already weakened condition. That case was both rightly decided and rightly reasoned because it recognized that the high probability that the harm had been caused by some nonresponsible agency (either the plaintiff's own condition or a properly administered injection) precluded the application of *res ipsa loquitur* to the facts of the case. By applying the doctrine broadly, as in *ZeBarth*, the courts have shifted the wavy line between inevitable accident and culpable conduct so that injuries once regarded as inevitable are today regarded as actionable. The English courts, which have rejected this invitation, use a law of negligence, and so do we; yet there is no doubt that the two systems have very different substantive rules of liability.

A third illustration of the general proposition that the doctrine of negligence is known by its subrules is the way in which the customary standards of practice within the medical profession are treated in setting the applicable standard of care. In England, as *Hatcher* v. *Black* indicates, the courts have not sought to challenge practices that conform with accepted medical standards. Thus, in *Roe* v. *Minister of Health* the plaintiff was paralyzed when phenol solution made its way through invisible cracks into an ampoule of spinal anesthetic which was subsequently injected into the plaintiff.[11] At the time of the injection, the defendant had visually inspected the ampoule to see if it contained cracks. It was only four years later that the possibility of invisible cracks became generally known in the profession and that the practice of adding colored dye to the phenol was instituted to guard against its secret contamination. The court refused to apply standards developed after the case and affirmed the judgment given to the defendant in the trial courts.

There was a time when American courts and commentators generally took this view of the relationship of custom to negligence in the law of medical malpractice. In 1932 Judge Learned Hand remarked in the *T. J. Hooper* case: "a whole calling may have lagged in the adoption of new and available devices," and further, "there are some precautions so imperative that even their universal disregard will not excuse their ommission."[12] Yet for the most part this hostility to custom was reserved for cases involving harm to strangers or arising from industrial

---

[11] [1954] 2 Q.B. 66.
[12] 60 F.2d 737 (2d Cir. 1932).

accidents; medical malpractice was generally treated as a special situation in which the norms of the profession should, if only because of their technical nature, be accepted universally.

In recent years the courts have tended to move away from that position in malpractice cases. We have already noted that professional standards of disclosure are not conclusive upon the jury in informed consent cases. There are also many circumstances in which the very definition of custom has been narrowed. Practices that prevail within a substantial portion of the profession are no longer treated as constituting custom for the profession as a whole, and the jury is free to make its own judgment of the desirability of a particular practice in a particular case. In my view, the law should protect from liability the physician whose practices are recognized by any portion of the medical community. Yet there are hints in the recent cases that the jury is entitled to find one mode of treatment negligent because of its belief in the greater wisdom of some alternative, a position which in effect makes the jury not only a finder of facts, but an arbiter of medical practice.[13]

The distrust of custom has gone even further. Here special mention should be made of the recent Washington State decision in *Helling* v. *Carey*, where the court found that a defendant ophthamologist was liable as a matter of law to his patient, who had suffered visual impairment from glaucoma, when it was established that the defendant had not administered to her an eye test ordinarily sufficient to detect the condition.[14] The decision not to administer the test was in conformity with the general rule of the profession that the probability of the condition is so low (1 in 25,000) in persons under forty that the test is not required unless there is some special reason for its use. Here the court, in a novel application of risk theory, argued that in determining the desirability of this precaution, the likelihood that the plaintiff had glaucoma was immaterial. Reasoning that young and old are entitled to the same level of protection, it held that a test required for one group of patients was required for all. The decision is, of course, suspect because it assumes that the glaucoma test is well nigh riskless. One does not need any medical knowledge to know that no procedure is absolutely safe. The probability of a mishap in the administering of the test might well have been equal to or greater than the probability that the disease would be discovered, and the rough and ready calculations of the profession might have made more sense than the court's own painstaking assessment.

---

[13] See, for example, Incollingo v. Ewing, 444 Pa. 263, 282 A.2d 206 (1971).

[14] 83 Wash. 2d 514, 519 P.2d 981 (1974).

More important, the decision illustrates a major shift in attitudes about *who* should make the calculation of costs and benefits. Rejecting the custom of the profession, the court in effect decided that any physician acts at his peril when he follows customary practice in routine procedures, for a court or jury is free to conclude that the procedures themselves were negligently conceived. The negligence standard once said that where there were several alternatives, each of which was reasonable, the defendant could escape liability if he had embraced one of those alternatives, even though one of the rejected alternatives had subsequently proved superior. *Helling* v. *Carey* revises the standard so that the court has the final say on the trade-off between risk and safety, cost and benefit. The Washington legislature quickly passed a statute which made customary practice within the profession the standard in malpractice cases, but it is always an open question whether any statute can, by the force of its words alone, restore the situation that existed before court decisions spurred its enactment.[15] Outside of Washington, *Helling* v. *Carey* remains a warning of the extremes to which liability can be extended in malpractice cases.

One last difference between the English and American systems of tort law cannot be illustrated by reference to single cases, but it is perhaps as important as any of the doctrinal considerations that we have already canvassed: it concerns the law of damages. The English courts try most tort actions without a jury and are inclined to award damages that are but a small fraction of the awards received by successful plaintiffs in the United States. Thus, there are two major reasons for the much greater exposure to medical malpractice loss in this country: in the first place, the liability rules are systematically broader in this country than they are in England, and in the second place, the adverse financial consequences of negligence are far greater here than there. Since both liability and damages add to the total cost of error, the burdens placed upon the medical system are vastly greater here than in England.

Economists, following the lawyers' lead, are apt to think that they can analyze the functioning and purpose of a tort doctrine such as negligence by concentrating on the general contours of the legal rule and the judicial or legislative reasons for its adoption. The point of this discussion is not only to show the quiet transformation that has taken place in the law of medical malpractice, but also to remind us once

---

[15] See, *Washington Revised Code,* (1975 Supplement) section 4.24.290, which provides that in all medical malpractice action that the plaintiff must establish that the defendant failed to exercise that degree of skill, care, and learning possessed by others in the same profession; the statute excludes from its operation causes of action based upon a failure to obtain informed consent.

again that a sound appraisal of a legal doctrine requires a detailed examination of its inner workings as well as a grander appreciation of its social function.

Alternative Solutions

The transformation of certain legal rules is one of the origins of the current medical malpractice crisis. But it is one thing to understand the origins of a problem and quite another to find a cure. In this section I should like to examine possible ways out of the current medical malpractice dilemma.

There are three possible approaches to the current situation. The first is to work around the edges of existing law by making piecemeal statutory reforms designed to undo particular medical malpractice rules. Thus, it has been proposed to limit contingent fees, to place maximum limitations upon the amount of recovery, or to allow juries to take collateral benefits (such as payments from health insurance or employment plans) into account in setting the recoverable amount of damages. Laws can also alter the substantive elements of the malpractice cause of action. We have already noted the passage of the Washington statute designed to reestablish the custom of the profession as the standard of care in malpractice cases. Other statutes have been proposed to cut down on the rigors of informed consent and restrict the use of *res ipsa loquitur*. I do not propose to spend any time here examining these changes, except to say that they will probably prove to be too little and too late to solve the problem.[16]

Instead of considering interstitial legal reforms, I shall examine two major approaches to reforming the medical malpractice system: private agreement and a general no-fault insurance system for medical injuries.

The Contractual Approach. The contract proposal I have outlined in my article in the *American Bar Foundation Research Journal*. Its fundamental premise is that we have been mistaken all along in looking at the problem of personal injury in malpractice cases as though it were a problem for tort law. Instead, we should both permit and encourage private agreements between physicians, hospitals, and patients to set the terms on which medical services are rendered. Virtually all of the general discussions of malpractice law and virtually all of the judicial opinions upon the subject take it for granted that the specification of the substantive rules of medical malpractice rests, in the absence of legislative

---

[16] Epstein, "Medical Malpractice," pp. 128-43, includes a more systematic evaluation of some of the reforms.

command, upon the courts and that the parties themselves are not free to vary those terms by private arrangement. Although most courts have not expressly stated the extent to which specific provisions in the physician-patient contract are void and unenforceable for reasons of public policy, some uneasy combination of the doctrines of unequal bargaining power, contracts of adhesion, economic duress, and unconscionability today block any private effort to contract out of the judicially mandated liability rules for medical malpractice.[17]

The consequence of this judicial attitude—which should be condemned in itself as an unwarranted intrusion upon the principle of freedom of contract—is to create distortions of a kind that arise so often in regulated markets, for the consequences of regulation are the same whether imposed by judicial or legislative command: the regulators, for reasons of their own, decide that certain relationships should proceed only upon certain terms; it then turns out that they are mistaken in their assessment of the needs of both the parties and of the complexities created by the rules that they impose. Were such errors made in private agreements, they could be corrected by more responsive alternative private arrangements. But where the original distortions are created by public command, private correction is effectively precluded. Instead, we are required to go to the legislature or the courts for modifications of the original standard-form arrangement. Judging from the piecemeal reform that has thus far been the norm, this effort produces only makeshift political compromises. In the area of medical malpractice, there is

---

[17] See, for example, Tunkl. v. Regents of University of Californa, 60 Cal. 2d 92, 32 Cal. Rptr. 33, 383, P.2d 441 (1963). In that case the court struck down the contractual provision whereby a charitable research hospital sought to exempt itself from liability for medical malpractice. In its opinion the court said: "In placing particular contracts within or without the category of those affected with a public interest, the courts have revealed a rough outline of that type of transaction in which exculpatory provisions will be held invalid. Thus the attempted but invalid exemption involves a transaction which exhibits some or all of the following characteristics. It concerns a business of a type generally thought suitable for public regulation. The party seeking exculpation is engaged in performing a service of great importance to the public, which is often a matter of practical necessity for some members of the public. The party holds himself out as willing to perform this service for any member of the public who seeks it, or at least for any member coming within certain established standards. As a result of the essential nature of the service, in the economic setting of the transaction, the party invoking exculpation possesses a decisive advantage of bargaining strength against any member of the public who seeks his services. In exercising a superior bargaining power the party confronts the public with a standardized adhesion contract of exculpation, and makes no provision whereby a purchaser may pay additional reasonable fees and obtain protection against negligence. Finally, as a result of the transaction, the person or property of the purchaser is placed under the control of the seller, subject to the risk of carelessness by the seller or his agents."

a complete unwillingness to abandon the original assumption that direct public control is required.

In my view private arrangements, with their different priorities, would take a very different course. Private parties would realize that the difficulties of medical malpractice actions render them largely ineffective as a means of quality control. Instead of pressing for government regulation, the parties involved would attempt to deal with the problem by reducing the number of situations demanding legal intervention. It is quite conceivable that the parties would contract for medical services on an "as is" basis, with the patient agreeing that no action would be brought for medical malpractice, no matter how adverse the outcome of a medical procedure and no matter how egregious the conduct of the physician. The rule of total immunity does not say that gross violations of medical procedures are a good in themselves. It only recognizes that courts cannot weed out unsound claims without barring proper ones as well. Private parties, assessing the trade-offs, might well opt for agreements that allowed no malpractice claims whatever. Under such agreements, the checks upon the conduct of physicians would be market constraints, as individual patients, knowing that they were without legal recourse, would exercise greater care and caution than they do now in choosing their physicians.

It might also turn out that patients and physicians would opt for some contractual protection, albeit less complete than that which is currently required by the malpractice law. Thus, it might well be that private arrangements between doctors and their patients (like so many commercial arrangements), would hold the physician liable only for willful infliction of harm or gross (that is, very great) negligence. This system, in principle, would allow for successful actions against physicians who amputated the wrong leg or who omitted to take some universally recognized precaution—who failed to put silver nitrate drops in a newborn's eyes for example—which they themselves concede should be observed. Yet a standard of this sort would repudiate all of the recent judicial extensions of malpractice liability. A gross negligence standard, faithfully construed, would not allow, under an informed-consent theory, actions against physicians who failed rightly or wrongly to disclose. It would not permit the extensive use of *res ipsa loquitur*, be it on the issue of negligence or causation, in the host of delicate circumstances to which it is applied today. And it would preclude attack on any practice that is in conformity with the uniform standards and customs of the medical profession, or even in accordance with one respectable school of thought. In effect, the gross-negligence standard says that the individual patient puts his trust in the skill and judgment of the physician he chooses and not in any after-the-fact determination of right and wrong made by judge and jury.

In my view, private contracts would probably produce agreements of the two basic types I have just described. But regardless of its specific results, the contractual approach is superior in principle. The strength of contracts is that they allow individuals to determine solutions for themselves that are better than any we, as legislators, economists, or lawyers, might wish to impose. Private parties make mistakes under contract, and the legal system cannot after the fact correct the misfortunes of those who have entered into inadvisable agreements. On the other hand, it is equally clear to me that substantial mistakes are made in regulation, which—aside from the loss of individual freedom that regulation necessarily entails—impose large administrative and allocative costs. Even in an area as complex as medical services, I think we should seek solutions through the market, for, whatever the problems confronting private individuals in evaluating and pricing services, they are problems that any scheme of regulation must face as well. I do not think that judicial regulation has done much to reduce the problem of medical malpractice; I have little hope that the more sophisticated forms of regulation, such as Professional Standard Review Organizations, imposed at great cost, are apt to do any better.[18]

No-Fault Medical Insurance. Let us turn now to the second type of response—no-fault medical insurance. The recent proposals for such insurance are instructive because, unlike the contractual schemes, they seek to expand the number of cases in which physicians must compensate their patients. The central conception of all no-fault systems is that of "iatrogenic injury": in essence, the physician is required to compensate the patient for any injury caused by medical treatment, whether or not occasioned by the negligence of the physician. Many of the "inevitable accidents" that the common law of negligence has refused to treat as compensable would become compensable under the proposed systems. The no-fault rules thus would accelerate the tendency already observable in case law, but instead of merely shifting, *sub silentio*, more and more cases into the class of avoidable injuries, no-fault insurance would eliminate the line between unavoidable and avoidable injuries altogether by regarding both types as compensable. By so doing, the systems of medical no-fault insurance would place greater pressure upon the definition of medical causation than does the common law of medical

---

[18] James F. Blumstein and Clark C. Havighurst, "Coping with Quality/Cost Trade-Offs in Medical Care: The Role of PSROs," *Northwestern Law Review*, vol. 70, no. 1 (1975), pp. 6-68.

malpractice, because the absence of physician negligence would no longer be a barrier to compensation. Making causation rather than negligence the test for compensation would increase, of course, the administrative burdens on the system. The supporters of the various no-fault plans understand that their success rests in large measure on the realization of two supposed advantages: the first is the reduction, through various causation tests, of the costs of resolving any individual claim; the second is some express limitation on the personal damages obtainable in any given case.

In my view, no-fault insurance is counterproductive at every point. To begin with, it would create a more comprehensive compensation system than we already have—when one of the major problems we face under the current system is the high cost of dispute resolution, measured in terms of both direct expenditure of resources and utilization of physician and patient time. It hardly seems wise to attempt to achieve goals more ambitious than those ever envisioned by the tort system at the very time when that system is itself overburdened. Believing as I do that we ought to adopt private solutions for the medical malpractice problem, I am convinced that it would be a step in the wrong direction to create administrative agencies to handle individual claims against physicians. The burden of proving the benefits of this step must be upon those who would thus vastly extend the compensation system.

For purposes of analysis, the no-fault proposal can be broken down in two different ways.[19] On the one hand, it is possible to distinguish between elective and nonelective no-fault plans. On the other hand, it is possible to distinguish between plans (whether or not elective) that rely upon broad coverage formulas and those that specify detailed lists of adverse, compensable events.

---

[19] A third possible breakdown, on the basis of collateral benefits under no-fault plans, deserves brief mention. Under some versions of medical no-fault insurance, including the O'Connell proposals, (see note 20) and the Kennedy-Inouye bill, collateral benefits are deductible from the amount which the eligible patient otherwise receives. Under the Havighurst-Tancredi proposal (see note 21) collateral benefits would not be deductible, the double payment being eliminated, if at all, by repayment to the collateral source from the individual benefits received under the no-fault system. Where the sole end of the no-fault system is compensaticn, the O'Connell solution of deductions from no-fault payments is possible, but by no means necessary; the Havighurst-Tancredi alternative is workable as well. Where any desire is retained to fashion appropriate incentives for medical care, as with the Havighurst-Tancredi proposal, it would be wrong, as the authors recognize, to permit deductions from the no-fault scheme for collateral source payments even though (in the short run at least) it might reduce the total cost of the plan. Note, too, if the collateral source is entitled to repayment it may have to be given the right to pursue the injured party's cause of action under the no-fault plan, much as a workmen's compensation employer can pursue his employee's tort rights against third parties.

Let us consider first the desirability of elective plans.[20] The major reason put forward for making no-fault coverage elective is a commendable caution about making compulsory such a far-reaching reform when so little is known about its actual operation and impact. In its most robust form, the elective proposal, therefore, contemplates that certain physicians will opt into such a plan, which would allow them to escape from all medical malpractice liability (except, for example, in informed-consent cases) and would allow patients to decide indirectly through the selection of their physicians whether they wished to participate. The argument in favor of election is all to the good; indeed it allows for a contractual solution, on a limited scale, and in this is consistent with the approach that I have advocated. Yet the puzzling point about the proposal is that it would limit both physician and patient to the choice between medical no-fault and medical malpractice insurance when they might well wish to choose a much cleaner and simpler legal relationship. If the parties are entitled to choose between these two alternatives, why not a host of others? Contractual freedom should not be limited but complete.

It may be said that the law will allow a medical no-fault contract but not, to take the extreme case, an "as is" contract because in the first instance the patient receives a quid pro quo for the waiver of his malpractice action in the form of increased coverage even at reduced levels, whereas the patient receives nothing in exchange for the reduced legal protection under the "as is" rule. Yet the argument is utterly wrong in principle because it presupposes that courts should make independent judgments about the substantive merits of private bargains before enforcing them. The emphasis on the quid pro quo is also misplaced because it fails to recognize as a benefit the reduction in price that is necessarily coupled with the elimination of the malpractice action. It takes a peculiarly rigid mind to assume that a quid pro quo must take the form of some tangible and distinct obligation (like broader coverage) instead of the reduction of an existing obligation. The important thing is only that a quid pro quo will be present, for sellers simply cannot charge the same price for services that will not entail tort actions and for services that may.

From what has been said above, it should be clear that I have little faith in *compulsory* no-fault medical insurance. That system may be defended on the ground that it is only possible to get a fair measure

---

[20] See Jeffrey O'Connell, *Ending Insult to Injury: No-Fault Insurance for Products and Services* (Urbana: University of Illinois Press, 1975), pp. 96-111. See also, O'Connell, "Expanding No-Fault Beyond Auto Insurance: Some Proposals," *Virginia Law Review*, vol. 59 (May 1973), pp. 749-829.

of the system's efficiency if all of the physicians in a given jurisdiction are required to join, but the consequent loss in contractual freedom and the dangers of massive regulatory blunder are quite sufficient to outweigh benefits of this forced experiment.

Let us turn now to the form of the coverage formula under no-fault insurance. The original no-fault proposals attacked the problem of medical causation by adopting a straightforward definition, patterned upon the time-honored formula of workmen's compensation: the employee recovers damages "for any injury arising out of or in the course of his employment." The analogous phrase in medical no-fault insurance is in effect that the harm in question is compensable "if more attributable to the treatment that he received for the condition than to the prior condition of the patient." This definition has startling implications. The negligent failure to diagnose a dangerous condition is actionable under the malpractice law. Does it follow that *any* failure in diagnosis is actionable under medical no-fault insurance? Would the no-fault system, then, require the physician to compensate the patient for all undiagnosed glaucoma? And what about the early stages of cancer or heart disease? Similar problems would arise with the side effects of beneficial drugs. Properly administered, drugs create no cause for action under the current law of medical malpractice, because it is understood that the patient assumes the risk of adverse side effects as part of the price of adequate medical treatment. However, a concept of medical causation that makes no allowances for negligence or the assumption of risk will have a dramatic effect on the types and number of claims. Again, there is the question how one makes difficult judgments in uncertain circumstances: Is it possible to argue that so long as there is in principle any better treatment (at any cost) available for a given case, the requisite of medical causation is satisfied?

These unsettling questions illustrate the point that it may be impossible to ascertain in advance precisely the dimensions of the enterprise to which the general causal formula would commit us. The success of the no-fault system, therefore, appears to depend upon some refinement of the original position, expanding liability beyond the traditional limits of negligence but cutting off the open-ended problems raised by the hypothetical compensation formula.

One approach, originally put forward by Professors Havighurst and Tancredi and elaborated by Professor Havighurst, would replace the original open-ended coverage formula with a detailed list of the adverse consequences of certain medical procedures for which the physician would be required to compensate the patient.[21] By establishing a list of compensable events, the authors hope to achieve several ends. Thus they wish to distinguish between outcomes that are in general avoided by the exercise of reasonable care from those which are not, by including only the former on the list of compensable events. In effect the program is designed to achieve the incentive effects of an ideal negligence system, not on a case-by-case basis, but on an aggregate basis, by identifying as compensable those consequences usually, but not always, associated with negligent treatment. Then by eliminating the negligence issue, and perhaps the causation issue from the individual case, they hope to generate substantial administrative savings which can in turn be used to provide the additional benefits called for by the plan. They hope, too, that eliminating the need for case-by-case judgments about negligence will remove the stigma from physicians who were required to pay compensation in individual cases. Yet, by keeping compensation tied to iatrogenic injuries, they seek through the no-fault system to create strong incentives for all physicians not only to avoid the embarrassment of negligence suits by complying with the minimum process standards of the profession, but to go beyond those standards by delivering the best possible service in the individual case. One can hardly quarrel with the objectives of this type of plan. My objection to it is that I do not believe it would be able, at an acceptable cost, to achieve them.

It is doubtful first that the precise specification of compensable events would excuse a trier of fact from confronting the difficult questions of causation and negligence central in today's medical malpractice suits. Let me give two examples. The first involves the compensability of the paralysis suffered by the patient given the aortogram in *Salgo* v. *Leland Stanford Hospital*; [22] the second concerns a hypothetical patient who contracts infectious hepatitis within six months of a surgical procedure—one of the compensable events cited by Havighurst himself.[23]

The problem that would arise under no-fault insurance in the *Salgo* case emerges most clearly if we first note the three possible causes of the plaintiff's paralysis. In that case the court said, and quite rightly, that the paralysis could have been (1) the result of a stroke that the

---

[21] Clark C. Havighurst and Laurence R. Tancredi, " 'Medical Adversity Insurance'—A No-Fault Approach to Medical Malpractice and Quality Assurance," *Milbank Memorial Fund Quarterly,* vol. 51 (Spring 1973), reprinted in *Insurance Law Journal,* no. 613 (February 1974), pp. 69-77. Clark C. Havighurst, " 'Medical Adversity Insurance'—Has Its Time Come?" *Duke Law Journal,* vol. 1975, no. 6 (January 1975), pp. 1233-80.

[22] 154 Cal. App. 2d 560, 317 P.2d 170 (1957).

[23] Havighurst, "Medical Adversity Insurance," p. 1254.

patient suffered because of his own (deteriorated) natural condition, (2) the result of a stroke induced by the nonnegligent injection of the contrast material into the artery, or (3) the result of a negligent injection into the artery.

Under the traditional law of medical malpractice, the plaintiff recovers damages only if he can show that the harm is attributable to the third of these possible causes. Under no-fault insurance, if "paralysis from stroke" were included on the list of compensable events, the plaintiff would be entitled to compensation if he could show that the second or third possible cause had occurred, but not the first. Causation, then, must still be determined. The fact that the first possibility is treated differently from the last two leaves the no-fault case with all the complications it would possess if it were tried as a negligence action, for the source of the injury still remains the issue upon which liability turns.

It may be countered that no-fault is still defensible because it nonetheless eliminates the negligence issue. Yet I believe that conclusion, too, is incorrect. True, the negligence question is no longer an ultimate issue of fact in the case; yet the question of negligence remains crucial to the causal inquiry that the no-fault system requires. Thus, suppose that the physician is able to show that the injection in question was properly performed, and that the inserted needle was a safe distance from the exposed nerves. While that piece of evidence does not resolve the question of causation, it makes it less likely that the defendant's conduct (possibilities two and three) was responsible for the harm and more likely that the patient's natural condition (possibility one) was. Since the question of performance levels is intimately bound up with the proof of causation, negligence issues cannot be eliminated from the case.

This point is neatly illustrated by a related development in the law of products liability. Broadly speaking, one of the great developments of the 1960s was the formal elimination of the negligence issue from most actions involving harm caused by defective products. With the elimination of negligence as an ultimate issue, it might be thought that the doctrine of *res ipsa loquitur* which it had spawned would fall into disuse. Yet recent case law indicates that both are very much with us.[24] Negligence retains its importance not as the ultimate issue upon which liability turns in products cases, but as evidence on the causal question: negligence, with its *res ipsa* doctrine, is a means of proving whether there

---

[24] See, for example, Jiminez v. Sears, Roebuck, and Co., 4 Cal. 3d 379, 482 P.2d 681. 93 Cal. Rptr. 769 (1971); see also Jagmin v. Simonds Abrasive Co., 61 Wis. 2d. 60, 211 N.W. 2d 810 (1973).

was any defect in the defendant's product at the time that it left his possession and control. If the defendant were careless in his techniques of manufacture or quality control, it is much more likely that his product contained the defect needed to establish liability. If the product were manufactured with all possible care, the probability increases that the fatal defect was the doing of some third party or the plaintiff himself. Given the importance of negligence for determining causation in products liability cases, it should not surprise us that the use of *res ipsa loquitur* continues to be of major importance today, for it is proper for the plaintiff to use circumstantial evidence to exclude his own conduct, that of third parties, or natural events as the cause of injury. Plaintiffs continue to frame their complaints with negligence and strict liability as alternative counts in large measure, I believe, in order to take advantage of *res ipsa loquitur*, which they believe is expressly tied to negligence liability by judicial pronouncement.

The persistence of negligence issues is also illustrated in our second example, the case of hepatitis contracted within six months after transfusion. Here the problem is that the plaintiff is required, under no-fault insurance as well as under tort law, to show that the blood furnished by the defendant contained the hepatitis virus. This is by no means easy to establish, since it is quite clear that hepatitis can be contracted from a variety of sources, including previous transfusions, and even random contact. In order to rebut, therefore, the implication that the source of the virus was the blood he supplied, the defendant will attempt to prove that he went to all possible lengths to collect uncontaminated blood from acceptable donors, to store it under ideal conditions, and to administer the transfusion in the safest possible way. Likewise, the plaintiff will attempt to demonstrate negligence with respect to any of these items, for example, by showing that the blood in question was not kept in a properly sealed container.

One possible escape route is open to the defenders of medical no-fault. In both the stroke and hepatitis cases it might be possible to eliminate the inquiry into source simply by presuming that all strokes that occur during operations are surgically caused and all hepatitis contracted within six months of a transfusion is caused by the transfused blood. This, I believe, is Tancredi's and Havighurst's final position. Yet there is a significant associated cost: if health care providers are held accountable not for what they have done to a patient, but for what has befallen him for reasons beyond their control, it cannot be argued that the system rates health care providers on the strength of their performance. If the simplification in proof is allowed, it will undermine the claim that the system deters physician misconduct. The law of medical malpractice could have incorporated conclusive presumptions on difficult questions of fact, but the belief that ultimate judgments of responsibility should only be made on the basis of all the evidence has effectively precluded the use of blanket procedural devices to bar defendants from presenting evidence in support of their factual contentions. There is no reason why the same consideration should not preclude its use within the no-fault framework.

Assume, however, for the moment that the use of such presumptions is in principle allowable, at least if it has the desired economic effect. One major peril still promises to undermine the scheme.[25] Any useful list of compensable events must be such that the designated adverse outcome is usually the consequence of medical negligence. There are today literally hundreds of complicated medical procedures carrying with them inevitable risks of unfortunate results no matter how carefully they are carried out; and there is no evidence that the major cases of negligence are uniquely associated with any identifiable subset of these procedures. The closed-claim study of the National Association of Insurance Commissioners indicates that the medical malpractice cases with large awards have arisen over a very broad range of medical procedures, and no single procedure was involved in more than a small handful of cases. In other words, the study seems to suggest that no particular procedure is so clearly associated with actionable adverse effects as to justify its inclusion in a no-fault list. Does it make any sense, for example, to place hepatitis within six months of transfusion on a list of compensable events if less than half the cases of hepatitis are in fact attributable to blood transfusions and only a tiny fraction of those are attributable to negligence? No-fault liability may eliminate the error of allowing negligent providers to escape liability, but it does so only by holding careful providers liable for consequences they would never be considered responsible for under a medical malpractice theory. The erratic distribution of medical malpractice appears to preclude the formulation of a workable list of compensable injuries under any system of medical no-fault insurance.

There are other drawbacks to medical no-fault insurance even when it specifies which events are compensable. Two of the specific ends of the system are (1) the creation of incentives to elicit the best possible performance from doctors and (2) the elimination of the costly and unnecessary medical tests that are currently being administered by

---

[25] This point was suggested to me by Patricia Munch at the AEI conference in December.

doctors who are threatened by the law of medical malpractice. In my view, no-fault insurance will not accomplish either of these goals. Consider first the question of defensive medicine. Generally, the view today is that the malpractice system encourages physicians to perform certain tests upon their patients not to advance the patients' interests, but to allow the physician to rebut any potential malpractice claim. In effect, the increased standards of performance demanded by the system have made imperative certain tests that were once thought optional. The no-fault system, which would only increase the incentive to move to ever higher standards, will reinforce this tendency. If a physician knows that his involvement in a no-fault case can be prevented by his ordering more tests, why should he refrain from ordering them? One of the reasons why excessive precautions are accepted so easily by individual patients is that they know some form of third-party insurance will pay. Since this would remain true under no-fault insurance, there would be little resistance to increased costs at the consumer level. The pressure can only increase upon those systems of direct regulation which have already shown their utter inability to control medical costs.

The second point is that there is little reason to expect no-fault systems to provide incentives to improve the ultimate performance of physicians. The success of a given procedure is a function not only of the care with which it is performed but also of the condition of the patient on whom it is performed. Heart surgery performed on a young person in fair health has a much greater chance of success than that performed upon an elderly person in a weakened condition. To cite the success figures in these operations without taking into account the original condition of the patients is therefore to give a misleading impression of the proficiency of the parties who provided the treatment. A physician who saves 50 percent of difficult cases may be quite superior to one who saves 90 percent of easier ones. In one sense the negligence law, with its vague definition of reasonable care, tried to take into account the composition of the physician's caseload in measuring his performance. The no-fault law, by removing case difficulty from consideration (except to the extent that it is reflected in the categories of compensable injuries, certain procedures, for example, not being compensable for persons over a certain age), tends to *undermine* the connection between levels of performance and the obligation to make compensation. Indeed, there is a very real danger that a physician operating under the no-fault system would decide to turn away difficult cases precisely because they could have an adverse effect upon his overall ratings and involve him in complex compensation proceedings.

265

There is yet a further delicate question, that of incentives involving substitute procedures. Suppose that treatment A or treatment B could be used for a given condition, and that only one of them carries the risk of no-fault liability. In this situation there will be a strong incentive for the physician to adopt that treatment which does not expose him to liability, even if it is not the treatment that promises the patient greater hope of success. Unless therefore one treatment is added to the list, or the other one removed, the existence of the liability rules could lead to the selection of inferior treatments. Yet to establish the parity between A and B may yet lead to a distortion between B and C, where those are substitutable under some other circumstances. There may well be no way to control incentives created by these unfortunate substitution effects. The best solution may indeed lie in retreating to the grosser rules adopted of a sensible malpractice system, which though it attempts less, may achieve more.

To the objections just mentioned must be added the obvious point that, the high cost of the enterprise to one side, the system suffers from a great disadvantage in that it relies upon cumbersome administrative mechanisms to define the rights of individual parties. Under a no-fault system one could expect medical compensation issues to involve fierce interest-group politics over what are ostensibly technical problems. Consumer groups, medical groups, and insurance groups all would lobby for a system they could live with. I fear too that it would be virtually impossible to keep the larger question of income distribution out of the discussion. One need only cite the precedent of the legislative treatment of the medical malpractice issue in California, where, in negotiating with medical groups, the governor (through the state HEW) sought to tie relief from the medical malpractice problem to a promise by medical groups that they would forgo increases in state reimbursement for medical care. Those two issues are not essentially related, but interest-group politics at the legislative level will tend to link them for political ends.

My final objection to no-fault medical insurance plans has an ironic twist: they would not in themselves eliminate the need for the ordinary medical malpractice action. In order to define the class of compensable events to which the no-fault system applies, it would be necessary at the outset to circumscribe severely the initial coverage of the system. It would remain possible in principle to say that whatever adverse consequences fell outside medical no-fault coverage would go completely without redress. But that course is one that even the supporters of medical no-fault find difficult to accept—particularly in cases involving questions of informed consent or gross negligence in treatment

Clearly, it would be necessary to retain the ordinary tort system (or its contractual reformulation) to cover the many additional risks not included in the plan. Given that the no-fault systems would probably have one set of benefits and the malpractice system quite another, there would be efforts on both sides to move particular cases in or out of the two separate compensation systems. Let there be a case of severe injuries and possible negligence, and the injured party will argue that the no-fault coverage does not extend to the case, such that a negligence action is proper. The defendant in turn will argue that only the no-fault benefits should be awarded. Let there be serious injuries without obvious negligence and the forensic roles might be reversed, the injured party claiming that the injury is listed as compensable, the defendant replying that compensation is payable only if medical malpractice is established. The problem of coordination here is by no means an easy one, particularly as there are often multiple defendants in medical cases who might be sued either under the no-fault rules or under ordinary malpractice law. By the same token multiple injuries might be attributable to separate events, some covered by no-fault and some not. The complications that have arisen under workmen's compensation when some injured parties have sought redress under the tort laws and others from workmen's compensation remain formidable even after half a century of litigation. We can expect similar results if we adopt two separate systems of compensation for medical injuries. Anyone who is aware of the dissatisfaction aroused by the unhappy marriage between workmen's compensation and the common law of tort knows that the coordination of two distinct systems of individual compensation will never be an easy matter once the hard cases come before the courts.

I have said enough to show that there are major, indeed fatal, defects in the various schemes for medical no-fault insurance that have been proposed. I hope that such schemes will not be hastily enacted by legislatures looking for dramatic solutions to the medical malpractice problem. Conclusions similar to those I have presented here could, I believe, be reached about various schemes of direct public regulation of the practice of medicine as well. One would hope that the experiences of the last several years would heighten the willingness of legislators to think more favorably about private solutions to difficult problems. Yet in the current political environment there is a well-nigh irresistible attraction to taking dramatic public action, however misguided, even if "doing nothing" is, as a matter of both legal theory and political prudence, the best possible course.

COMMENTARIES

Ross D. Eckert

I want to confess at the outset that I do not fully understand the purpose of medical malpractice law. I conjecture that I am not alone in this ignorance and that this is one reason our society is having so much difficulty formulating solutions to this troubling issue.

There appear to be two possible rationales. The first is equity: most of us would agree that people should not have to bear the total costs of injuries which can be traced to the carelessness of others. These costs used to be shared by physicians and their insurers, but the trend is toward spreading them over society at large. If equity is the goal regardless of who picks up the tab—and the size of some recent malpractice awards suggests strongly that it is—then it appears that we have provided this equity at a heavy cost that includes distortions in the practice of medicine and surgery and possibly the career choices of potential physicians. These distortions represent a "dead-weight loss" to society, a use of resources that does not increase the total output of goods and services. Society might be able to "purchase" more equity if the same value of resources had instead been devoted to compensating the victims of birth defects. The plight of a child who is paralyzed as a result of a surgeon's negligence in performing a spinal tap does not tug more at my heart-strings than that of a child born with *spina bifida*, a deformity of the spinal tract which, among other things, prevents the draining of fluids from the brain and dooms its victim to a miserable and short life of disfigurement, low intelligence, and prolonged institutionalization. The family of the second child usually gets ongoing medical care largely at society's expense. But the family of the first child can in addition probably be "made whole" by, as one of the conference participants would say, the "legislative grace" which permits them to sue the surgeon or his insurance company. Both situations create productivity losses to society of roughly the same magnitude. However, the compensation of birth defects raises fewer questions of fault, moral

269

hazard, distorted incentives, and other factors which raise transactions costs and contribute to the extent of the dead-weight loss. (Of course, there would still be the problem of determining what constitutes a birth defect.) I say this not to advocate compensation for birth defects but to emphasize that society has decided to tackle the more difficult and perhaps the less important problem.

The second principal rationale for medical malpractice awards is that they are a means of punishing negligent physicians. The threat of suit supposedly induces physicians to be more careful, and successful prosecution may force them to bear the full costs of their incompetence. It seems to me that this shift in liability for iatrogenic illnesses from patients to physicians represents a clear-cut application of Roland McKean's well-known analysis of the economic effects of changes in product liability.[1] With buyer liability, potential patients would exercise what they viewed to be the economical degree of caution in the choice of physicians, treatments, hospitals, drugs, and so on. This search would be relatively expensive (especially in emergencies) owing to the complex nature of medical products, the layman's unfamiliarity with them, and the restricted conditions of supply. Reversing liability for iatrogenic illnesses on the grounds that the physician and hospital have lower-cost access to the crucial information, malpractice law has produced results that coincide with McKean's predictions: the costs of producing riskier medical treatments have risen; the range of product quality has contracted; more resources have gone into issuing disclaimers in the form of defensive medicine; and some consumers presumably have chosen to search less efficiently in the knowledge that the cost to them of selecting unsafe physicians and treatments has declined sharply. The results are ironic: many "unsafe" medical products and services have been taken off the market, but the accident rate appears to have risen for the goods and services that have remained. This reversal of liability appears to have increased the total resource costs of medical practice— the sum of injury costs, transactions costs, and the distortions caused by the insurance system. (There also appears to have been a contemporaneous and exogenous shift, however, in the public's demand for more advanced and risky medical and surgical procedures.)

It is interesting to note the shifting and incidence of these higher costs. The results cited by professors Greenwald and Mueller suggest that higher insurance rates do not directly punish incompetent physicians, if this was ever the purpose of insurance. An insurance company that loses a malpractice suit will probably spread that loss over a group

---

[1] Roland N. McKean, "Products Liability: Trends and Implications," *University of Chicago Law Review,* vol. 38 (1970), pp. 3-63.

of doctors and their patients, including those who are careful in their choice of medical supplies and services. Evidently, it is rare for marginal physicians to be removed by their colleagues from hospital staffs, and there is little evidence even that they shift their practices to localities where insurance rates are lower.

In sum, I do not think we now have a satisfactory rationale for the existing system. Its equity premises are weak and probably have been implemented at a cost that is too high. The economic arguments, if they ever were taken seriously, have largely backfired. Economists probably take the economic arguments more seriously than other analysts, however, and my chief disappointment is that few of the conference papers that I have read tell me anything about the size of the dead-weight losses. Estimating at least some of these costs ought to be high on the research agenda.

The main question before us is whether the problems of medical malpractice can be permanently resolved. After reading the papers by Professor Epstein and Professor Calabresi, I tend to share their pessimism. Our national policies toward medicine, health, and litigation have been so inappropriate for so long that the malpractice problem probably cannot be solved even temporarily. Each policy change that offers some promise is likely either to be rejected or to be adopted in some watered-down, ineffective form. Of course, there is also the distinct possibility that further public intervention in this arena will distort the allocation of resources even more.

We appear to be watching an enormous struggle between two quasi cartels. On the one hand is a small group of physicians, hospitals, and other suppliers who obviously want their customers to continue to bear liability for iatrogenic illness or, failing that, to transfer most of the costs of their own liability to their customers in the form of higher fees. This cartel has been effective, according to several of the papers, only in achieving the second goal. The other cartel is a large, loose-knit group of personal-injury trial lawyers who have enough clout to prevent sweeping changes in our existing medical and automobile insurance systems. The members of this group also have the ultimate advantage that the rules of the game are written by their colleagues, the legislators. The public, shortsightedly, has little direct sympathy with either group as long as the flow of medical services is not drastically altered and as long as the federal government continues to pay roughly half of the hospital bills.

A number of proposals for the reform of the malpractice insurance system have been mentioned in the conference papers. I would divide these proposals into two categories: those which would reduce the total costs of injuries and malpractice transactions and those which would redistribute existing costs without reducing them. Naturally, the trial lawyers want to shift more of the burdens to doctors, and vice versa. The problem is analogous to the economics of tax incidence and burden shifting, and on very few points do the papers give us anything more than a clue as to what the economic impacts of the reforms would be.

One of the most sweeping proposals in the first category was made by Professor Epstein, who suggests that we should return to a system of unfettered contracting and caveat emptor. This would reduce litigation costs, but it is likely to raise the cost of private bargaining over liability between physician and patient, especially for risky surgical procedures that have risen in demand and have high search costs on the patient's side of the transaction. To some people, this would represent a reversal of burdens that would be unacceptable in equity terms. As I see it, the chief attraction of Epstein's proposal is that it goes to the heart of the malpractice problem by attempting to restore a rational set of incentives for patients and physicians alike, therefore reducing the current level of dead-weight losses for society at large. Professor Reder's proposal to abolish the malpractice attorney's system of contingent fees also would give us the caveat emptor system that Epstein recommends. This is because the contingent fee makes it attractive for attorneys to continue to supply their services to this "industry," and removal of the fee would essentially wipe out this form of legal practice. Professors Shavell, Epstein, and others appear unanimous in their opinion that a no-fault system would be worse than the system we now have, in terms of both transactions costs and distortions of physicians' incentives. Shavell also argues that ceilings on awards and changes in the statutes of limitations would cut transactions costs at the expense of major losses in equity, especially for the "big ticket" malpractice cases. (As my earlier remarks suggest, I think that this is a loss in equity that we could stand, although many people believe just the opposite.)

The recent experience with malpractice legislation in California suggests which types of reform may have the better chances of adoption.[2] A special session of the legislature was called in 1975 in anticipation of a strike—against just whom was never clear—by 9,000 physicians and surgeons in Southern California who had received notices that their malpractice insurance rates would rise by about 400%. The California Medical Association (CMA) favored a broad set of reforms that included the abolition of contingency fees and the requirement that

---

[2] See Barry Keene, "Malpractice Mess: Raw Nerves Still Waiting for a Real Cure," *Los Angeles Times*, December 28, 1975, pt. VII, p. 1. I am indebted to Diane Richey for providing me with source materials on the California experience.

a patient give his doctor notice of intent to sue within sixty days of the claimed date of injury. Instead, the CMA narrowly won a bill that (1) tightened the statute of limitations, (2) limited pain and suffering awards to a maximum of $250,000, (3) established a sliding scale for attorney fees, (4) required juries to take into account the plaintiff's other sources of income, the nontax status of awards, and the remarriage of spouses in wrongful-death cases, (5) eliminated huge awards to nondependent heirs of dying patients, and (6) made it easier to substitute arbitrators for juries. The common effect of these changes would be to reduce transactions costs, but an overall assessment of their economic impact is impossible at this point. I should add that the trial attorneys are challenging the constitutionality of the new law. Earlier in the special session they were able to kill a bill that would have created a board to settle malpractice awards, similar to the one that deals with claims for workmen's compensation.

The California experience also sheds light on the possibility of securing reforms of the second type mentioned earlier. These would reshuffle the existing bundle of costs and thereby postpone a final reckoning with the high and rising total costs of health care. A second California statute created a Joint Underwriting Association (JUA) designed to subsidize high-risk physicians and to prevent the complete withdrawal of insurance carriers from the medical malpractice field. As Patricia Munch's paper explains so clearly, the need to subsidize these physicians out of the premiums paid by purchasers of other lines of insurance would vanish in an unregulated insurance market. Insurers would raise the premiums or adjust the deductibles for this group of physicians until all risks were covered. However, local medical societies have opposed experience-rating for physicians and have pressed state insurance commissioners to limit premium increases. The natural reaction of insurers to this regulation is either to write insurance on a selective basis or to withdraw from the market. What will happen under the California JUA remains to be seen. Its effectiveness in reshuffling costs, if it is ever activated, may be only temporary since insurers will have incentives to discover new and unregulated methods of raising premiums for high-risk physicians.

At one time the governor of California proposed a more ambitious risk-reassignment package that would have kept the average insurance premium at $4,000, funded by a $120,000,000 physician-controlled insurance pool backed by the state government. Three political strings were attached to this "gift." First, a physician could no longer refuse to treat a person who was a recipient of Medi-Cal. I understand that 33 percent of all Californians are such recipients and that the most statistically significant trait of malpractice plaintiffs in California is that they are also on Medi-Cal. It was, therefore, not surprising to find little enthusiasm among physicians for this proposal. The second string was an implicit tax: the requirement that physicians whose practices included fewer than 10 percent Medi-Cal patients would have to offer twenty days of free services each year to low-income people. (Paradoxically, the governor proposed that this activity be financed by raising the states annual license fee for physicians.) Third, physicians would have to demonstrate that they had passed their reduced insurance costs on to their patients in the form of lower professional fees.

The CMA was prepared to agree to the governor's package of proposals only if three conditions were met: (1) the implicit taxes were removed; (2) participation in the plan were voluntary for county medical societies; and (3) the legislature promised to work on significant reforms of the tort liability system in the time that remained before the $120,000,000 fund became insolvent (one of the principal controversies being just when insolvency would occur). The doctors were not given any of these assurances (particularly the promise that the entire tort system would be revised to their satisfaction). As a result, the governor's bill died in committee. (Fortunately there is no basis as yet for malpractice claims against politicians who let bad bills die in committee.)

The strong incentive of both of the cartels to litigate to death any fundamental change in the system—especially any change in the monopolistic conditions of medical societies of which Reuben Kessel wrote so well—makes an even broader spreading of risks to the federal taxpayer the most likely outcome. Under this system, as McKean argued, there would be even fewer gains to the careful searcher than under the present system, warnings that physicians directly give to patients about the risks associated with certain procedures would fall sharply, and the demand for riskier procedures would skyrocket. The enormous transactions costs under this system would lead the government carefully to regulate the nature of treatments, product and service warnings, warranties on medical services, and so forth. Some risky procedures would be banned entirely, and the procedures that the bureaucracy permitted would often be inappropriate to the cases and the times. In addition, I suspect that the total costs of the medical malpractice insurance system that we have now would pale beside those of a system that was federalized for keeps. As McKean said, "Whatever the product liability rule, the world will still be full of accident, tragedy, and disappointment."[3]

---

[3] McKean, "Products Liability," p. 45.

Dennis E. Smallwood

The papers by Mark Kendall, Patricia Munch, Judy Mann, and Jerry Green represent, in that order, a transition from an extremely broad and atheoretical discussion to a theoretical treatment of one specific issue. Kendall uses an extremely broad brush to paint his impressions of the causes of the medical malpractice crisis, using a mixture of economics, social psychology, and history. Munch dissects the malpractice crisis from the point of view of economic theory, with particular attention to explaining events in California. Mann presents a sophisticated theoretical treatment of the relationship between the frequency of claims and the economic losses of insurers using queueing theory, and applies it to data collected in San Diego County. Having moved from the United States to California to Southern California, we finally forsake the real world altogether and enter the wonderland of pure theory in Green's paper, which analyzes a model of the costs and benefits of having different standards of care applied by the courts.

Kendall provides a useful overview of the controversies surrounding the recent strains in the medical liability insurance markets; the main charges are succinctly explained. As an introduction to the debate, this paper has several virtues. First, Kendall attempts to interrelate diverse factors: the behavior of insurers and of insurance regulators, the attitudes of consumers, the behavior of the American Medical Association (A.M.A.), the performance of licensing boards, and changes in legal doctrine. Second, he does not shrink from drawing conclusions; the traditional academic custom of qualifying conclusions until they are invulnerable to objection is bravely ignored. Third, I agree with what seems to be his basic conclusion, namely that "there is no overwhelming reason for exempting physicians from large portions of our liability laws." In fact, the moderateness of the conclusions surprised me, given the tone of the discussion. Indeed, the only specific recommendation, for a federal reinsurance mechanism, comes as a distinct surprise since Kendall does not argue that the reinsurance market has played a role in the crisis. In fact, this recommendation is offered as "a short-term solution," which should be used because "it does seem unfair to force individual physicians and individual insurers to bear the burden of these changes." Coming after such judgments as "It would be easy to infer from the Senate hearings on medical malpractice insurance that the major cause of the medical malpractice insurance crisis is the insurer," such generosity is unexpected. The call for federal reinsurance appears implicitly to involve major subsidies, since otherwise it would not shift any burdens, but the details are not specified.

275

Whether one agrees with Kendall's conclusions, the quality of his supporting evidence ranges, in my opinion, from mediocre to worthless. He begins by alluding to confused testimony about the average cost of insured claims by insurance representatives, which was gradually clarified "with more than a little help from the committee chairman." In fact, a reading of the testimony suggests that the source of the confusion was simply that the committee chairman did not understand the nature of an occurrence policy. At another point, Kendall concludes that "Until the formation of the American Medical Association in 1847, there seems to have been no popular dissatisfaction with this relatively free market for medical services," using as evidence a quotation from Benjamin Franklin. After stating that "The plausibility of the monopolization argument is obvious," he notes that licensing restrictions on physicians followed the formation of the A.M.A. In fact, the states began to license doctors and lawyers during the latter part of the eighteenth century; so much for relying on one of Ben Franklin's letters. Interestingly, most of these statutes were repealed in the early nineteenth century during a wave of sentiment against centralized control, so that by 1830 legal restrictions on the practice of medicine were at a minimum. It would thus be as easy to argue that the formation of the A.M.A. and the subsequent licensing laws were a reaction against the performance of the unbridled market as that they were tools of monopolization. To Kendall's credit, he acknowledges the validity of either explanation of licensing restrictions.

Similarly, he argues that shifting legal doctrine has played a major role. He emphasizes the relaxation of the locality rule from its original version, which referred to the standard of care used in the same locality or community. According to Kendall, the strict locality rule together with control over local physicians by county medical societies effectively curtailed malpractice litigation. In fact, the strict form of the locality rule was overturned in Minnesota in 1896, in North Carolina in 1898, in Rhode Island in 1904, and in most other states soon thereafter. While it is true that the remaining forms of the locality rule have been weakened recently, the rule as applied to specialists—the defendants in most malpractice claims—has been loosely construed in most states since the fifties. Kendall relies on the concentrated summary of legal doctrine provided by Dietz et al. in the *Secretary's Report* as his source, which is misleading on several points.

With respect to insurance rating practices, Kendall discusses the Insurance Services Office (ISO) rates and procedures as if the ISO rates were effective rates. In fact, they are simply suggested rates and are not reliable guides to actual rates. For instance, in California, suggested ISO rates have been about twice the actual market rates. Thus when Kendall asserts that "investment income on loss reserves was not reflected in the standard rate-making procedures for medical professional liability insurance," one should realize that he is not necessarily talking about actual market rates.

Kendall's reliance on information from the ISO and on a superficial legal synopsis can be forgiven, but it is hard not to allege fraud when, to support an argument, he notes that "For example, in 1972, researchers warned . . . " and the footnote indicates that the researchers in question were Kendall and Haldi.

In contrast to Kendall's attempt to identify the underlying causes of the malpractice experience, Munch focuses on the responses and adaptations to the explosion in malpractice claims. In part, her purpose is to rationalize an apparent paradox: during a period when the risks from liability were clearly rising, why has the market for risk spreading contracted in various ways? Explaining the rise of physician mutuals, she notes that the correlated component of claims against different physicians—which arises because of the common effect of changes in legal doctrine, and possibly because of the epidemic effect—has probably become more significant. Given the implied increase in variance even when many physicians are underwritten, a mutual may represent a more efficient diversification of the overall risk than the standard insurance market can provide. Similarly, the claims-made policy allows insurers to shift part of the risk arising from uncertainty about shifts in the claims distributions to physicians in the aggregate. I agree with this analysis, but I would also argue that the ability of physician mutuals to effectively underwrite may be crucial. Munch tends to dismiss this effect, noting that physician mutuals have usually replaced programs sponsored by medical societies, in which the peer review committee was actively involved in underwriting. But the incentives for the mutuals to be strict are greater, there are fewer problems of confidentiality, and there is less reluctance to allow the underwriter—who is now completely under the control of professionals—to become involved in the control of professionals.

It is interesting to compare Munch's fundamental premises with those of Kendall. Her objective "is to determine to what extent these institutional changes are an efficient response to the changed environment. Those developments that cannot be rationalized in terms of economic efficiency must be attributed to regulatory constraints." By contrast, Kendall argues that it is impossible to make confident statements about the appropriate level of insurance premiums, in part because insurers have been poor data collectors. He maintains that "By the late 1960s, the forthcoming crisis in medical malpractice insurance should have been obvious—if anyone had been paying any attention." Munch provides some support for the position that insurers seem rather inept, at least in retrospect. During the years 1970–1974, claim frequency and severity increased at clearly observable rates. She finds that on the basis of these increases, the huge increases in 1975 appear justified, given the levels of the original rates. The question is why premiums were not adjusted sooner. Unlike Kendall, however, she seems to find no lack of competitive pressures. His premise—that if a group is written by a single insurer, a new insurer will be very reluctant to bid because it has not had experience in the area—is simply contradicted by the history in California. This fact is probably due primarily to the sensible precaution by the insured group of keeping a claims history.

Mann provides an analysis of the effect of an increase in the frequency of claims on the cost of claims to insurers. Because claims enter a queue, doubling the rate of claims filed does not simply double the insurer's claims cost in present value terms, because at the higher filing rate it will take longer for the average claim to work its way through the queue. But using estimates for the parameters of her queueing model, and a monthly discount rate of .01, Mann estimates an elasticity of expected payout with respect to claims costs of .9985, so the apparent effect in steady state is not significant. However, Mann notes that during the transition period from one steady state to another, the justified premium rate does depend on the queueing effect. She concludes that the requested premium increases are justified, although she is comparing San Diego experience to national premium increases. Since she takes only increases in claims frequency into account, her inferred premium adjustments clearly understate the appropriate increases.

The application of queueing theory is an interesting exercise, and the data which Mann painstakingly compiled provides a valuable sample in an area where useful statistics are amazingly difficult to find. I feel she overstates the value of a statistical model in computing "valid" premium rates, however. Mann argues that the "long tail" in the closed-claims distribution is not, per se, a problem. If one moves from one steady state to another, a reading on frequency in the new steady state provides an immediate basis for the proper premium adjustment, she notes. That is true, but only under very restricted assumptions: namely, that a reliable estimate of the new frequency distribution is available, that the severity distribution is unchanged or is also predictable, and that the pattern of closed claims for a particular policy year is unchanged. In other words, if the insurer *knows* that a transition from one steady state to another has taken place and that the *only* difference is observable from the claims closed during the first year or two, then predicting total claims costs is, indeed, reasonably easy. But insurers do not know that those statements are true, which is why the long tail causes nightmares. To assure them that total claims costs are predictable—given some very strong assumptions—is not likely to provide much consolation.

Green's paper is a brilliant contribution to the law and economics literature; his innovation is to explicitly introduce the "fact-finding" function of the courts by distinguishing between the a priori level of care as perceived by the plaintiff (or, more appropriately, by the plaintiff's lawyer) and the ex post level as determined by the court. The traditional way to treat the function of the courts in economic analyses of liability law is effectively to ignore them, by implicitly assuming that the standard of care exercised by the defendant is known and verifiable without cost. Green's method of modeling the function of the court should prove useful, perhaps in a modified form, in analyzing many other issues which have been previously treated with inappropriate models.

In fact, Green's framework permits one to consider an aspect of setting different standards of care which he ignores. He notes that in malpractice, "it is quite likely that some . . . serious incidents of malpractice will escape the system, disguised as bad luck." As the standard of care rises, the likelihood that this will happen falls. On the other hand, the converse error becomes more likely. Cases of simple bad luck will more likely be interpreted as malpractice. Thus there is a tradeoff between these "Type I" and "Type II" errors, which involves not only issues of efficiency—on which Green's paper focuses—but also issues of equity. Indeed, the belief by physicians, that they are increasingly being held liable where bad luck is primarily involved, is a major source of dissatisfaction, possibly more significant than the economic burden of liability.

Whether the standard of care has increased dramatically in recent years is less obvious than Green alleges, in my opinion. The allusion to "a large body of evidence," indicating that doctors are responsible for damages in some situations in which they would previously have escaped liability, refers to what is essentially a large body of propaganda. While it is certainly true that the law has become more strict in its application recently, careful survey of the law with respect to medical malpractice suggests very few fundamental changes in the past two decades. While a few striking cases have occurred, the overwhelming majority

COMMENTARY

of successful cases would have been successful two decades ago, if pursued. While that assertion is obviously arguable, I feel quite confident in asserting that the conventional wisdom with regard to the importance of legal changes is based on very superficial grounds.

Green analyzes the nature of an optimal standard of care, with emphasis on the litigation costs involved in different standards and on the effects of different standards on physician behavior and patient-plaintiff behavior. Of course, a higher standard of care employed by physicians also involves direct costs of medical resources, a fact that is not sufficiently emphasized in Green's discussion.

There is an aspect of the analysis which deserves further consideration. Very few cases go to trial. But the social costs of litigation for those settled out of court are surely much less, *ceteris paribus*, than the costs of those which go to trial. Green implicitly assumes that the transactions costs of each claim are equal. But let us distinguish between "contested" claims (those which go to trial) and "uncontested" claims (those which are settled out of court). As the standard applied by the courts is raised, the number of claims surely increases, holding constant the level of care applied by physicians. But it is quite possible that the proportion of contested claims would go down substantially because more incidents are now clearly identifiable as malpractice. Thus, total transactions costs could easily go down even if plaintiffs do not adjust for a higher care level by physicians. This lack of monotonicity is not implausible. In fact, it is the essential argument for strict liability.

In analyzing the transactions costs of applying the law, it may be crucial to distinguish between transactions costs at two levels: the level of transactions costs which *temporarily* prevails while the law appears to be in flux is much higher than the level that occurs under a stable system. The high level of claims during the early 1970s—which appears to have slackened recently—may reflect uncertainty about just what the law of liability was. Many claims may have been based on hopes that possible precedents would be followed or that "natural extensions" of apparent precedents would be accepted.

H. E. Frech, III

I am scheduled to discuss four papers. However, the Burghardt paper reached me very late, so I will have little to say about it. I will discuss it first, then go on to the Greenwald/Mueller paper, and finally spend the bulk of my time analyzing the related contributions of Calabresi and Epstein.

280

Let us concentrate on the theoretical sections of the Burghardt paper. Its main point is that placing liability on the physician rather than on the patient is unlikely to raise the quality of medical care and may indeed lower it. Therefore, the liability change that has occurred in recent years cannot improve economic efficiency. I believe that Burghardt's results come from his assuming away some of the interesting real features of the medical care market. In his world, a tort system would never have arisen.

First, Burghardt assumes that incentives do not induce physicians to exercise greater care. Thus, the only possible use for malpractice law is to improve the distribution of patients among physicians and to drive some physicians out of certain types of practices. But, improving incentives to be careful is the fundamental purpose of tort law. Furthermore, if incentives really had no effect, it would be difficult to justify any liability system whatever.

Next, when Burghardt considers the effect of uninsurable malpractice costs on the physician's choice of cases, he does not relate the physician's perceptions of the uninsurable costs of suits to negligence or low-quality care. Clearly, a malpractice system in which the success of suits was totally independent of the quality of care would not be very helpful. But, what does that have to do with the actual system?

In a later section, Burghardt adopts the following model. Two classes of patients choose high- or low-quality care on the basis of their preferences and prices. They are perfectly informed about which physicians supply which type of care. The assumption that each individual physician does not respond to incentives for quality is maintained. Such an economy is, of course, optimal. Malpractice law cannot improve an already optimal situation. But the consumer's *lack* of information is fundamental to tort law. The purpose of the law is to require the supplier to act in the manner that would have been contracted for had information costs and transactions costs been low enough.

In short, Burghardt's models assume away all the important considerations. Thus, his conclusion that physician liability cannot improve quality is irrelevant. Now, let us turn to an almost purely empirical paper.

Initially, the Greenwald/Mueller paper aroused my enthusiasm. It promised to tell all one would want to know about the effects of higher malpractice pressure on physician pricing, physician migration, hospital pricing, and defensive medicine. Skipping to the results, I was astounded to learn that, not only are malpractice premiums shifted to consumers, but a dollar increase in premiums appears to raise prices by enough to recoup the losses many times over. This is found to be true for both

281

physician and hospital care. Further, the size of a physician's malpractice premium is a major determinant of the complexity of the medical treatment he administers. The authors believe that complexity here measures defensive medicine. Both of these results attribute more power to the threat of suits than I would have expected. Some slight biases in the econometric tools of analysis tend to exaggerate the importance of malpractice premiums, but the authors have demonstrated that these cannot account for an overstatement of more than a few percentage points.

There are a number of less serious econometric problems which I should like to mention. First, some very important variables appear and disappear in various equations, with either no discussion or a very strained argument. Most important in this respect is the variable for the depth of insurance coverage (the proportion of private medical expenses paid by private health insurance).

A probably minor problem with the hospital equations is that the bed-days variable is adjusted for demographic factors following Martin Feldstein's example.[1] This introduces biases since demographic factors are correlated with the economic variables. The benefit of the technique is a gain in efficiency through more precise estimates. It would be useful to see regressions with unadjusted data as well.

What can we conclude? The results indicate that malpractice premiums have a very large effect in raising prices and increasing the complexity of medical care. It is difficult for me to believe that effects are so great, but Greenwald and Mueller's work is competent. The effects of malpractice premiums are apparently fairly large.

I would like to make one point about the normative or policy implications of the Greenwald/Mueller paper. The statement that the authors' work "justifies the search for actions to deal with this crisis" is not warranted. Indeed, the results do not even establish that there is a crisis. The current system may be close to optimal, for the benefits of the current malpractice system in increasing the quality of health care must be considered. A finding that malpractice premiums are being shifted and that defensive medicine is being practiced is not damning evidence against the system. Indeed, one purpose of a tort system is to change the way medicine is practiced. The Greenwald/Mueller finding that defensive medicine between 1970 and 1974 increased resource costs by about 1 percent of health expenditures certainly seems reasonable.

---

[1] Martin S. Feldstein, "Hospital Cost Inflation: A Study in Nonprofit Price Dynamics," *American Economic Review*, vol. 61 (December 1971), pp. 853-72.

At this point, let us turn our attention to a pair of papers with a much more explicit policy concern, those of Epstein and Calabresi. These interesting papers seem to get very close to the essence of the problem. Close, but not precisely there. There is a certain amount of agreement between the two authors, largely their opposition to no-fault schemes, especially that of Havighurst and Tancredi.[2] However, I find neither paper entirely convincing. Let us examine the common ground between them.

First, both authors believe that the current fault system "has failed," "has done a miserable job," that malpractice law faces a "crisis" or "dilemma." I attribute this alarm, which is expressed by most commentators, to the conservatism of social scientists. (That these writers are called lawyers is mere disguise. Clearly, they are excellent students of human behavior.) Like the octopus, which is essentially blind in the absence of movement but strikes at every shadow that moves by, the social scientist not only notices whatever moves but usually considers it bad. Thus is it with malpractice. Malpractice law is held in low repute largely because it has recently changed. In these papers there is little evidence on which to base an argument against the current malpractice system.

Epstein provides no direct support for his pessimistic view. However, his engrossing analysis of court cases supports the notion that some are decided in ways that appear to be wrong. This can be interpreted as evidence against the existing system, although one needs to know how frequently the courts reach such silly decisions.

Calabresi marshalls against the current system a fascinating theoretical analysis. Unfortunately, his argument is incomplete. Let me restate it briefly and then go on to show where it goes wrong. The courts will punish certain types of malpractice but not others, Calabresi says. The reason is that certain types of bad medical practice are observable—they leave traces in records, in the memory of witnesses, and so on. Other types of bad practice are very costly for the courts to detect. From this Calabresi deduces that there is a bias in the incentives. Types of treatment that are unconducive to prosecution because of the difficulty of establishing error will tend to be favored by physicians. Therefore, the system is inefficient. Setting up incentives which do not have this bias—"rounding out the circle"—is necessary for efficiency.

[2] See Clark C. Havighurst, " 'Medical Adversity Insurance'—Has Its Time Come?" *Duke Law Journal*, vol. 1975, no. 6 (January 1975), pp. 1233-80, and Clark C. Havighurst and Laurence R. Tancredi, " 'Medical Adversity Insurance'—A No-Fault Approach to Medical Malpractice and Quality Assurance," *Milbank Memorial Fund Quarterly*, vol. 51 (Spring 1973), reprinted in *Insurance Law Journal*, no. 613 (February 1974), pp. 69-97.

This conclusion depends on the costs of the relevant alternatives to the current system, with all its biases. Calabresi believes that there are essentially two alternatives—assigning liability to the patient and setting up health maintenance organizations (HMOs) with complete responsibility for the patient. Calabresi's argument establishes the superiority of a *costless* HMO system to the current system, but not the superiority of either patient liability or a costly HMO system. I will concentrate on the argument that patient liability would be superior to the current tort system.

Let us suppose that patients are liable. Next, impose the present tort system. Presumably physicians will be more careful than they were without the tort system to avoid errors that are observable by courts. This is a gain. However, they will also abandon some modes of treatment that are beset with possibilities for observable errors and adopt instead less efficient modes seldom associated with errors detectable by a court. This shift produces inefficiency. Only if the loss from the latter outweighs the more appropriate care induced in observable ways will the tort system produce a net loss. Calabresi's paper presents no evidence on how the comparison of these costs and benefits would come out. I suspect that the tort system would win in such a comparison. To quote Epstein, "a sound appraisal of a legal doctrine requires a detailed examination of its inner workings as well as a grander appreciation of its social function." It is just such a detailed examination that we lack.

The second area of common ground between the two authors is that they oppose no-fault malpractice insurance, including the version proposed by Havighurst and Tancredi. Calabresi's main objection is that no-fault insurance would simply create new issues for litigation over the boundaries of the compensable events without offering any advantage over the current system.

Epstein presents the interesting idea that under a no-fault system arguments as to negligence would still be important in the court's determination of whether an injury was iatrogenic. He refers to product liability cases where, even under a strict liability standard, negligence is argued since a negligent firm is likely to have produced a flawed product. The parallel seems appropriate to some models of no-fault medical liability, though not to the Havighurst-Tancredi proposal.

The Havighurst-Tancredi plan envisions a drastically simplified evidence rule: the plaintiff would not be required to prove that an injury was iatrogenic, merely that it had occurred. This simplified rule, in fact, is the essence of the proposal. It seems very likely that it could reduce the costs of litigation, as Havighurst and Tancredi claim.

Epstein criticizes the simplified evidence rule on the ground that it would create bad incentives for physicians. This is not so. The fact that a physician were liable for purely random injury to the patient would not impair the incentives to avoid damage where possible. On the contrary, the incentives and the savings they would entail would be identical whether or not the physician were also liable for random events.

The real problem with no-fault schemes, including that of Havighurst and Tancredi, lies in the selection of patients and treatments. Epstein notes in passing, "there is a very real danger that a physician operating under the no-fault system would decide to turn away difficult cases precisely because they could have an adverse effect upon his overall ratings and involve him in complex compensation proceedings." This is more than a danger—it is a virtual certainty.

Depending on the flexibility of pricing, there are two ways in which this discrimination might work. If prices were perfectly flexible, physicians would simply charge difficult patients more—which would require costly bargaining on an individual basis. If prices were not flexible enough (and the influence of third-party payers, professional pressure against price cutters, government regulation, and bargaining costs all tend to keep prices rigid), physicians would simply refuse to treat difficult cases. Presumably, this would mean that some physicians would specialize in difficult patients at higher, but still rigid, prices.

In either case, resources would be wasted in determining the probability of a compensable outcome. Physicians would expend time and money to determine whether or not it would pay to serve a patient, even after it was known that treatment would be in the patient's interest. Further, if prices were rigid, more than one physician might expend these resources before the consumer actually received treatment—*if* indeed he ever did.

This is a serious drawback to no-fault approaches. However, my (Harvard) colleague Steven Shavell points out that patients and physicians are not perfectly matched under the tort system either and that some additional incentive for certain physicians to specialize in high-risk patients might be a good thing. How great an effect the selection bias would have is difficult to determine in advance.

Epstein and Calabresi diverge substantially in their own proposals for reform. Calabresi half-jokingly proposes "rounding out the circle," by which he means making the physician responsible for all the losses and injuries in the patient's life, regardless of whether they could be traced to medical care. Since Calabresi's jokes are more interesting than many scholars' solemn statements, this idea is worth serious consideration. Calabresi's suggestion would eliminate the bias in favor of treatments with unobservable errors which occurs under a fault system. His would be a sort of super no-fault system, going beyond medical care to anything that could cause observable losses to individuals, including accidents and laziness. In effect, physicians would become competing welfare states, with cradle-to-grave responsibility for their customers. Consumers would be forced to join HMOs which would be required to carry life and disability insurance in large amounts. The probability of medical errors that could lead to any bad outcome would be taken into account by the HMOs.

Such a scheme sounds very costly. First, many consumers and physicians do not favor HMOs. Second, for the HMOs to have the proper incentive to prevent the death of their clients they would have to offer extremely high life insurance, perhaps as high as $200,000—compared with the $30,000 or so typical today. So great an expansion of life insurance would be very wasteful.

Further, the internal management of a large HMO would pose many of the problems that beset the current system. For example, someone would have to determine fault in complex medical situations and administer punishment. (This would also be true if all physicians were to become government employees in a centralized health care scheme.)

One could argue that an HMO should be small so that supervision of the physicians would be relatively easy. However, small HMOs could not bear the tremendous risks that Calabresi would have them assume. So a small HMO would have to sell the risk by reinsuring. However, to the extent that experience-rating is imperfect (and it must be imperfect for insurance to have meaning), the small HMO would no longer have the optimal incentives. In fact, under Calabresi's scheme, the HMO might have less incentive than today's solo practitioner since the uninsurable loss of reputation from a successful malpractice suit would be eliminated. Thus, the HMO with a rounded circle of incentives might well be so costly as to be worse than the status quo.

I might note here that negotiation between customers and providers, which Calabresi denigrates, might work reasonably well if the providers were organized in HMOs and the customers were represented by employer and/or union groups. In this situation, the HMO would have a strong incentive to perform well to keep and attract informed customers—and its reputation would be even more important to an HMO than the solo practitioner's is to him since the HMO has a longer-lived brand name to preserve. Thus, quality competition among HMOs, especially for group clients, thus might accomplish what might be very difficult to achieve through individual negotiation between patients and solo practitioners. HMOs without rounded circles of incentives might do quite well.

Taking a different tack than Calabresi, Epstein argues for the freedom of the parties to contract out of the initial allocation of liability. Of course this should be established; the current tendency for the courts to disallow it is scandalous. One might even say that the courts' behavior has been unconscionable. Yet however great the need for free contract may be, contracts are not a complete solution. In fact, they might make considerably less difference than Professor Epstein envisions. This pessimistic view is based on transactions costs of two types. First, emergencies, especially when the patient is unconscious, eliminate the opportunity for contractual agreement. Second, the costs of informing the consumer and securing his agreement are not zero. In many situations they may be prohibitive. Thus, the initial allocation of liability (in the absence of agreement to the contrary) will continue to be important. On this matter Epstein suggests that the area of liability of the physician ought to be restricted. He prefers the older American boundaries of physician negligence to the wider ones now popular in this country. Several states which are moving by statute to restrict the types of events for which physicians are held liable apparently share his view. The legal doctrines that are being affected include informed consent and *res ipsa loquitur*.[3]

At this point, I would like to draw attention to the apparent disagreement between Calabresi and Epstein on physician-consumer contracting. The dispute is only apparent. The two authors have different types of transactions in mind. The contracting which Calabresi thinks ineffective involves complex agreements about the level of *care and accident avoidance* provided by the physician. A meaningful arrangement of this kind would require a great deal of medical information, at least for a contract between an individual and a physician (as mentioned above, consumer groups dealing with physician groups may do better): Professor Calabresi's skepticism is well placed. On the other hand, the type of contracting Epstein advocates would involve agreements in advance of the delivery of medical care on the legal *liability rule* that would apply. Since this latter type of transaction would require no great medical knowledge on the part of the consumer, it would be much more likely to be effective and reasonable. The disagreement between the two authors, then, is only superficial; the contracts rejected by Calabresi and those favored by Epstein are very different.

[3] See William J. Curran, *How Lawyers Handle Medical Malpractice Cases: An Analysis of an Important Mediolegal Study*, NCHSR Research Report Series, DHEW publication no. (HRA) 76-3152 (Washington, D.C., 1976), pp. 38-41.

My own views about malpractice are twofold. First, it goes without saying that contracting out of the initial liability assignment ought to be allowed. But the initial definition is still important. Currently we do not know that the existing system is less than optimal. Only our natural conservatism tells us it is. The rapid increase in malpractice judgments and awards and the inflation of insurance premiums seem somehow bad. What we need in order to decide if the status quo is faulty is the "detailed examination of its inner workings" that Epstein calls for. He has made a start by examining specific cases, but this analysis must be pursued systematically with a view to answering the following questions: Are many frivolous cases filed? How costly are they? Do they have adverse incentive effects on medical practice? Are cases decided in a reasonable way, in the main? To what extent are treatments involving unobservable errors favored as a result of the current fault system? What legal rules can be developed to reduce litigation costs and/or improve incentives?

Most of the speakers contend that the current system is a failure. My own hunch is that a detailed legal, economic, and medical investigation would show the opposite. I suspect that research would uncover some new rules of law that would improve the system and some old ones that deserve wider application, such as the defense of customary practice which Epstein discusses. And I suspect Epstein's view that physicians are too often held liable would be supported. But I predict that a serious investigation would show the current system to be quite reasonable overall.[4] I would not be surprised if we found that the alarming explosion of malpractice litigation in recent years has been moving us towards optimality.

---

[4] A recent survey of plantiff and defense lawyers indicates that they believe juries generally to have a good grasp of the medical and legal issues involved in malpractice proceedings. See ibid., p. 19.

LIST OF PARTICIPANTS

Abraham, Kenneth S., *Professor, School of Law, University of Maryland, Baltimore, Maryland*

Abrams, Paul F., Esq., *Administrator, Office of Medical Malpractice Arbitration, Commonwealth of Pennsylvania, Harrisburg, Pennsylvania*

Backus, Robert C., Ph.D., *National Institutes of Health, Bethesda, Maryland*

Baldwin, Roy J., Esq., *Kahaner, Nord & Baldwin, Fairfax, Virginia*

Bazzle, Nancey, *Subcommittee on Health, State Capitol, Charleston, West Virginia*

Beck, Fred W., *Vice President and General Counsel, American Mutual Insurance Alliance, Chicago, Illinois*

Bedwell, Theodore C., *Director, Medical Relations, Pharmaceutical Manufacturers Association, Washington, D.C.*

Bernzweig, Eli P., *Special Assistant to the Administrator, Federal Insurance Administration, Department of Housing and Urban Development, Washington, D.C.*

Blumstein, James F., *Professor, School of Law, Vanderbilt University, Nashville, Tennessee*

Braverman, Jordon, *Senior Policy Analyst, Health Policy Center, Georgetown University, Washington, D.C.*

Brooks, Jack, M.D., *Phoenix, Arizona*

Brown, Melissa, *Insurance Services Office of Washington, D.C., Washington, D.C.*

Brown, Murray, *Professor, Department of Preventive Medicine, Dalhousie University, Halifax, Nova Scotia*

Bruse, Charles, *Washington Representative, Allstate Insurance Company, Washington, D.C.*

Cabot, Edward, *Equitable Life Assurance Society, New York, New York*

Chapman, Carleton, M.D., *President, The Commonwealth Fund, New York, New York*

Chen, William Y., M.D., *Chief Occupational Medical Officer, Government of the District of Columbia, Washington, D.C.*

Chien, Robert I., Ph.D., *President, Institute of Health Economics and Social Studies, Skokie, Illinois*

Chollet, Deborah, *Syracuse, New York*

Cohen, Barbara, *Malpractice Study Director, Institute of Medicine, Washington, D.C.*

Craig, John, *Health Policy Group, National Planning Association, Washington, D.C.*

Demlo, Linda K., *Quality Assurance Study, Institute of Medicine, Washington, D.C.*

Denenberg, Ellen, *Bradley, Woods & Co., Inc., Washington, D.C.*

Dornette, William H. L., M.D., *Shaker Heights, Ohio*

Dyckman, Zach, Ph.D., *Council on Wage and Price Stability, Washington, D.C.*

Eglin, William C., *National Association of Blue Shield Plans, Washington, D.C.*

Eichenholz, Joseph, *Department of Health, Education, and Welfare, Washington, D.C.*

Ein, Marion, *Washington, D.C.*

Feldman, Roger, *Professor, Department of Economics, The University of North Carolina, Chapel Hill, North Carolina*

Fisher, Catherine, *Danville, Pennsylvania*

Foster, David R., *Prudential Property and Casualty Insurance Company, Woodbridge, New Jersey*

Frederick, Charles, *General Conference Risk Management Services, Takoma Park, Maryland*

Freiberg, Lewis, Jr., *National Association of Blue Shield Plans, Washington, D.C.*

Fu-Huang, Lien, *Professor, Department of Economics, Howard University, Washington, D.C.*

Goldstein, Evelyn M., *American Association of Medico-Legal Consultants, Philadelphia, Pennsylvania*

Goodman, Lou, *Director, Statistical Service Bureau, American Medical Association, Chicago, Illinois*

Grabowski, Henry, *Professor, Department of Economics, Duke University, Durham, North Carolina*

Green, Daniel B., D.D.S., *Robert Wood Johnson Health Policy Fellow, Institute of Medicine, Washington, D.C.*

Green, Leo Arthur, M.D., *Chairman, Malpractice Insurance Committee, Medical Society of Queens, Forest Hills, New York*

Hadley, Jack, *The Urban Institute, Washington, D.C.*

Hall, Charles, *Professor, School of Business Administration, Temple University, Philadelphia, Pennsylvania*

Harris, Frederick, *Professor, Department of Economics, College of William and Mary, Williamsburg, Virginia*

Harris, Mark, *Roche Laboratories, Nutley, New Jersey*

Heilman, Ronald, *Professor, School of Business Administration, University of Wisconsin, Milwaukee, Wisconsin*

Hilton, Robert, *Treasurer, Hospital Affiliates International, Inc., Nashville, Tennessee*

Holen, Arlene, *Center for Naval Analysis, Arlington, Virginia*

Holman, Thomas D., *Medical Economics Specialist, American Mutual Insurance Alliance, Washington, D.C.*

Holloway, Sally, *Manager, Division of Human Resources Management, American Hospital Association, Chicago, Illinois*

Hu, Teh-Wei, *Professor, Department of Economics, Pennsylvania State University, University Park, Pennsylvania*

Huang, Lien-Fu, *McLean, Virginia*

Huffman, Odell, *Subcommittee on Health, State Capitol, Charleston, West Virginia*

Isaacs, Marion, R.N., *Washington, D.C.*

Johnson, William G., *Director, Health Statistics, Syracuse University, Syracuse, New York*

Kaminsky, Irving, *American Hospital Association, Washington, D.C.*

Kanarck, Larry, *ABT Associates, Inc., Cambridge, Massachusetts*

Kaplan, Alan K., *PSRO Letter, Washington, D.C.*

Kessel, Shirley, *Chevy Chase, Maryland*

Kilstein, Sol, *Washington Business Group on Health, Washington, D.C.*

Kirson, Stanley, *Silver Spring, Maryland*

Klar, Robert, *Department of Health, Education, and Welfare, Rockville, Maryland*

Korper, Samuel P., *Washington, D.C.*

Knowles, Robert, *Insurance Information Institute, Washington, D.C.*

Lachman, Judy, *Professor, Department of Economics, Vanderbilt University, Nashville, Tennessee*

Lang, Donald, *Maginnis and Associates, Chicago, Illinois*

Lee, Robert, *The Johns Hopkins University, Baltimore, Maryland*

Lerner, Richard E., J.D., *American Arbitration Association, New York, New York*

Lewin, Lawrence, *Lewin and Associates, Washington, D.C.*

Lundberg, Carol, *Department of Health, Education, and Welfare, Washington, D.C.*

Lynn, JoAnn, M.D., *Clinical Scholars Program, George Washington University, Washington, D.C.*

Madden, J. Jerome, *Director, Government Relations, Eli Lilly & Company, Washington, D.C.*

Mangold, John H., *Administrator, Emergency Physicians, San Leandro, California Department of Economics*

Marchand, James R., *Virginia Commonwealth University, Richmond, Virginia*

McIver, Diane, *U.S. Senate, Special Committee on Aging, Washington, D.C.*

McLoughlin, Paul, *College of Physicians and Surgeons, New York, New York*

Miike, Lawrence, M.D., J.D., *Berkeley Springs, West Virginia*

Miller, Frances, *Professor, School of Law, Boston University, Boston, Massachusetts*

Miller, Joseph L., *American Insurance Associates, New York, New York*

Nielsen, Shyrl, *Arizona Medical Association, Phoenix, Arizona*

Oi, Walter, *Professor, Graduate School of Management, University of Rochester*

Olson, William J., Esq., *Jackson, Campbell and Parkinson, Washington, D.C.*

O'Neill, Dave, Ph.D., *Center for Naval Analysis, Arlington, Virginia*

Pelovitz, Steve, *Office of Research and Statistics, Social Security Administration, Washington, D.C.*

Platt, Roger D., M.D., *New York, New York*

Reed, Edgar, M.D., J.D., *Director, Medical and Legal Affairs, Veterans Administration, Washington, D.C.*

Robeson, Franklin, *College of Business and Management, University of Maryland, College Park, Maryland*

Robbins, David, *Vice President and Controller, Health Insurance Association of America, New York, New York*

Robinson, Lupi Phillips, *Institute of Medicine, Washington, D.C.*

Roth, John, *General Conference Risk Management Services, Takoma Park, Maryland*

Roussil, Rosemary, *Washington Insurance Newsletter, Washington, D.C.*

Schwartz, Edward, Ph.D., J.D., *National Center for Health Services Research, Rockville, Maryland*

Segal, David, *Highland Park, Illinois*

Semkow, Brian, *Professor, Department of Economics, Queens University, Ontario, Canada*

Shearer, Gail, *Policy Analyst, Consumers Union, Washington, D.C.*

Sheffler, Richard, *Professor, Institute of Medicine, Washington, D.C.*

Simpson, Bruce, *Legislative Analyst, Health and Welfare Committee, Legislative Research Commission, Frankfort, Kentucky*

Singer, Burton, *Washington, D.C.*

Small, Arthur, *Legislative Service Bureau, State House, Des Moines, Iowa*

Sparks, Robert D., *Program Director, W.K. Kellogg Foundation, Battle Creek, Michigan*

Steffes, Donald G., *President, Pennsylvania Hospital Insurance Company, Camp Hill, Pennsylvania*

Stein, Eric, *Arlington, Virginia*

Steslicke, William E., Ph.D., *School of Medicine, Wayne State University, Detroit, Michigan*

Steves, Buddy, *Myron F. Steves and Company, Houston, Texas*

Sumner, Michael, *ABT Associates, Inc., Cambridge, Massachusetts*

Schwartz, Edward, Ph.D., J.D., *National Center for Health Services Research, Rockville, Maryland*

Toping, Frances, *National Economists Club, Washington, D.C.*

Turen, Milton, *Institute of Medicine, Washington, D.C.*

Unger, Walter, *Special Assistant to the President, Institute of Medicine, Washington, D.C.*

Virts, John, Ph.D., *Economist, Eli Lilly and Company, Indianapolis, Indiana*

Wallack, Stanley, *Congressional Budget Office, Washington, D.C.*

Watford, Thomas, *President, Hospital Association Risk Managers, Camp Hill, Pennsylvania*

Waugh, David K., *American Medical Association, Chicago, Illinois*

Weiss, Sophie Carroll, *Texas State Board of Insurance, Austin, Texas*

Weltman, Robert, *Associate Director, American Medical News, American Medical Association, Washington, D.C.*

Whipple, David, *Naval Postgraduate School, Monterey, California*

Wickens, John A., *Director, Group Underwriting, Prudential Insurance Company of America, Newark, New Jersey*

Cover and book design: Pat Taylor